Small Business Solutions

E-Commerce

Brenda Kienan

PUBLISHED BY
Microsoft Press
A Division of Microsoft Corporation
One Microsoft Way
Redmond, Washington 98052-6399

Copyright © 2000 by Brenda Kienan

All rights reserved. No part of the contents of this book may be reproduced or transmitted in any form or by any means without the written permission of the publisher.

Library of Congress Cataloging-in-Publication Data
Kienan, Brenda.
    Small Business Solutions for E-Commerce / Brenda Kienan.
       p. cm.
    Includes index.
    ISBN 0-7356-0846-6
    1. Electronic commerce.   2. Small business--Technological innovations.   I. Title.
HF5548.32 .K54   2000
658.8'4--dc21   99-059494

Printed and bound in the United States of America.

1 2 3 4 5 6 7 8 9   MLML   5 4 3 2 1 0

Distributed in Canada by Penguin Books Canada Limited.

A CIP catalogue record for this book is available from the British Library.

Microsoft Press books are available through booksellers and distributors worldwide. For further information about international editions, contact your local Microsoft Corporation office or contact Microsoft Press International directly at fax (425) 936-7329. Visit our Web site at mspress.microsoft.com.

Chevrolet is a trademark of the Chevrolet Motor Division, General Motors Corporation. bCentral, FrontPage, Microsoft, Microsoft Press, MSN, NetMeeting, Outlook, PhotoDraw, PowerPoint, Slate, Visual Basic, Visual J++, Visual SourceSafe, Windows, and Windows NT are either registered trademarks or trademarks of Microsoft Corporation in the United States and/or other countries.

The example companies, organizations, products, people, and events depicted herein are fictitious. No association with any real company, organization, product, person, or event is intended or should be inferred.

This book describes the author's opinions about products and services that can be used to create an e-commerce website. Publication does not imply an endorsement by Microsoft for any specific approach or product.

Acquisitions Editor: Christey Bahn
Project Editor: Kristen Weatherby

For Dan, who quietly occupies my heart,
And for Claire, who dances there.

Contents at a Glance

Part 1
Plan Your E-Commerce Initiative
1 Focusing Your E-Commerce Goals 3
2 Setting Up a Budget and Sticking to It 33
3 Knowing the Legal Issues 53

Part 2
Create Identity and Attract Customers
4 Creating Online Branding 77
5 Providing Customer Service 101
6 Building Traffic and Community 129

Part 3
Build Your E-Commerce Website
7 Organizing Your Site's Framework 157
8 Creating the Site Yourself 179
9 Working with Web Shops, Developers, or Teams 205
10 Understanding the Back End and Hosting 229

Part 4
Maintain, Promote, and Succeed
11 Managing and Maintaining Content 261
12 Promoting to Your Target Market 281
13 Assessing Your Success 311

Appendix
Amending Your Site with an Intranet or Extranet 329

Contents

Acknowledgments . . . . *xvii*
Introduction . . . . *xix*

Part 1
Plan Your E-Commerce Initiative

1 Focusing Your E-Commerce Goals 3
   Just What Is E-Commerce? 4
      What It Takes to Win 5
      What E-Commerce Can Do 6
   What Do You Intend to Accomplish? 8
      Choosing a Business Model 9
      Selling via the Internet 14
   Who Is Your Customer? 21
      The Internet Is International—Are You? 21
      Identifying Your Target Market 22
      Reaching a Local Market 23
   Who Is Your Competition? 23
   Aligning Your Resources with Your Goals 24
   Focusing Your Expectations 25
      Setting Benchmarks for Success 26
      Writing a Mission Statement 26
   Making a Plan of Action 29
      Creating a Business Plan 29
      Creating a Project Plan 30
   Is It Really Feasible? 31

2 Setting Up a Budget and Sticking to It 33
Where Do You Start? 34
    Follow a Known Format 34
    What's in a Website Budget 35
Setting Realistic Expectations 35
    What Can You Do for Around $500,000? 36
    What Can You Do for $50,000 or So? 37
    What Can You Do for $5,000 to $10,000? 38
    What Can You Do with a Minimal Investment? 39
    How Can You Keep Costs Down? 40
Looking at a Model Spreadsheet 42
    Grouping Costs by Activity 43
    Categorizing Costs by Type 47
On E-Commerce Revenue Models 48
Considering the Return on Your Investment 51
Using Microsoft Excel 52
Using Small Business Financial Manager 52

3 Knowing the Legal Issues 53
What Is Intellectual Property? 54
Who Owns What on a Website? 56
    Ownership of Look and Feel 57
    Ownership of Back-End Systems 58
    Ownership of Content 59
    Ownership of Ideas 59
Can Copyright Laws Protect You? 60
    What Is a Copyright? 60
    How Does Copyright Law Work? 62
    Marking Your Site with a Copyright Notice 62
    What About Copyright Infringement? 63
    What About Fair Use and the Public Domain? 64
    Can You Use People's Images? 66

Why Does Licensing Matter? 66
What Does Trademarking Mean to You? 68
    What Can You Trademark? 69
    Deciphering Trademarks: ™ and ® 70
    Registering Trademarks 70
How Does the Law Affect Linking? 71
Where Does Business Liability Begin and End? 72
Should You Worry About Slander and Libel? 72
Avoiding Trouble 73

Part 2
Create Identity and Attract Customers

4 Creating Online Branding 77
What Are the Elements of Successful Online
Branding? 80
Naming Companies, Products, and Domains 81
    Do You Need a Domain Name? 82
    Choosing Memorable, Meaningful Names 83
    Understanding the Domain Naming System 87
    Is Your Prospective Name Taken? 88
    Registering Your Domain Name 89
Determining Look and Feel 90
    Clarifying Your Audience and What They Want 90
    What Does Your Logo Say About You? 91
    Defining Your Website's Look and Feel 92
    So What Works? 95
Considering Quality of Experience 96
Establishing Integrity and Trust Online 98

Contents

5 Providing Customer Service 101

Why Customer Service Matters—Especially in E-Commerce 103
- You Are Your Web Site 103
- First Impressions Are Lasting 104
- If the Industry Looks Bad, Business Is Bad 105

Provide the Best Product or Service 106

Build Customer Loyalty 108
- Communicate Positively 109
- Be Easy to Reach 110
- Respond Immediately 113
- Offer Customer Service via Email 114
- Offer a Searchable, Easy-to-Use FAQ 119
- Set Up Your Systems So Service Is Easy 122
- When a Problem Occurs, Make Good 123

Ask Your Customer—and Listen! 125
- Track Email Feedback 125
- Conduct Surveys 125
- Keep Things in Perspective 128

6 Building Traffic and Community 129

Building Focused Community 130
- Choose a Technology 132
- Identify Communities of Shared Interests 137
- What Are Your Community Goals? 138
- Invite a Community to Gather 139
- Welcome the Community 140
- Provide the Community with Security 141
- Offer Value to the Community 141

Sending Email Newsletters 142
- Track Down Content 143
- Format for Effect 144

Contents

    To Opt In or to Opt Out? 145
    Provide Options for Unsubscribing 146
    Address Privacy Issues 146
    Tools to Use 146
Offering Discussion Groups 148
    To Moderate or Not to Moderate? 149
    Options for Hosting 151
Leveraging Archived Email as Valuable Content 152
Community-Based Websites 153
Measuring Community Success 154

Part 3
Build Your E-Commerce Website

7 Organizing Your Site's Framework 157
    The Value of Pre-Production Planning? 158
    Keep in Mind Your Goals and Expectations 159
    Acquire Content 160
    Organize Content 161
        Identify Pages by Type 162
        Refine Your Plan 164
    Define the Site's Architecture 168
        Create a Site Map 169
        Build a Directory Structure 172
        Think About the Back End 174
    Should You Build It Yourself? 175
    Write Specs or a Design Document 177

8 Creating the Site Yourself 179
    HTML 101 179
        How HTML Works 180
        Required Tags and Their Order 182
        Opening and Closing Tags 182
        Tags That Do Special Jobs 183

Contents

    Limitations of HTML (and a Few Workarounds) ... 184
    Page Layout Tricks 187
    Posting Your Pages 190
Understanding Images 191
    The Basics of Image Files and Formats 191
    Preparing Images for the Web 193
    Other Image Types You Will Encounter 194
Creating and Managing Your Site with Microsoft
FrontPage 195
    Conventions of Microsoft FrontPage 195
    Using FrontPage to Create a Site or a Page 196
    Mapping the Site and Its Navigation 196
    Adding a Catalog, Transaction System,
    and Shopping Cart 197
    Working with FrontPage and HTML 197
    Managing Your FrontPage Website 197
    Making the Site Live 198
Designing for Multiple Browsers 199
Jazzing Things Up with Interactivity 201
Including Microsoft Office Documents 203
Relying on Microsoft bCentral Site Manager 203

9 Working with Web Shops, Developers, or Teams 205

Assess Your Needs 206
    Consider Outsourcing and Insourcing 206
    Consider Outtasking 208
Use Microsoft Products to Facilitate Collaboration ... 209
Who's Who Among Shops and Developers 209
    What Are ISPs and IPPs? 210
    What Ad and Marketing Agencies Do 211
    What Specialized Web Shops Do 212
    About Independent Contractors 213

Contents

Using Multiple Vendors 214
Find the Right Vendor 215
   Define the Project 215
   Look at Style 217
   Evaluate Skill and Experience 217
   Judge Quality of Interaction 219
Evaluate Quotes 221
   Negotiate Fees 222
Get References that Count 222
Deliver Specs and Firm Up Details 224
Understand the Contract 225
Remember Maintenance After Launch 226
Manage the Project 227

10 Understanding the Back End and Hosting 229
What Is a Server? 230
Selecting a Platform 232
Choosing a Server 233
   Issues of Performance 233
   Issues of Reliability 235
   Issues of Support 236
All About Hosting 238
   Hosting Your Server at Your Location 238
   Hosting Your Server at an ISP 240
   Hosting Your Site on an ISP's Server 240
Choosing and Working with an ISP 241
Consider a Database 243
   The Power of a Database-Backed Website 244
   Relational Databases vs. Flat File Databases . 245
   Introducing Middleware 246
   Maintaining a Database 247

Contents

    The Basics of Transaction Systems 248
        Security in E-Commerce Transaction Systems 250
        How Credit Card Transactions Work 251
        Credit Card Setup, Step-by-Step 253
        About Fees and Charges 255
        Other Forms of Payment 256
    Will You Build or Buy Your Transaction System? 256
    Keeping Your Site Running Night and Day 257

Part 4
Maintain, Promote, and Succeed

11 Maintaining Fresh, Compelling Content **261**
    Create Effective E-Commerce Content 263
        Writing for E-Commerce 265
    Keep It Fresh 269
    Keep It Organized 270
    Assure a Smooth Reader Experience 271
    Monitor Quality and Assure Credibility 272
        Create and Use a Style Guide 273
    Tools for Managing Site Maintenance 279
    Archive and Purge Content 280

12 Promoting to Your Target Market **281**
    Attract Traffic with Your Site and Your Message 282
    List Your Site 284
        What Are Search Engines, Directories,
        and Portals? 284
        How Search Engines Work 285
        Get to the Top of the List 285
        Protect Some Pages from Searchability 290
        Submit Your Site 290

Get Others to Link to You 291
   Get Backlinks and Trade Links 291
   Form Partnerships and Join Alliances 292
   Offer or Achieve Awards 293
   Check Your Backlinks 293
Create Affiliates 294
Use Banner Ads 296
   The Basics of Banner Ads 296
   Get Real Results 297
Sponsor Another Website 300
Leverage Newsletters and Discussion Groups 301
Make Your URL Prominent Everywhere 302
Get Coverage in Magazines and Newspapers 303
   Gather Materials 303
   Write a Press Release 304
   Launch Your Press Campaign 305
   Post to Your Online Press Room 306
Become a Presence in Discussion Groups 307
Mix Online and Offline Promotion 308

13 Assessing Your E-Commerce Success 311
What Does Success Mean to You? 312
   The Benefits of Measurement 314
   Getting to Know Your Audience 315
What Can You Know? 316
Understanding Measurements of Traffic 320
Analyzing Hits, Impressions, and Page Views 322
   Looking into Log Files 322
   Selecting Tools 323
   Auditing Your Data 324
Soliciting and Analyzing User Input 325

Contents

    What to Do with All That Information 326
    Is the Customer Always Right? 328

Appendix
Amending Your Site with an Intranet or Extranet . . . 329
    What Are Intranets and Extranets? 331
    Typical Uses of Intranets and Extranets 331
    Assess Cost and Return 334
    Address Management and Technology Issues 335
        Providing for Security 338
        Getting the Support of Management 341
    Be Conversant: What You Must Know 341
    Measure Intranet or Extranet Success 343

Glossary 345
Index 359

Acknowledgments

Many fine people contributed their energy and expertise to the book you hold in your hands. It is their accomplishment as much as it is mine; I am indebted to them all.

Christey Bahn, Barb Ellsworth, and Kristen Weatherby, all at Microsoft Press, provided opportunity, encouragment, guidance, and a glimpse into life around Rain City. Anne Hamilton and David Clark have been respected colleagues through many venues. Joyce Cox, Leslie Eliel, and Steve Lambert, at OTSI, kept the language, the schedule, and the facts all on track. R.J. Cadranell and Mary Rasmussen shaped text and art into an actual book, and Rachel Moorhead and Gabrielle Nonast proofed to perfection. David and Sherry Rogelberg at Studio B provided their usual fine and wise counsel.

Maureen Nelson has been a true collaborator in this book; it simply would not have happened without her. Bob Walker, Bruce Molloy, Brian Jeffries, Christina Cheney, Gloria Keene, Leslie Hamilton, Kathleen Beal, Mitchell Levy, Alicia Eckley, and Dennis Woo all contributed keen insight or commentary that influenced the text. Michael Gross provided invaluable advice regarding the legal chapter, and Erma Takeda kindly translated an article from German.

Caroline Heller, Bob Huber, Thaisa Frank, and John High made a writing career a possibility (though this probably isn't quite what they had in mind), and long ago, Stephen Zelnick first suggested "technical" writing—perhaps I should have listened to him. Rudy Langer and Barbara Gordon opened the doors that finally led here.

John and Aida Bjorklund, Kent Gerard, Ana Ortiz, and Charlie Wright make the daily grind both possible and surprisingly enjoyable.

And finally, my special thanks to Dan Tauber, Claire Tauber, Lonnie Moseley, and Cordell Sloan, who kept humor and perspective intact while wife, mother, sister, and friend vanished behind a computer screen; and to friends and family who make life the adventure it ought to be: Joani and Jessica Buehrle; Sharon Crawford and Charlie Russel; the Cunninghams; Dames Who Dine; Rion Dugan; Fred Frumberg; Jessica, Martin, and Lori Grant; Mai Le Bazner, Katri Foster, and Peter Bazner; the McArdles and Undercoffers; Carolyn Miller; Wynn Moseley and her family; Margaret Tauber; Ron and Frances Tauber; Judy Tauber; and Robert E. Williams III.

Introduction

E-commerce, some said, would level the playing field, allowing even the smallest business to stand tall next to corporate giants. But these days, launching an e-commerce website can seem daunting to small and mid-sized companies. To read much of what has been written, you might think e-commerce involves hiring a staff of dozens, thinking up a slick gimmick, building a relational database from the ground up, and paying a fortune for promotion and maintenance. As of this writing, 68 percent of small businesses have Internet access; within three years, according to Jupiter Communications, that figure will have jumped to 85 percent. For small to mid-sized businesses, e-commerce holds promise: those that want to grow *and* those that cater to a local clientele can find opportunity online. But how do you choose the tools that are right for you, and where can you find guidance for forming strategies that focus on your concerns?

> **Note**
>
> E-commerce isn't just *selling* online—it's any kind of business conducted online. So whether your business is consumer-oriented or business-to-business, and no matter what its purpose (sales, information, distribution, manufacturing, education, or entertainment), this book has something to offer. This book was written for small to mid-sized businesses with as many as 100 employees or as few as one. Whether you are doing business primarily online or in the brick-and-mortar world, if you need guidance in making decisions about e-commerce, this book is for you.

Introduction

While many e-commerce principles forged in the big-budget corporate world can be successfully applied to small-business concerns, small businesses have their own unique issues, ranging from keeping staff size small to knowing how to target and attract just the right type of visitor. Many small businesses are looking at the most basic issues. They are considering, for example, whether their goal should be to sell online in any of a variety of venues, to provide purchase support and expect customers to buy at brick-and-mortar locations, to take business-to-business orders online, or any of several other options.

What This Book Can Do for You

Enter *Small Business Solutions for E-Commerce*, the book that will show you, the e-commerce manager or entrepreneur, where to start, which end is up, and which tools and technologies can help you. Whether your e-commerce endeavor is consumer-oriented or business-to-business, this book covers what you really need to know to get into the e-commerce game. It offers you valuable information about everything from how to develop online strategies to how to organize content and oversee a transaction system. It shows you what to consider in building a site, as well as how to maintain freshness and quality, mind legal matters, promote the site, and decide whether to house it on your own server or have it hosted elsewhere. Along the way, this book highlights the products and services that make building and maintaining an e-commerce site an easily manageable task.

Small Business Solutions for E-Commerce does not offer across-the-board answers, because each e-commerce initiative requires solutions tailored to it and to the business goals it serves. This book provides you with the means to ask yourself the right business questions to form strategies and solutions that will meet your needs. It offers real-world solutions and options in undaunting language, and provides pointers to additional information available online. It also includes tips and advice gleaned from interviews with people who've been there and people who work extensively with e-commerce issues.

Introduction

Who You Are and What You Already Know

You might be a manager in a 50-person company with overall operations and profit and loss responsibility or the Mom or Pop of a mom-and-pop store. You might envision a quickly expanding digital market for your company's products, or perhaps an online venue for focusing a local market on your company's services. In any case, you are probably responsible for managing the website and focusing its content, production, and perhaps some technical implementation, as well as the day-to-day matters of running a business. You might be conducting business exclusively online or planning to expand an existing brick-and-mortar operation to include an online component. Whatever your objectives, you need to be conversant in e-commerce issues and you need pointers to easy-to-use tools.

You know how to use a web browser and have used the Internet; you might even have a little background in creating web pages. But you aren't a programmer, and you don't want to be one. You already know business; no one needs to tell you that you have to keep costs down to make a profit. You do need a guide to making business decisions about your company website—a guide written by someone who's been in the business arena and has the Internet expertise to offer savvy guidance.

What This Book Covers

Written by an Internet professional with years of business experience in companies small, large, and in-between, this book covers launching and running an e-commerce website *from a management perspective*. You'll find out what it takes to succeed in e-commerce and how to know you have succeeded. This is not a technology book, it's a business book. It describes, soup-to-nuts, how to forge a strategy and how to follow through on it successfully. It also describes technologies that will help you in your e-commerce endeavors, but it covers them from a business strategy perspective. To use this book, you don't have to be a developer—or even know one. This book introduces you to the issues and challenges you'll encounter as you develop and implement your e-commerce website and conduct business online, no matter what your line of business might be. The book is written in four parts that cover planning the site, establishing an identity, building the site, and what to do after launch to promote it, maintain its quality, and measure its success.

Part One: Plan Your E-Commerce Initiative

Part One starts with setting goals for your site, because that's the foundation on which success is based. (The goals you set will also determine how you'll measure your success.) Guiding you onward, Part One delves into identifying your target market, competitors, and goals, and deciding how to write a business plan or project plan. Pointers for budgeting lead into what it costs to build small, mid-sized, and large websites. Part One ends by introducing you to the new spin e-commerce puts on traditional issues of intellectual property, copyright, trademark, and business law.

Part Two: Create Identity and Attract Customers

Part Two is all about customers—establishing an identity they'll recognize, providing excellent customer care, and building a customer base. E-commerce puts new emphasis on the classic marketing strategies for *branding* (creating an immediately recognizable identity). In Part Two, you'll read all about how to brand your e-commerce endeavor. The user's experience is a big part of online branding, for example, so you'll find out how customer care and after-sale customer service fit into the equation.

Email newsletters and discussion groups offer a unique opportunity for you to have a one-on-one relationship with your customers; Chapter 6 tells you how. You'll also discover how to create that powerful but elusive experience called *community* as well as how to transform the phenomenon of community "bonding" into long-term customer loyalty to your site and your brand.

Part Three: Build Your E-Commerce Website

Planning is vital to building a website. From beginning to end, Part Three describes organizing content, creating directory structures, and working up a design document or specs that will guide the building process. Whether you want to build the site yourself or take the project to a designer or developer, you'll find the guidance you need. Because you'll want to be conversant with developers and be able to assess their work, you'll need a general understanding of the technical infrastructure of a website. You won't need to do hands-on development but you will want to know what the issues are. Chapter 10 walks you through what you need to know about platforms, servers, hosting, databases, and transaction systems, giving you a management overview.

Part Four: Maintain, Promote, and Succeed

As you know, a business does not simply have a grand opening and then experience assured success. Daily, ongoing attention is required. An e-commerce website needs attention after its launch, too. To build your customer base and reach for success, you'll want to promote your site to your target audience. In Part Four, you'll learn what keeps users coming back and how to reach them, even if your promotional budget is limited. You'll find out about listing your site with search engines and directories (AltaVista, Yahoo!, and the like). You'll discover how to check how many backlinks lead from other sites to yours. And you'll get tips for promoting your site in creative ways, ranging from traditional print media to so-called "new" media.

You'll also want to keep your site's quality up and spruce up the online merchandising after launch. Part Four covers keeping your website's content and appearance fresh. And finally, you'll need to know how to measure your success. You'll find out in Part Four about the various ways you can assess your site's achievements based on the goals you set in Chapter One.

Appendix and Glossary

As a bonus, the Appendix at the end of the book describes how you can amend your e-commerce website with an intranet to provide internal information to your staff or team, and with an extranet that will provide vital information to vendors, sales reps, or buyers. For your quick reference, a glossary lists all the e-commerce and business terms you'll want to be familiar with as you venture into this field.

Contacting the Author

This book is meant to act as a guide to e-commerce management. As you meet the challenges inherent in e-commerce, if you'd like to share tips and strategies that you find useful, you can contact the author. Simply send email to the following address:

ecommerce@tauberkienan.com

For e-commerce articles, tools, and new strategies, visit the E-Commerce Management Center:

www.tauberkienan.com

Part 1

Plan Your E-Commerce Initiative

1. Focusing Your E-Commerce Goals
2. Setting Up a Budget and Sticking to It
3. Knowing the Legal Issues

Chapter 1

Focusing Your E-Commerce Goals

It's a *bonanza*. That's the public's perception of e-commerce, and market researchers agree. International Data Corporation (IDC), a research giant, projects overall e-commerce sales of $220 billion in 2001. According to Giga Information Group, e-commerce revenues will reach between $580 billion and $970 billion in 2002. And these figures don't even account for the revenues and cost savings associated with e-commerce ventures such as marketing, procurement, customer service, and improvements in operations. Your question might well be whether (and how) you can get your piece of this enormous pie.

At first glance, large companies might appear to dominate e-commerce. Advertisements for "dot coms" and "brick-and-mortar" companies with booming online divisions are everywhere. But even smaller businesses, according to Giga, can parlay niche specialties and local service into consumer-oriented and business-to-business success. According to IDC, by 2001 over 4.3 million small businesses will be online.

Part 1: Plan Your E-Commerce Initiative

> ### Tip
> An online resource devoted to growing businesses, Microsoft bCentral (*www.bcentral.com*), goes beyond the typical information portal model to provide a comprehensive set of integrated services that can help companies improve their business. bCentral delivers real, practical services geared toward getting an e-commerce venture started, building a website, promoting and marketing online, and simply managing a business more effectively.

Just What Is E-Commerce?

E-commerce is, basically, doing business online. In its most obvious form, it is selling products online to consumers, but in fact, any sort of business conducted electronically is e-commerce. E-commerce is simply the creating, managing, and extending of commercial relationships online.

Successful e-commerce ventures might involve purchasing, developing and designing products, managing production or manufacturing, marketing and comarketing, sales, service, collaboration among businesses or affiliates, distribution of products, research, dissemination of information, setting up commercial communities, educating, entertaining, and probably all sorts of other businesses that haven't yet been thought up. Here are just a few examples of e-commerce in action:

- Consumers learning about products online before buying at a "real world" location
- Consumers ordering products online and receiving them either via traditional shipping or via the Internet
- Students participating in online education programs to receive degrees or professional training
- Citizens renewing their drivers' licenses, registering their cars, filing their taxes, applying for building permits, or conducting other business with government agencies online
- Businesses selling products and services to consumers or to other businesses
- Businesses tracking projects online or transferring electronic files (images, database records, or text files) via the Internet

- Businesses providing technical or customer support 24 hours a day, seven days a week
- Entertainment and other venues promoting their events online, or even creating online events
- Governments and their agencies receiving and processing requests for proposals and other procurement documents via the Internet
- Educational institutions integrating online components and research techniques into the everyday classroom

Perhaps because it is an emerging industry, e-commerce also spawns a lot of myths. Novices to e-commerce might think that it's all about taking online orders and that once anyone sets up shop, scores of customers will buy out warehouses full of widgets. Not so. Successful business in the virtual world takes as much savvy as successful business in the "real" world. Some people think that because e-commerce is technical, it must be expensive. Also not so. Fantastic e-commerce sites don't always require expensive programmers, but they aren't built on the cheap by any handy college student, either. And finally, a solid e-commerce venture does not have to include all the latest technical marvels—Java applets, Flash, Extensible Markup Language (XML), and whatever's next. None of this is necessary for a winning e-commerce site. What is necessary? Smart planning, implementation, promotion, and maintenance. Read on.

What It Takes to Win

To win in e-commerce, it is said, you must be first, be the best, or be different. Being first gives you the extra edge of defining a market and setting a benchmark against which others who follow will be measured. But remember this: Even if you are first to offer a product or service and define a market, if your offering is mediocre, someone else can swoop in with a better product. And that someone else will also have the benefit of selling to a defined market—the market you have so graciously identified. You will have mapped out a road others can follow, and if they are smart, they will look over your target market and come up with ways to serve it better and differently. Your best bet in e-commerce is to be first, of course, but you also want to be extremely adaptable so that, as times and technologies change, you can be the best and be unique.

> **Tip**
>
> Microsoft's websites offer e-commerce insight, tools, events, and information about e-commerce communities; to find out more, start at *www.microsoft.com*. Tauber Kienan Associates provides an E-Commerce Management Center which also offers strategy, insight, and tools at *www.tauberkienan.com*.

What E-Commerce Can Do

A 1999 survey showed that 90 percent of Internet users expected to make an online purchase that year. And according to Forrester Research, in 1999 more orders were placed via the Internet than by phone or fax for 10 percent of Fortune 500 companies. Growth of e-commerce revenue over the years following the writing of this book is projected at between 74 and 125 percent. The numbers are just stunning—and so are the innovative uses of e-commerce. Consider these examples:

- A company that delivers gravel to its construction customers sets up a website that allows foremen to place orders any time, day or night, for next-day delivery.

- A nonprofit social services agency provides teenagers with a forum in which to ask questions anonymously via email, with responses posted in a searchable database for others to see.

- A printer accepts a file from a designer via a website, and the printer then tracks the job online so that the designer can see the job's progress and know when to come in for press checks.

- A small boutique designer of fashion accessories and gift items puts her catalog online so freelance reps can show her new line to buyers all over the country.

- A community organization provides its members with information about meetings, services to the community, and upcoming events.

- A company provides a business-to-business auction outlet for the buying and selling of chemicals used in industry.

When many people think of e-commerce, they think only of traditional retail sales in an online setting. But consider the California gold rush. In the mid-nineteenth century, a wave of people hoping to strike it rich flocked to California, where gold had been discovered in a riverbed. Most imagined themselves quickly staking a mining claim and easily finding gold. Most didn't find any. But others saw the opportunity created by the sudden influx, and companies such as Levi Strauss & Co. (the jeans maker) and Wells Fargo (the financial institution) got their starts serving the needs of those who headed west to seek their fortunes.

The moral: Think outside the box. Your e-commerce venture might best be developed not to sell to consumers online, but instead to serve others already in e-commerce or brick-and-mortar businesses that hope to get involved. Of course, you probably won't want to change directions altogether if your business already exists and you simply want to extend your offerings to new, online markets. But even so, consider imaginative opportunities for creatively serving your customers. Don't simply sell flowers online; sell fresh flowers direct from the flower market, or track special events for your repeat customers so that you can send them reminders and offer to fill their flower needs. Think about your specific customer base and what would set you apart from your competitors. Give people what they want and need.

Also, keep in mind that while technology is great—without it, there would be no e-commerce—technology is a tool, not a business model. It's easy to be blinded by super-cool bells and whistles, but technology can't guarantee the success of your e-commerce venture. In e-commerce, as in the 3-D world, success comes from smart thinking and a dash of good luck. You'll need a plan for your e-commerce venture, and this plan should be based on a workable strategy.

As innovative business models and solid practices evolve for e-commerce, public acceptance is widening, and more and more companies are joining the fray. Before you jump in, ask yourself some key questions.

Will E-Commerce Improve Your Business?

You almost certainly would not open additional branches or create a franchise program without solid indications that success would result. Yet it's remarkable how many people launch websites without thinking through what it will take and how the site will impact their business. Before you launch an e-commerce venture, read through this book. Also, take a good look at Microsoft's online e-commerce resources. Consider how you will build and fund your venture, how it will serve your customers, and what return you can expect on your investment.

Part 1: Plan Your E-Commerce Initiative

Do You Have What It Takes?

Do you have the time and resources required to accomplish your specific e-commerce goals? To answer this question, you must know as much as you can about your goals and what it will take to fulfill them. You need to know what technology, time, funding, and promotional resources you will need to make a go of things.

Creating a business or project plan (as discussed later in this chapter) might not seem like a trip to the beach, but it is essential if you plan to seek funding for your venture. Even if you plan to fund the venture yourself or launch it as an adjunct to your existing business, going through the exercise of thinking through the issues will help you focus on answers to the relevant questions. To start your deliberations, consider what you plan to accomplish by building an e-commerce website.

> ### *Not Every E-Commerce Purchase Takes Place Online*
>
> What do people shop for online more than anything else? Cars and car parts. Despite the fact that you can't test drive a car online and most actual car purchases take place in traditional dealerships, a 1999 CommerceNet/Nielsen Internet Demographic Survey study showed that 18.2 million shoppers had checked into cars and car parts on the Internet. The numbers for more easily deliverable products, such as books (12.6 million shoppers), computers (12.4 million), clothes (11.6 million), and CDs and videos (11.4 million) lagged behind cars. Online shopping—comparing prices, features, and services—sometimes results in a sale in a traditional store. But this is an e-commerce event, too—the sale was, after all, driven by the convenience of comparison shopping via the World Wide Web, or simply, the Web. Almost half the respondents in a study by market researchers Roper Starch Worldwide said that they conduct online research as their first step in making a large purchase.

What Do You Intend to Accomplish?

Focusing your e-commerce goals is step one toward creating a successful commercial website. If you think you can zip past this step and move on to building the site, think again. Creating a site is a lot like building a house, in that starting without a well-engineered plan will leave you with an unsound structure. If you don't have a good plan, at best you'll only wind up spending time later undoing the unpleasant results of your impatience. At worst you'll find yourself in a real spot—for example, you might even be several thousand dollars poorer with no viable website to show for it. Without a clear strategy, no amount of technology will produce success.

If your website is an extension of your existing business, you probably have a clear sense of where to begin. Perhaps you have a restaurant where you serve a specialty sauce that you'd like to bottle and sell. That's a no-brainer; all you need is an easy-to-use selling site. Perhaps you have a painting company and you want to attract more upscale clients. In that case, providing general-interest information about your field—such as how to choose a painting contractor or the special preparation that distinguishes a Cadillac paint job from an ordinary paint job—could do the trick.

Choosing a Business Model

Lots of potential business models exist; your task is to identify a model that makes sense for your company. Let's look at some possible paths your e-commerce venture might take.

Tip

Identify between one and three goals for your e-commerce endeavor, and then rank them according to their importance. Keep in mind that although they might change as you go along, focusing on a few goals will prevent you from being spread too thin.

Generating Revenue

Making money through product sales, service charges, subscription sales, and other models, is obviously attractive. These methods of conducting e-commerce are perhaps the most apparent routes to take. But not all of the business models suggested by these ventures have proven successful. Retail sales—sales of hard deliverables such as books, CDs, clothing, and so on—have worked and worked well when branding and customer service have been good (see Chapters 4 and 5). However, as of this writing, it's been more difficult for newspapers and similar publications to persuade the online public to pay for information. Although historically people have

On E-Commerce Sales Cycles and "Back Ends"

In a typical e-commerce retail sale, the customer makes a purchase using a credit card to make payment. Other methods of payment can be used, but this one is the most common. It has the advantage of being familiar to the customer, which shortens the actual process of the sale—the customer doesn't have to read an explanation of how the payment method works because it is reassuringly well known. Behind the scenes, the online merchant and the merchant's bank conduct business pretty much as they do in the brick-and-mortar world.

The big difference between an online retail sale and one that occurs in a traditional setting is that the online transaction occurs over the Internet via computers, modems, and servers—it involves hardware and software that might be unfamiliar to you or your customers. Basically, an e-commerce site includes a *front end* that the users see (the web pages), and a *back end* that's like the behind-the-scenes workings of a retail store in the real world. (The customer never sees the "back end" of a traditional store, but it's there, and the store won't function if the back end doesn't function.) The sales systems, warehousing, delivery systems, and so on that make sales to the customer possible in the brick-and-mortar world are not duplicated exactly in e-commerce, but there are similarities. In a sales website (see Figure 1.1, shown at the top of the next page), the back end includes a *database* (which stores information about your products and tracks a customer's purchases while they occur), a *transaction system* (the hardware and software that enables online sales), and some scripts or other programming that make them work together.

You, as the storeowner, also have to have a relationship with the bank in order to make the transaction system work. You'll need an account similar to (but often separate from) the relationship with the bank that enables credit card sales at a traditional store.

What, you might wonder, pushes your operation over a threshold into needing a database and transaction system? The answer is that a certain level of complexity of information and function starts to require a database. If your operation is very simple and all you need is a few web pages with basic text and a picture, you don't need a

(continued)

On E-Commerce Sales Cycles and "Back Ends" (continued)

database. The more pages there are and the more complex the material you present on them, the more likely you are to need a database. And for simple sales via phone or email, you don't need a transaction system. But to gain credibility and provide your customers with a means for giving you credit card numbers online to close a sale, you do need a transaction system. And to run a transaction system, you again need a database.

Chapter 11 describes transaction systems in detail, but from a business perspective rather than from a programmer's perspective. That ought to help you to understand them better, but you may also need to help your customers understand what is involved in completing a transaction. Many e-commerce sites offer a page that describes their specific transaction system and its level of security in language the public can understand; this can go a long way toward building customer confidence.

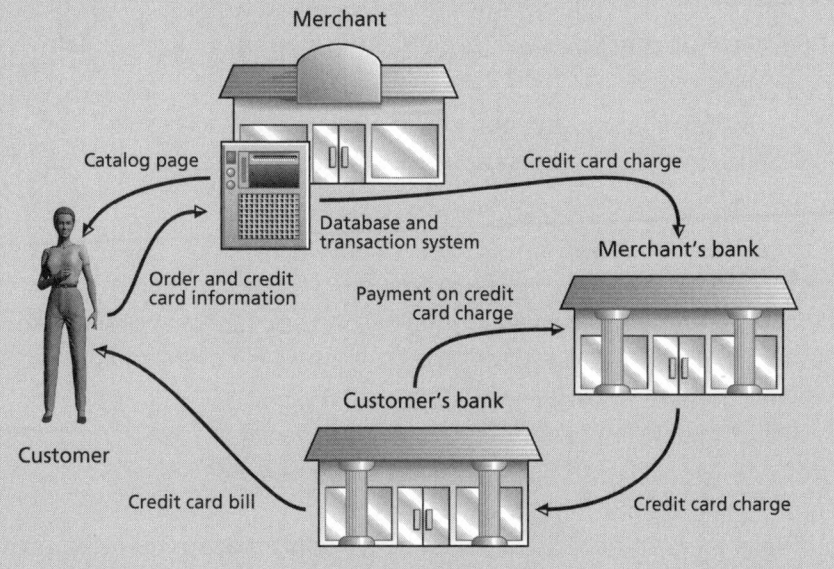

Figure 1.1
An e-commerce site's "back end" often includes a database and transaction system.

been quite willing to pay for magazines and other printed sources of information, the Internet's origin as a method for freely disseminating information seems to have inclined the online culture to expect just that.

Revenue-producing e-commerce ventures can include:

- Selling products or services directly online.
- Selling advertising space. (But remember that advertising on your site won't be an attractive proposition unless your traffic is high, and to create a lot of traffic, your content has to be very, very compelling.)
- Selling sponsorships of sites (or of content) to others, as the Public Broadcasting System (PBS) does on TV.
- Selling product placements, like those that occur in some entertainment venues when certain products casually appear in a scene. (Yes, companies pay for those placements.)
- Selling subscriptions to periodical information, reference information, or site services.
- Licensing content, such as text, information, images, video, sound, and so on, to others.
- Providing community in the form of a customer-to-customer or business-to-business auction site and taking a commission on sales.

Caution

Whatever your planned endeavor, don't expect an overnight windfall. Like every business venture, e-commerce businesses take a while to pay off. More about this as we go along.

Reducing Expenses

Cutting costs is an often overlooked but tangible way for an e-commerce venture to pay for itself. For example, if your product is deliverable over the Internet—meaning that it is digitized, like software, or it can be digitized, like images or other printed documents—costs to produce and distribute your product can be saved. Time-to-market also improves, because you won't have to go through traditional channels to manufacture and package your product.

Chapter 1: Focusing Your E-Commerce Goals

Cost savings can also result from online communications with your sales people; improved document management and workflow processes; project management; and tracking of projects, services, and people. *Intranets* (internal websites available only to staff, not the public) and *extranets* (websites that extend to clients, specific customers, or off-site staff) often come into play for such purposes. (See the Appendix for more information on intranets and extranets.)

Note

E-commerce can increase the efficiency of selling to existing customers by reducing the number of sales calls needed. That alone can be a cost savings.

Cost savings can also occur through the improved efficiency of your customer service program (see Chapter 5), as well as through the expedited delivery of information directly to customers.

Enhancing Customer Relations

Better relationships with your customers can lead to more revenue or lower costs, and is certainly a worthy endeavor on its own. Most successful sites think of the customer first. They make it easy for customers to get the information they need, and just as easy to buy. Customer service can take as simple a shape as an email form directed to the site manager or customer service rep. Answers to the ten most often asked questions might also be listed on a Frequently Asked Questions (FAQ) page to save time and make life easier for you and your customers. More complex customer service initiatives can include tracking customer preferences, suggesting items for purchase related to the customer's interests, and offering special services to repeat customers.

Tip

E-commerce allows you to have a unique one-on-one relationship with your customers. You can glean valuable marketing information from customers based on their answers to simple online surveys, and an email address or an easy form provides a convenient method for your customers to give you quick feedback. See Chapter 5 for more information about customer service.

Supporting Your Business

E-commerce initiatives that don't show a direct profit but that enhance or enable your business can include:

- Providing company information and making it easy for customers, clients, job seekers, partners, and others to contact your company.
- Shortening the sales cycle by providing in-depth product information to support purchases that will be made via reps or in a retail setting. You can reach prospects via e-commerce that you might not reach otherwise. To succeed, make getting product information easy and attractive.
- Offering top-notch customer service in an online setting, as described earlier in this section and in more depth in Chapter 5.
- Enhancing connectivity with business associates through strategic partnerships, shared resources, improved systems, and more.

Tip

Keep in mind your long-term goals as you form your strategy. But remember, too, that Internet time is a little like dog years. Things change quickly, and technologies change at the speed of light. The "long term" on the Web is perhaps a year from now, and the "short term" is the immediate future.

Selling via the Internet

How ambitious are your goals? A sales site can range from a simple listing of products with a "call for prices" notice, to a sales site created using Microsoft bCentral Site Manager or Microsoft FrontPage, to a full-blown, customized site that offers recommendations to customers based on their previous purchases. (See the sidebar "On E-Commerce Sales Cycles and 'Back Ends'" for more information.) Because sales sites are so commonly of interest to e-commerce entrepreneurs, let's take a closer look at two options: selling to consumers and selling business-to-business.

Chapter 1: Focusing Your E-Commerce Goals

Note

Creating a site that offers a simple listing of products with the option to send email for more information generally takes fewer resources and less technical skill than creating revenue-producing sites. However, the easier you make it for your customers to buy—and buy now—the more likely they are to bite. Take a look at the services offered at bCentral for convenient one-stop solutions to getting an e-commerce storefront up and running.

Selling to Consumers

If you already sell products via a catalog to consumers, e-commerce is a logical extension to your existing business. Self-directed consumers come to websites seeking something; they are sales waiting to happen. In a traditional setting, most selling occurs when customers (either the public or other businesses) approach a business location with the intent of shopping and perhaps making a purchase (see Figure 1.2).

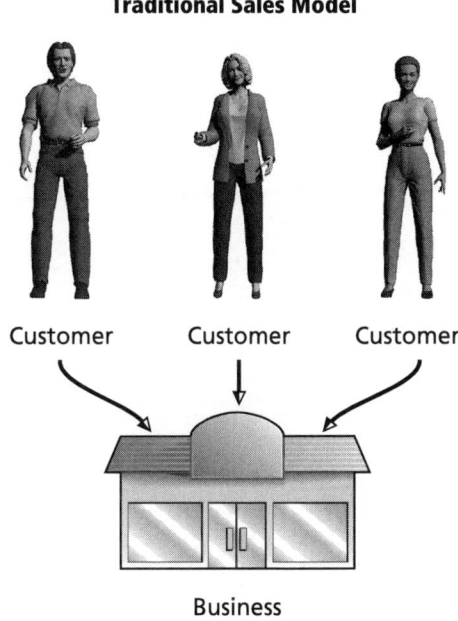

Figure 1.2
Many customers approach one retailer in a traditional model.

Part 1: Plan Your E-Commerce Initiative

E-commerce introduces the possibility of other sales models. For example, a number of businesses might form partnerships or a business cooperative (as shown in Figure 1.3), or various companies might form more extended partnerships to add services, value, and functionality to specialized sites (as shown in Figure 1.4, on page 17).

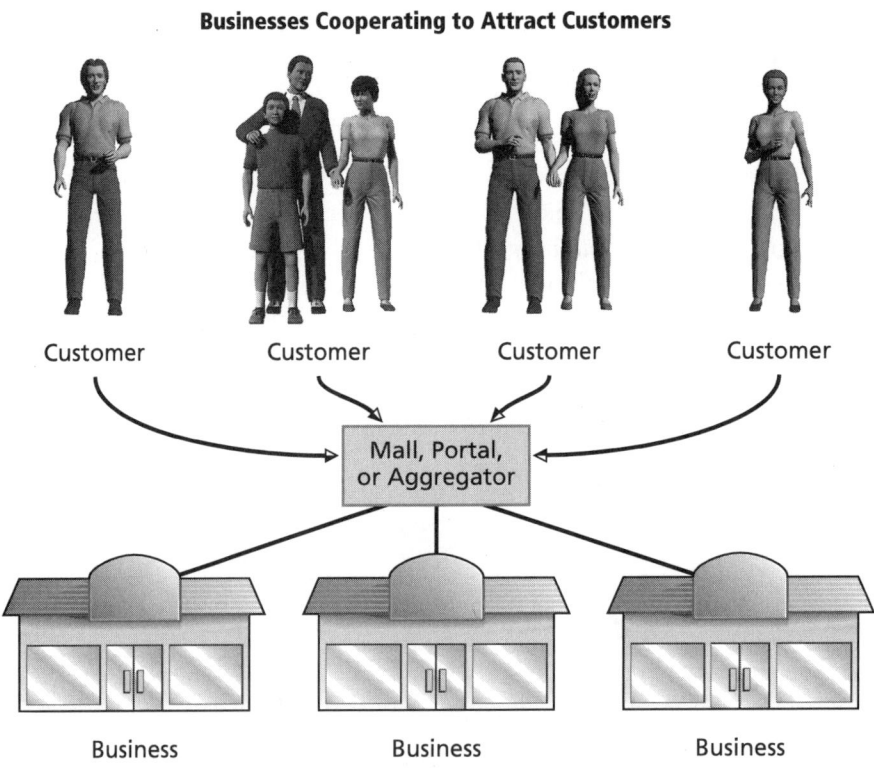

Figure 1.3

Many customers approach several online retailers cooperating to attract business.

Creating a website is only one part of online selling; remember that you must also address order fulfillment, customer and technical service, and so on. Order fulfillment must be quick—it can't depend on someone remembering to check for orders. Also, customer service expectations are high—people expect immediate responses via email or phone. To create an online sales environment that works, you must establish trust and integrity online. Take a look at successful online sales sites, such as Lands' End (*www.landsend.com*), Amazon.com (*www.amazon.com*), Barnes & Noble (*www.barnesandnoble.com*), and Beyond.com (*www.beyond.com*), to see what instills confidence in customers.

Chapter 1: Focusing Your E-Commerce Goals

Obviously, you have to look credible. Create an image for your site that is professional and appropriate to your audience, and use a design that serves your audience and your products. Don't junk up your site with unnecessary clutter such as visitor counters, gratuitous animations, and meaningless links. Have your site edited for typos, confusing grammar, and factual errors, and make your transaction system understandable and convenient to use. Put your site through an all-around quality check, and make sure your users will find your establishment trustworthy.

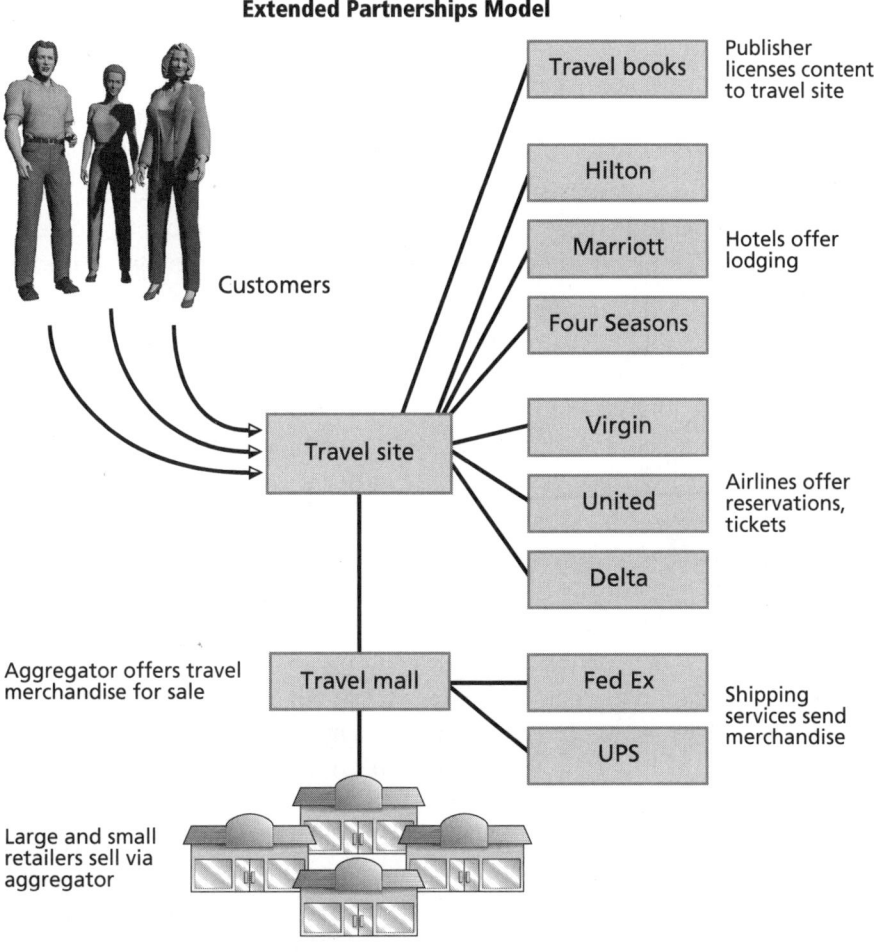

Figure 1.4
Businesses form strategic partnerships to leverage assets and offer more value and functionality to customers.

17

Part 1: Plan Your E-Commerce Initiative

Leverage your assets. If you are locally recognized, play that up. Post reviews of your restaurant, testimonials from your business's clients, endorsements by people known in your industry, awards from professional or industry associations, recognition by the Better Business Bureau or the American Academy of Optometry, or whatever says that you are a solid business entity.

Play on what's familiar. Perhaps your company or product is already well known. Good. Then you might not have to push the issue of establishing identity. But if your endeavor is new and you are going to have to work to make yourself known, you might want to form a strategic partnership with a larger, more established company or solicit testimonials. If nothing else, use established vendors for your site development, hosting, transaction system, and delivery. Creating your site with bCentral Site Manager, to use the most convenient example, is an excellent way to gain the credibility that comes with having a back end (the database, transaction system, and the programming that makes them function) powered by Microsoft, a company known the world over for its technology solutions.

Give your customers all the information they need to make a purchase. Provide images of your products. Consider using *thumbnails* (small images the size of postage stamps) that link to larger images appearing on a separate page to give a closer look to those who want one. Place price, size, description, and materials used right where customers can see them. Offer any other information that might entice a sale.

Make buying easy. Never put a barrier in front of a sale. Don't demand marketing information or ask customers to fill out a survey or register before they buy. Place Buy buttons where they are most visible, especially on pages that present product information. Remove or edit any language or images that might confuse people. (A confused customer does not ask questions—a confused customer leaves.) Make your forms simple but complete. Walk people through your ordering system quickly and, if possible, provide them with a way to buy with one click.

Offer convenient, known methods of payment. Don't make people send a check by surface mail, then wait for the check to clear, and then wait another four weeks for delivery. Set up a payment system that allows customers to use their credit cards on a *secure server*—a computer that's set up with software that enables the transaction while protecting the customer's credit card number and other personal information. (For more information on secure servers, see Chapter 10.) Consider keeping their credit card and delivery information in a database so that customers don't have to enter the information the next time they order, but do this only if

Chapter 1: Focusing Your E-Commerce Goals

you have a secure server that protects confidential data. (Again, see Chapter 10.) Make it easy to buy and the convenience of your online sales system will become an attractive alternative to getting in the car and shopping around at the local mall.

Let the customer know when the transaction has been processed. Don't make customers wonder whether their orders were successful. Provide them with the opportunity to review their orders, make corrections as needed, and then actually execute their purchases. When their purchases have been processed, say so, and give them unique confirmation numbers that they can use to track their orders during the fulfillment process or if something goes wrong (as it sometimes does).

Explain your delivery system. It's amazing how much more confident people feel when they know what you plan to do to get their purchases to them. Use familiar shipping methods such as the postal service or delivery services such as Federal Express Corporation (FedEx) or UPS, and tell people how long they might have to wait for delivery.

If something does go wrong, tell your customers that you'll fix any problems. Describe (perhaps by linking to your customer-service FAQ) what you'll do if an error occurs with their order. Post your return policy. (For a great example of how returns can be handled well, take a look at how Lands' End does it.) Treat people with respect. Post and stick to your privacy policy, describing how you will (or preferably *won't*) reuse your customers' email addresses and other information, and how you otherwise protect their privacy and security in your online store. Rather than simply including all customers in your mailing list, during the transaction, provide people with a check box labeled "Notify me of future sales, promotions, or specials." They can "opt in" if they want to get that information.

Caution

However tempting it might be to sell or rent your mailing list as a revenue source, don't sell or give your customers' email addresses to others without offering the customers the option not to be included. Providing your mailing list to others is one sure-fire way to turn off your customers, and you might not survive the onslaught that will result from this faux pas, no matter how innocent your intentions.

Finally, make sure your content is appropriate. For example, lawyer jokes might be appropriate if you are a self-help legal publisher selling books to consumers online, but they might undermine the credibility of a legal firm that handles corporate or criminal law. Running a contest is not the right lure for many sales sites; instead, the products should be the lure. (What's more, the contest will drain valuable resources that should be used to spiff up your customer service.) If you consider using email messages, chats, or other efforts to create online community to bring customers in and keep them coming back (see Chapter 6), also consider whether those methods are truly in line with your site's intended purpose. Common wisdom says that each time a user returns, you should show them something new, but the new feature should be *something that supports your site's mission*. For a sales site, for example, it can be simply a new product or a new idea for using an existing product.

Selling Business-to-Business

Market studies by Forrester Research, Inc. indicate that by 2003, 90 percent of e-commerce will be business-to-business. Business-to-business e-commerce ventures include industries such as transportation, electronics, leisure, engineering, and energy, each of which is currently worth billions or even trillions of dollars. In a business-to-business setting, you can forget about measuring success by the number of click-throughs or page views (see Chapter 14); getting and keeping customers is what counts. Branding and service make all the difference.

In that sense, business-to-business e-commerce couldn't be more traditional, but its applications can be very innovative. Consider the example of ChemConnect, a portal for the chemical industry that enables business-to-business chemical transfers. PartMiner, another business-to-business venture, searches for electronic components for its customers. A third example, VerticalNet, reported in 1999 that it had generated 47,000 qualified leads for buyers and sellers in vertical markets and had auctioned two items worth more than $30 million each via the Internet.

A successful business-to-business e-commerce site can minimize routine sales calls by making ordering quicker and easier via online forms that are available 24 hours a day, seven days a week. It can transfer electronic files to speed up production processes. It can consist of virtual enterprises, virtual cooperatives, virtual markets, or communities of commerce that are combined for mutual benefit. Some of these ideas are not so new in the world of business, but historically they have been considered too expensive to implement. The technology of today's Internet lowers the barriers and makes new models possible.

> **Note**
>
> Remember: Your site's offerings should be driven by your business goals. These goals determine what functionality and features are needed in your website.

Who Is Your Customer?

To serve your customers, you must understand how and why they do business with you. Then you must build your website based on those needs. E-commerce provides a unique opportunity to have a one-on-one relationship with your customers, and you can empower them to control the relationship by providing convenient methods to communicate with you via email and forms on your site.

As you learn more about your target market, it will become easier for others within your market to do business with you. You'll want to find out about your customers' age group, income, education level, gender; desire for accessibility versus sophistication in your products and site design; how they access the Internet (using what Internet service providers (ISPs) and what browsers), and more. For more on identifying your market, see Chapter 4, which discusses *branding* (creating a message and image that reaches the market and defines your company and products).

The Internet Is International—Are You?

Your customers in the brick-and-mortar world might be local to your area, but your website might attract a national or international audience. You'll have to make some decisions about selling to this broader market. If your operation is in Boise, Idaho, will you ship to overseas American military bases? To areas the United States Postal Service treats as domestic (though they are not part of the fifty United States) such as Puerto Rico and Guam? To France? How will you present your content? Will you translate it into other languages so that foreign customers can read it? Will you accept various currencies? How will you handle sales tax, value-added tax (VAT), and other taxes? Gathering marketing data for other countries requires a different level of respect for privacy than it does in the US, so you will need to consider cultural differences. For example, in France, asking someone what he or she does for a living is considered very rude. (Supposedly, this knowledge provides you with insight into the person's income level, which you would never ask about.)

Research by IDC indicates that by 2002, Internet users outside the US will outnumber US users. Western Europe's growth in Internet use is especially strong. It is tempting to try to capitalize on this information, but doing so changes your market and makes e-commerce more complex. People in many countries don't have credit cards, for example. Accepting international orders will bring up numerous issues. Are you prepared to handle them?

> **Note**
>
> You don't have to do business internationally just because the Internet is international. But you should post your policies about international sales on your site. If you accept orders only from within the 50 United States, say so. (And be polite about it.)

Identifying Your Target Market

After launching your website, you'll know your customers through a variety of electronic means (see Chapter 13). You might also know your customers through an existing brick-and-mortar business. However, your online customers might differ from your other customers. To find out about Internet users in general and to investigate whatever data might exist about online customers in your industry, seek out statistics via sources on the Internet. (The statistics presented in this chapter were all obtained via Internet searches.) Good starting places are the usual suspects: Yahoo!, Alta Vista, and other search services.

For recent information regarding web usage—including the top ten most-visited sites this week, how many hours people are spending online each week, and how many sites they visit and for how long—try the Nielsen/NetRatings reporter (*www.nielsen-netratings.com/hot_off.htm*). You can also try the websites of the various market research companies mentioned in this chapter. Be forewarned, however: These companies often charge a hefty price for their published reports, which they sell online. But sometimes you'll find sample data on their sites that's actually quite useful and free.

Reaching a Local Market

You need to know where your customers are and how to get to them. If your audience is local, you can list your site with local search services and use a variety of other methods to promote your site locally (see Chapter 12). When you create your site, though, remember to include your location *on your home page*. Customers who wander onto your site will need to know that your operation is local, and they'll need to know where "local" is.

Who Is Your Competition?

The good news is that if your competitors are already online, you can check out their sites and conduct a speedy competitive analysis. For that matter, if your operation is local, you can look at the sites of companies that are in your industry but in other towns and cities to get an idea of what's happening in similar companies. You might be able to adapt an idea or two to your own purposes. (Hey, *ideas* aren't copyrighted; it's their expression that is. See Chapter 3.)

The bad news is that if your competitors are already online, they were there first and defined the market, and now you'll have to be better and different to succeed against them. You'll have to be clever about it. (See Chapter 4 for ideas about how to differentiate your image or brand. See Chapter 5 for ideas about how to set yourself apart with superior customer service.)

If you have an innovative idea for doing business online, you might have no visible competitors. But if the idea is innovative enough, your "competition" might be public perception or public ignorance. A few months ago, I saw a demonstration of a product that had been described to me earlier. The product was nothing like I'd imagined it to be. It was so new and different that the makers had no way of describing it easily. To sell it, they had to demonstrate it in person. Similarly, a few years ago, I co-wrote one of the very first books about web browsers. My co-author and I had to explain in painstaking detail what the Web was, what a browser did, what an ISP was. Public perception has now caught up with those concepts, but in those days, a web browser's stiffest competition came not from other web browsers but from what the public did not know. Take this into account as you plan your endeavor.

> **Caution**
>
> The e-commerce industry is highly competitive. If you have an innovative idea, keep it under your hat until you can launch it. Announcing the features of an innovative venture two weeks before launch gives competitors time to upstage you. I've seen it happen.

Remember: In an online setting, your competition might become national if not international. (See the section "The Internet Is International—Are You?" earlier in this chapter.) It's up to you whether you accept the challenge of a larger sphere of operations; just make sure you've communicated to your customers what the boundaries of your business are.

Aligning Your Resources with Your Goals

Reality check: You might want to build the next eBay, but if you have only one person with little Hypertext Markup Language (HTML) experience to build your site, it isn't going to happen. You'll need to redefine your goals or find and allocate additional resources. On the other hand, you don't need unlimited resources or a $5 million budget to launch an e-commerce site. See bCentral for solutions to building an economical, easy-to-launch storefront site.

> **Note**
>
> Keep in mind the ultimate goal, which is that you want your e-commerce endeavor to be, if not immediately profitable, then at least not a burden to your business.

You do have to think about your resources as you plan your e-commerce endeavor. Think about where funding will come from: Will it be from the profits of your brick-and-mortar business? From investors? Or perhaps from a second mortgage on your house or the liquidation of assets? Think, too, about staff time: What will it take to create your site, launch it, promote it, and maintain it? And what technologies do you anticipate needing? (See Chapter 2 for budget insight; information about technologies appears throughout this book.) Other than your business acumen, what expertise do you have? Will you hire people, outsource, or keep your

Chapter 1: Focusing Your E-Commerce Goals

endeavor scaled back enough to make it manageable without extra staffing? Will your budget allow for equipment? What do you have already? What do you need?

> **Note**
>
> Chapter 2 includes a description of what you can expect to build based on your overall budget—for example, what does $500,000 get you that $50,000 doesn't, and what can you do for $10,000, $5,000, or even less than $1,000?

An often-overlooked cost associated with pursuing any venture is the *opportunity cost*. This is the cost of pursuing that venture as opposed to other opportunities that might arise at the same time. Of course, it is common business sense to weigh the relative value and risk of pursuing one opportunity rather than another. However, this weighing process is especially important as you launch your e-commerce venture. Would you be better off opening a second location of your traditional store instead? Only you can make that call.

Building a website site includes, at the very least, design, branding, programming, and *hosting* (placing the site on a computer that delivers it to the public). You'll need to weigh the cost of performing these tasks in-house (which has a time cost) versus contracting outside services (which can have a substantial monetary cost). For the smallest businesses, much of the work will probably fall to unqualified in-house staff. (Again, see bCentral for potential solutions.)

To focus on allocating resources appropriately, ask yourself these questions: What would you spend to grow your business without the e-commerce option? Would you hire a sales rep? Would you spend more on advertising, marketing, or outreach? Would an e-commerce site save some costs? Include both savings and costs in your budget as you plan your site.

Focusing Your Expectations

Let's talk about return on investment (ROI). Although you might usually judge success by the numbers at the bottom of your Microsoft Excel spreadsheet, some types of web success aren't so apparent. For example, how do you really measure the value of advertising? Various sites have various purposes, and success has to be measured differently for sites that don't make producing revenue their primary goal. Customer service sites can survey customers to measure success. Business-to-business sites can ask partners about their level of satisfaction.

> **Caution**
>
> In e-commerce, measuring the number of "hits" is often irrelevant. A site that is getting millions of hits can nevertheless be a drain on your business resources. How can you consider that a business success?

Long visits might be a measure of the success of a marketing site, where you want customers to spend time viewing information. But on a sales site, you want customers to make purchases. Too much browsing can distract customers from completing the sales cycle.

Setting Benchmarks for Success

How do you spell success? Traffic, sales, acceptance by the public, savings in cost, media presence? Set benchmarks that are attainable and that correspond to the goals of your site. (See Chapter 13 for more information on measuring success.) Set realistic goals, and err on the conservative side. Give your site time to ramp up to its potential—six months is really minimal. In many industries, it is believed that it takes at least three to five years to become profitable, which in Internet time, translates to a minimum of 18 to 30 months.

Writing a Mission Statement

We've probably all heard the metaphorical thud when someone in some group suggested writing a mission statement and the idea went over like a lead balloon. In truth, a mission statement can be a terrific tool for helping you to focus. It's true that a mission statement that uses dull language, includes everything, and offends no one is probably a mission statement that will also inspire no one. Nevertheless, any mission statement will help you focus.

Far better is the mission statement that has vision. Visions lead. They drive your endeavor. They offer inspiring focus and help everyone understand how they can contribute. To inspire people to do their best, when

Chapter 1:   Focusing Your E-Commerce Goals

you create your mission statement, focus not on the creation of the document but on the creation of the vision. The language matters less than the ideas. If you are stuck for ideas about where to begin, ask these questions:

- What service or product does your company provide?
- What are three to five goals that your company wants to achieve? (Rank them in order of importance.)
- What does success look like, given the nature of the company's goals?
- How will the website help achieve the company's goals?
- What are three words that describe the company's image?
- Who is the target market?
- What content or technology is available?

After you've answered those questions, throw away the answers. (The point of the exercise was to start you thinking.) Most mission statements are overly descriptive. They are written by committees and include everything the company wants to do now and forever. Instead, a mission statement should be very short, and should get right to the point. It should prescribe which path, of the many the company might take, it will focus on.

Here is an example:

XYZ Unlimited provides the finest experience in extreme sports by creating and building safe, high-performance equipment, and by helping sports-equipment users find new and better ways to use the equipment XYZ manufactures.

Your mission statement should be specific. Simply saying you'll market your products or services online is much too vague: To whom? How? To what end? Look again at XYZ Unlimited's statement. It really ought to describe results that are defined and measurable:

XYZ Unlimited is the number one manufacturer of equipment for extreme sports. Quality, the safety of our customers, and providing a fine extreme sports experience are our first concerns.

Note the measurable results: The *number one* statement is measurable through sales figures, and the *quality*, *safety*, and *fine experience* statements are strategic directives. As you shape your mission statement, reach for such measurable goals and defined strategies, but don't overreach. Don't aim for things you can't deliver. Declaring your commitment to 24/7 (24 hours a day, 7 days a week) technical-support access is good only if you can keep that promise. Increasing penetration into national or international markets is good only if that's a realistic goal. Can you handle it?

Your mission statement should not be a memorial tacked above your desk. It should be a living document. As your e-commerce venture changes, so should your mission statement. It should be equally dynamic, growing (or shrinking) with the company. Remember: It is a tool to help you focus on your goals and the strategy you will use to accomplish them.

Ten Common E-Commerce Errors

The path to success in e-commerce is full of potholes. To make the journey smoother, here are ten things you want to avoid:

- Ignoring your existing business model or sales channels, your marketing, fulfillment, inventory, and accounting procedures, or your customers.
- Building a site with bells, whistles, cutting-edge design, or complex navigation that obscures your message.
- Creating web pages that download slowly.
- Making it hard to find your products, product information, service information, and so on.
- Confusing customers who are trying to make a purchase. For example, creating a transaction path that isn't brief and orderly, not providing customers with acknowledgment of their purchase or order, or not letting them know if an item is out of stock.
- Not giving your customer confidence in the security of the transaction.
- Failing to build a back end that's easily managed as well as powerful enough for your current and planned needs.
- Charging higher prices for purchases made online than you do for traditional purchases.
- Not providing customers with a means for communicating with you.
- Building a site that's harder to use than ordering or communicating via phone or fax.

Chapter 1: Focusing Your E-Commerce Goals

Making a Plan of Action

By now, you should have thought through your site's goals and your overall strategy for achieving them. Will your site be built on a cornerstone of community providing people with like interests a place to gather)? Will it be a portal to information or perhaps to other sites? Will you be selling via secure transactions? A catalog offering purchase support? Taking orders from other businesses? Now that you have in mind what you want to do, what's the next step?

Building a website site involves these basic phases:

- Planning
- Design
- Development
- Deployment
- Promotion
- Maintenance

You're ready now to take the next step in the planning phase. Whether you are getting ready to launch an entire online business or simply an online project, you owe it to yourself to write a business plan or project plan.

Creating a Business Plan

Traditionally, every business, large or small, begins with the creation of a business plan that can be presented to bankers or investors. Even if an entrepreneur has no expectation of ever seeking investment capital, a business plan will help him or her focus ideas and form strategies for starting the business. A business plan includes such subplans as a marketing plan, a balance sheet, an income statement, a statement of cash flow (which calculates true expenses against income and then projects that calculation into the future), and so on.

The four major steps in planning a business are:

- Defining the business (mission statement)
- Setting goals, objectives, and milestones (focusing the expectation of return on investment)
- Identifying key staff positions, employees, resources, and associated costs
- Finalizing the plan of action

Writing a mission statement, setting goals, and focusing on expectations of success (return on investment) have been covered earlier in this chapter. As far as resources are concerned, considering key staff or team members, the reasons why they are needed, what other employees might be essential, and what their qualifications and job descriptions will be depends on the scope of your endeavor.

Although the specifics of how to write a detailed business plan and what form it should take are beyond the scope of this book, having read this chapter, you are already well on your way. The remainder of this book will help you define and clarify your plan. Remember to allow for expansion as you outline your plan. Give yourself plenty of time to write everything down—several weeks or more is commonly needed. Time invested here, although it might compete with your day job or existing business, will pay off when you launch your e-commerce endeavor and find that you have all your ducks in a nice, neat row.

> **Note**
>
> Remember: Sales volume alone does not create a successful business. Profits must sustain necessary staffing, labor, fixed costs, and so on before return on investment occurs. Also, start-ups take work. Two years of 80-hour weeks is common.

Creating a Project Plan

Define your project plan just as you would a business plan. Think about your goals, time lines, budget, technology needs, and who will do what, both before launch and after. How will you build the skills or team you need to carry your project through? Is your endeavor so large or complex that you need a project manager or some kind of "general contractor" to keep it coordinated and on track? Will you be that person? Will that job take you away from other, more profitable ventures? Evaluate or define your process for accomplishing tasks. Eliminate unnecessary steps, but focus on your objectives, including quality. Define requirements. Think about staff, technologies, equipment, and the functionality needed to make your project work. How will you select good vendors who will not bleed you over the course of months or years? Above all, understand your goals.

Chapter 1: Focusing Your E-Commerce Goals

Is It Really Feasible?

It's important not to fall in love with your e-commerce plan. Instead, be its harshest critic. Show it to your accountant, your lawyer, your spouse. Put it in a drawer for a few days; then take a fresh look, and think hard about any potholes you see along your path. If you know in your gut that you must proceed or live with regret, go forward. If you have doubts, revamp your plan and try again.

Then ask the same questions all over again. Will you kick yourself in years to come if you don't do this? Is the risk worth the return?

Above all, don't be wowed by reports of enormous success. And do think carefully before you jump.

Chapter 2

Setting Up a Budget and Sticking to It

E-commerce is an industry that is still in its infancy. As a result, few models exist for creating budgets for e-commerce endeavors. Other industries have formulas that have been tested over many years. For example, the food service industry has its famous ratio of thirds, where one third of every expense is allocated to each of three categories of costs: food, labor, and other. (This formula, by the way, provides a simple method of dividing costs but doesn't specify a particular profit margin.) Although at least *some* models have recently evolved for e-commerce budgeting, it will probably be a few more years before formulaic budgeting tricks can offer entrepreneurs and managers a leg up in planning their e-commerce ventures.

Budgeting is not the most glamorous aspect of e-commerce. However, it is a vital tool for determining whether your venture is going to be a profit center, a cost center, or an expensive hobby. Let's take a look at the ins and outs of today's e-commerce budgeting.

Part 1: Plan Your E-Commerce Initiative

Where Do You Start?

The specific format for your budget (how it's set up, what categories are included, and so on) often depends on whether your online endeavor is an extension of an existing company or a brand-new start-up. It also depends on the size of the project and what components of e-commerce you will include. Different types of e-commerce ventures require different levels and types of funding. For example, a site that publishes information of interest to a trade or professional group will need an editorial budget, while a site that sells hand-knit baby items will need a budget for shooting and processing photographs of the items. Similarly, some sites require a hefty budget for customer service or technical support of products, and some require a big technology budget for a heavy-duty server that can take an intense load and for the technical staff to support it.

Follow a Known Format

Your company or your accountant might have a prescribed format for budgeting—one that's easy to understand because it's familiar. If so, you should probably follow that format as best you can. Some tweaking might be necessary to make the format fit a web initiative, but getting in line with the tried and true at this level can help you get budget approval or the kind of advice you need from your accountant before you proceed.

Be aware that a lot of e-commerce lingo is new to executives and accountants. They might not understand, for example, why you need a *staging server* (space on a server where you can post pages for testing before going live; see Chapter 10) or *redundancy in your database* (duplication of the system so that if one part breaks, the system will still function; see Chapter 10). Anticipating their needs by providing supporting documentation for any special needs is generally a good idea. (If you need to define terms, check the Glossary of this book.)

If you plan to solicit bids from outside contractors (web shops, design firms, programmers, and so on) for your e-commerce project, you will probably want to set up a sample budget first. Doing so offers three advantages:

- It allows you to test your plan to see if it's out of whack with your resources.
- It allows you to walk into meetings with some preconceived idea of the scope of your project and its general, potential cost.
- It allows you to review bids intelligently.

Chapter 2: Setting Up a Budget and Sticking to It

What's in a Website Budget

What appears in a website budget depends first on the scope of the project. What are your goals for the site (see Chapter 1)? What resources or personnel are already on hand? Be specific. Will you be building a small, simple site; an e-commerce department; or a standalone e-commerce company? If you will be managing a very small endeavor by yourself, talk to others who've done the same. If you will be building a department within an existing company, talk to people in other departments (especially accounting!) to find out whether you have to figure office space, desks, phones, and equipment into your budget, or whether the company spreads these expenses across all operations without requiring you to specify them for your department.

You simply cannot do too much research. Read everything you can—this book, others, Microsoft's online resources, *everything*. Then move out from there. The world is full of people who have experience and opinions. Talk to everyone who might help you consider all the angles. If you'll be hiring a team or contracting with a web shop, pick their brains as you interview them. Ask about projects they've worked on, the scope of these projects, the resources that were available, and what was accomplished with those resources. You probably won't get an answer to a question like "What was your budget?" Answers to such questions are usually squelched in advance by nondisclosure agreements (NDAs). But you can get an idea of the money involved by asking peripheral questions. In the course of all this research, your own budget will begin to gel in your mind.

Tip

During budgeting, keep your company's values in mind. A company that practices branding or believes deeply in customer service is going to budget more for those aspects of its web endeavor than a company that feels research and development are most crucial.

Setting Realistic Expectations

Have you ever wondered what those big, slick, corporate websites actually cost? Brace yourself. Building one of those sites can easily cost $500,000; maintaining the site (for example, creating fresh content, upgrading functionality, promoting the site, managing the hardware and connection, and so on) commonly costs in excess of $5 million a year. And, interestingly, not all of those sites reap a profit. In fact, many of them are listed by the company's bean counters as *cost centers*, not profit centers. They might serve the purpose of marketing the company or its products or services, but they are often seen as expensive necessities that don't contribute in any direct way to the company's bottom line.

Let's take a look at how much bang you can expect for your buck. For the most part, the discussions that follow refer to the cost of creating a site, not promoting it and not updating or maintaining it. Building a site and then not promoting it doesn't make sense because you are unlikely to develop much traffic (or business). And building a site but not maintaining it has about the same effect as building a house and not maintaining it: things will fall apart. Text will go out of date, links will rot, the site will look old and stale, and functionality will go bad. So as you consider the following budget categories, remember that your budget should also include the ongoing costs of promotion and maintenance. (See section "Budgeting for Promotion and Maintenance," later in this chapter.)

What Can You Do for Around $500,000?

For the really big bucks, you can hire a world-class web design shop, or you can even combine the services of a branding consultant and a top-notch designer. If your goal is selling products or services, you'll also be able to support that by buying the custom development of a slick transaction system and a powerful database to serve your product catalog. Whatever your goal, you'll be able to afford a back-end system that can handle a great deal of traffic so that millions of users per month can access your site and use it to its full potential. Your investment will also allow you to hire professional copywriters, editors, and artists to develop snappy content targeted to your market (as defined by the research your branding consultant has conducted to identify your customers). You will probably have to add more money to your budget if you want to use custom photography (as opposed to stock photos purchased by your designers from a catalog of images). But hey, when you're in this league, what's a few dollars more?

Chapter 2: Setting Up a Budget and Sticking to It

What Can You Do for $50,000 or So?

For $50,000, you can hire a respectable web shop to create your site. It will be professionally designed and will probably have a thoughtful navigational system that enables visitors to get around easily, but it might not be cutting edge in its look or functionality. That's fine; not all sites have to be visually stunning. In most cases, strong content and ease of use are preferable.

Your $50,000 investment won't buy a powerful back end that can handle millions of users per month, but it will probably buy one that can handle hundreds of thousands. Your transaction system won't be as quick to use as the more expensive, highly customized types; customers might have to traverse seven pages instead of three to complete a transaction. You won't be able to afford a branding consultant, but your designers will be able to use the "look and feel" elements (colors, fonts, logos, and so on) that define your company's identity. (This assumes, of course, that the elements are translatable into web colors and fonts—not all colors and fonts work on the Web; see Chapters 7, 8, and 9 for more information.)

Remember: Presenting simple text and straightforward content is more economical than offering complex functionality and lots of special effects. An informational site with approximately 2000 pages of content (that's quite a lot), including regular articles and special reports, will run perhaps $50,000 per year (in ongoing costs). However, the initial design costs for this type of site would be quite low, because the design work would involve nothing more than coming up with a handful of fairly simple page templates. A content editor could then paste purchased content into the appropriate template. Keeping the process of creating new pages very simple and providing the editor with a powerful computer would keep time costs as low as possible and would therefore help keep ongoing costs down. Although the site would first call on the time of at least one staff person, for a mid-sized organization that presents only information—a trade organization, for example—this type of site could be an excellent e-commerce solution.

What Can You Do for $5,000 to $10,000?

For $5,000, you can create a small site with approximately 10 or 20 pages of professionally designed content—that's *content*, not bells and whistles such as animations of your product in action. You might include, for example, an About the Company page, a small roundup of simple catalog pages (not in a fancy database), a Tech or Customer Support page and a FAQ page to support your products, and a form that allows customers to order products or catalogs via email. Your budget can support hiring a designer to apply your company's look to the site, by coming up with a simple page layout that includes your logo, chosen font, and identifying color scheme. But for $5,000, you won't get custom technical development of your back-end system, and you can forget about a custom-built database and transaction system. You can't expect the designer to create the company look from scratch or every page to look unique, and you can't expect to include lots of art or nifty effects such as *mouseovers* (text that changes color or form when a mouse pointer passes over it).

For $10,000, you can get all the things a $5,000 budget will buy, and you can also hire a programmer to create a few forms that allow your pages to be updated by someone who has no HTML skills. You won't be able to afford a big, complex database with lots of functionality, but you can add a simple database that is useful nonetheless. You can then store information in the database for efficient presentation on your web pages, and you'll be able to present richer information about your products to your customers. For example, you can offer a larger and more sophisticated product catalog, with photos and descriptive information. Having a database will also enable your site to handle online transactions—for example, your customers will be able to make purchases at your site using their credit cards.

In addition, with a budget of $10,000, you might even be able to augment your site with a simple *extranet* (a site that is available not to the general public but only to those people you designate). Typical uses for an extranet are to support sales by making key information about your products available to your reps and to allow buyers to enter and track orders. The extranet you add to your $10,000 website might access the database that contains the product information you present to the public, but can present additional data to those who have entered the password required to access your extranet. Your extranet can have the same look and feel as your public website, or it can be more utilitarian or more upscale. (See the Appendix for more on extranets.)

Chapter 2: Setting Up a Budget and Sticking to It

What Can You Do with a Minimal Investment?

For less than $1,000 of initial investment, you have three basic options:

- You can hire a designer to create a single, basic page template for a very simple site with perhaps five pages, including a list of your products along with contact information that urges customers to call or send email to find out more. (You will pour the content of the five pages into the template that was designed.)

- You can use a web-authoring program such as Microsoft FrontPage to produce a site with basic functionality yourself. FrontPage lets you create your own design or use any of a number of pre-designed looks called *themes*.

- You can use Microsoft bCentral Site Manager, a service that allows you to create a fully functional e-commerce site even if you don't know anything about HTML, back ends, branding, design, or programming. (For details about how bCentral Site Manager makes this possible, see Microsoft bCentral, at *www.bcentral.com*.)

If you decide to hire a designer, you might want to look around for an entry-level designer who can do HTML coding or who knows enough to work with a novice coder to create the pages. Don't hire a designer who has no web design experience at all. Web pages are simply not the same as printed pages, and the design issues are numerous.

If you decide to go the FrontPage route, you might still want to hire a designer to create the template you'll use when building your pages yourself. (Be sure the designer knows and uses FrontPage.) Before you spring for a designer, though, check out the themes, or pre-designed pages, that FrontPage provides.

If you opt to use bCentral Site Manager, you'll be stepped through a series of wizards (like those that help you with many Microsoft products) that will help you set up your site, choose among the pre-designed looks offered, and enable a transaction system. bCentral Site Manager lets you make choices among looks tailored to your industry. It also lets you set up a site with a back end powered by Microsoft server software and a credible transaction system. For smaller businesses, bCentral Site Manager can provide a good deal of cost-effective bang for a minimal investment.

Remember that if you build the site yourself, you'll be investing time in both the learning curve and the actual work of creating the site. You probably need to evaluate the opportunity costs of this time.

No matter how you decide to proceed, keep the number of pages small—fewer than 10, for example—and include no animation, gimmicks, or custom graphics. If you decide to work with a designer, make sure to interview him or her carefully; read both the chapter of this book on jobbing out work on your site (Chapter 9) and the following section in this chapter, and consider all the angles. A lousy site that costs only $1,000 isn't a bargain; it's a waste of $1,000.

How Can You Keep Costs Down?

To rein in costs and keep them reined in, follow these guidelines:

- **Remember that text costs less.** Text is cheaper to produce than art, video, sound, animation, special visual effects like mouseovers, and anything that requires programming. It's not that hiring a writer is necessarily cheaper (rates range from, say, $25 per hour to $75 per hour or more), but rather that the cost of producing the pages is less. Creating the simple HTML code required for text is just not as expensive as art preparation, programming, and the other work required to make more complex pages work.

- **Clarify your goals and stick to them.** Chapter 1 described the process of developing your site's goals. If necessary, go back to that chapter, read it again, and move on from there.

- **Get bids for project costs by the page rather than by the hour.** When a contractor bids by the hour without a cap, you don't know what the site is going to cost until the game's over. Hourly costs can really stack up, and the contractor has no real incentive for keeping the hours (and the cost) to a minimum, or for completing the project quickly.

- **Organize and prioritize your content.** Before you speak to designers and before you get bids, gather together all the existing content you want to include (company information, product information, customer service documents, contact information, and so on). Then make a list of the new content you plan to create. After that, take a look at Chapter 7. Think carefully about how each piece of information will serve your site's goals, whether it is needed in an online setting, and how customers will use it. Toss anything that isn't crucial into a folder, and set it aside (just in case you really need it after all). When you talk to designers, having a plan in mind will make it easier to get a real bid, and having a bid will make it easier to monitor costs.

- **Avoid gimmicks, bells, and whistles.** The special programming required for nifty effects, such as personalizing web pages with the customer's name, can cost a bundle. What's more, extra effects require a more powerful back end, which can drive up costs. And because effects make the site more complex, they make maintaining it more complex, which can involve more maintenance time. You should think carefully about adding bells and whistles anyway. Ask yourself what they add to the site. Is it real value and functionality, or are you just draping your store with twinkle lights?

- **Don't include features you aren't prepared to maintain.** A weekly article about caring for roses might be just the type of content that will keep customers coming back to an online garden store, but are you prepared to take time away from your family or from actually tending your store to write the article every week? Are you prepared to hire a writer?

- **Keep staffing costs low.** Staffing is a commitment. Hiring people means you will have them, their salaries, their benefits, and their taxes as constant obligations, even when business is slow. While you are ramping up and until you know your e-commerce venture is a go—until you are prepared to commit to payroll, management overhead, human resources staff, and so on—keep your operation lean.

- **Avoid feature creep.** We've all experienced this insidious circumstance. You're remodeling your kitchen, and the contractor suggests real granite for the counter instead of faux granite Formica; or you go to a car dealer to buy a basic sedan and wind up with a convertible with an elaborate stereo system; or you start a programmer on a simple project, and along the way you add bells and whistles without considering your bottom line. These are all examples of *feature creep*—the creeping in of features that weren't originally in the plan. As you build your site and as you maintain it, avoid this phenomenon. It can bloat any budget in no time.

Part 1: Plan Your E-Commerce Initiative

Looking at a Model Spreadsheet

Budgets are often developed in a spreadsheet that includes a line item for each expense. Expenses are logically grouped to make reading the budget easier. As mentioned earlier in this chapter, different companies and accountants use varying methods, but no matter what method is used, the spreadsheet should paint a clear picture of the project. Take a look at the sample spreadsheet in Figure 2.1, which might help you in devising your own budget.

Item	Hours	$/Hour	Fixed Cost	Total Cost	Notes
PLANNING					
Concept					
Define Target Audience	20	75		1500	
Investigate Competition	24	25		600	Intern will research
Test Concept			2000	2000	Use focus group or customers
Needs Assessment					Include time for concept
Staff	4	75		300	In-house and freelance?
Hardware	10	125		1250	
Connectivity	8	125		1000	See attachment re ISP options
Software	6	125		750	
Project Management	100	100		10000	20% of project budget
DESIGN					
Architecture and Navigation	24	100		2400	Flowchart, schematics
Look and Feel (concept)	16	100		1600	Includes creating "roughs"
Storyboarding			2000	2000	
DEVELOPMENT (CONTENT)					
Write Content	80	65		5200	
Edit Content	40	75		3000	Use freelance copy editor
Art			4000	4000	Purchased or licensed illustrations
DEVELOPMENT (TECH)					
HTML	50	75		3750	HTML outsourced
Media Conversion	20	100		2000	

Figure 2.1
A sample spreadsheet showing the budget for a mid-sized e-commerce site.

Tip

No one will ever ding you for coming in *under* budget. To give yourself some leeway, you might want to boost your estimates by as much as 20 percent. Also, if your budget process involves seeking approval from a higher up, you might want to include a few line items you can compromise on or even sacrifice during negotiations.

In the sample spreadsheet, each item is named, its costs are categorized, and categories are summarized as totals. Budget items are also grouped by activity. General categories include *fixed* expenses (one-time costs such as a piece of software), *hourly* expenses (such as the per-hour cost of programmers), and *ongoing* expenses (the expenses you incur regularly, such as rent, utilities, salaries, benefits, and so on). You'll learn more expense categories in the section titled "Categorizing Costs by Type," later in this chapter.

> **Tip**
>
> For your convenience, the spreadsheet shown in Figure 2.1 is posted in the E-Commerce Management Center at *www.tauberkienan.com* and at *http://mspress.microsoft.com/mspress/products/3757*. You are welcome to use it as a model for your own budget spreadsheet.

Grouping Costs by Activity

In Figure 2.1, line items are listed in the leftmost column, and they are grouped by row according to the activities that are generally involved in building and maintaining a website. (Of course, your line items will be different, because they will be based on your site plan and e-commerce goals.) This method of organizing financial information provides a clear picture of what will happen and what each task will cost. It is also an easy way to remember the categories for which you must have a budget.

As mentioned in Chapter 1, building a website involves the following basic steps:

- Planning
- Designing
- Developing
- Deploying
- Promoting
- Maintaining

Consider the activities involved in each step as you devise your budget. The following sections will help you focus on those activities.

Budgeting for the Planning Stage

Remember to budget for both needs assessment and project management. Project management can include needs assessment, in the sense that you might assign the project manager the task of conducting the needs assessment. But the two activities are actually separate, one being performed before the site is built and the other being an ongoing task performed throughout the project.

The discussion in Chapter 1 of setting goals and writing a business plan or project plan will set you on the road to assessing your needs. Needs assessment includes brainstorming, research, project planning, and perhaps the budgeting process itself. Specifically, it consists of these activities:

- Researching Internet demographics and statistics, industry trends, and information on Internet marketing
- Identifying target markets and ferreting out information about your potential customers, such as how they access the Internet, how they find your existing business, and how they currently buy
- Identifying your competitors, the traditional methods they use in business, and the methods they use online
- Identifying your project's goals, the potential advantages and risks in proceeding, and any advantages and risks in not doing the project

If your endeavor is large enough, you might hire professionals to conduct some of this research for you; otherwise, you'll have to budget your own time or a team member's time to do it.

Project management can eat up as much as 20 percent of the overall time it takes to complete a project. Project management includes managing staff, contractors, schedules, and the budget, but also involves meetings, phone calls, executive summaries and presentations, and so on.

During the planning stage, you'll also need to plan and budget for the following:

- Staff and personnel (in-house or contracted)
- Hardware (the computers that act as servers, workstations for your staff, and so on)
- Connectivity (your site's connection to the Internet via an ISP, hosting service, or another of the options outlined in Chapter 10)
- Software (HTML editors, graphics programs, word-processing software, email systems, traffic analysis systems, transaction and database servers, web servers, and so on)

If the project is being handled in-house, this planning time can be built into the general work schedule. If the project is being handled by freelance contractors or a web shop, the planning time is billable, and you *will be* billed for it. Some contractors build project management charges into their rates, while others charge separately for it.

> **Tip**
>
> If you are creating a budget for someone else's approval, tie expensive items (such as hardware) to a return on the investment. Point out what specific benefit will result from the expense, and what consequences might result if the purchase is not approved. (For example, the server might crash and interrupt service to customers.) Provide detail in an attachment to back up what you predict.

Budgeting for Design and Development

After you've read Chapter 8 on creating a site, you will find it easier to understand some of the terms used in this section. For now, here is a list of the general activities involved in designing and building a site, all of which have an associated cost in dollars or time:

- Planning the site's size, architecture, and navigation
- Designing the site's look
- Creating a *storyboard* for the site (mocking it up as sketches)
- Writing (and editing) or licensing the content
- Coding in HTML
- Integrating any graphics and multimedia (and perhaps licensing images, video, or sound)
- Programming *scripts* (small programs written in languages such as Microsoft active server pages (ASP) or JavaScript to provide some of the site's functionality, such as forms users can fill out)
- Creating interfaces to databases or a transaction system

> **Tip**
>
> Remember that your staff's time isn't free; it has a labor cost *and* an opportunity cost. (While your web team members are building the site, they won't be performing other potentially profitable tasks.) You'll want to think realistically about their time as you develop your budget.

Budgeting for Deployment

A number of activities occur just before a site is launched in preparation for "going live." These include:

- Testing the site on a staging server, including looking for typos, checking links, verifying that all functionality is in place, and making sure all systems are "Go."

- Preparing marketing materials. (This is a deployment activity because it must begin well before the actual launch, but the marketing materials themselves are a line item of the promotion budget.)

Then after all the preparations have been made, the actual launch includes:

- Placing the site on the live server and checking areas that might have been troublesome in development. (This quality check should turn up no new problems.)

- Announcing that the site is now available to the public.

Caution

After you've made a plan and started to build the site, changing your mind won't be cheap. Feature creep can bloat a budget quickly and horribly, and switching hardware, software, or a database product mid-project can be a setback for both your budget and your timeline. Again, this is why planning is crucial to the success of your e-commerce venture.

Budgeting for Promotion and Maintenance

Unfortunately, many people think that after a site is launched, it is "done." Not so. To remain competitive, your website must, at the very least, be maintained with fresh content and attention to technical matters. It must also be promoted. "If you build it, [they] will come" might work for baseball diamonds in the middle of Iowa cornfields, but it is simply not true for websites.

The hows and whys of maintenance and promotion are discussed throughout this book. Suffice it to say here that, according to a 1999 study by Forrester Research, 54 percent of respondents said they are motivated to frequent sites that are updated often. And how did those people say they found sites? Via search engines (57 percent), email messages (38 percent), links from other sites (35 percent), word of mouth (28 percent), and magazine ads (25 percent). Not, you will notice, by stumbling across them. (By the way, respondents were able to indicate more than one method of finding sites, so the percentages noted don't tally to 100 percent.)

As you consider the categories involved in your budget, take into account these issues of promotion and maintenance:

- Fixing bugs and broken or outdated links
- Responding to feedback from customers
- Updating content and adding to product lines
- Reprinting existing marketing materials to include your web address (known as a Uniform Resource Locator, or URL) and promote your e-commerce venture
- Forming partnerships to exchange links with other sites
- Advertising via traditional media as well as online
- Initiating and monitoring listings in search engines and directories

Again, remember that staff time will be required to do all these tasks, as well as to monitor server logs (see Chapter 13) and deal with any contractors you retain after launch.

Categorizing Costs by Type

In addition to grouping line items by row according to the activities described in the preceding sections, the sample budget shown in Figure 2.1 groups costs by column according to their type, or category. As mentioned earlier, the basic categories include fixed expenses, hourly expenses, and ongoing expenses. The sample spreadsheet includes these column headings:

- **Item**, under which is listed each of the budget items noted in the preceding sections.
- **Hours**, under which is shown the *estimated number of hours* needed for in-house staff (if they are paid hourly) or contractors to complete a task. (The fees you might pay to a web shop are listed in the Fixed Cost column, discussed below.)
- **$/Hour**, under which is shown the *estimated cost per hour* of in-house staff or contractors.

- **Fixed Cost**, under which is shown the cost of an item—for example, computer equipment or software. If you contract with a firm to work for a fixed bid, show that cost here. If both an hourly cost and a fixed cost are associated with a particular item, indicate each cost in its appropriate column, and then enter their sum in the Total Cost column.
- **Notes**, under which details are provided about each item.
- **Total Cost**, under which appears the sum of all the costs shown in the spreadsheet. This number indicates the projected cost of your web endeavor.

On E-Commerce Revenue Models

Revenue issues are not addressed in the sample spreadsheet shown in Figure 2.1 because, quite simply, it is impossible to show every revenue model in one example. But of course it is important to know what revenue model you will be using—in other words, how will your site make money, and from what source will revenue emerge? Revenue models for online ventures are in a state of flux; let's take a look at a few possibilities.

Product sales is the simplest revenue model in town; basically, a merchant sells products and makes a profit by keeping costs lower than the gross income from sales. This model translates nicely to web endeavors, except that, as mentioned at the beginning of this chapter, the standard formulas used in other industries to help entrepreneurs understand and manage their costs simply aren't available yet for e-commerce initiatives. The methods you know and love for keeping costs down in your florist shop won't translate neatly into methods for keeping costs down in your online florist business. Watch Microsoft bCentral and other online sources for insight into managing costs in specific types of sales sites.

Ad sales as a revenue model seems an obvious option to many who venture into e-commerce. After all, a lot of people are online, and they'll see the ads, so advertisers should be willing to pay for ad space, right? The flaws in this reasoning are threefold. First, to attract advertisers who will pay for premium (or even mid-level) ad placement, you need *big* traffic numbers. To get that traffic, you must first invest a lot of capital in building your site, creating compelling content, and promoting your site. Magazines often run on this model. (You don't really think your paltry little

Chapter 2: Setting Up a Budget and Sticking to It

subscription pays all the cost of running a magazine, do you? If so, what are all those ads doing there?) And a general rule in launching a new magazine is that it will bleed money for three to five years before the publisher can expect a dime of profit.

The second challenge to those going after ad sales as a revenue model is that advertisers want outside confirmation of your traffic; your word is fine, but they want an external audit or some other verification to back it up. In the magazine and broadcast world, trusted companies like ACNielsen sell just such a service. In the web world, technologies and standards are emerging to enable the verification that advertisers want. Companies such as Arbitron, Media Metrix, and ACNielsen provide auditing, but it might be cost-prohibitive for small to mid-sized companies.

The third challenge in ad sales may be that the very nature of the Internet, historically, has been to provide information for free. Of course advertising can also be seen as an intrusion in broadcast and print, but somehow it's more resented online than elsewhere. Users often resent ads because they are a gauche reminder that this is, after all, a commercial venture. Ads can also be a distraction; usually the advertiser wants the ad placement to be at the top of the page, and that is exactly the placement the site's creator wants, too, to establish identity for the site. With time, a solution to all of these challenges will surely come. In the meantime, ad sales are a possible revenue model, but unless you can afford to wait until your traffic ramps up, you might want to look at other options as well.

Paid *sponsorship* works on a model much like that used by the Public Broadcasting Service (PBS), where a company or individual pays for the privilege of being listed as a sponsor, perhaps in a highlighted way. For example, the sponsor's name might appear in a special font or in a box that highlights the company's often generous donation. The prestige of being associated with a certain site might compel an advertiser to sponsor the site; again the issues of the site's traffic numbers, and user perception of the site come into play.

In a *paid placement* scenario, companies pay to have their products or brands actually appear in key places. For example, in a game site, within images of the game, images of certain products would appear—a brand of beer, a type of car, the name of a hotel. Like ad sales and sponsorship, the issues of traffic numbers, verification of the numbers, and user perception are some drawbacks; an additional drawback is that you have to somehow fit the products into your images—if you can make that a feature of your site instead of an intrusion into your presentation, all the better.

Part 1: Plan Your E-Commerce Initiative

At one point, the *subscription* model—where users pay for information delivered daily or weekly, for example, like a newspaper—seemed to many like an obvious winner online. After all, it was reasoned, the Internet was a fast medium for delivering information, and people were used to paying for journalism and reference materials. So what went wrong? Again, the inherent nature of the Internet as a source of *free* information may have disinclined users to pay for the very same information they'd be willing to pay for if it were printed on paper. Some sites have gotten around this by offering premium information—newer, larger, or more recent versions of reports or newsletters, for example—to subscribers who have paid while offering smaller samplings to those who have not paid a subscription fee.

Fee for services is a model that works perfectly well in cases like ordering new registration for your car, and it shows a lot of promise in the area of online education or training. There, perhaps, the customer knows what will be delivered. A very tangible item or product (the car registration or the educational materials and experience) will be received. However, it's a bit trickier in cases such as, for example, offering consulting services online for a fee. (The clients of consultants seem to prefer to see the consultant in person; perhaps this is because they want an in-person assessment or because of the generally high cost of consulting suggests in-person service.)

Licensing is an interesting option for people who have something of such interest that others are willing to pay for its use. Content can be licensed—so can software, code, services, images, music, video, and so on. Licensing can be for a specified length of time, specified venues, specified uses, and so on. The keys to making licensing work are having offerings others want, having licensing models that work, and having a solid contract. If you don't have any licensing experience, it's best to get professionals involved. A lot of blues singers licensed all rights to their work in the '50s only to find in the '70s that others had gotten rich on their talent while they were still scraping by. This example would give anyone the blues.

Affiliate and affinity programs involve one company setting up a system to sell their products through other companies (usually by linking to the first company's sales site). The seller often gets a small royalty, bounty, or commission for each sale that comes from the seller's site. Examples of this include the programs set up by big online booksellers to encourage other, smaller sites to sell books through them. The larger bookseller is able to extend its reach enormously via its affiliates; this has the effect of creating many sales outlets without the expense of creating many sites.

Cost savings via online ventures can be very compelling. Anything that can be digitized (software, music, art, and so on) can be distributed over the Internet, saving manufacturing and packaging costs as well as improving time to market (because the manufacturing, packaging, and distribution cycles effectively vanished). But other cost savings can also occur. In one scenario, a company that had been printing a customer service registration card to include in its product packaging found that while the product still had to be packaged and distributed, the registration card could be posted online instead of being printed. Enormous savings were realized with little set-up expense.

Whatever your site's goal, your revenue model must line up with the type of site you are creating. You'll want to play with spreadsheets that consider various what-if scenarios to determine which revenue model or combination of models will result in a reasonable return on your investment.

Considering the Return on Your Investment

Your venture might not have the turning of a profit as its primary goal. The goals of many sites don't include profit. Some are cost centers whose purpose is to make a product or a company's identity (its brand) known to a wider market, to gather research data that will be analyzed and published as a report, or to allow a city's citizens to easily obtain information or such items as business licenses or building permits. However, every e-commerce site must return *something* on the investment that was made to create it. Increased branding, retail sales, maintenance of wholesale accounts, public relations—these are all legitimate reasons for building a website. They are also all activities that demand a return. If there is no return, financial support for the website will evaporate.

In the course of developing your budget, you must account not only for costs but also for revenue or some other return. For the site to survive, you must be able to show that it brings value to the company, and that value must be clearly justified by an understanding of the site's goals, the site's costs, and the standards the company has established for measuring the site's success (see Chapter 14). Remember: An e-commerce venture that does not realize a return on its investment is nothing but a hobby.

Using Microsoft Excel

Microsoft Excel offers a comprehensive set of tools for creating spreadsheets and analyzing business scenarios. You can convert a spreadsheet to HTML via a simple menu choice and then post it on a website—for example, on an extranet that provides sales reps or buyers with information, or on an intranet that keeps web team members up-to-date as they build or maintain your site.

Building an Excel spreadsheet involves labeling the columns and rows (see Figure 2.1 on page 42), then entering the appropriate numbers into *cells* (the junctions of columns and rows), and finally writing a few simple formulas that use the numbers to perform calculations. You can manipulate the *data* (the numbers in the cells) in all sorts of ways—for example, by running "what if" scenarios such as "What if the website gets 200,000 visitors a month; how much revenue can I then expect from ad sales?" Or "What if costs exceed revenue by 20 percent; how much of a cushion will I need to keep things going for a year?"

To find out more about using Excel, see Microsoft's website (*www.microsoft.com*) or one of the bigger Excel books, such as *Running Microsoft Excel 2000* or *Microsoft Excel 2000 Step by Step* (both published by Microsoft Press).

Note

Microsoft's website also offers tools and products tailored to help smaller businesses use Office (and Excel) effectively. There you can find information on how to run "what if" scenarios and how to do the same kind of financial modeling that large corporations are able to do.

Microsoft Small Business Financial Manager

Smaller businesses can use Microsoft Small Business Financial Manager in conjunction with Excel to do the kind of financial modeling large corporations do. This sort of financial modeling helps businesses analyze various scenarios and make sound business decisions. Small Business Financial Manager offers easy-to-use tools for bringing financial information from other popular accounting programs into Excel. Using Small Business Financial Manager, you can create reports and perform "what if" analyses that can tell you the effect of pursuing various scenarios (for example, building an e-commerce site) on your bottom line.

Chapter 3

Knowing the Legal Issues

You might not own what you think you own, even if you've paid for it. Further, not everything that is easy to take and use can be taken and used legally. And yet, your ideas and the tangible assets that make up your website can often be taken and used by others quite easily—sometimes without repercussions.

These seemingly paranoid realities are at the core of a set of issues you must understand and deal with in order to protect your investment in your e-commerce venture. However large, small, or even altruistic your venture might be, if you do not know and attend to legal matters, you might open yourself up to a world of legal trouble.

As a businessperson, you've probably dealt with the laws that govern setting up and running a business. If your company is of the brick-and-mortar variety, you are probably well aware of the ongoing legal issues that affect your business. For example, it's only common sense that you cannot defraud your customers, that you must honor your guarantees, and so on. You also know that to protect your company and your merchandise, you have to lock the door and provide security systems. In e-commerce, a new twist is added to these familiar business practices—e-commerce involves *publishing* (when you make your website public, you are publishing it), so some issues arise that might be less familiar to you than standard business practices. This chapter introduces the general legal issues involved in launching and maintaining an e-commerce website.

Part 1: Plan Your E-Commerce Initiative

> **Note**
>
> I'm no lawyer, and what you read here is not meant as legal advice. For legal advice pertaining to your particular situation, consult an attorney who practices Internet or e-commerce law. Internet law is rapidly changing, so it is especially important to stay on top of the issues. For general legal information, one great online source is FindLaw at *www.findlaw.com*. But again, the best resource is an attorney who is versed in Internet and e-commerce law.

What Is Intellectual Property?

Intellectual property is, quite simply, something that is owned (at least at first) by the person who thought it up (its creator). From the content that attracts traffic to your website to the code that drives the back end, someone owns every bit of everything that comprises the site, and it isn't always clear who owns what. For example, at one level the creator of a page "owns" that page, but the page might include a licensed image, a piece of public domain text, or a bit of code that was created by a programmer who assigned the rights to use it in a limited way. (Whoever creates a piece of code or text owns it, though the creator can transfer ownership to another person or other people.) You want to be sure that you have legally created, bought, or licensed all the components of your website, and you want to be sure that no one is going to steal them from you.

Intellectual property is a business asset. But unlike "tangible" property, such as inventory or real estate, intellectual property is not something you can necessarily hold in your hand, walk on, or point to, though you can usually document it or capture it in an art form. Intellectual property can be the plans for a specific kind of computer, the operating system running on it, or a specific piece of the code that makes up that operating system. It can also be a piece of art, music, or writing—say, the verses a poet types using a word processor (a piece of software that is, of course, another type of intellectual property).

> **Note**
>
> Unlike tangible property, intellectual property is infinitely reproducible; it can be consumed by one user and still be available for use by any number of other users.

In contracts, a creation that is intellectual property is often called *the Work* (with a capital W), and the Work is owned by its creator. (For the rest of this chapter, the term Work will have this connotation.) Essentially, intellectual property laws address ownership and control over the *representation* and implementation of ideas. (Not the ideas themselves—read on.) As the owner or manager of an e-commerce website, you should be aware of five areas of intellectual property law:

- **Trademark law**, which protects identifying symbols, words, and names of businesses, products, and services.
- **Trade dress law**, which protects how a product or its packaging or presentation looks. (In e-commerce, the product might actually be the website itself.)
- **Trade secret law**, which protects information of value kept secret by a company, such as the exact formulation of the Colonel's eleven herbs and spices in Kentucky Fried Chicken.
- **Copyright law**, which protects original Works created by an author or artist, such as written material, illustrations, music, or videos. Note that copyrights are more commonly licensed or sold than some other intellectual property; we'll get into that later in this chapter.
- **Patent law**, which protects inventions and processes. Patents, too, are commonly licensed or sold.

> **Caution**
>
> To play it safe, assume that everything on the Internet is owned by someone. That someone, however, might be willing to grant you permission to use their property or might agree to a licensing contract (perhaps with fees).

Part 1: Plan Your E-Commerce Initiative

Who Owns What on a Website?

A website is made up of a lot of bits and pieces. The most obvious components are the art, text, and page layout that users see. Behind the scenes is a lot of code—HTML and other code—that makes the page layout work. Behind that is usually a database (holding the pieces that make up a catalog of products, or even holding some of the content of the site) and a transaction system. More code and a variety of tools (software, forms, and other stuff) make the database and transaction system work. What seems simple and easy to use on the surface is actually a complex system of components, all working together. Any of these pieces—and the bits that make up these pieces—can be owned. And the various bits that make up a single, larger piece are not necessarily owned by the same person.

Here's what it all boils down to: When you purchase a piece of "original" commercial art from a designer, the designer might use as a departure point or as an integral part of the final image any combination of "stock" photography, clip art, or original images. Different *fonts* (styles of type) might also be used to incorporate text into the piece. The designer has to pay a fee for the use of stock photography and might have to pay to use other types of images or some fonts. If an original photograph is taken, a fee might also have to be paid to the photographer and to anyone who appears in the photo. Each of these fees might be for a one-time use in a limited venue (for example, in a print brochure to be distributed only in the United States) or for unlimited use.

Along the same lines, when a designer creates a web page, it might include text that was purchased for one kind of use, a piece of art that was purchased for another kind of use, yet another piece of art that was purchased for a more narrow use, and so on. In fact, a single piece of art could contain several small images, each licensed for a different kind of use!

Similarly, a developer hired to create your site's back end (see Chapter 1) might use *proprietary* code or tools. (Proprietary means privately owned and controlled.) The developer might, for example, use code or tools that are owned by his or her own company. In a worst-case scenario, you might find after you've paid for your site that pieces of it are not actually yours. In fact, various pieces might belong to an assortment of different entities and might be licensed to you for only limited uses. These uses might not all match up with each other or with your plans.

Chapter 3: Knowing the Legal Issues

Regardless of who actually creates your website, you need to know what you can and can't legally use and whether you have to pay fees for the use. You don't want to get an unpleasant letter from a lawyer demanding that you either dismantle your site or pay for the unwitting use of material that belonged to someone else.

Caution

Whether you hire a firm to create your website or you create it yourself, it's imperative that you know the details about what makes up your site and what legal rights you have to use or reuse text, images, code, and tools. An attorney can help you sort this out by reviewing any contracts you set up with developers or designers.

You Can View the Source, but Don't Use It

Unlike the specifications for a computer or a building, you can easily see a web page's specifications. (You can view the workings of the page itself, but not those of the back end.) Simply choose Source (or a similar command) from your browser's View menu to display the source code that makes up the current web page. Technically, you could simply cut and paste that code into a new document and use it yourself. In fact, in days gone by, some web design students were told by naïve instructors to do exactly that. But the code was created by someone else—not you—and if you use it, you are stealing.

Some people—including "open source" proponents—do allow others to use their code, but they usually post a notice offering permission on their web pages or in the underlying code.

Most people, however (and particularly their lawyers), believe that stealing and reusing their code, content, or even the "look" of their pages is a violation of intellectual property rights. So remember: You can look, but unless you've been given permission, you cannot touch.

Ownership of Look and Feel

In the e-commerce industry, the public face of a website, including both its design and functionality, is often called its *look and feel*. Look and feel are closely tied to branding (see Chapter 5). The elements that make up look and feel (colors, graphics, navigation tools, layout, typeface, and anything that visually distinguishes one site from another) are often referred to in legal documents as *trade dress*. The 11th Circuit Court of Appeals defines trade dress as the "total image of a product [, which] may include features such as size, shape, color or color combinations, texture, [or] graphics."

To understand this, think about the differences between an online gaming site and a site devoted to working moms. One wants to convey excitement, competition, speed, power, and hyperreality. The other wants to present itself as a resource for overextended women who are trying to juggle career and family and still somehow find time for refreshment and renewal. Both sets of concepts can be telegraphed to the user by the purposeful choice of colors and graphics. A company that realizes that the look of its website is part of its branding devotes attention and resources to defining and refining that look. The company then pumps even more resources into keeping the look consistent and extending it into the world. It is not about to let anyone muscle in on that look and feel, because it's part of the company's intellectual property.

Ownership of Back-End Systems

As mentioned in Chapter 1, *back end* is a catchall term for the technical underpinnings of a website. A back end can be as simple as a few *scripts* (simple programs) that enable a customer to add her name to a mailing list via a form, or it can be as complex as the machinations of a large catalog database and transaction system that facilitates credit card purchases and electronic interactions with suppliers and distributors.

When you hire a web shop or individual programmer to create a back end (or modify an existing back end), either of them might use pieces of code or tools that they own or that are owned by someone else. You must know who owns what, including what pieces of code the web shop or programmer has developed and licensed to you for a specific purpose or a specific time and what tools they have licensed on your behalf for your use. How can you acquire this information? You have to ask. Ask during the initial interview, before the contract is written. Ask a lot of questions, and then make sure your understanding is clearly spelled out in the contract. (See Chapter 9 for more about hiring a web shop or programmer and about what you should ask before entering into a contract.)

> **Note**
>
> If you use an off-the-shelf back-end product, such as Microsoft SQL Server, you are *licensing* the technology. The manufacturer still owns it; you have simply paid for the privilege of using it (probably within specified limitations).

Ownership of Content

Content is a nebulous term. It refers to the images, verbiage, video, and sound on a page, but it also refers to the *expression* of ideas those elements contain. Note that no one can own an idea. It is the expression of the idea that is owned, and the expression becomes owned the moment it is fixed in tangible form. (See the section "Can Copyright Laws Protect You?" later in this chapter.) An artist, musician, or writer owns any original Work he or she creates. Technically, any individual who writes an original sentence (even in the form of an email) owns his or her "Work" (the sentence). In traditional media—books, maps, lyrics, poetry, screenplays, images, written instructions, and others—a Work is owned by its creator until and unless the creator assigns, sells, or licenses rights to the Work to another entity. Most employment contracts require employees to assign the company the rights to any Works they create on the job. Similarly, some publishing contracts assign rights to a written Work to the publisher.

> **Note**
>
> If a person writes email at work, the terms of his or her employment agreement might specify that the email, like other Works created on the job, is the property of the company.

Ownership of Ideas

As stated in the previous section, in legal terms, no one can own an idea. Only the expression of the idea can be owned and protected. You cannot protect a claim to ownership of the idea of a story about star-crossed lovers on a sinking ship, but you can of the movie *Titanic*. (Don't you wish!) The tangible form, expression, or implementation of an idea can be owned and protected, not the idea itself. Even when an invention is patented, it is not the idea that is protected by the patent; it is the tangible implementation of the idea. To obtain a patent, you must have fixed the idea in the tangible form of a drawn or written plan for a process. Likewise, to hold a copyright, you must have expressed the idea in a tangible form.

Can Copyright Laws Protect You?

Although you might not think of yourself as a publisher, copyright laws figure strongly into your e-commerce site. Generally, intellectual property is divided into two types: industrial property, such as inventions, industrial designs, trademarks, trade dress, and trade names; and copyright, which protects a variety of creations, such as plays, music, books, poems, photographs, movies, maps, and more. Copyright laws don't protect your inventions, processes, back-end systems, and look and feel. Copyright does address the *content* of your website. To hold the copyright to that content, you must be its creator, or you must have been assigned rights to it by the content's creator(s). Before you assign rights or have them assigned to you, however, make sure you understand what copyright is, what you are protecting when you hold copyright, and how the law protects copyright. Above all, when rights are being assigned, be sure that the party assigning them actually owns the rights being assigned.

What Is a Copyright?

A *copyright* is a right of intellectual property that, for a limited time, provides the creator of a Work (or someone to whom the creator assigns rights) specific, exclusive rights to the Work. Copyright does not cover ideas, facts, blank forms, specific words, titles, or names. It also does not cover existing material the creator of the Work incorporated into the Work. It covers only the *original expression of an idea* (a creation) and only once it is *in tangible form* (a Work).

Caution

Simply placing a copyright notice on your website does not mean you own everything on the site. You cannot protect your rights to something you don't actually own. Ownership comes first, and copyright notices signal the intention to protect ownership.

Chapter 3: Knowing the Legal Issues

Originally, the term *copyright* meant the right to make copies—to produce or reproduce a Work. Copyright law came into being with the invention of the printing press and was created to sort out who had the right to make, and profit from, copies of Works that could be printed. In today's world, a Work is owned by its creator, who holds the copyright as soon as the Work is created and fixed in *any* tangible form. For example, a piece of writing does not have to be printed to be in tangible form. If it is written on a word processor and exists only on a hard drive, it is still considered "fixed in tangible form." Similarly, digital art or music that is distributed over the Internet—Works that exist only in digital form—are considered fixed in tangible form and are owned by someone.

Works in new media—websites, for example—present new twists in the copyright story. One dilemma, as described earlier in this chapter, is that each page is created from a number of other elements—text, images, code—that might each be a Work in and of itself. Another problem is that a web page viewed in one browser might look different when it is viewed in another browser. Can this "changing" web page be considered an original Work fixed in tangible form? The consensus has been that it can, because the web page is fundamentally a fixed arrangement of elements, laid out by a creator as an original Work and fixed in a tangible (if digital) form. Websites, like printed Works, are covered by copyright.

Copyright law recognizes the following rights:

- The right to reproduce the Work by any means and in all media
- The right to prepare derivative Works based on the copyrighted Work
- The right to distribute copies of the Work
- The right to perform the Work in public
- The right to display the Work in public
- The right to claim authorship and to prevent use of the author's name on a Work that he or she did not create
- The right to prevent distortion of the protected Work

Tip

The United States Copyright Office is part of the Library of Congress; you can find it at *www.lcweb.loc.gov/copyright*. Also, attorney Ivan Hoffman maintains a website full of useful articles on copyright and other intellectual property issues at *www.ivanhoffman.com*.

How Does Copyright Law Work?

In the United States, which (like most countries) supports the Berne Copyright Convention, almost all Works created after March 1, 1989 are protected by copyright, whether or not they are marked with a copyright notice. (Placing a copyright notice on a Work does, however, make it easier to defend the copyright. More on this in a moment.) Copyright is a federal law. It is also a civil law rather than a criminal law, so those accused of violating copyright law might be sued but do not face potential jail time. (Although criminal charges can be filed in cases of commercial counterfeiting, such as when someone prints counterfeit CDs.)

The term of a copyright is, as of this writing, the life of the creator of the Work (or his or her heirs) plus 50 years. Copyright is transferable to heirs or others and can be sold or licensed. (Rights to a good deal of the Works created by the Beatles were sold decades ago when the lads were young. The rights to some have since become the property of pop icon Michael Jackson.) In some special cases, as when an independent contractor is hired to create a Work, the terms of copyright can differ. If you are an independent contractor or are hiring one, you can find out more by consulting online resources or, preferably, an attorney.

Marking Your Site with a Copyright Notice

To notify visitors to your site of your copyright, it is advisable to place a copyright notice on the site. A typical copyright notice looks like this: *Copyright [date] © [author or owner's name]*. (Replace *[date]* with the date the Work was created and *[author or owner's name]* with the name of the person or company that holds the copyright.) Whether you need the © symbol varies from country to country, but it isn't a problem to have it, and it can help. Also, in the United States, you don't have to use the phrase *All rights reserved*, but in some other countries it is required, and it doesn't hurt to include it, especially because the Web knows no boundaries. You might also want to include more lengthy and specific legalese; your attorney can advise you on what's best for your situation.

> **Note**
>
> HTML does not include a code for the © symbol. You can produce the symbol in many browsers using the code *&#169* or, better yet, *&copy*. However, because not all browsers recognize those codes, the safest route is to use the word *copyright* in your website's copyright notice.

Chapter 3: Knowing the Legal Issues

You can register a Work with the Copyright Office (*www.lcweb.loc.gov/copyright/*), which is a part of the Library of Congress. Doing so provides extra proof that you are the creator of the Work, and more importantly, is necessary to protect your Work in court. In fact, before you file suit for infringement, you must have your copyright registered. Registering a Work also brings additional rights, which you can investigate via the Copyright Website (*www.benedict.com*) or other resources.

What About Copyright Infringement?

Copyright infringement is like poaching; it's taking something you don't own. The best way to avoid infringing a copyright is to create something new. Don't cut and paste someone else's code, don't nab someone else's image files and use them, and don't copy someone else's text. As you are putting together your web pages, keep in mind these points:

- Don't delude yourself into thinking that the owner of the Work you copied will be flattered that you took it. More likely, he'll be peeved.

- Don't lull yourself into thinking that because you altered the Work a tad, you're not stealing. You can paint that blue Buick red, but it's still stolen.

- Don't think that merely giving credit (or *attribution*) for the Work on your site is good enough. For one reason or another, the owner of the copyright might not want to be associated with your site.

Admittedly, it's tough to be original. Even George Harrison might have said, "Oh, was *that* the song I was humming?" when he was accused of plagiarism. In that case, Bright Tunes Music Corp., copyright owner of the Chiffons' song "He's So Fine," sued and won against Harrisongs Music for lifting harmonies and using them in "My Sweet Lord." The plaintiffs did not have to prove the infringement was purposeful; the ruling was based on unintentional infringement.

And don't think that the Web is so big that no one will know you took and used something. Copyright owners frequently search the Web for their own names and sometimes for key phrases from their Works. What seems like a tiny needle in the huge web haystack can come right to the top of a list of search results. Your best bet, if you're enamored of some content and want to use it, is to email the Work's owner and *ask* if you can use it.

Legal matters get worked out in the courts, and lawyers turn to precedents set in the courts for guidance in interpreting the laws. Because the advent of the Internet—and the Web in particular—brought about situations no one had considered before, the application of copyright law to the Internet has had to be tested in the courts. Cases have addressed such questions as whether an ISP is responsible or liable for infringement on the part of its subscribers. How all this unfolds will be up to the courts.

> **Note**
>
> The development of a new technology, for example, could bring up the question of whether a website's visitors can embed notes on a site's pages for others to view. If the notes are displayed in such a way that they appear to be part of the pages' content, but they were not put there by the pages' creator(s), visitors probably can't embed the notes.

Can you ever use someone else's Work without first getting formal permission? Under some circumstances, it is permissible. When the use of a portion of a Work is what's known as *fair use*, the portion of the Work can be used without first getting permission. When the Work is in the public domain, anyone can use it.

What About Fair Use and the Public Domain?

Fair use refers to the granting of the privilege (not the right) to use a small portion of a copyrighted Work for the purpose of reviewing the Work, teaching, reporting events, or creating a parody. While reviewing a book, a reviewer can quote a brief passage. She cannot reproduce the whole Work, but a few lines from a poem or story might be acceptable. Although a person cannot photocopy another person's poems and sell them, an instructor can reproduce a few lines for the purpose of teaching about that poem. To report on the news, a journalist can quote a brief passage from another Work. (Again, the whole Work cannot be reproduced.)

Under fair use, you cannot copy a passage from someone else's Work and simply put it on your e-commerce site because you like it. To recap why:

- You cannot copy someone else's Work without their permission.
- You cannot profit from someone else's Work without their permission.

In fair use cases, the portion of the material you use in relation to the size of the whole Work is generally important, as is the actual use to which you put the quoted Work. Anything that could be construed as decreasing the income of the Work's creator is unacceptable. Here is an example: in the book you hold in your hands, screen shots appear as illustrations. Within the book, they are generally considered to fall under the fair use umbrella, because the book is instructive, and it reports on or reviews web pages. However, printing any of the same screenshots on the book's cover would not be fair use, because the purpose of the cover is not to instruct or review but rather to sell the book.

Caution

It's quite difficult to know when fair use is applicable. The privilege grants limited use in limited ways of limited amounts of material, but the specifics of each case vary, and judgment calls are not easy. It has been said that copyright is the one branch of the law you really know you're violating only when a judge tells you so.

Some Works are in the public domain. These Works can be used by anyone for any purpose. A Work can enter the public domain in any of several ways:

- The copyright was defective (for example, the owner might not have followed the copyright laws in effect at the time and so might not really own the copyright).
- The copyright might have been granted before 1909 and not renewed.
- The copyright expired without being transferred to heirs or sold.

Very old Works (for example, the Bible and the plays of Shakespeare) are generally in the public domain, but the Works of Ernest Hemingway (and indeed his personal letters) are not. Publications of the United States Government are in the public domain, but only because the United States Government said they would be.

Caution

The laws of public domain vary from country to country and can be very complex. As always, seek professional legal advice to be safe.

You can publish public domain Works on your website without repercussions. But be very careful: Don't simply assume that a Work is in the public domain; make sure of it. For example, clip art sites have cropped up all over the Web. They offer snippets of art that you are told you can use without paying a fee or for a very small fee. Be very careful. In some cases, a practiced eye can see that what is presented as clip art is actually a photo scanned from a national magazine. True clip art is public domain because its creator put it in the public domain; photos scanned from magazines are not clip art.

Can You Use People's Images?

Can you use someone else's image on your website? This is a stickier question than it might at first seem. Obviously, using a picture of Tom Cruise or some other celebrity to sell cars on your site will bring lawyers to your door. Celebrities profit from their images and protect them as a business asset. In fact, the heirs of deceased celebrities do the same, so don't imagine you can simply substitute James Dean for Tom Cruise. In some states and countries, people also have a *right of privacy*, which prevents disclosure of embarrassing private facts, casting someone in a false light, intrusion, and (of most interest here) misappropriation, which is also known as the *right of publicity*. According to the right of publicity, each person has a right to control the use of his or her name, likeness, voice, biography, and overall persona such that others cannot use them for commercial purposes. This means that you should probably get permission from your Aunt Matilda before you use *her* image to sell your products on your website.

Why Does Licensing Matter?

You might be the owner of a Work that someone else wants to use, or you might want to use a Work owned by someone else. In either case, a written agreement, however simple, keeps the lines of the deal clear. It does not always involve payment, but it does always involve rights.

When you want to use a Work that someone else owns, you can simply request permission, which is easy enough to do and often results in success. Sometimes the granting of the permission will involve restrictions on the use.

If the owner of a Work prefers to *license* its use rather than simply grant permission to use it, the licensed use can involve special restrictions or require payment. Generally, licensing specifies length of time, types of use, geographic location of the use, and so on. It does not transfer ownership. The owner can license as many uses to as many people or entities as he or she likes, and several licensees can license similar or identical uses.

Typical licenses provide for any of the following types of rights:

- **Nonexclusive rights** grant permission to one of perhaps many licensees the right to use the Work in certain specified ways. Restrictions might include such items as length of time, type of use (for example, print or electronic), use within a geographic area, or a specific venue (for example, only this particular brochure or print ad).

- **Exclusive rights** grant permission to one licensee, who has exclusive use of the Work for the time and perhaps the use specified in the agreement.

Note

Assigning copyright is not licensing; it is transferring the copyright itself, usually for a one-time payment or royalties or other payment based on income the Work produces. Note that when a copyright is transferred, the entity to whom it's transferred can actually assign (or transfer) it to others unless the written agreement says otherwise. When you "sell" your copyright, you are actually assigning it.

Licensing, then, provides a way for the creator of a Work to allow others to use it without giving up ownership rights to it. To the owner of a Work, licensing provides a method for gaining profit from it; to the licensee, it provides an opportunity to gain use of the Work without having to pay a larger sum to own it. Many companies choose to acquire the use of Works, such as graphics, text, video, and audio, by licensing them instead of buying them. Licensing is cheaper than outright buying, and is the sort of deal that results in your favorite rock songs showing up in car, footwear, and jeans ads. Most licenses include lots of legalese; you will almost certainly want to consult with an attorney before entering into a licensing agreement.

Note

Debate rages about whether license agreements like those you "accept" when you click on a dialog box in a piece of downloaded software are actually enforceable. Some people contend that because there is no piece of paper with a signature on it, an actual agreement hasn't been signed. However, as a user, you probably don't want to test this matter in the courts yourself, so it might be wise to treat these licenses as real agreements.

About "Work for Hire"

In one distinct situation, a Work is not owned by its creator. According to the Copyright Act, a *Work made for hire* is "a Work prepared by an employee within the scope of his or her employment." It can also be "a Work specially ordered or commissioned for use as a contribution to a collective Work, as a part of a motion picture or other audio-visual Work, as a translation, as a supplementary Work, as a compilation, as an instructional text, as a test, as answer material for a test, or as an atlas, if the parties expressly agree in a written instrument signed by them that the Work shall be considered a Work made for hire." You can hire someone to create a Work and specify in the contract that it is a "Work for hire." In that case, you (the employer or commissioning party) will hold the copyright to the Work just as if you were its creator.

What Does Trademarking Mean to You?

A *trademark* is a right of ownership protecting a word, phrase, or symbol that represents a product or company in the marketplace. Examples might include the red-ring Lucent Technologies logo or the *It's the real thing* tagline of Coca-Cola. McDonald's has trademarked everything from its golden arches to its clown spokesman to the prefix *Mc*. The title of a specific book cannot be copyrighted or trademarked, but the title of a series of books can be. And of most interest to you, a domain name can be trademarked. The U.S. Patent and Trademark Office attempts to apply to domain names the same standards it applies to other trademarks.

Trademark rights become important and valuable when the trademark gains commercial worth. *It's the real thing* was worth nothing until it became a company asset. The Coca-Cola Corporation invested huge amounts of money to make that asset a commercially successful brand identifier, and then it gained value. The asset issue has bearing on the trademarking of domain names, because if a private person registers a domain name that includes a trademarked term, the courts have ruled that the holder of the trademarked term can basically demand the right to use the domain name.

> **Note**
>
> Related to the trademark is the *servicemark* (SM), which protects the representation of a service instead of a product.

If you use an image, logo, tagline, or other identifying element on your website, you might well want to trademark it. Downloading just about anything from your site is easy for others to do, and once you've made the investment in an identifier, it might be worth going to the extra trouble of protecting your investment as best you can.

Consider this example of trademarking. A few years ago, two industry leaders merged. Company A and Company B were distinguished by different looks; a new brand with yet a different look was created to signal a merged identity to their customers. The new brand's look consisted of specific colors, with the name of the merged company and a logo of curved stripes or *arcs*. "The arc," as the logo became known to the marketing team, became a defining element of the look of all printed pieces produced by the company, and eventually, of the look of the company's website. Even the company's intranet sites were redesigned to include the arc, so that all employees would have a consistent user experience. The arc became the company's identifying symbol; it was part of the company's identity.

If you were to use *an* arc on your site or in your logo, you probably would not bring the wrath of this company down on you. But if you were to use *the* arc, or any arc accompanied by the company's color scheme, font, layout, and other elements in such a way as to duplicate the company's look or user experience, you would probably be told to "cease and desist" or explain yourself in front of a judge.

What Can You Trademark?

You can trademark a word, phrase, symbol, or design, or a combination of those elements that distinguish your products from the products of other companies. A trademark must, however, distinguish and identify rather than simply describe. You cannot protect a trademark for banana chips, but you can trademark and protect DynoChips. (Assuming someone else hasn't gotten to it first.) You can also protect dynochips.com. Your trademark (and *trade dress*, or look and feel) must be clearly distinguishable from those of others, especially others in your line of business. Although Domino Sugar and Domino's Pizza are both trademarked, Domino's Sugar or Domino Pizza can't be. You cannot register or protect a trademark that causes confusion to consumers.

In addition to preventing consumer confusion, the purpose of a trademark is to protect commercial identity, including goodwill, reputation, and marketing investments, by ensuring your exclusive right to use the trademarked item to identify your goods and services. An infringement of trademark occurs when a trademark is used or copied in a way that causes consumer confusion. An infringer can be sued to stop the infringement, and if the trademark holder prevails, the infringer might have to pay both costs and damages.

> **Tip**
>
> The Nolo Press Self-Help Law Center, at *www.nolo.com*, discusses trademark, copyright, patent, and other issues and provides resources and forms for setting up businesses.

Deciphering Trademarks: ™ and ®

What's the difference between ™ and ®? The ™ symbol can be used before a trademark has been registered with the U.S. Patent and Trademark Office. You can replace the ™ with the ® symbol when the registration process is complete. Companies that have registration pending will use a ™ until they can legally use the ®.

Registering Trademarks

To register a trademark, you can simply file an application for registration with the Patent and Trademark Office in Washington, D.C. and pay the requisite fee. You can file for a trademark before you start using it. Because paperwork seldom moves quickly, you might want to file early. Searching the database of existing trademarks to determine whether yours is unique might save you time and money in the long run. You might need the help of a legal professional for the process, but it does provide the strongest possibility for protecting your asset.

How Does the Law Affect Linking?

The Web is, by its very nature, a set of linked documents. In days gone by, it was widely believed that anyone could link anywhere. Linking was the way of the Web. Many thought that the mere act of publishing a website implied permission to link to it. But it turns out that in some situations, links are not welcome. For example, if your site is concerned with family values or presenting material of interest to children, you probably don't want links to your site on pornography sites. If you're trying to establish an environmentally conscious business, you might not want links to your site on the website of the local toxic dumping kings. Similarly, if you are a chemical company, you might not want environmentalists intent on debunking you to be able to link to your site to illustrate their points. An irony of the Internet is that the larger the Web gets, the smaller the world gets—and the faster word can travel about a product's defects, a company's practices, or an executive's foibles.

Here's yet another twist on the issue: Although some sites encourage others to link to specific "buy" pages in their online catalogs, thinking that these links encourage sales, other companies feel quite differently. Why would a company discourage others from linking to its site's internal pages? Perhaps because part of the company's revenue comes from the advertising it sells on its home page, or because the company delivers an important part of its overall marketing message on its home page.

> **Tip**
>
> You can find out about backlinks to your site quite easily. See Chapter 12 to learn how.

If unwelcome links are leading visitors to your site, a simple email message requesting unlinking might do the trick. Remember: it's often best to make your first request polite and even friendly. There's no point in offending the linking party, and alienating them might result in a more unpleasant link before you can finally resolve the issue.

And if you are considering linking to someone else's site, it doesn't hurt to ask permission. You might find, in fact, that asking permission results in a link back to you.

Part 1: Plan Your E-Commerce Initiative

Where Does Business Liability Begin and End?

Like brick-and-mortar stores, your online business must be concerned with *liability*. Liability is essentially *accountability*. You are accountable to customers, co-owners, business affiliates, the government, and the public. If you violate agreements, break laws, cause damage, deceive, or engage in other poor business practices, you might be liable. At best, you might lose customers or have to pay fines; at worst, depending on the infraction and your degree of liability, you could lose your business or be jailed. Doing business on the Internet has opened many new legal questions with which you must be concerned, some of which have been described in this chapter. To protect yourself and your investment, a consultation with an attorney might be a wise investment indeed.

Should You Worry About Slander and Libel?

Slander and *libel* are, respectively, spoken or written messages that reflect on someone negatively or falsely. (TV and radio are technically "spoken," but defamation that occurs via TV or radio is considered libel.) To prove defamation, the offended party has to prove that what was said was damaging. If someone insults you in a forest, has defamation occurred? Probably not. Defamation laws specify that the disparagement must be revealed to a third party.

Defamation is a matter of serious concern in the publishing industry, and journalists are trained carefully to avoid it. Given that your website is a publishing venture (you are "publishing" electronic material when you make your website public), the prudent move for you is to avoid it, too. If you get into trouble, most states have retraction statutes. If you are accused successfully, you can be forced to retract what you said and even to post an apology on your website or elsewhere. In some cases, a retraction might spare you punitive damages but not compensatory damages. Consider this: the Web is a community of 40 to 90 million users, depending on whose estimate you believe. If a lawyer asks for damages of even fifty cents for every person who might have seen your libelous remark, the bill for the remark can get very expensive very fast.

Avoiding Trouble

With most legal matters, it is usually fairly clear under which set of laws and in which court of which state or country any particular matter falls. By its very nature, the Web is without boundaries. An e-commerce company can be in one state, the server(s) hosting its website can be in several others, fulfillment of orders for its products can occur in another, and the customer can be, quite literally, anywhere in the world. As a result, it is unclear where a single transaction has occurred, and that in turn makes it difficult to know just whose laws govern the transaction. This does not mean that *no* laws govern the transaction. It does mean that you, as a businessperson, might be subject to laws you are unaware of. It is always best, in this context, to err on the side of caution. Follow the industry's best standards and practices, and watch for overall developments in the regulation of e-commerce.

All this legal talk might seem daunting. Keep in mind that as a businessperson, part of what you do is assess risk. The laws are there to be used and interpreted; that very fact drives the entire legal profession and the court system. You have to make judgments about whether a given situation is worth the business risk. The more you know about the law, however, the more informed your assessment of risk will be and the more likely you will be to stay out of trouble. It is always easiest and cheapest to simply avoid trouble to begin with.

Part 2

Create Identity and Attract Customers

4　Creating Online Branding
5　Providing Customer Service
6　Building Traffic and Community

Chapter 4

Creating Online Branding

When a product, company, or service is immediately recognized by customers and potential customers, its identity has been successfully established by a process known as *branding*. Branding has a direct effect on a website's traffic and on whether customers will make a purchase.

To understand how branding works, imagine that you need to buy laundry detergent. You'll probably go to a store you know. In a new town, especially, you'll most likely head for a store that's part of a familiar chain. When you get there, you'll probably select a product you recognize, one that looks familiar and whose name rings a bell for you. Branding will make this sale, because it has created an immediately recognizable identity for a particular store and a certain type of detergent, to such an extent that you will choose that store and that brand instead of an unknown store and brand X.

Part 2: Create Identity and Attract Customers

Consider these statistics:

- 42 percent of online buyers say that they plan their purchases in advance, and they know ahead of time what brand they want and from which merchant they'll buy (10th Graphics Visualization & Usability Center [GVU] Survey).

- 82 percent of online buyers indicate that recognizing a product's brand name is an important factor in making their buying decision (Ernst & Young).

To create a brand presence, you must differentiate your website, your product, and your service. You must also create an identity that your customers can and will remember. Admittedly, a corporation with a big budget has an advantage when it comes to creating slick ads and buying media space. But with ingenuity and the pointers in this chapter, you can create effective branding for your e-commerce endeavor. The bottom line is that you must be creative, consistent, and aggressive. And remember: Your competitors will be doing the same thing, so go as many extra yards as it takes.

Tip

Microsoft FrontPage and Microsoft bCentral Site Manager both offer options for the quick and easy creation of a consistent look and feel throughout a website.

Chapter 4: Creating Online Branding

The Case of Martha Stewart

Martha Stewart is not just a person, she's a brand. As recognizable now as Betty Crocker was in the 1950s, Martha can put her stamp on anything related to fine homemaking or living a comfortable, pleasant life in town or country. For a lesson in online branding (and branding in general), open your browser and look at *www.marthastewart.com* and look especially at *www.marthabymail.com* (see Figure 4.1). On Martha By Mail, products are easy to find, the information customers need is right there, the product photos are clear (users can see a larger photo quite easily), and the transaction system runs like clockwork. When a customer makes a purchase, he or she receives an immediate email confirmation, a follow-up snail mail postcard, and quick delivery. If shipment will be delayed for any reason, the customer finds out about it quickly via both email and surface mail. Martha's smiling (and highly recognizable) face, the user's experience, and the design all establish and support Martha Stewart's branding message. And Martha extends her brand relentlessly, through appearances, books, her magazine, and other means. Now that's branding.

Figure 4.1
Martha By Mail, an excellent example of branding.

Part 2: Create Identity and Attract Customers

What Are the Elements of Successful Online Branding?

In the brick-and-mortar world, branding includes *differentiation* (making your product stand out from the crowd), recognizable packaging, and a relentless releasing of messages (TV and print ads, media announcements, and so on) to make sure that the name and appearance of your product are firmly rooted in the minds of the buying public. (Can you sing the Oscar Mayer hot dog jingle?) It's no accident that UPS trucks and FedEx trucks look completely different from each other. Each company—UPS with its brown trucks and staid look, and FedEx with its white trucks and bright colors—is trying to distinguish itself from the other. One look seems to say "Reliability"; the other says "Energy." Each company, through its look, advertising, and messages about its service, underscores those themes at every opportunity. Creating those opportunities and taking advantage of them is known as *extending the brand*.

In an online setting, branding includes:

- Identifying the *goal* of your e-commerce endeavor and making sure that the identity you're creating furthers the goal without muddying the image

- Selecting an appropriate, easy-to-remember *domain name* and making your site's URL a snap to find

- Creating a *look and feel* that is appealing to your target audience, is recognizable, is differentiated from your competitors, and, again, furthers your goal

- Providing your customers with the right *quality of experience*—in other words, making sure they have a positive experience when they enter your place of business (your website)

- Maintaining *integrity of service* by seeing to it that your business practices are up to par with your customers' expectations, that your systems and products deliver, and that your customer service is solid

- Putting forth the *relentless message* that your product is good, your service is good, and your company has its customers in mind

Christina Cheney, an executive producer with Simulations Interactive Media (*www.simmedia.com*), says of online branding, "First impressions are critical and so is the ease of use of navigation and information design. Every aspect of a site, from the functionality to the logo placement, communicates your brand."

Banner Ads Can Boost Visibility

Banner ads can be an effective tool in getting your message out to the public (see Chapter 12). Don't expect a lot of people to click those ads to get to your site, however. A "click-through" rate of *half a percent* is considered more than decent. (That's half a person (!) for each 100 people who view the ad.) Think of banner ads—along with print ads, and if your budget allows it, radio and even TV ads—as a method for putting forth your image. For tips on using banner ads effectively and on swapping ad space with other sites, visit Microsoft bCentral at *www.bcentral.com*. Do you need a "hook"? Well, you do need a targeted message. A recognizable tag line or jingle can't hurt, and a certain attitude that is communicated in your text, color scheme, and product and domain names can definitely help. Appropriately applied product demos, coupons, downloadable freebies, or entertaining animations can add pizzazz to your identity and can be a way to get attention, which also helps. Just make sure that whatever you use is appropriate and not distracting. After all, you want *positive* attention. Don't festoon your site with gimmicks. One striking image or animation is an accent. Too many is just…too much.

Tip

Associate your site with an attitude or point of view. Stand for something. Just make sure it's an attitude or point of view your target audience will find appealing. Having some people disagree with you is not so bad. You can't be all things to all people, and trying to do so leaves you *un*differentiated.

Naming Companies, Products, and Domains

When people think of your website (and therefore your e-commerce venture), one of the first things that will pop into their heads is the site's domain name. Choosing and registering a good domain name might be the simplest thing you can do to brand your site and make it easy to find. Your domain name might be based on your existing company's name, or you might prefer that your website have a different name. If your site sells a single product, you might want to use that product's name as the site's domain name. (But if you have more than one product or you'll be expanding your product line, consider the implications of having a domain name for each product. Supporting a website for each of your products can be unwieldy, expensive, and labor intensive.)

> **Note**
>
> Internet *domain names* are not at all related to Microsoft Windows or Microsoft Windows NT *network domains*. Network domains provide a method for organizing groups of network users, whereas Internet domains describe the location of a network or server that's attached to the Internet.

Do You Need a Domain Name?

Your domain name will be your online address and will provide you with a business location as well as credibility and an opportunity to create branding. So for the highest level of e-commerce positioning, yes, you need a domain name that fully distinguishes your site.

However, not everyone who wants to engage in e-commerce should feel compelled to set up and maintain a website (see Chapter 1). If you plan to sell only a few hand-loomed scarves, you probably won't want to spend much for site setup and maintenance, and the $70 investment in registering a domain name might be too big a bite out of your budget. You'd be better off selling your product via a page on a site that aggregates craftspeople into an online mall. You would then use the mall's domain name and would have no need for your own.

Let's say you are planning to launch a site later, but you aren't quite ready yet. You might be concerned that someone else will nab your chosen domain name before you get around to building your site. The dictionary, after all, has only so many words in it and many of them are already registered as domain names. So are a lot of people's names. There is simply no time like the present when it comes to nailing down a good domain name. Register your chosen domain name now, and you can let it sit like a piece of real estate on which you plan to build *someday*.

> **Note**
>
> You can "reserve" a domain name for a limited time; this is not the same as registering a domain name. Reserving a domain name is a bit like reserving a hotel room; you have a reservation but you actually register at the hotel when you take possession of the room. To actually register the domain, you must have a server lined up as the machine that will host your site.

Choosing Memorable, Meaningful Names

Whether you are building your site now or next year, you need to consider the issue of your domain name carefully and make sure it represents your business well. Your company and product names should convey what you're all about. So should the name of your site and your domain name. It's no accident that many online companies now include *dot com* in their names, so that their company name and their domain name correspond. Think about what a name such as Amazon.com conveys. The company's tagline says it is the "Earth's Biggest," like the Amazon River (which carries more water than any other river on earth and has more than 500 tributaries), and the *dot com* in its name says it conducts business on the Internet.

In some cases, using generic words as a name is a great way to instantly communicate what your company does. For example, 1-800-Flowers is clearly the name of a flower company that you can reach by phone. Translating that name into 1800flowers.com for the company's e-commerce incarnation works mainly because the brand was already so well established. If you provide a product or service and your name is already known and trusted, you might want to capitalize on that fact when naming your e-commerce venture.

> **Tip**
>
> These days, Internet users often dispense with search engines and simply guess at a domain name. If you want your customers to have a reasonable chance of getting your name right, it especially important to choose a name that is logical or easy to remember.

Tips for Successful Naming

In devising the perfect name for your e-commerce venture, keep in mind the following guidelines for naming domains and e-commerce products:

- **Make it memorable.** Your domain name can be your company name, a brand name, or a word that describes your product or service. But make it something people don't have to write down.

- **Make it easy to spell.** Keep the name's spelling simple and easy. If your product is commonly spelled two ways (for example, *donuts* and *doughnuts*), consider registering a separate domain name for each spelling, along with domain names for any common misspellings. Avoid domain names that include hyphens (such as coffee-express.com) or even underscores to separate words.

    Robert Walker, executive director of The Management Center, a consulting firm for nonprofit organizations, has this to say regarding the difficult-to-spell domain names: "We're changing the name of our publication, OpportunityNOCs, to OpportunityKnocks." (OpportunityKnocks, which can be found at *www.opportunityknocks.org*, is a publication aimed at job seekers in the nonprofit sector.) "NOCs was an acronym that made sense when we started in print. But when we began publishing online, we realized most people would spell out k-n-o-c-k-s, and we made that spelling our domain name to make it easier for our audience to find us."

- **Keep it short.** The perfect domain name is less than six letters long, followed by *dot com* or some other suffix. Short domain names are easier to remember and type. However, let's be realistic: There are fewer and fewer one-word domain names left with each passing hour. So…

- **Be flexible.** If your perfect domain name is taken, dream up alternatives. Consider concepts and creative variations. If your company name is Beauchamp Automotive, it's a virtual certainty that beauchamp.com, automotive.com, and cars.com are all taken. You might be forced to break some rules and go with beauchampautomotive.com or beauchamp-automotive.com (shudder). You might also consider a solution such as the one that Ryder (the truck rental company) came up with when it named its domain yellowtruck.com after the distinctive coloring of its vehicles. You might even score with a clever domain name that reflects what you do—for example, an earthquake retrofitting company might decide to go with something like stopquake.com, if it's available.

- **Think about the future.** You don't want your name to be too limiting. What once was called Software.net is now called Beyond.com because the company has visions of selling more than just software (and, perhaps secondarily, because they wanted a *dot com* name instead of a *dot net* name).

- **Give products their own names.** Your website can have the same name as your company, or it can have the same name as your product (if the website is about that product alone). But give your company and your product distinct names. Giving them the same moniker makes it difficult to distinguish the two, and if and when you have more than one product, you'll have a hard time associating your company with the new products. For example, Netscape the company originally marketed only Netscape the web browser. When the company introduced other products, it renamed the browser as Navigator, but many people continued to call the browser "Netscape."

- **Investigate the competition.** To succeed in business, you must have one eye on the competition. Point your web browser at their sites and take a look at their domain names. If a rival grocer has registered bobsgroceries.com, you might have an opportunity to grab perfectproduce.com.

- **Avoid trademarked names.** Single words cannot be copyrighted, but they can be trademarked (see Chapter 3). Phrases and domain names can also be trademarked. What's more, *styles* of naming can be more or less trademarked (at least enough to defend in court). For example, it's best to stay away from Mc-anything or Gadgets R Us to avoid the unwelcome interest of lawyers representing McDonalds and Toys "R" Us. Note, too, that even if a big company hasn't yet registered its trademarked name as a domain, that company will defend its right to do so with great legal vigor. (See Chapter 3 for more information about trademarks and intellectual property.)

> **Caution**
>
> Do your homework. Research a potential domain name. Investigate whether the name is taken (You can do this via bCentral.com), whether it's the name of a corporation that might legally take the domain away from you, and whether it infringes on trademarks or copyrights. Conducting a trademark search might involve a lawyer but can be worth the savings in anxiety and lawsuits.

- **Consider registering more than one name.** Registering variations of your chosen name will help guide users who might otherwise stray to sites with similar domain names. If your domain is propertymgt.com, then you might want to register propertymanagement.com and property-management.com, as well. (You don't have to actually post your site at all the different domain names; talk to your ISP about *redirecting* traffic from the variations to the main domain name.) Registering a lot of domain names gets expensive (see the section "Registering Your Domain Name" later in this chapter), but you might also want to consider registering negative versions of your domain name. The online publication Slate (*www.slate.com*), had it also registered stale.com, might have stopped a scathing parody in its tracks. Disgruntled people have also expressed their hostility by registering company or product names in unflattering variations; you might or might not want to go to the trouble and expense of preempting that kind of registration.

To Dot Com or Not to Dot Com

Whether your company already exists and has a name or you are starting and naming a new company, product, and website, you must think carefully about your domain name. It's your primary identifier on the Internet. You might wonder why some companies use *dot com* in their URLs and others use *dot net* or even *dot org*. The next section, "Understanding the Domain Naming System," explains what the different terms mean. Suffice it to say here that most users in the U.S. assume that URLs end in *dot com*. Some organizations (and individuals) that are not "commercial" at all (*com* stands for *commercial*) use the .com designation simply to make it easier for users making that common assumption to find the site. You certainly have alternatives, and some alternatives might suit you better than *.com*, especially if your perfect domain name is taken in its *.com* form. To get a grip on how domain names actually work, read on.

Understanding the Domain Naming System

A *domain* is a network or single computer that's represented as a *server* on the Internet. (For more about servers, see Chapter 10.) The system that keeps all of the domains distinct from each other is the *Domain Naming System* (DNS).

To see how the DNS works, look at this URL:

http://www.microsoft.com/catalog/product/superstuff.html

URLs go from the specific (a document, which is shown on the rightmost end of the URL) to the general (the protocol used to access the document on the Internet, shown at the leftmost end of the URL). The document is in a subdirectory, which is in a directory, which is on a computer, which is part of the network of computers that make up the Web. This URL shows the document *superstuff.html* within the subdirectory *product* within the directory *catalog* on the server *microsoft.com*, which is a web server (*www*) accessed by using the Hypertext Transfer Protocol (*http://*). The *www.microsoft.com* portion also indicates that, in this case, the web server is in the domain *microsoft.com*. The domain name shows who "owns" the URL, but it can also be used for other purposes. For example, in the email address *someone@microsoft.com*, the user *someone* receives his or her messages on the email server whose domain name is *microsoft.com*.

The suffix *.com* in the URL example indicates that this domain is commercial and presumably, but not necessarily, located in the United States. (Because a *com* suffix is expected by so many users, many European, Asian, and other companies now use it.) Domains that use *com* are very common, but other suffixes do exist. For example, most countries have a suffix that can be used by the domains registered within that country. Here are a few examples:

de	Domains registered in Germany
jp	Domains registered in Japan
ru	Domains registered in Russia
uk	Domains registered in the United Kingdom

You can find out more about domain suffixes at *www.iana.org/top-level-domains.html*.

Domains originating in the United States are so numerous that the *us* country suffix is rarely used. Many U.S. domain types are instead identified by the following suffixes:

com	Commercial (profit-making) domains
gov	United States federal government domains
edu	Educational institution domains
mil	United States military domains
org	Not-for-profit organization domains
net	Network provider domains

> **Note**
>
> As mentioned, some European, Asian, and other companies register their sites with the *.com* suffix. Nothing prevents them from using this or any of the other suffixes commonly presumed to be for United States sites. Paris.net is as likely to be in Paris, France as in Paris, Texas.

Domains are assigned names because names are easy for humans to remember. The domain name must be unique among all domain names so that the computer(s) it represents are not confused with other computers on the Internet. However, computers are machines, and machines understand numbers better than names. For this reason, in the DNS, each domain name corresponds to a unique numeric address—called an *Internet Protocol (IP) address*—that specifically identifies each computer to all the others. In other words, a domain name is a kind of pseudonym for an IP address. As an example, *www.microsoft.com* is a pseudonym for the computer known to other computers as 131.107.1.240, which lives in the domain *microsoft.com*.

Is Your Prospective Name Taken?

One simple (but not foolproof) way to check whether a domain name has already been registered by someone else is to open up your web browser, enter the name as a URL (preceded by www. and followed by .com), press Enter, and see if your browser locates a website. This method isn't completely accurate, because not every domain has a currently operating website, but it is quick and easy.

Another method is to use any of the domain name registration services listed in Yahoo! (*www.yahoo.com*), but why pay extra fees for tasks you can perform yourself quite simply for far less money?

A better way to check whether a prospective domain is available is to use the service provided by bCentral. It's fueled by Network Solutions, the firm that has traditionally been responsible for maintaining the central domain-naming database. You can also go directly to Network Solutions at *www.networksolutions.com*.

Registering Your Domain Name

After you've determined that your prospective domain name is available, registering it is a simple matter. You can usually do it through the ISP that will host your site (see Chapter 10). They will provide the appropriate form(s) and might charge you a small service fee for getting your domain set up. They'll also provide the domain naming system with all the information (the IP address and so on) that's needed.

Tip

You can also use the service at bCentral to register your domain name.

No matter who registers your domain name, you will receive a bill. As of this writing, you can expect that bill to run at least $70 for two years of registration; it will cost perhaps $35 per year thereafter.

Note

The process for registering a domain name might have changed by the time you read this book. Check *www.icann.org* to find out more.

If you prefer to register your domain yourself (for example, if you're hosting the site on your own server at your own location, rather than through an ISP), you can do it through the Network Solutions website (or bCentral). The forms there will step you through the process. You'll need information about your IP address and other items, so check what's needed and gather that information together before you start.

So now you know what your e-commerce venture is trying to achieve, and you know what you are going to call it. The next question is "What will your site look like?"

Determining Look and Feel

The look and feel of your site starts with the *palette* (selection of colors) you use. Web design books are full of information about selecting a palette. For a calm, soothing look, the experts suggest choosing cool blues, greens, and grays. These are classic, corporate colors. (Think IBM.) For a hipper, more modern look, choose the colors in the current week's ads on MTV. Also consider a general look that conveys the image you want to present: if your site is chock full of stuff, go for a busy look; to convey that your site is backed by a stable, trustworthy company, go for an uncluttered look.

> ### Use Browser-Safe Colors
>
> Web browsers recognize only a certain range of colors—216 of them, to be exact. That range, known as *browser-safe colors*, includes yellows, blues, purples, and so on. It even includes ranges of fuchsias, magentas, and the like. But it does not include all tints or hues of all colors. Yellow, for example, is a notorious problem. There are only a handful of browser-safe yellows and they are not all terribly attractive. When you select your site's palette, and the colors of logos and other identifying elements that you will represent on your site, your best bet is to stick with browser-safe colors (see Chapter 8). You might even want to check these out before selecting the colors you will use in your signage and print materials. More than one large company has found that its signature color simply cannot be reproduced on the Web, causing no end of dismay in those companies' marketing departments.

Clarifying Your Audience and What They Want

Go back to what you know about your target audience (see Chapter 1). Select a visual style that appeals to that audience. Set aside your personal preferences in favor of what works for that audience. If you hate purple but your site sells herbal products and the color lavender will work for your target market, so be it. If you love chartreuse but your target audience is not that adventurous, you might have to go with cobalt. Presumably, your e-commerce site is not a vanity site. It's there to serve your customers. Know your customers, and meet their needs. Think about the following questions:

- What is the product?
- Who is the audience?
- How and why does the product appeal to this audience?
- Are you already reaching an audience you'd like to retain?
- What new audience do you want to reach?
- Does most of your audience already know you?
- How do they see your company or product?
- How do you want them to see your company or product?
- Do they have any general or specific attitudes you ought to take into consideration?
- Where are the greatest opportunities for growth, given your current or projected audience?
- What is the risk that you might lose your audience?

The answers to these questions will help you form a basis for thinking about the development of your website from a branding perspective.

As your business grows, stay close to your customers. FedEx changed its name (and branding) from *Federal Express* to *FedEx* at about the time its customers were commonly referring to *FedEx* and had even coined the verb *to FedEx* (to send) a parcel.

Tip

Brand messages (ads, for instance) take two general forms: those that tell you about a company, and those that tell you about its product. Company messages might mention the products ("the makers of Just Togs") if they are well known, and product messages might mention the company name ("brought to you by MightyFlight Toys") if the name will help sell the product. But seldom does one brand message try to do all things. Consider this separation as you create your online brand messages.

What Does Your Logo Say About You?

Your logo (visual identifier) is the stamp you place on all your products, including your website, to identify them as yours. For online purposes, your logo must be available in a horizontal form (to fit pages, banners, and ads more conveniently). It can also be in a vertical form (but that can't be

Part 2: Create Identity and Attract Customers

the only form available). Think about how it will work in postage-stamp-size ads. (See Chapter 12 for more about advertising.) Also think about how it will look with a tag line attached to tell people who you are or what you do. Try out different versions of your logo so that you have flexibility in advertising and page design.

Take a look at the two logos—both for online brokerage sites—that are shown here:

The logo for Charles Schwab, the more traditional company of the two, uses a font with *serifs* (those little dangly things hanging off the corners of each letter), which is an older, more traditional style. The logo itself is in one color, on a conservative, navy blue, pinstriped background. The E*Trade logo is in a more modern *sans serif* font (one without serifs), uses three colors (one of which is lime green!), and although navy blue does appear on the site, most of the page backgrounds are black or white, heightening the contrast of the lime green accent color. The differences between these two companies are obvious from their logos. Both are dealing with people's money, so they must inspire trust. But E*Trade, the *electronic* brokerage firm, is a tad more modern than Schwab, the more established, brick-and-mortar company.

Defining Your Website's Look and Feel

The design of your site's pages should be consistent with your logo's look. Remember: the key to branding is to be relentless in conveying the branding message. If your site is company-oriented, carry over the look of the company's logo to the site. Repeat the color scheme, the design elements, the fonts, and so on. If your site is product-oriented, repeat that product's look in the site design. It's all about identity.

Go back once more to what you know about your target audience, and ask yourself the following additional questions as you consider how to create your site's look and feel. (If you are using a web shop, you might also want to provide this information to the designers before they begin the project.)

- What is most unique about your company or product? What are its strengths and weaknesses?
- Who is your competition? What are their strengths and weakness?
- What products or services do you offer? Do you plan additions? (If so, describe what and when.)
- Where are you located? Do you prefer to market and sell locally, nationally, or internationally?
- What is the main purpose of your website? Is there a secondary purpose?
- Think about the image you'd like to convey to your audience. Which of these words describe it: conservative, contemporary, modern, creative, elegant, innovative, exciting, earthy, calm, warm, casual, witty, personal, confident, formal, sophisticated, serious, professional, educational, technical, artistic, smooth, dramatic, sympathetic, fun, energetic, easy? Can you add any other words to the list?
- Is there a general image that should be avoided?
- What photographs or illustrations might convey the site's message? Are there any types of photos or illustrations to be avoided?
- In order to convey its message, should the site include the company's history or philosophy? What about staff biographies?
- Will case studies, testimonials, or other evidence of customer satisfaction help convey the site's message?
- How long do you plan to keep this site running after launch? Do you plan to minimize maintenance or add fresh content frequently? What sort of content and how often?
- Will the site need to be tied in to other branding efforts, such as print brochures, the look of your real-world location, or the look of other sites?
- What are your overall marketing objectives?

Part 2: Create Identity and Attract Customers

> ### Sound and Video as Part of Your Branding Message
>
> Identifiers certainly can be audio or even video, as evidenced by the Oscar Mayer hot dog jingle and those computerized tones that identify the Intel Pentium Processor. But don't use bells and whistles you don't need. Sound and video might be appropriate for high-tech sites, especially if bells and whistles are the product, and you might want to use them to deliver a message that adds a personal note to your site. Excellent use has been made of animation, sound, and video, but usually as an accent. And accents, by definition, are sparsely applied.

For an example of an e-commerce site with a consistent look, strong branding, and a good audio accent, take a look at the Fresh Flower Source site (*www.freshflowersource.com*), shown in Figure 4.2. And for an example of an elegantly designed and highly functional site that was created for a nonprofit organization, have a look at the Redland Baptist Church site (*www.redlandbaptist.org*), shown in Figure 4.3.

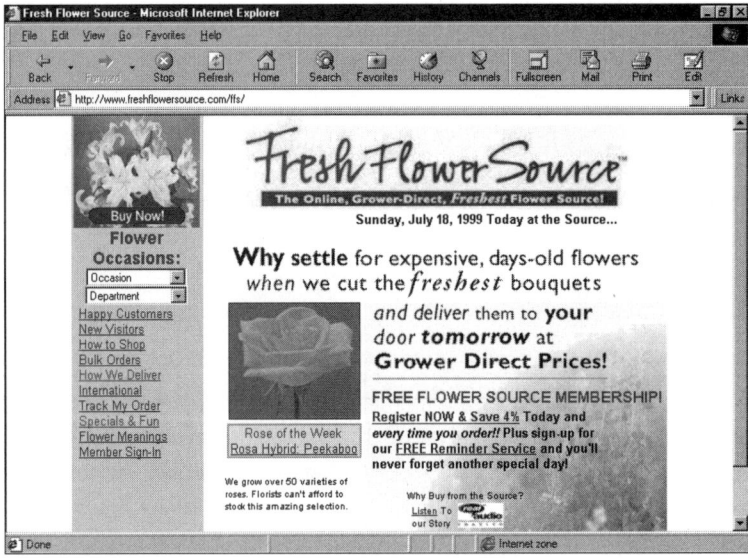

Figure 4.2

Fresh Flower Source, a site branded with fresh service.

Chapter 4: Creating Online Branding

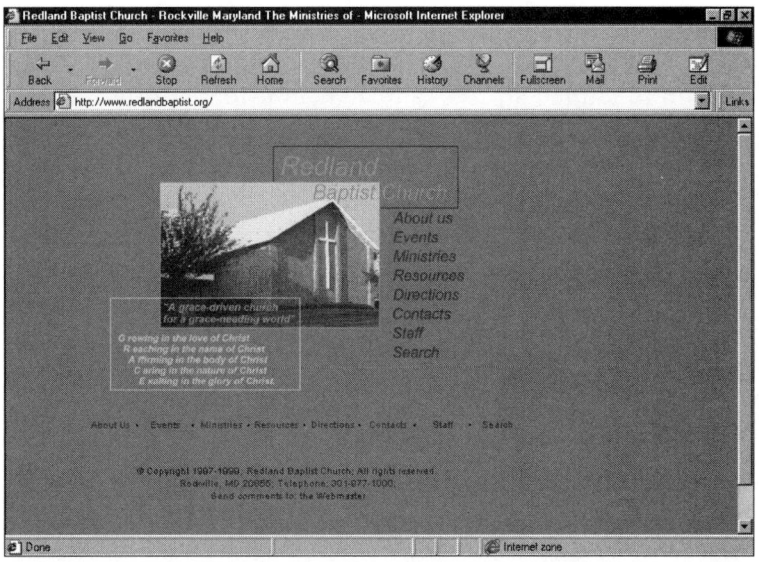

Figure 4.3
Redland Baptist Church, a site with smooth navigation and elegant, consistent design that wasn't pricey.

So What Works?

As you define your branding message, take a look at what works for others. Consider what you might learn from the campaigns of companies that hire high-priced branding consultants. Along with what has already been described in this chapter, your research will tell you:

- **Trade on what you have.** If you are number one in your industry, say so. If you are not, you might be able to turn a seeming disadvantage into a source of inspiration. Remember the Avis campaign from years gone by. Avis was number two (behind Hertz) in the rental car industry and very cleverly made a whole campaign out of "trying harder."

- **Get there first to own the space.** It's always easier to stake a new claim than to take one from someone else. Yahoo!, Amazon, and eBay are all examples of companies that were first to market and defined the playing field for others.

- **Market your brand offline.** Use your signage and any print advertising to further your online brand. If your company isn't in a position to launch a print campaign, consider partnering with a company whose brand is already known or a company that is also putting in the effort to get known.
- **Relentlessly get out there.** Make friends, affiliates, and linking partners. It's the Web, so you should follow links, get reciprocal links, share content, barter for ad space, and build some co-marketing agreements. Work with suppliers to co-market. Create your own affiliate programs. Curry favor with the press. Offer freebies to users who will display your logo or text link on their sites, and never give up the cause.
- **Be consistent.** Maintain a consistent look and message among your packaging, products, ads, and site design. Within the site, don't confuse people by switching the design and color scheme from page to page or from area to area. Make your site's style of writing consistent with its look and feel. A conservative site should have a formal look and more formal writing; a site with a cutting-edge attitude should have an intrusive look and in-your-face writing. Be sure your transaction pages follow through with whatever style you choose for the rest of your site.
- **Actually deliver value to your customer.** Now there's a concept! Make your product(s) strong, your service impeccable, and your site's operation smooth. Nothing does more for branding than being the best.

> **Note**
>
> Chapter 12 discusses techniques for promoting your site both online and by traditional promotional methods.

Considering Quality of Experience

In the world of e-commerce, the customer's experience is a major component of branding. You need to create a positive experience by making sales easy and service solid. Take a look at successful mail-order companies such as Lands' End, and then consider these guidelines:

- **Don't keep people waiting.** Pages should load quickly (in less than a minute). Don't assume that customers will have the fastest connections. Unless your audience is primarily high-end techies, design for a low common denominator. You don't have to take into account every browser that ever existed and modem speeds that went out with the last century, but do figure out (as best you can) the likely *range* of browsers and modem speeds, and design for the slowest systems your audience might have.

- **Put the goods out in the open.** Make it easy to find what you're promoting or selling. Put links to sales pages at the top of your home page. Present pertinent information clearly. A confused customer is a customer who will simply walk away. Don't let that happen.

- **Create multiple ways to search your online catalog.** Make it easy to find items based on the price, size, color, brand name, year, topic, and so on.

- **Don't place barriers between the customer and a sale.** Make it easy to pay in as few steps as possible. Don't require registration (the providing of email addresses and marketing information) before the customer can make a purchase. Reduce the number of hoops that a customer must jump through to a bare minimum.

- **Build trust.** Online shoppers are a skeptical bunch, and rightfully so. Like all customers, they want to know what they're getting, when, and how it will be delivered. They want to know how you're protecting their credit card information. They also want to know to whom you're selling their name and email address (they'd prefer you didn't do that, by the way), and what you're doing with any marketing data you might have gleaned from them. According to a survey by IntelliQuest, people who do not buy online cite the following reasons for their reluctance:
    - Concern about fly-by-night retailers (81 percent)
    - Don't want to deal with returns (72 percent)
    - Concern about using their credit card online (69 percent)
    - Concern about getting a lot of junk email (63 percent)
    - Prefer to see and touch what they buy (62 percent)

Given that data, it seems evident that the e-commerce industry as a whole must provide reasons for Internet users to become Internet customers. And that means that e-commerce businesspeople have to instill trust in their customers.

Establishing Integrity and Trust Online

People want to know what they're getting. In an online setting, the most tangible way to convey what you are going to deliver is via pictures and words. There are, however, other methods for gaining the sort of trust that inspires people to do business online.

First and foremost, be predictable. Follow through on your promises and deliver what you said you would, on time, without fuss. According to online branding pro Christina Cheney, "The most common mistake people make is to overhype and overpromise. Don't launch too fast—make sure you're ready. And don't offer anything you cannot deliver. Of course, time to market is incredibly crucial to an online brand, but follow-through is even more important."

In general, make sure yours is a quality operation. Show your merchandise in detail. (Provide thumbnail-size photos as links to larger images if necessary.) If you are a retailer, feature name brand products the customer will recognize. Make communication with you or your staff easy; make an email address obvious, and include both a surface mail address and a customer service phone number on your site. Display testimonials from satisfied customers. Publish your privacy policy, telling customers what you will and won't do with their email address and any personal information they have provided by registering on your site or making a purchase. (bCentral offers resources for creating a privacy policy.) Assure customers that if they are victimized by fraud while shopping at your site (an unlikely event if you've addressed security issues; see Chapter 10), you'll cover any charges. Create, stand behind, and publish a *no-hassle* return policy that allows customers to send back merchandise for a refund or exchange. If possible, affiliate yourself with a respected association or a large, known, and trusted company.

Here's a thought: Use a face—if not the face of a celebrity, then your own. Consider the example of a website for a real estate consultant. His smiling face appears beside a brief description of his credentials and the various associations he belongs to. A navigation bar provides links to standards of practice and other information that can inspire trust in potential clients. If you're shy, perhaps a cartooned likeness can step in for you. But don't use Mickey Mouse, Ronald McDonald, or any other trademarked image. They are part of someone else's brand, and using them will both muddy up your brand and cause the company that owns those images to defend their brands by coming after you. (For information about trademarking, see Chapter 3.)

One final tip: when you use technology to bolster your branding by providing a strong user experience, you have to constantly look ahead. Don't rely on whatever created last year's buzz. And don't just toss in the latest bells and whistles for the sake of bells and whistles. Make sure they count for something, that they further the brand message, and most importantly, that they add quality to the customer's experience.

Chapter 5

Providing Customer Service

Whatever your business, if you are *in* business, you have customers. How you treat them has a profound, immediate, and lasting impact on whether your business thrives. If your business involves e-commerce, you have a significant opportunity to identify, track, target, and stay close to your customers. And, quite significantly, you can interact directly with your customers, rather than communicating with them via buyers from your distribution channels, who might be filtering or interpreting your customers' feedback.

Online shoppers are an attractively affluent market. In the United States, they control more than 50 percent of household income. They are also becoming more savvy every day. Because of these factors, you might do well to think of your *customer service* program less as a fallback measure for when things go wrong and more as a *customer care* program that tends to the needs of customers from the moment they approach your site until they buy, receive, and use your product or service. Customer service actually extends beyond the sales cycle to include these possible goals:

- Expanding and retaining customer loyalty
- Boosting profit by increasing sales and decreasing costs

Part 2: Create Identity and Attract Customers

- Minimizing the time it takes to get a product or service to market
- Improving products and services in step with what the customer needs and wants

Let's consider for a moment what service really means. Whatever your e-commerce website's purpose, when a customer approaches your site, service should be its goal. Naturally, for a sales site, having service as a goal means making your products easy to see, experience, and buy. But suppose yours is a company that sells, installs, and services heaters. You might think that all your website has to do is list your company contact information and describe your services. If so, you are missing an opportunity to provide service, attract traffic, and telegraph to potential customers that your company is service oriented. On your website, you can post seasonal reminders of the services a homeowner or company might need, you can provide a scheduling service via a simple online form, and you can offer tips about keeping heating costs in line by regularly maintaining heating systems. You can also display the products you use so that customers don't have to wait for you to mail or drop off a brochure. (And you don't have to check your supply of brochures, either.) In short, you can market your service and products much more effectively.

Here are some other examples of customer service at work in the overall strategy of a website:

- A health insurer's website can provide listings of doctors who accept the insurance plan. Similarly, a pediatrician's office can provide a list of the insurance plans it accepts, along with immunization schedules and other information of interest to its patients.
- A local utility company or an electrician can describe how businesses, homeowners, and renters can arrange for electrical service after a move.
- A small company can do without a sales force by posting product or service information online and then sending out direct mail postcards to potential customers, guiding them to the website.

Doing as little as using your website for standard customer service can save on costs. Forrester Research, Inc. reports that online customer service efforts can cut overall customer service costs by 43 percent. The savings result primarily from reductions in staffing and phone-service costs. But other, less obvious savings can result from offering extended customer service via a website. In the case of the health insurer in the list of examples just presented, you can easily see that providing an online list of doctors associated with the insurance plan can save on the cost of printing pamphlets and distributing them. It also allows the insurer to update the list more frequently and less expensively, and it gives clients multiple ways to search the list (by ZIP code, medical specialty, or other criteria). Now that's customer service!

Your website might have customer service as its central goal rather than as just part of its offerings. Online customer service sites can effectively communicate with existing customers and prospective customers, provide service and support, augment traditional customer service communications, and offer internal communications about customer service or other topics. But remember: a customer who wants information is likely to use an online option for getting it, while a customer who wants to discuss a bill or invoice will invariably want to talk to a human being.

Why Customer Service Matters—Especially in E-Commerce

E-commerce is a new industry, and the public has been somewhat skeptical about embracing it. Who wouldn't be? Aren't we all reluctant to do business with companies that we don't know? It just makes sense that we want reassurances before we entrust our credit card numbers and purchasing power to an entire industry that's less than familiar. Individual companies engaged in e-commerce are up against the same challenges that face the industry as a whole: how do you build trust? The public is flocking to the Internet and has enormous purchasing power; how do you sell to them effectively?

You Are Your Web Site

Your online customers experience your website as if they are walking into your place of business. In fact, to them that's exactly what it is; your website might be their only experience of you and your business. Like customers in the brick-and-mortar world, they decide to buy based on their impression of your products and services, your pricing, and how it compares with similar products. But they also decide based on the experience they have while they are at your website.

Chapter 4 discussed the importance of making your site functional, persuasive, easy to use, and easy to navigate. These points come to bear here. Just as a "real-world" storefront and the merchandising within can either persuade customers to come in and make purchases or drive them away, so can a website and its "merchandising." If the site's pages are geared to its audience, if its information is easy to find, and if the catalog of products or services is easy to use and attractive, online customers are more likely to stick around and buy. For pointers on attracting traffic and creating a striking identity for your site, see Chapter 4. For more information about serving your customers effectively, read on in this chapter.

First Impressions Are Lasting

Perhaps you've had the experience of walking into a store, glancing around, not seeing what you want (either the actual product or the level of merchandising and store maintenance you expect), and walking right back out again. If you're like most people, you probably won't give that store another chance. Similarly, you might have had the experience of trying a new restaurant, thinking it was okay but not great, and without being able to put your finger on just why, knowing you aren't interested in trying it again.

> **Note**
>
> The first impression you make is both the lasting one and the easiest one to get right. If a first impression is good, customers will come back. If it's bad, you might not get another chance. Even if you do, you'll be fighting that first failure. It's a lot easier to get it right the first time than to correct a mistaken or disappointing first impression later.

The bottom line here is that if customers doubt your integrity, can't find what they want, or feel misunderstood or confused, they won't stay and they won't buy. Make your website look inviting and trustworthy. Make it function well, and not just look good. And make it so that a customer who clicks in to your site sees what he or she wants—the style, the information, the products and services, and the benefit of being there—immediately. That's the way to keep customers clicking in, and stop them from clicking right back out again.

Chapter 5: Providing Customer Service

If the Industry Looks Bad, Business Is Bad

No one wants to buy from hucksters. If the e-commerce industry doesn't adhere to solid business standards, including customer service, the industry as a whole will suffer, as will each e-commerce endeavor. Because e-commerce is such a new industry, not only is every e-commerce endeavor creating a first impression, so is the industry as a whole. As well-known companies begin doing business online (bringing with them their reputations for integrity), and as more people have positive experiences with online business in general, the credibility of the industry as a whole rises, which in turn leads to more and more business being conducted online. To continue this trend and enhance the e-commerce industry as a whole, each e-commerce venture must conduct itself with integrity and treat each customer with respect. What else but that, after all, is customer service?

The National Association of Consumer Agency Administrators reports that the top complaints about e-commerce from consumers are that the customer:

- Did not receive the goods or services ordered
- Received damaged merchandise
- Experienced problems obtaining refunds on returned goods
- Was overcharged
- Believed advertising was false or misleading

Perhaps the truest test of customer service is how returns are handled. A post-holiday survey by Jupiter Communications showed that 42 percent of e-commerce sites never responded to customer inquiries about returns, took more than five days to reply, or didn't offer to respond by email to reported problems. Of course, your employees will occasionally make mistakes. Customer service is about addressing those errors, but it's also about preventing them from happening again.

Remember: Bolstering customer service on your website—taking care of each customer from the moment he or she enters your front door (your home page) until well after he or she has received your product or service—will benefit both your business and the entire e-commerce industry. "Making Up for It Later" gets expensive.

Consider the case of a neighborhood restaurant. This restaurant does no advertising but draws customers from a 50-mile radius. How do they know about the place? It's simple: word of mouth. The owner of the restaurant feels strongly that his best shot at building a strong customer base is to provide good food and good service, pouring the money that might have been used for advertising into the product. And if something goes wrong—for example, if the cooks misread an order and prepare the wrong entrée, and the waiter doesn't notice the mistake but the customer does—the restaurant's policy is not only to correct the error, but to offer dessert on the house. That's great customer service. But is it great *customer care*?

From the viewpoint of the customer, the restaurant has made amends for its error. It would have been better if the error had not occurred, but hey, people make mistakes. It is better to acknowledge mistakes, correct them, and learn from them. From the viewpoint of the restaurant, the customer service gesture preserved the customer's loyalty but lost the profit margin on the meal.

You're always better off providing good customer care and getting things right the first time than having to pay for customer service after a poorly executed transaction. Bruce Molloy, of Brigade Solutions (*www.brigadesolutions.com*), a provider of outsourced customer service via email, says, "In the case of low-profit-margin items like a $75 piece of software, many companies find that responding to just two or three customer service calls can kill the profit margin on a specific sale." Molloy goes on to suggest that providing customer service response via email can cut costs dramatically. However, industry experts, including Molloy, agree that the best way to keep overall customer service costs down is to provide good customer care in the course of everyday business, rather than in response to a mistake.

Provide the Best Product or Service

A good start in providing excellent customer care is to offer customers the options and quality they expect. Make sure you and your product are actually available. You or your staff must be "in the store," items must be in stock, and your products and services must be deliverable. That might seem obvious, but it's remarkable how often the simple issue of order fulfillment trips up a business plan (see Chapter 1). Make sure you can service all of your accounts, and make sure your products are usable. Pour resources into making your product or service the best. And above all, understand what your customers want and what will bring them back for more.

Chapter 5: Providing Customer Service

E-commerce provides a unique opportunity to stay close to customers. Customer service professional Bruce Molloy suggests, "Focus on customer care, on problems and inquiries, but also on getting a base of information about the customer—how happy are they, and what other services or features might they want?"

You might think you know your customers very well indeed. But asking them what they want can yield surprising results. You might find, for example, that customers want phone support for your high-tech product, when you thought they preferred just online support. Build simple forms into your website to conduct online surveys, and you'll find out more about your customers as the results roll in.

Options for how to build online survey forms range from off-the-shelf software and simple tools to big-ticket software to outsourced solutions. At the low end, you can use a program such as Microsoft FrontPage to build the form, have the results from each form emailed to you, and save the results in a file. (Figure 5.1 shows a survey form created with FrontPage.) You can also use Microsoft Access and Microsoft Excel to track and analyze the information compiled from the survey.

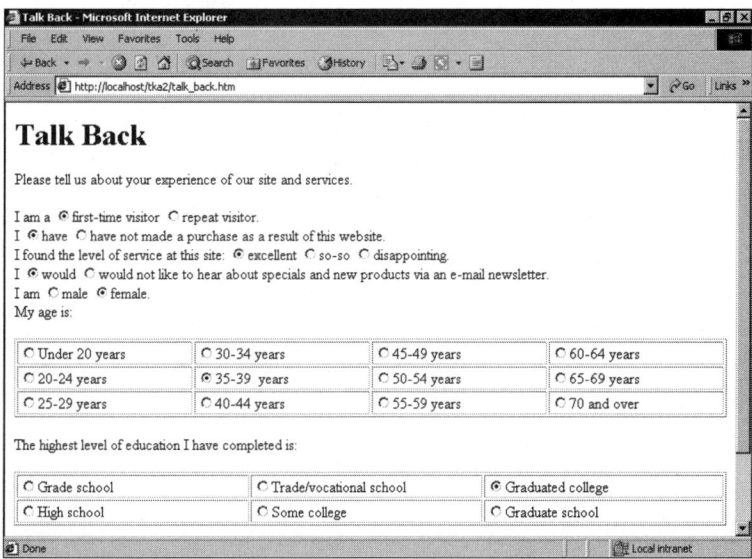

Figure 5.1
Create an online survey to get feedback from customers about your site as well as your products and services.

Whether or not you choose to find out about your customers through surveys, it's a good idea to provide customers with an easy method for emailing inquiries to you. (Again, you can use FrontPage to create an online form that lets customers send email directly from your site to you in a snap.) You can even send customers email responses with small surveys embedded in them.

It goes almost without saying that your decisions have a profound effect on your product, your company, and your customers. Remember: it is how well you fulfill your customers' needs, not how well you satisfy your personal beliefs about what they *might* need, that will make or break your business.

Build Customer Loyalty

Every customer is a good customer: They are all spending good money at your business. To keep them coming back, treat each customer as though he or she is your most important, most valued customer. It's common wisdom in customer service circles that customers respond well to key phrases such as these:

- Welcome. (Use whatever form the target market expects.)
- How can I help? (Let them talk!)
- I understand. (This builds rapport.)
- Is this what you had in mind? (If not, find ways to improve it.)
- Is there anything else I can help you with? (This ends the communication without alienating the customer.)
- Has this transaction met your expectations? (Communicate that your goal is to serve the customer's needs.)

To each customer, his or her own needs matter most. Your goal in providing excellent customer care is to show the customer, via your website's design, its functionality, and its content, as well as through the quality of your communications, that his or her needs matter most to you, too.

> ### *Breaches in Privacy Cost Sales*
>
> Rushing to get online at the expense of protecting your customers' privacy simply does not pay. Take the time to make sure your systems are secure. Give any programmers you hire the time and resources needed to build and test your transaction system and to address all security issues before you go live. Inadvertently leaving holes in your systems can allow unscrupulous hackers to get to names, addresses, phone numbers, card numbers, and other purchasing information. A breach of security like this is the kiss of death in e-commerce customer care. And it doesn't even take a knowledgeable hacker to break into a system—innocent users can sometimes get to sensitive information accidentally by using certain keywords in searches, for example.
>
> Interestingly, large businesses tend to be more aware of these issues and often spend more to make systems secure; smaller businesses must make the same conscious effort. The United States Department of Commerce and the Federal Trade Commission are discussing how to encourage privacy protection. If the e-commerce industry does not set its own standards and provide the public with good security, these governmental bodies might step in more strongly to enforce privacy standards.
>
> If you hire programmers to build your transaction system, question their credentials and get references. If you hire friends or an untested agency to create your site, be aware of the pitfalls. For example, nonprofessionals might not know the intricacies of security well enough to provide you with the means to protect the privacy of your customers. If you are building the site yourself, be sure to use only those products and turnkey solutions that can back up their security claims with experience and proof. Not protecting the security of your customers is the surest way to lose them. Your customers must trust you in order to do business with you.

Communicate Positively

On your e-commerce website and in customer service emails, phrase communications positively to get the best results. Consider the difference between the more reassuring "We'll have it in stock on Tuesday" and the more abrupt "That item is out of stock." In the first case, the customer knows he is being taken care of and will get what he wants; in the latter case, the customer has to fend for himself by asking further questions or just forgetting the whole matter. Consider, too, the difference between "No smoking" and "Thank you for not smoking" (or better yet, "Smoking is permitted in the outdoor courtyard").

The Negative Version	**The Positive Version**
Our product isn't for everyone.	Our product appeals to connoisseurs.
We don't accept American Express.	We accept Visa and MasterCard.
No, we can't walk it down to the mailroom to shave a day off shipping.	Expedited shipping is available for a small fee.

What's an example of the worst kind of customer service failure? Blaming the customer. Here's a true story: a customer ordered a pizza for delivery, and it didn't arrive. The customer called to inquire about the order, and the dispatcher insisted that the delivery person had arrived and knocked, and that the customer "hid" behind the door. The customer replied that no one had knocked on his door. The dispatcher said he was lying. The customer asked to speak to a manager. The dispatcher said he was the manager. The customer pleaded, "All I want is my pizza." The dispatcher (who later turned out not to be a manager at all) answered, "Then you should have answered the door." In this outrageous example, the dispatcher had several opportunities—missed at every turn—to right the situation. It's remarkable that this customer remained calm, and that his reaction was only that he vowed never to call or recommend this pizza chain again.

Be Easy to Reach

In many ways, the Internet is all about communication. In traditional sales, communication tends to flow in one direction from company to customer, and getting feedback from the customer often involves drawing together expensive focus groups or waiting for communication in the form of complaints or sales figures. In e-commerce, not only can communication flow easily in both directions, but the channels can be more open and immediate. Your website can and should provide customers with several methods for contacting you. Online forms, email addresses, phone numbers, postal addresses—each has its place in customer interaction, and offering customers a variety of methods to contact you empowers them to communicate

Chapter 5: Providing Customer Service

Handling the Disgruntled Customer

Things sometimes go wrong, and at times even the most service-oriented company finds itself facing an angry customer. Perhaps the customer had a lousy experience with the company, or perhaps the customer is simply an angry, unhappy person. In either case, the customer service representative must handle both the complaint and the customer's outrage.

Responding to an angry customer effectively is an art. Start by listening. Look for an opportunity to tell them they're right—about something. You obviously don't want to tell them that they're right about something that isn't true or that opens the company to legal liability, but find something, even if it is just to say "I'm glad you're calling this to my attention." At the very least, don't disagree. Instead, ask for details. Getting the angry customer to talk about the situation shifts him or her out of yelling and into problem solving. Next, commit to solving the problem. Instead of "We'll see about it," say something that starts with "I will...." Something as simple as "I will make a note of that" can help. Ask for the customer's input in coming up with a solution. "How would you like this resolved?" goes a long way toward allowing someone to let off steam and move the conversation forward. Finally, if this is an important issue or an especially loyal customer, drop everything and deal with it right away, perhaps even face-to-face. Keep in mind that only one thing matters to the customer: that the problem be solved.

effectively and appropriately. The faster, more convenient, and more complete your service is, the more likely casual browsers are to turn into loyal, returning customers. Even more important, providing the means for easy communications provides customers with the *sense* that their input is valued. In many cases, simply having a way to contact you is so reassuring that a customer's actual need to contact you is diminished. Just as offering a money-back guarantee persuades many people of your good intentions but is an option that few will take advantage of, offering easy communications telegraphs your accessibility to many more people than you will ever hear from.

There are, of course, situations where personal interaction is most effective and even quite necessary. Complex negotiations, the resolving of complicated problems, and addressing concerns about bills are all best done by phone or in person. Further, though purchase of big-ticket items like cars and capital equipment can be supported via online information, closing the sale is generally more effective via a personal contact. A survey of online shoppers by NFO Interactive revealed that approximately 50 percent of those surveyed preferred to shop for cars online but to buy at a dealer. They liked to gather dealer-invoicing information from the Web, get the inside scoop, and avoid the stereotypical sales hype, but only 11 percent would actually buy the car online without visiting a dealer. (Of course, the key draw to the dealer might simply be the lure of the test drive.)

Another survey of online shoppers by NFO Interactive found that some retail customers shopping for items much smaller than cars simply want someone to talk to. Nearly 35 percent of those surveyed said they would buy more if they could interact in real-time with an e-commerce salesperson. Of those who had not yet purchased anything online, almost 14 percent said they would if they could speak directly to a customer service rep. Online chat, direct phone (as in conventional catalog sales), and email are all options for providing personal interaction.

Caution

Keep in mind that real-time, interactive support can be very labor intensive and by extension, very costly. It's a great option for some e-commerce businesses, but it's not for everyone.

One option for providing interaction with service and sales reps can be found in Microsoft NetMeeting, a product that offers online conferencing, web phone capabilities, an online whiteboard, text chat, and file transfer, as well as point-to-point audio and video. Software companies (such as the Baan Company) routinely use NetMeeting to remotely train value-added resellers (VARs) by introducing and demonstrating new products over the Internet. Companies can also provide real-time training and support to in-house and freelance team members (including customer service staff). Customer service reps can provide interactive support to customers via chat sessions and, if necessary, can draw on an online whiteboard that customers can view via their web browsers.

Respond Immediately

Customers see response time as an indication of what it will be like to do business with your company, and the overall promise of the Internet is speed and convenience. Make that the promise of your company, too. When customers contact you, they expect you to answer right now. Confirm orders and answer email immediately. Remember: big-ticket items demand the quickest response. The more someone spends, the more service they expect. But in general, your goal should be to respond before your customer logs off.

Not too long ago, I ordered a couple of items from Martha By Mail (www.marthabymail.com). Before I had time to switch to my email window, I'd received a message confirming my order. A follow-up email told me when to expect delivery, and a postcard arrived a few days later reiterating the same information. One item was on backorder and had to be delivered later. I received an email to that effect, with the same type of follow-up generated by my initial order. By contrast, that same week I ordered a digital music player from a major distributor of hardware and software. They sent no confirmation email and no notice that the item was out of stock. When it didn't arrive, I called to follow up. They insisted they'd sent out a letter via the postal service, but over a week had passed and the letter had not yet arrived. I canceled the order.

Caution

The urgency of generating an email confirmation should not inspire you to disregard quality. Incorrect information creates a poor impression; so do poor spelling and grammar.

As you plan your communications strategy, remember to account for possible spikes in traffic. For example, anyone who's bought a house will tell you that the last few days of closing the deal are a frantic time of papers moving back and forth among many players, including the mortgage lender. And any mortgage lender can tell you that the most popular time to close deals is the end of the month. There is always a surge in business then. Using electronic methods to move communications around during the home buying process can be a real boon, but for mortgage lenders, the end-of-the month spike can be a problem. Suppose responses at the end of the month take 24 hours. The deals on dozens of houses might be closing in that 24-hour period. To manage this email problem, one lender installed a smart system that "understands" customers' email questions and automates responses. That lending company can now answer many routine emails within a minute. More complex inquiries are directed to a customer service center that handles questions by phone or personal email.

> **Note**
>
> In addition to offering email support for their products, more and more companies are staffing chat rooms with technical support staff. Be aware, though, that this can be an expensive solution—staff time costs money, and a real-time conversation can get stretched out with unnecessary back-and-forth chatter.

Offer Customer Service via Email

Email is far and away the most-used Internet application. The number of email users eclipses the number of Web users, and many new users cite wanting email as their reason for going online. The popularity of email does not mean that email is the best solution for initial contact with customers or even for presenting or selling your products or services. For one thing, users deeply hate *spam* (unsolicited commercial email); for another, email is often text-based and allows for little or no visual presentation of what you are selling.

The popularity of email does, however, mean that email is a communications tool with profound possibilities. Some businesses already use email as their customer service communications medium. They might use email instead of telephone call centers or in addition to them. Email customer service can be more cost effective than telephone call centers, because long-distance phone charges are not typically associated with email. Furthermore, because email responses can be automated or stored in a database and then mixed and matched by reps, staff time is reduced. "Phone support typically costs three to five times as much as email support," says Bruce Molloy of Brigade Solutions. Others agree that costs can drop in excess of 50 percent when email support is implemented.

Chapter 5: Providing Customer Service

Some typical uses of email in customer service scenarios include:

- A maker of extracts used in cooking and sold via retail channels and catalog sales has staffed an email service center with customer care representatives to augment its phone call center.

- A local realtor offers prospects the usual listings of homes for sale and interior and exterior views of the homes via the company website, but also hosts a live chat area where home buyers can ask questions and get quick answers from the realtor's staff.

- A car dealer follows up with customers who have bought cars by sending service reminders and special offers via email rather than postal mail.

You have many options when organizing the flow of customer service information via email. You can hold email messages overnight and send them in the morning, automate responses to go out instantly, and prepare stock responses for the issues customers raise frequently. You can also cross-sell via customer service email. As long as your style suggests that you are performing another service (instead of pushing another product), you can, for example, suggest another product if one hasn't met the customer's expectations.

Tip

Email newsletters can be a very effective tool for reaching customers to notify them of changes on your site, new products, sales, trends in your industry, and so on. See Chapter 6 to find out more about staying in touch with customers via email newsletters.

Customers who send you email are giving you an opportunity to talk to them. Grab it. Offer special deals to those who sign up for email newsletters, or point to an online survey customers can fill out via a simple form. Take care, however, to avoid offending your customers or intruding on their privacy. Remind people of how you got their email addresses, and don't send out email unless you're asked to. As mentioned, spam is universally disliked, and far from helping your cause, its use will backfire on you. You'll find more on this in Chapter 6, but for now, keep in mind that the customers who opt in to email offers are the most receptive to receiving them. You'll get more response from 1000 people who want to hear what you have to say than from 10,000 who are annoyed to find your message in their inboxes.

> **Caution**
>
> If you begin to depend heavily on email for your customer service program, have accounts with more than one ISP. If your line is accidentally severed by construction workers or your ISP has some technical trouble, you'll want a backup.

The Big-Ticket Solution

To understand the potential of email customer service, consider the big-league case of a large auction site that receives anywhere from 40,000 to 75,000 customer emails per week. Its customer service staff numbers more than 200 people, including 60 independent contractors across 27 states. Its systems include a central database of scripted and semi-scripted replies. It also has a public message board where customers can post questions to service reps; answers appear within minutes. This use of email and message board communications has improved support staff productivity by as much as 50 percent. It's also had an impact on business: happier customers return to the site more frequently, and they buy more, too.

> **Tip**
>
> If you get more than 100 email inquiries per day, you might want to consider automating or outsourcing responses.

What does all this technology and people power cost? Big software solutions that provide an automated email response system can cost between $100,000 and $250,000 to buy and install. The price of outsourced email customer service varies according to the level of service you want and often involves a setup charge as well as monthly fees. Both are probably beyond the budget of many smaller companies.

A Mid-Level Solution

Assuming that either your in-house network or your ISP uses Microsoft Exchange as its mail server software, you can use the AutoReply feature in Microsoft Outlook to automate responses to customers who send you email. (Many ISPs, including MSN, do use Exchange as their mail server software, but check with yours to find out if it does.) Setting up AutoReply is simple—the one-two power combo of Outlook and Exchange offers a number of features that automatically monitor, organize, and process email. For example, via a series of simple check box "rules and actions" you can specify that when certain words or phrases appear within the To or From boxes in an incoming email, or within the Subject line or the text of the message, a certain response will be sent. It's even possible to monitor the date and time the email was received and have responding messages sent out at certain intervals after that time. This can be very useful when, for example, you want to acknowledge an order, get a confirmation of some aspect of the order from your customer, and nudge your customer gently until you receive that confirmation.

You can also create personalized, prewritten email responses to various customer questions or requests. The incoming email will be searched for a designated word or phrase, and based on that word or phrase ("send me a catalogue," for example), an outgoing message will be sent automatically.

In addition, you can include value-added attachments to your automated responses. When customers make requests for certain kinds of information, you can send them images, spreadsheets, documents, or slide presentations, all without any human intervention.

Mail Often, With Ease

Gathering customer information is tedious for some retail businesses but essential for e-commerce companies. Again, Exchange makes this easy. You can specify that when a customer sends email, the email address will be stored, and you can even indicate that certain addresses be stored in one or more distribution lists. This makes it possible to send out information to those lists on specific dates or at regular intervals, and before you know it, you have a newsletter mailing list. And to make this very nifty, you can specify that not every name and address on the list appear on every message, so that each message can seem to be directed only to each individual customer who receives it.

A Few Things Microsoft Outlook Can Do Without Microsoft Exchange

Most of the features described here require both Outlook and Exchange to work properly, but you can use Outlook to create distribution mailing lists without Exchange. Outlook's distribution list feature lets you quickly create and name distribution lists and then as an incoming email arrives, you can assign it to one or more distribution lists.

Using the Contact List feature in Outlook in conjunction with Microsoft Word offers another cool option; you can store names and addresses with Outlook and then do a mail merge in Word to send out printed mailings the old fashioned way, via surface mail. Alternatively, you can first export your list of names and addresses to an Access database, sort and analyze the information as you like, and then export only a certain type of address (such as all international addresses) to Word for your print mailing.

A Low-Cost Solution

You can look into Microsoft bCentral (*www.bcentral.com*) for low-cost solutions. For example, ListBot, a tool provided by bCentral, helps keep email efforts manageable by automatically collecting visitor email addresses and managing existing mailing lists. It allows you to send email

> ### *The New Customer Service Employee*
>
> Email changes the customer service job description. A pleasant voice and unflappability have been the traditional hallmarks of excellence in customer service employees, but in an email setting, these qualities make way for good writing, spelling, and grammar. As you hire and train your customer service staff, ask how they've handled situations in past—not just on the phone but in writing. Ask for writing samples, and look at the samples for both content (what did they say?) and quality (how did their use of language represent the company? Is the message clear and spelled correctly?). You may find that salaries are higher for those with solid communication skills, but those people will be faster and more productive at answering email.
>
> Once you've hired good customer service employees, provide them with written guidelines, but don't overscript; that is, don't prescribe every word and insist that overly specified, "boilerplate" sentences be included in every message. Give them the authority they need to actually solve problems. Above all, listen to your customer service employees—they're often your front-line personal contact with your customers. Despite the contention that every customer is a good customer, some people simply aren't worth the trouble they cause. Your customer service people will tell you when a customer is truly impossible to please. The customer who consistently wastes time with nuisance complaints or who abuses employees with foul language isn't likely to be worth the time and hassle in the long run.

messages to multiple addresses with one click and conveniently stores your messages for re-use later. So even if your operation is very small, you can manage your email and send mail to a targeted list regularly, quickly, and with professional grace.

Whatever the size or complexity of your endeavor, your email customer service program can be a proactive measure for gaining customer loyalty and cross-selling products and services. You can also take the responses to the questions asked most often and build them into a FAQ page that your customers can access via your website. Read on.

Offer a Searchable, Easy-to-Use FAQ

Giving people answers to their questions up front saves time and money. It also makes them happy. Including a FAQ page on your website solves a basic customer service problem. It relieves you (or your staff) of the burden of answering the same questions over and over, and it gives your customers quick, hassle-free answers.

Savvy e-commerce sites use FAQs as their first line of defense in customer service. This just makes sense. Many people prefer not to have to ask someone for help, and most prefer quick answers. If the answer to a customer's question is easy to find and understand, they won't call you or send email, and you'll have one less thing to do today. You might also stop a wondering customer from turning into a wandering customer.

Given that a customer who can find a quick answer via a FAQ won't have to contact you, it's probably obvious that providing a FAQ will save money. But a well-constructed FAQ can also increase sales by providing more information about your products and services. It can't close a sale, and it can't answer every question known to humanity, but a FAQ can be a very important tool for customer service and sales.

A typical FAQ is a simple list of questions with each question followed immediately by an answer (see Vanguard's FAQ in Figure 5.2, on the next page). It can include information such as who you are, where you are, how to contact you, how you process orders, what shipping methods you use, how you handle returns, what your privacy policies are, how you maintain the security of your transaction system, and so on. It might also include specific answers to often-asked questions about your products—for example, how to launder the linen/rayon blend garments you sell, or why your painting company prefers to use premium products despite their extra cost.

Part 2: Create Identity and Attract Customers

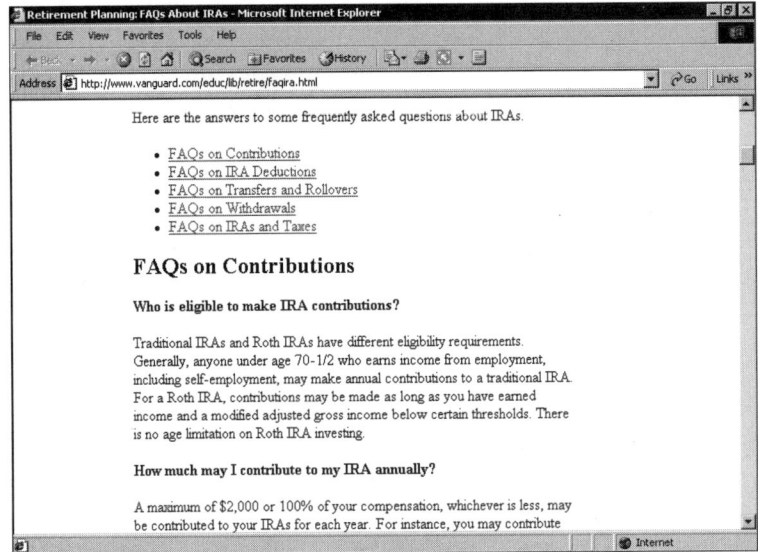

Figure 5.2
This FAQ from Vanguard is their customers' first resource for answers to their questions.

As you build your FAQ, keep in mind the following pointers.

- **Make it easy to find.** Don't bury your customer service FAQ in a section titled "About the Company." Instead, place it in an obvious location, for example, as a link from your home page and from your storefront page. At the very least, provide a distinct customer service page or area with a link to the FAQ. Your FAQ should never be more than three clicks away from your home page.

- **Make it quick to access.** Don't gunk it up with art, animations, and gimmicks. This page is meant to offer fast answers. It should load especially quickly. To make this so, stick to simple text with just enough look and feel to establish your company identity. If you find you have so many questions and answers that the page gets long, break it into several pages and provide an index page that shows only the questions—as links your customers can click on to find answers.

- **Make its organization obvious.** List the questions at the top of the page with links to the actual question-and-answer entry. Group questions according to their subject, with brief headings. Keep similar questions together so they flow naturally—for example, go from buying figs to eating figs to removing fig stains from carpets. Don't group questions according to how often they're asked. Although it might seem that placing the questions customers ask most often at the top of the list will help them find those answers quickly, that method of organization also makes finding answers to other questions harder. If you can't come up with a natural flow, organize alphabetically or according to some other easy-to-see system.

- **Focus on the customer.** Write answers from the user's point of view, not that of the sales rep, the engineer, or the programmer. Start with what customers want to do, and tell them how to do it, rather than starting with how your system works and describing its components and processes.

- **Tailor the FAQs.** Prospective customers want different information from existing customers who might have already had experience with your product or service and seen its flaws. Channel buyers or sales reps might want the same information as customers, but you'll want to use different language and terminology when you're talking to them than you do with end customers. If you need to offer FAQs to more than one audience, place the FAQ list for each audience on its own page and perhaps even in a different area of your site.

- **Provide brief, to-the-point answers.** If the answer to a question stretches to more than a few short sentences, break it down. Create subquestions and answer them separately, below the original question. (You can either indent the subquestions so that they appear to be part of the primary question and answer, or somehow make them distinct from the original.)

- **Be clear, be honest, be complete.** Your FAQ isn't doing its job if, after reading it, customers are still confused or doubtful, and they have to call you (or worse yet, if they leave). If your product has a bug or includes an error, give them a workaround. Product weaknesses don't have to be the first thing a customer sees on your FAQ, but the answers customers need should be there.

- **Keep it fresh.** Maintain your FAQ by adding current information. As customers ask new questions and you or your customer service staff answers them, add the questions and answers to your FAQ (not every question, but those you find to be truly

FAQs). Take a tip from local fire departments who, when the twice-yearly time change occurs, remind the public to change the batteries in their smoke alarms. Tie major overhauls of your FAQ to some twice-yearly event to make sure they happen.

- **Link, link, link.** There is simply no point in rewriting existing text, especially on the Web. Link to other areas of your site that offer the information customers need. Answer the question "How can I contact your company" by linking to the Contact Us page. And if your customers frequently ask questions for which you don't have answers or don't want to answer, consider linking to other sites that do have answers or who are in the business of answering that type of question.

In the end, though, remember that your FAQ is not meant to be documentation. It doesn't have to answer every question anyone might ask, and it doesn't have to tell your customers everything they ever wanted to know about you and you company. It covers only the FAQs. For deeper insights, specific how-to information, and predictions of industry trends, you can direct users to manuals, books, or oracles.

Set Up Your Systems So Service Is Easy

Rule Number One for selling anything (and by extension, for customer care) is never, ever, put a barrier in the way of a sale. In e-commerce, that rule translates into making transactions quick, easy, and painless. To address this point, e-commerce ventures have created systems that take advantage of their technological underpinnings. For example, storing the password and account information customers provide with their first purchase means that, on return visits, the customers don't have to enter them again. They can buy by clicking a single button. Making buying easy includes making the forms customers fill out in the course of a transaction simple to use and so uncluttered that they are a snap to read. It also includes keeping customers informed—for example, by telling them how shipping occurs and letting them track where their purchases are in the fulfillment process. ("It's been shipped. It will be delivered in two days. It will be delivered in one day. It's arrived!") As mentioned, telling people how to make returns is crucial to good service.

To prevent customer service snafus, integrate your e-commerce systems smoothly with your supply chain. Carefully plan and execute your venture so that all systems flow together to avoid mixed-up orders, late deliveries, and damaged goods. If your operation is large enough to have several departments each with a profile of the same individual customers, build yourself a nice central database so that all customer data is stored in one location. This will prevent conflicting or erroneous data from creeping into your systems (for example, three departments storing varying information about the same customer under the names *bkienan*, *brenda kienan*, and *brenda keinan*). It will also prevent your employees from acting on different data and either giving different responses one day and the next, or—gasp!—revealing that your operation is badly organized. Integrating all of your back-end systems, including tracking customers for customer service, shipping, order taking, and marketing, will make your whole operation smoother and allow you to provide far better customer care throughout your business cycle.

When a Problem Occurs, Make Good

A dollar spent on correcting an error today can retain a customer who might spend ten dollars next week. Moreover, that customer will probably tell a friend that at the end of the day, yours is a very good company. The dollar you spend might also forestall the spending of ten more dollars on damage control.

Everyone makes an occasional mistake. A wrong item might be shipped, a piece of a ceramic candelabra might arrive broken, a misunderstanding might result in the wrong type of service being provided. ("Oh! You wanted our one-hour consultation? We thought you wanted our three-hour assessment.") Be prepared to make amends. What exactly those "amends" are will vary from business to business, but you must have policies and procedures in place for correcting errors, responding to the customer's annoyance, and addressing any inconvenience you have caused.

In brick-and-mortar retail, 10 percent of what's sold during the December holidays is returned as soon as the holidays are over. If your e-commerce venture is a shopping site, make sure you are prepared for similar return rates. If you don't have a smooth method for handling those returns and processing customer credits, 10 percent of your customers are going to be very annoyed indeed.

Whenever possible, use existing systems. Companies that sell via traditional print catalogs are famous for good return policies and systems, and that makes all the difference in customer confidence. Include return information with every shipped item on the back of the shipping form, as Lands' End does. On that form, ask why the customer is returning the item.

Provide options for getting the correct size, color, or product, as well as the option to simply get the money back. If you have to require that customers call before they return a purchase, or if you have to keep systems to a minimum and can't offer online management of returns, provide a toll-free phone number and have staff on hand to respond. For damaged products, arrange for pickup and pay for it. Customers who have to pay to return something that was damaged through no fault of theirs will be turned off to buying from you again.

> **Note**
>
> In some cases, taking returns isn't cost effective. For example, what's the point of returning a dead or dying plant or melted chocolate? The cost of having the customer return such items exceeds the cost of simply replacing them. Some online retailers simply accept their customer's word that an item arrived damaged. They then replace the item without asking for the return of the damaged one. Of course, those companies also keep track of returns, so that if a customer starts to report a suspicious number of "broken" items, the matter can be investigated.

Everyone does things a little differently, and there is no "right" way to handle returns. One retailer has a nifty system set up so that customer service staff need only press a button to process a refund, another to process an exchange, or another to arrange for company credit for broken or returned items. Another retailer allows returns of online purchases only to the website's distribution center, not to a local brick-and-mortar store. Yet another retailer allows returns only to a store and not to the website distribution center. You can tailor your policy to suit both your customers' needs and your own, but just be sure you've told your customers what your return policy is and how returns are processed.

> **Tip**
>
> Remember: You can turn a problem into a sale. When an item is returned because it doesn't meet the customer's needs, You or a customer service rep have the opportunity to offer an add-on, upgrade, or newer product in place of one that's old and has finally broken down. Just be sure these options are presented as a service and not as a hard sell.

Ask Your Customer—and Listen!

Part of the beauty of e-commerce is that you can build systems that help you to know and build your site around your customers' patterns and preferences. Of course, the first time you launch a site, you probably won't know your online customers as well as you know your own family, but assuming that you include opportunities for customers to contact you and provide you with feedback, you'll soon find out what gets people to click. Pay careful attention to patterns in your customers' feedback. Not doing so risks building a site that customers will visit only once—and no repeat business means diminished returns.

Track Email Feedback

What are you going to do with all that great feedback you'll receive from customers who will email you about this or that? Don't just toss those messages; file them. You might find that numerous people are asking the same question repeatedly, perhaps in different ways. If that's the case, you can add that question and its answer to your FAQ page. You might find that many people are requesting a new flavor in your gourmet coffee line, or a change in your method of offering accounting services, or a better explanation of how to make payment in your online transaction system. To track comments you can file paper copies of customer emails, or you can sort them into Outlook folders. Whatever your method, don't toss aside that valuable information.

Conduct Surveys

If you collect and analyze customer information as it comes in, you will be able to personalize sales, marketing, and distribution strategies in ways that add value and inspire customer loyalty. Because of the immediacy and convenience of online communication, surveys are often easier to conduct in e-commerce than in the brick-and-mortar world.

It can be tricky, though, to get a random sampling. Surveys are often skewed, for example, because they indicate the preferences of the people who have the time or inclination to fill out the survey form. The value of a survey depends on the quality of both the questions and the sampling, and in many cases you want the most random sampling possible. Site-based surveys of customers and visitors can be as skewed as any others, but they are also a good tool for getting feedback, and they are relatively easy and inexpensive to conduct compared to focus groups or offline surveys.

One clever method for gathering more representative information might be to conduct surveys by intercepting every twentieth or so online visitor and asking them to complete a quick survey form. In one case, two-thirds of the intercepted visitors agreed to participate in the survey just because they were asked. Alternatively, you can offer an incentive for participation, but keep in mind the costs of fulfilling that obligation. (See "Car Talk: A Case Study in Cleverness" for an example of how to get around the real costs of incentives.)

In addition, be aware that participants who seek gimmicks or giveaways will respond, skewing results. You might get some "participants" who are there only to collect the prize and a few who enter repeatedly under different names to get more prizes. These are probably not people who are offering quality feedback.

Asking visitors to "Leave your comments" is a fine technique for making people think you're listening, but be aware that it often draws few responses and sometimes draws responses only from those with axes to grind. This feedback won't be representative of all your users—at least you hope not!

Keep any requests for feedback very short. Less than ten questions or five minutes of a customer's time works best. Include multiple-choice questions in your survey, but also include open-ended questions. (For example: How can we improve our product or service?) And if you're a car dealer asking whether visitors to your site would buy a car online, remember to ask: If you wouldn't buy online, is it because you want a test drive, or are there other reasons?

Tip

You might want to embed a few survey questions in your outgoing customer service email. For example, you can ask customers about the quality of your service or for feedback about your site. For the best response, though, keep your questions especially short or consider providing a URL or link to a survey page on your site.

> ### *Car Talk: A Case Study in Cleverness*
>
> Speaking of cars, a popular radio show, Car Talk, has used an interesting technique for surveying customers on its website (*www.cartalk.com*). On the surface, the feature is presented as an amusing service to users of the site. "Car-O-Scope," says the site, "is here to help you determine if you're driving a car that fits your psychographic profile." The user is promised a personalized email telling her whether the car she is currently driving suits her personality, and suggesting alternatives if it doesn't. To participate, the user begins by filling out an online survey form about how well various statements apply to her, statements such as "If there were only two jobs in the world—accountants and social workers—I'd want to be an accountant." Like any good survey, this one includes questions about how much money the user makes and what car she currently drives, but rather than ask away, it offers such an enticing incentive that the user might not even realize she is actually being surveyed. The website managers get a great deal of demographic and "psychographic" information about the site's audience (its "customers"), which allows them to tailor their site's offerings. It also allows them to provide a remarkable amount of information about the audience to companies interested in purchasing ad space. And, as a special bonus, they get an enormously long list of email addresses that might be of use (depending on how it fits in with their privacy policy) in other ways.

Try to get feedback from repeat customers; their viewpoint will be very different from that of first-timers. Repeat customers have had experience with you and they know your warts. Analyze the data you receive from repeat customers and first-timers separately. And get viewers to look at the site before responding—you want feedback based on an actual impression of the site, not just on someone's general beliefs or preconceived notions.

And finally, remember that your competitors can respond to your survey, and they might well do so. This may sound like a sitcom episode, but an unscrupulous competitor can easily seed your survey with multiple responses, throwing you off track about what your customers want or need. To prevent distortion such as this, weed out responses that come from competitors' domains and any multiple responses from a single address or computer.

Admittedly, site-based surveys of customers and site visitors can be as skewed as any others, but they are also a good tool for getting feedback, and they are relatively easy and inexpensive to conduct compared to focus groups or offline surveys.

Keep Things in Perspective

In the end, many customers will tell you many things. One might want your site to be blue; another might prefer green. You simply cannot be all things to all people, and part of being in business is determining which of the many paths you could take is your best bet. Providing excellent customer care involves listening and responding to your customers, but it also involves setting clear guidelines—creating policies and procedures that will work for most of your customers. You can then bend your policies for special cases and you can build triage systems to handle any errors that crop up. As mentioned at the beginning of this chapter, whatever your site's business purpose, service should be its goal. To be successful, you must serve as many of your target customers as well as you can.

Chapter 6

Building Traffic and Community

There's been a lot of talk about *community* in online circles. It's a terrifically compelling concept. However, community is also a buzzword that is frequently tossed around in conversations, meetings, and even business plans without much thought given to what community is and how it will be created.

Community, when it thrives, is a powerful force for building traffic and retaining the loyalty of a target audience. CNET's Builder.com site (*www.builder.com*) reports that while the Web itself is growing at 50 percent per year, online communities are expanding at 20 percent per month. That potential is very attractive to the managers of e-commerce ventures.

The very history of the Internet is one of community. Long before web browsers debuted and the first e-commerce sites opened shop, bulletin board services (BBSs)—networked communities with shared interests—pulled together groups of people with like interests who talked online in text-based messaging systems. Usenet newsgroups (another type of online discussion system) were also very popular on the Internet before the advent of the web browser.

Part 2: Create Identity and Attract Customers

> **Note**
>
> You know, of course, that the Internet is actually more than 25 years old. Its popularity with the general public boomed when the first web browser made it possible to see pictures and nicely laid out type rather than just plain text in documents that were difficult to navigate.

As online tools became more sophisticated, audiences came together and new online alliances formed in new venues. Communities formed in email discussion groups, in discussions on web pages, in chat areas, and so on.

It's not too surprising that community is of such interest to users. However, many website managers, business owners, and corporate executives talk of building community on their sites without a clear understanding of what the word means. A community is a group of people who interact online. But community is more than just clusters of people. Communities don't form just because you put out chips and salsa and throw open your door. They need a reason for being that draws an audience. For example, a community can begin to form around a common interest. For the community to thrive, frequent interaction between community members must also occur, and they must begin to identify with the community. Let's look at the issues surrounding building online communities more closely.

Building Focused Community

Community requires interaction among a group of people who share a common interest or purpose. The first and perhaps most important key to building community is to provide an environment or forum that encourages a reciprocal exchange of information. Users who get involved in online communities might want to meet people, exchange information on a given topic, argue, or even seek out romance. In general, they want electronic interaction with other people with whom they share *affinity*. In this context, affinity can be thought of as a bond or alliance forged of common interest and often a drive toward achieving some common purpose.

As examples, let's consider two very powerful online communities: a community of open-source software developers, and a global community of expectant mothers all due to deliver babies in the same month. In both

Chapter 6: Building Traffic and Community

cases, the groups formed around a common interest, and members have plenty to talk about—the developer community shares information about the software it's creating and passes code back and forth, while the expectant mothers share insights about the symptoms, hopes, and fears they are experiencing on the same timeline. In both cases, too, individual members experience a powerful identification with their group. The developer group sees itself as building something valuable and important; each member is proud to be a contributor to the effort. The expectant mothers become so attached to each other that they create a virtual baby shower, set up regional and national in-person meetings, help each other through personal crises, and sustain their community well into the toddler years.

Commonality of interest and frequent interaction, then, are clearly crucial for bonding to occur. An individual can be an ex-Marine, but if he hasn't had contact with other ex-Marines lately he might not feel strongly about the community of ex-Marines. True identification with the group must also occur for a community to form. A woman isn't a feminist unless she says so, for example. Other people might think she walks and talks like a feminist, but if she doesn't identify with the group, she isn't part of its community.

To create an online community, you must start by targeting specific groups based on their affinities. Affinities can include interests; gender, age, or other demographics; shared experiences in the past, present, or future; or social groups that people identify with or join. Commercial communities are as viable as noncommercial communities. Consider the possibilities of a community of physicians sharing information about their specialties (with behind-the-scenes talk about unusual patients and cases) or of a community based on a professional association; the Association of Internet Professionals (*www.association.org*) is such a community. Women who work on websites have formed a strong national community in the form of Webgrrls at *www.webgrrls.com* and strong regional communities such as San Francisco Women on the Web (SFWoW) at *www.sfwow.org*. They share technical and career development information, but also "off topic" tips for finding housing, painless dentists, and alluring vacation spots.

Auction sites such as ChemConnect (*www.chemconnect.com*) and eBay (*www.ebay.com*) represent another type of community—a community of buyers and sellers. In fact, eBay turned the entire notion of community on its ear when it opened shop with the model of bringing together buyers

Part 2: Create Identity and Attract Customers

and sellers of all sorts of goods in a commercial community where they could transact sales of individual items. In yet another take on community, VerticalNet (*www.vertical.net*) creates commercial communities that target specific, narrow markets (*vertical markets*), such as bakeries, environmental engineers, nurses, laboratory science, solid waste, tool shops, and so on (see Figure 6.1).

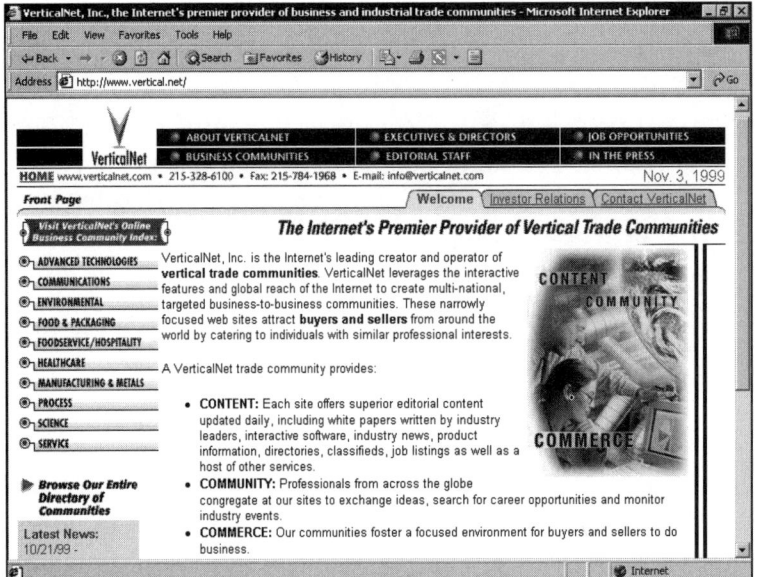

Figure 6.1
VerticalNet targets specific markets and creates commercial communities for those markets.

Choose a Technology

Much of this chapter addresses how to build, leverage, and respect a community. To kick off the discussion on choosing a community for you, let's start by describing the gathering places where communities grow—the types of technologies on which they exist. Large sites like eBay, ChemConnect, and VerticalNet use technologies that might not be within the range of smaller sites, but many options exist for creating community on sites of all sizes.

Chapter 6: Building Traffic and Community

Email Newsletters: From One to Many

Email newsletters are pretty much what they sound like—outgoing messages. The industry term "one-to-many" describes them well; they are broadcast from one computer to many recipients. Newsletters can contain news or announcements, but they don't have to. Infobeat, TipWorld, and other companies have built entire businesses around sending subscribers brief (usually one-paragraph) tips on a variety of topics.

The defining factor for an email newsletter is that communication is one-way at regular, stated intervals, from sender to recipients. No discussion takes place among the recipients. In the most sophisticated cases, "mailing list" software is used to send the newsletters; the To: line of the email message usually includes the email address of only one recipient because the mailing list software that sends the message takes care of obscuring the addresses of other recipients who've subscribed to the list.

How do you, the sender, get addresses for the mailing list? Usually, you offer the opportunity to get something of value and interest to potential subscribers. You can place a small sign-up box like the one shown here on this web page:

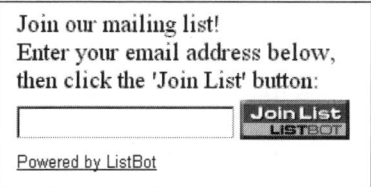

In addition, provide details about the benefits of signing up, a link for getting help, and instructions for unsubscribing.

To persuade people to sign up for your mailing list, you have to offer something of value *to them*. Getting your product information into the inboxes of a group of subscribers might be very valuable *to you*, but is it really attractive to them, or will the information just seem like more "junk email"? Here's the trick: A newsletter that blares a hard pitch on gourmet cooking equipment is less compelling than a rhapsodizing newsletter that offers a recipe, a tip about using a specific piece of equipment, and a special on, say, mandoline slicers.

It's important to allow people to sign up for your newsletter (*to opt in*), rather than signing up everyone who makes a purchase from your site and expecting those who don't want your wonderful newsletter to cancel (or *opt out of*) it. Later in this chapter you'll learn more about these issues;

for the moment, keep in mind that your customers will appreciate and respond better to opting in, as well as to the publication of your privacy policy (the promise you make to them about how private information such as their email addresses will be used).

> **Tip**
>
> You can learn more about privacy policies and even write your own using online resources; see TRUSTe, a non-profit organization that addresses such matters, at *www.etrust.com*. Or look into the Privacy Wizard on Microsoft bCentral at *www.bcentral.com*.

Email Discussion Groups: From Many to Many

In email discussion groups, one person (or a company) sets up a mailing list of subscribers (or "members"), but any member can send a message that will be received by all other members. Any member can then respond with comments or questions, and that response will also go to all other members. Voilà! It's a discussion.

> **Note**
>
> Some of the terminology here may be a little confusing. People use the term "mailing list" to describe a list of addresses to which they send out email newsletters (described in the preceding section). However, the same term can also mean an online discussion group that takes place in the form of email. In both cases a list of "subscribers" has signed up to receive the email. To clarify the differences between email newsletters and email discussion groups, this chapter uses mailing list to refer only to a list of email addresses.

The discussions that take place are often dynamic, even if they don't take place in real time. Messages appear in a member's inbox and can be read and responded to at the member's convenience. The discussions themselves can be *moderated*, meaning that someone sees to it that the "conversation" sticks to the stated topic, that administrative issues are handled, and even that disputes are resolved. Or they can be *unmoderated*, meaning that members regulate themselves. (To find out more about the implications of moderating or not moderating a discussion group, see "To Moderate or Not to Moderate" later in this chapter.)

Usually, subscribers join an email discussion group by signing up (opting in) just as they sign up for a newsletter. Again, enabling people to opt in is a much more effective strategy than requiring them to opt out. Presuming that people will want to join your email discussion group is a fatal faux pas. As with a newsletter, you must offer value. "Join my discussion group" isn't very compelling. To make a discussion group work, you must provide a forum in which a specific niche of people can discuss a powerful, shared interest (see the earlier section "Building Focused Community"). The discussion topic must be focused, and ideally it should remain focused. Discussion groups often get sidetracked into off-topic sub discussions; it is up to the group (or its moderator) whether to allow these tangents.

As the "host" of a discussion group, you should be sure to provide members with a list of ground rules, as well as a clearly stated privacy policy. (Sharing the email addresses of the people who subscribe to your discussion group is frowned upon and few people will subscribe if they think that's what you intend to do.)

A compelling email discussion group can work very well as a way to attract traffic to a low-volume site. In fact, more than one business that started with a simple email discussion group has grown into a powerhouse in its industry. But building traffic is only one of the advantages of hosting a community. You can also use the material obtained from the group in a variety of ways, such as in the development of site content. For information about transforming email discussions into site content, see the section "Leveraging Archived Email as Valuable Content" later in this chapter.

Message Boards: Threaded and Serial Discussions

Message boards differ from email discussion groups in that the discussion takes place not in email messages but in an electronic forum contained within a web page. Users typically don't have to subscribe to join a discussion; they can simply post messages and respond to the messages of others. Unlike chat sessions, these discussions do not take place in real time; users read, post, and respond at their convenience.

Typical formats include *threaded* discussions (where messages are grouped according to subject and users can click a subject to read all the messages pertaining to that topic) and *serial* discussions (where all of the messages appear in a single, unindexed list). Threaded discussions generally work best when users want to follow a "conversation" about a particular topic—for example, when users are interested in discussions about particular aspects of a topic or are likely to want to search the talk for answers to specific questions. Serial discussions have more appeal in cases where the talk is less focused and is perhaps more social.

Getting a threaded or serial discussion off the ground requires a site that already has a lot of traffic. This type of community building is more effective on a site that has many users with an interest in the discussion topics already passing through, than on a site that is still trying to attract users to in order to join the discussion. If you're thinking of offering threaded or serial discussions, be sure you have the audience, traffic, and compelling topics you'll need to launch and sustain them. According to Forrester Research, Inc., you need to have 2500 daily visitors to your site to support a *message board* (a threaded or serial discussion area). Note that if you set up a message board and no one shows up, the lack of traffic will be clearly visible to anyone who stops by. And a deserted forum holds little appeal for the people who happen upon it.

Chat Areas: Real-Time Interaction Among Users

In a chat session, users join an electronic discussion that takes place in the form of typed communications. Participants can see and respond to the discussion in real time, by typing comments and responses that appear on the participants' screens as they are typed. In addition, many users can chat simultaneously.

Chat can be effective in the right circumstances, but as in threaded and serial discussions, if no one shows up, the silence is deafening. Chat areas work well when a session has a *big draw*—someone or something that attracts participants. A celebrity name is a big draw ("Chat about ice skating with Brian Boitano!"). If you don't have a celebrity name to tout, you must market your chat sessions aggressively to a motivated niche audience (for example, tax tips for seniors) or find an underrepresented, compelling topic (bird watching, perhaps) and target the audience that cares deeply about that topic.

Another option for building community via a successful chat area is to place the area on a site or part of a site where traffic is already extremely heavy. Forrester Research says that supporting a chat area requires 55,000 individual, daily visitors to the website that's sponsoring the chat. (That's not hits; it's visitors.)

> **Caution**
>
> Chats can degenerate quickly into flame wars or other unsavory dialogues if they aren't moderated. For commercial ventures, it's probably best to moderate to avoid both getting too far off topic and potential liability.

Chat is an alluring technology but implementing it successfully can be time consuming and is probably not cost effective for smaller sites with less traffic. However, chat can be effective for distance learning sites, for providing real-time tech support, and for the press conferences of famous-name people. Chat sessions are also well known gathering places for electronic social communities. Let's face it: chat is fun.

Guest Books: Simple Sign-In for Others to See

Yet another type of community forms when users enter informational blurbs into an electronic guest book. Guest books are simple to set up and are often offered as an option by ISPs and other companies that provide tools for easy web-page set up. Guest books provide minimal interactivity for users and little opportunity for leveraging community to build traffic. Although they often appear on personal pages and amateur sites, they are rarely employed in professional websites, so they are not discussed further in this chapter.

Identify Communities of Shared Interests

Simply placing a "Community" button on your site does not result in the formation of a community. For a community to start to form, you must give users a reason to join it. As described earlier in this chapter (see "Building Focused Community"), you must offer users value, as well as provide a service in the form of a place to gather.

Although community can form around such affinities as gender, age, and shared experiences, shared interests are generally the most powerful affinity. Why would *you* feel compelled to join your immediate neighbors in an electronic forum? You probably would only find online discussions with your neighbors compelling if you shared a purpose, intent, or interest with them. For example, a neighborhood in Oakland, California used email newsletters and online discussion to coalesce a Y2K preparedness effort. Some members of the community who were unconcerned about potential Y2K problems nevertheless saw the opportunity to participate in general emergency preparedness under the umbrella of Y2K. The effort was a success; a small neighborhood initiative turned into a larger citywide drive toward emergency preparedness, with Y2K as the catalyst. This effort demonstrates that shared interests are as powerful—or more powerful—than geography. Its success was the result of a shared intent among a geographic community, not the opportunity to have "an online block party."

To build a successful community, find a niche and fill it. Go deep, not broad. Creating a broad community takes deep pockets—the kind of budget most e-commerce ventures don't have. How will you find the right niche? Think about your audience and its communities of shared interests. From among those potential communities, choose those that really, really care. Pregnant women with the same due date really care; open source software developers really care; birdwatchers really care; sales reps and buyers might really care. The question to ask is, "In my industry, who really cares?"

Caution

If someone else has beaten you to the punch by creating a popular community for the niche you would usually go for, forget about it. They got there first, and unless the current community is deeply flawed in some way that you can improve on, you're better off trying another avenue. (Remember, to win in e-commerce, you have to be first, be the best, or be different. But being first gives you the real jump. See Chapter 1.)

What Are Your Community Goals?

As in every e-commerce venture, defining your goals is crucial to building a successful community. You might want to create an entire site around a particular community, or you might want to leverage community discussions as free content for your site by archiving it into a searchable database. (See "Leveraging Archived Email into Valuable Content" later in this chapter.) You might have a more altruistic purpose. Among the possibilities you consider in defining your goals, think about whether any of the following are your true motives:

- Building a subscription base so that you can sell advertising that will appear within the community's discussion
- Building traffic to your website so that you can sell advertising, content, or your services or products

Chapter 6: Building Traffic and Community

- Building a commercial community that supports or sells your product or service
- Building a *destination website*, which is one that users seek out because of its appeal to a particular community
- Building an audience for your views, opinions, or beliefs
- Building a forum for promoting yourself as a consultant or personality

Note

Remember that not all groups can be reached electronically. Luddites (people who oppose or fear technology), the Amish community, and healthcare workers in underdeveloped countries would probably be better reached by other means.

For more information about setting goals for your e-commerce venture, see Chapter 1. For more on defining your audience and tailoring your offerings to that target audience, see Chapter 2.

Invite a Community to Gather

Once you have set your goals and defined your audience and your community offerings, it's time to invite people to join your community. The invitation you present to your potential community might be a simple button on your home page that offers the opportunity to join. Right there, beside that button, you should provide users with a quick, clear sense of the benefits of membership. In general, it's best to stick to a few words that specify the value. ("Free! Tips! Daily! Straight to your inbox!" But don't use all those exclamation marks; they lose their punch when they're bunched up.) Take another look at Figure 6.1 and notice that, although quite a lot of text appears on the page, VerticalNet emphasizes phrases and words such as **vertical trade communities**, **buyers and sellers**, **content**, **community**, and **commerce** by making them bold. One glance at that page, and you know what VerticalNet is offering.

Alternatively, you might want to notify potential participants via email. But remember: if you have a list of addresses you've gleaned from another source, use that list to announce your new community and invite participation if, and only if, those users have explicitly indicated their willingness to receive unsolicited email. Even if the message is an invitation, unsolicited commercial email is unpopular at best, and sending it out can do more harm than good.

Welcome the Community

Greet people as they join your community. Tell them how the community works, what its guidelines are, and how you deal with privacy issues. (Do you or don't you offer your mailing list to others for their use? Can users opt out? How?) Let people know how problem users will be handled; that may not seem very welcoming, but it can prevent some problems and will signal to everyone that your community is a safe place.

A workable discussion group takes between 3 and 200 users. A good 85 or 90 percent of the users in any given discussion group will be *lurkers* (they'll read but not write); perhaps 10 percent will actively participate from time to time, and a smaller percentage will form the core of the community. You might think your goal is to bring out the wallflowers and persuade the 85 or 90 percent to participate more, but it isn't. Focus instead on the perhaps 2 percent who are core participants. They generate the richest content, they are committed, and they provide something for the lurkers to read. They also attract additional lurkers through the liveliness and interest of their interaction. You might consider offering these core people some reward—perhaps a title and responsibility for moderating a group, or a community-within-the-community for moderators, or even special discounts on your products.

As discussions take place and digress into new topics, subgroups of the original community will spawn. Spin them off to create additional communities if needed and if multiple communities fit your business goals. Communities tend to fail when they get too big and lose their focus or sense of purpose; active participants get bored or annoyed, spam starts to fly, and things can get ugly.

Finally, provide a method for users to send you feedback, and listen to it. Remember: these people are the community you sought and built so carefully. Although you might not react to every whim of every individual participant, you will surely want to keep the group as a whole happy and thriving. Keep them busy, let them interact, give them a way to offer feedback, and they'll reward you with rich content and a lively community.

Chapter 6: Building Traffic and Community

Provide the Community with Security

As you sort through your options for setting up community, make it a high priority to choose a stable, reliable technology or hosting service. Users prefer stable communities; they also feel more confident about telling like-minded associates where the community is if it isn't a moving target. What's more, communities don't just up and move with ease. So before you make your final selection of technology or hosting options, be sure the service or software you're planning to use can handle the traffic load you anticipate and offers the features your users will expect.

Of course every vendor claims to have the most reliable, stable, full-featured product available. So how can you find out who's who among the more stable and reliable community technology providers? Ask around. Ask users of community software; ask community managers and moderators, too. You might have to join a community or two to do this research, but checking references now can save you valuable time in the long run.

Caution

Community software, like all software, sometimes crashes. Users don't enjoy the thought that their carefully crafted messages could vanish into the ether, and that's exactly what can happen if your community software goes down and you don't have a good backup system. Just as you would with any other important business software, make sure your community software is capable of making backups, and then back up regularly.

Offer Value to the Community

Specifically, what does your target community value? This is a strategic question you'll have to answer in order to build compelling community. For example, pictures of the heaters your company sells are compelling only to a target community of heating system sales reps (who, even then, probably look only when they have to, to make a sale). Tips for troubleshooting heaters or for seasonally maintaining heating systems are more likely to be compelling to heating contractors and the general public—especially as winter months approach.

Some other uses of discussion groups and chat can offer value; for example, they might be good venues for delivering training, news, or analyses of relevant issues. Communities can be formed around information libraries, searchable directories, virtual trade shows, or job fairs. Events calendars and event registration can punch up the offerings. Some communities might also be interested in editorial content such as career or commerce features, but that content can be expensive to create and keep fresh; so before you go for it, plan your budget carefully. Although classifieds and advertising might seem more like revenue options than community-oriented features, to a community of job seekers they can be very compelling. Similarly, for a community of association or trade organization members, special benefits, member sign up, and the advantages of joining the association can be rich content.

As always, start your search for content of value by carefully considering what your specific audience wants, and continue your strategizing by thinking "outside the box" of what's been done and overdone. Beyond being true to your audience, freshness is your main goal.

Sending Email Newsletters

Sending out email newsletters with compelling content that reminds readers at regular intervals to visit your site can be a powerful method for building traffic. A Forrester study of 8,600 Internet-enabled households showed that 38% found websites through email. (The only more common method for finding sites, through search engines, was cited by 57% of respondents.) However, no one likes spam, so you must offer value. You're also better off allowing people to opt in to your newsletter. And you should provide brief instructions for unsubscribing in every issue.

Email newsletters fall into the following two basic types:

- **Announcement newsletters.** This is the more traditional type. They generally include product or service information or some other sort of promotional material. They can also include a teaser that entices users to click to a site. Announcement emails are far more effective, however, if they are written so that they don't appear to be blatantly self-serving. Offer subscribers something of value in each newsletter—specials, news, tips, or some other content that is related to the product or service. Otherwise, your carefully crafted newsletter will go into the recycling bin as quickly as last week's grocery store flyer.

- **Value-added or content-driven newsletters.** These primarily provide users with free information, tips, news, or some other valuable content. They often include brief ads as their revenue producer, but they can also include teasers that drive traffic to the newsletter producer's website. As an example, a newsletter producer with 70,000 unique users offers top news stories, technical advice, how-to news, and fun feature articles. Half of the newsletter traffic clicks through to the associated website within 16 hours of newsletter delivery.

Tip

For best response, send out your newsletters on Monday or Tuesday, early in the day. Make sure the subject lines are intriguing, and that they indicate the benefit of the content—how and why this material will be of use. Keep the subject lines short and use appropriate tone. Verbs work well for how-to material, for example, whereas adjectives spice up food and travel information. If you send out several newsletters, differentiate them by topic or some other system.

Track Down Content

Stumped about where to find valuable content for your newsletters? You can use free press release services, such as PR Newswire (*www.prnewswire.com*), PR Web (*www.prweb.com*), Web Wire (*www.webwire.com*), Internet News Bureau (*www.internetnewsbureau.com*), Internet Wire (*www.internetwire.com*), and so on. Just visit these sites or subscribe to their services, and sift out newsworthy items of interest to your audience. Or you can sign up for push news sources or other free email tip newsletters, not to nab their material but to get inspiration from the topics they cover. A third alternative is to ask your audience to send in ideas and even stories and tips. People love the validation and thrill of seeing their own writing published; why not give them the chance to send you material that you might use?

Note

Of course, you should attribute any material you use to its creator. Doing so will inspire yet another bit of loyalty in your audience. What's more, writers whose work you publish in your email newsletter might well be inclined to send the newsletter around to friends and family to show off the accomplishment, widening your circulation base.

Format for Effect

Email newsletters can have the usual text-based email look (see Figure 6.2) or they can have an HTML-formatted look (see Figure 6.3). The HTML-formatted look is available for viewing only by recipients whose email programs are HTML-enabled. It's unlikely (though possible) that your entire audience is able to view HTML-formatted mail, so generally speaking, you'll either want to stick to text-based email or at least offer people the option of receiving your newsletter in that format.

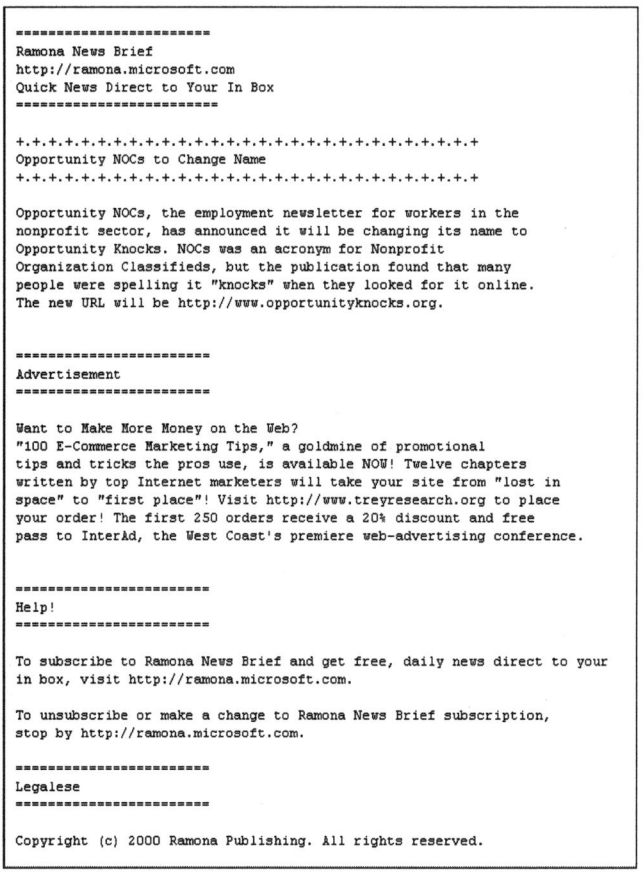

Figure 6.2
Text-based email can include some nifty formatting.

Figure 6.3
HTML-formatted email looks good but isn't available to everyone.

You can do various kinds of formatting in text-based email. Figure 6.2 shows a variety of vertical lines made with equal signs (= = =), plus signs and periods (+.+.+.+), and simple hyphens (- - -). Be careful not to junk up the message—readability is most important. But you can make the message more readable with judicious use of vertical lines. Note that, to avoid looking funny in some email programs, the lines should be no more than 65 characters long.

To Opt In or to Opt Out?

It certainly can be tempting to think that every customer who makes a purchase or an inquiry on your e-commerce website is "obviously interested" in your product and will welcome a newsletter. But this just isn't so. Take it from the pros who've researched this point: You'll get far better response from newsletter recipients who opt in than from those who are automatically included in your mailing list and have to opt out if they prefer not to be bothered. Click-through rates actually double or even triple when people opt in to newsletters.

To encourage people to subscribe and to willingly supply their email addresses, offer them something of value in exchange for their interest, as mentioned earlier in this chapter. You then have real permission to follow up with that person, and you have a far better opportunity to turn that person's interest into loyalty. No stigma of spam will be associated with your opt-in email newsletter, so you can send it out with a clear conscience and heightened optimism.

Provide Options for Unsubscribing

It's best to make it relatively easy for subscribers to your newsletter to unsubscribe. Clearly, you don't want to make that option the most prominent item in your newsletter, but do make it possible to find the information. Giving people an easy way to opt out increases credibility; it also decreases management overhead. Even those who remain subscribers will appreciate you making the unsubscribing process easy for them; they'll appreciate knowing that if and when they want to unsubscribe, they can.

Typically, you might place management information at the bottom of your newsletter, describing how to unsubscribe, how to subscribe, and even how to change the subscription (for example, if the subscriber changes email addresses). Or you might provide a link to a help page on your site (for example, to a FAQ like those described in Chapter 5), where subscribers will find all the help they need.

Address Privacy Issues

In your wildest dreams, you will wind up with a long list of interested, motivated, targeted subscribers to your newsletter. Sooner or later it will occur to you that the list is a gold mine. You will probably consider either trading lists with a non-competitor, or selling the list. Trading your list can get you more addresses, and selling your list can be a revenue producer, but either option can also irritate customers and drive them away, especially if your action comes as a surprise.

Perhaps in the future, Internet users will look on unsolicited commercial email the same way as printed junk mail—as a mild nuisance that comes with having a post box. At this time, however, Internet users are highly incensed by spam. In fact, sending out spam will probably alienate more people than it will ever persuade to take an interest in your product, service, or site.

Tools to Use

Microsoft offers several tools you can use to create and send email newsletters. For example, you might compose a newsletter in Microsoft Word without any fancy formatting, cut and paste a simple version into your email software, and then send out the text-based email newsletter to the subscribers who can read that format. Then you might format the newsletter as an HTML document and send that version to the subscribers who can read that format.

Create Simple Mailing Lists with Outlook and Exchange

The combination of Microsoft Exchange as mail-server software and Microsoft Outlook as email software can allow you to set up outgoing email newsletters to be delivered at regular intervals. You'll have to check with your ISP (or, if you have an in-house network, your network administrator) to make sure you have Exchange working in conjunction with Outlook, and if you do, you can take advantage of features that automatically monitor, organize, and process email. For example, you can use a series of simple check box "rules and actions" to specify when mail should go out; you can even create newsletters that will be delivered with personalized greetings. You can also attach value-added documents such as spreadsheets, images, or slide presentations to your newsletters, expanding your options for providing subscribers with rich content.

> **Tip**
>
> You can send email newsletters using Outlook simply by placing your own address in the To line and the list of all other addresses in the Bcc ("blind" courtesy copy) line. Recipients will see only their own addresses when they receive your newsletter, but they won't see those of the other recipients—just as if you had used special mailing list software to create the list.

With Exchange, you can also store email addresses in one or more distribution lists, making it possible to send out information to those lists at regular intervals. You can even specify that recipients should see only their own names and addresses and not those of everyone on the list, making the presentation clean and professional.

Even without Exchange, you can use Outlook to create distribution mailing lists. As incoming email arrives (say, from someone requesting a subscription to your newsletter), you can assign the sender's address to one or more distribution lists.

Manage Mailing Lists with ListBot

For a very powerful way of managing email mailing lists and newsletters (as well as email discussion groups), you might consider using ListBot, which is available through bCentral. ListBot comes in two versions: standard ListBot, which is free, and ListBot Gold, which you can use for a reasonable fee with the amount you pay depending on the number of outgoing messages per month.

The standard ListBot is a fairly full-featured product, it offers an easy web-page interface, archiving of past messages, gathering of demographic information, and so on, but attaches third-party advertising to messages. ListBot Gold collects email addresses automatically, sends email to the collected addresses with one click, provides an easy mailing list management system, stores outgoing messages (your newsletters, for example), lets you import existing mailing lists, and even collects demographic information from your subscribers for you. It also does away with the third-party ads. Both ListBot and ListBot Gold are very credible products that you can use to manage mailing lists and send newsletters.

Offering Discussion Groups

Discussion groups in general can take the specific form of email discussion groups, message boards or forums, or chat sessions. For details about the distinctions, see the section titled "Choose a Technology" earlier in this chapter.

One e-commerce website that offers discussion groups reports that more than 20 percent of its traffic is on the pages associated with the groups. The site offers between four and eight new discussion topics per week, rotating out those that aren't on fire. Each discussion is hosted by a staff member or "contributing editor"—actually someone chosen from among discussion participants for his or her especially lively and knowledgeable postings. Hosts are paid a minimal fee if they have true expertise and they sign a contract for a specified period of time. No registration is required of participants as they join in; they don't provide any demographic data. The discussion groups are heavily promoted on the site's home page with specific teasers that describe the current discussion topics.

In the course of setting up your discussion group, you must consider some of the same issues you'd consider in setting up a newsletter. For example, your privacy policy is going to be of concern to many of your discussion group's users, and you should provide easy instructions for getting in and out of the discussion, as well as links to a clear, well organized FAQ that specifically answers technical support and customer service questions.

Gathering demographic data from participants as they join the discussion is alluring to many e-commerce managers. That demographic data can be gathered by requiring participants to fill out what amounts to a survey on their way into the discussion, and it offers both a valuable tool for understanding your audience and valuable demographic data you can offer to potential advertisers interested in buying ad space in your discussion or on your site. The downside, though, is that you make participants jump through a hoop before joining the discussion. This isn't always wise, and it can drive traffic away from your group. Generally only the most compelling discussions will inspire users to answer questions before they join in the talk. But because demographic data is so appealing to potential advertisers, you'll have to decide which is more valuable—the extra traffic or the extra data.

To Moderate or Not to Moderate?

The advantages of having a moderator in a discussion group are that the moderator can keep the discussion on topic, monitor the discussion to avoid potential liability issues (slander, for example, as described in Chapter 3), and generally troubleshoot the discussion as well as the participants' experience. The disadvantage is that someone has to spend time moderating.

In some cases, having a moderator is necessary. For example, you wouldn't want an unmoderated discussion group for minors, because there is simply too much room for trouble to occur and too much likelihood that liability issues will arise if trouble does occur. On the other hand, some unmoderated discussion groups for adults have managed to stay generally on topic and avoid devastating conflict among the group members for years.

Discussion groups have distinct cultures. So much so, that newbies to discussion groups are often advised to lurk for a while to get to know the group before joining in the discussion. Many discussion groups develop their own shorthand for frequently used phrases. (The group of expectant mothers described earlier in this chapter refers often to their DHs, or their *darling husbands*.) The culture of a discussion group can shift like the weather; in fact, small or even large shifts occur with each posting. Discussions taking place in these groups are, after all, occurring within a community, which by definition is a group of people with relationships to each other. As any psychologist or human resources manager will tell you, group dynamics are deep, complex, and ever-changing, and although people generally prefer to get along, there is almost always one rabble rouser and a loose cannon or two in every crowd.

Moderators should be polite and appropriate; they also should have good written communication skills and knowledge of the topic of discussion. Handling difficult community members can be the most challenging aspect of moderating a discussion; remember that although familiarity can breed comfort and ease at first, later the fabled contempt is likely to erupt between at least some community members. A loose cannon might go off, a rabble-rouser might see flames and fan them, and someone else might misunderstand what is happening and jump to the undeserved defense of the loose cannon. The moderator's job in the midst of all this turmoil is to remain calm and smooth things out.

A moderator might have the option of subscribing or unsubscribing members manually as needed and will usually be responsible for troubleshooting subscription problems. The moderator might also be responsible for approving postings according to the discussion group's guidelines, which preferably will be written and posted as part of the FAQ. A moderator can (figuratively) slap the hands of those who post inappropriately, send out periodic reminders or notices, do outreach for the group, and even facilitate discussions by bringing up relevant or slightly provocative points. In groups of less technical people, there are always some who don't know how to use their own email software; the moderator might wind up troubleshooting even at that level. Depending on the breadth of responsibility, the culture of the discussion group, and phases of the moon, moderating can take very little time or as much as two or three hours a day.

Tip

One moderator reports success in handling flame wars by creating a board that includes a balance of types of people to dilute the effect of interest blocs. The board has a prewritten reprimand for unruly members, which avoids the likelihood that a reprimandee will take the notice personally.

Options for Hosting

When it comes to actually building your discussion group, you have the usual options. You can outsource or do it yourself, and you can select among BMW, Chevy, and Hyundai tiers.

Outsourcing offers the advantages of ease and expertise. If you outsource, you'll sign a contract with a hosting service that (presumably) has experience and knowledge you may not have. You'll have to sort out your business relationship with the hosting service, and you'll have to manage the service, as well as prepare a strategy for how to end your business relationship with the service when the time comes. But you won't have to guess what your budget will have to be, you won't have to learn the necessary software and technology, and above all, you won't have to struggle with the community-building learning curve.

Hosting service options range from those that are free but offer limited functionality and no expert staff, to those that cost in excess of $1,000 per month and come with friendly, experienced community development people to assist you in your endeavor. Some charge setup fees as well as monthly service fees. Features vary; in general, as you assess your options, you'll also want to look into how friendly the interface is.

> **Note**
>
> The "free" services almost always tack their own third-party ads onto your discussion group's messages; that's how they make revenue.

One excellent option for "outsourcing" email discussion group hosting is to sign up with ListBot (available through bCentral and described more fully earlier in this chapter). ListBot comes in a lower-end, free version, that allows you to set up moderated or unmoderated discussion groups and a higher-end version that lets you create your own demographic questions, as well as import your own lists.

> **Note**
>
> If you aren't in a position to create community but have some other offering that might be of value to a successful community developer, consider partnering. Strategic partnerships allow both companies to co-brand offerings so that they can each concentrate on their core business while broadening their online offerings.

Part 2: Create Identity and Attract Customers

If you prefer to run the whole shebang yourself, you can expect to have total control over the look and feel of your discussion group's interface, and you can avoid managing an outside vendor. But you'll be swapping those advantages for the complexities of staffing, writing workable usage and privacy policies, and keeping the software up and running. Unless your operation is fairly large or you have technical staff with time on their hands, a hosting service might be a better option.

Leveraging Archived Email as Valuable Content

Let's say you run a lively, focused discussion group and have a core group of subscribers posting quality comments regularly. Your discussion group software is storing all that email, and pretty soon you have gigabytes of it metaphorically lying around collecting dust. Isn't it a shame to throw away all that valuable content? (All that *free* valuable content?) Why not archive it, make it searchable, and leverage it as yet another reason for users to come to your site?

This type of leveraging can be accomplished in a number of ways ranging from the do-it-yourself to more sophisticated options. Using Microsoft FrontPage, you can add a full-text search option to a site with archived content. (You'd post the email as web pages on your site and then allow users to search the content. This would be time consuming, but it is possible.) ListBot automatically archives the messages posted to your discussion group and lets you provide group members with access to the archive. You can also (with some custom programming and database development) use Microsoft SQL Server for your database and Microsoft Index Server to make the database searchable. The SQL Server option isn't a do-it-yourself project (you'd need developers to work with SQL Server and Index Server), so it would take some investment, but after you've set up an archiving system, the strong, value-added content generated by your discussion group essentially provides your site with free, continually updated content that can increase interest in your site, involvement in your community, and your business credibility.

Community-Based Websites

It is, of course, quite possible to build an entire website around community. Successful examples of community-based websites include eBay, where the community focus is collaborating on the buying and selling of individual items; Infobeat, where users subscribe to daily email newsletters on a variety of topics; and SFWoW, where an association of women who work on the Web meets the needs of its members. Other collaborative communities are now fulfilling some of the Web's promise of innovation by creating electronic communities that have no parallel in the bricks-and-mortar world. As examples of these new types of communities, consider the following:

- Evite.com (*www.evite.com*), where users can get help planning social events, inviting guests, and recording events in photo albums and on web pages
- Exp.com (*www.exp.com*), where users buy and sell expertise and experience in an auction model
- Mercata.com (*www.mercata.com*), where e-commerce customers can gather to leverage volume buying into discounts on their purchases
- PredictIt.com (*www.predictit.com*), where users make predictions on sports and finance outcomes and find out how their predictions compare to those of others

As another example of how community can be the focus of a website, consider the sites that empower users to create content. Users read content that has been created by other users; submit their own comments, articles, reviews, and so on; receive acknowledgment for their contribution, which may then be put through an editorial cycle; and might later see their own contributions included as part of the site's content. In some cases, contributors receive special recognition or rewards; in other cases, publication on the site is apparently reward enough to win user loyalty. About.com (*www.about.com*) works on the model of making its audience into contributors and elevating some participants to a status known as "guides."

Part 2: Create Identity and Attract Customers

Measuring Community Success

Success can and should be measured differently for different types of websites. Gone (happily) are the days when all sites measured success in "hits." *Hits* (actually a count of the number of files served when a user accesses a page) were a poor and primitive measurement. Because every image, piece of text, and so on, on a web page is a file and one page can consist of dozens of files, some designs generate more hits than others.

How a given site's success should be measured depends a great deal on the site's goals. Measuring success is the subject of Chapter 13 and not a subject to dwell on here, but a few words on the specific measurement of success for online community endeavors are in order.

The most relevant measures for online communities might include such factors as the number of unique visitors to the site per month, week, or day; the number of *impressions* or *page views* that occur (meaning the number of pages that are seen by a pair of eyes in the course of a given time frame); how many registered members (or subscribers) exist; how many postings occur per month, week, or day (this measurement clearly does not work for chat); the length of time the average user spends in a session; the *posting ratio* (the number of posts that occur compared to the number of page views); or *audience penetration* (what percentage of the potential audience has this site or service reached?).

As of this writing, measurements for the success of online community ventures have not been standardized or accepted. In order for online communities to become as attractive to advertisers, sponsors, and others as they promise, such measures will have to become more generalized. Audit systems are also needed—the online community world needs a system like that used in broadcast or print, where third-party companies verify (by audit) the measurement of success for a given site, discussion group, or newsletter.

In the meantime, owners, producers, and managers of online community ventures must define for themselves what success means in the context of their particular endeavor. As always, go back to the goal you set for your venture. Which of the possible measurements of success corresponds to that goal? Has another success unexpectedly arisen from the venture? Which measure of success corresponds to that piece of serendipity? At this point, the question is open-ended: what is success to your venture?

Part 3

Build Your E-Commerce Website

7   Organizing Your Site's Framework

8   Creating the Site Yourself

9   Working with Web Shops, Developers, or Teams

10   Understanding the Back End and Hosting

Chapter 7

Organizing Your Site's Framework

You've focused your goals, created a budget, and set strategies for branding and service. Now it's time to pull your thoughts together into a tangible, viable site plan. There is no substitute for pre-production planning. Just as building a house without a blueprint is sure to produce an unsound, unlivable structure, building a website without a plan (on paper, in writing, and with sketches that spell out the details of the project) will produce an unsound, unnavigable website—one that customers won't visit.

Building a website is more complex than people realize if all they've ever done is view existing websites. This chapter walks you through the steps for planning a site, leading toward the question: who should do the building?

If you read this chapter and follow its steps, you'll have a plan that you can either implement yourself or take to a web shop for others to implement. In either case, you'll be far better off with a plan that is carefully thought through than if you try to make decisions on the fly.

Part 3: Build Your E-Commerce Website

The Value of Pre-Production Planning?

The pre-production planning process might seem like a lot of hoops to jump through, but it is the cornerstone of a workable website. When you read a book, a magazine, or other printed material, you generally read linearly. In English, for example, you read from top to bottom, and from front to back (see Figure 7.1). But when you read content on a website, you might jump from one page to another, following links in intuitive, nonlinear ways (see Figure 7.2). Given this, it might not seem to matter where you put what. But in fact, it matters a lot.

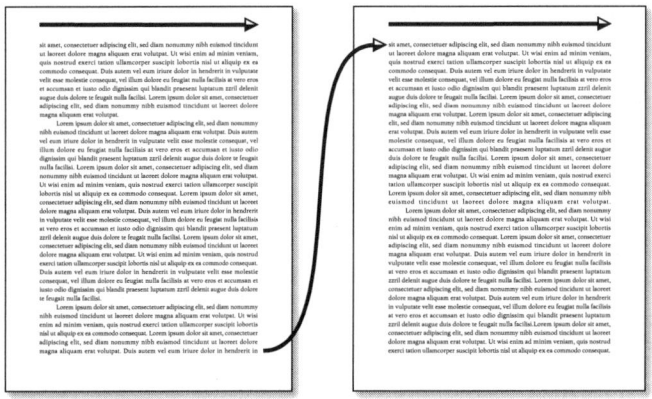

Figure 7.1
Printed material is usually read linearly.

As you know, having a good filing system in your office (or a good directory structure on your computer) makes life easier for everyone. Likewise, having a clear, functional, behind-the-scenes structure for your website makes maintaining the site and adapting it to changing markets far less daunting and difficult. Creating and maintaining a good site plan makes identifying and removing outdated content a snap. When you create new web pages, it also makes finding existing content, images, and other items, and linking to them a lot easier.

To begin the pre-production planning of your site, you first pull together the content you think you might use and organize it into a hierarchy. The process of organizing helps you identify the types of pages your site might have. You then build a site map, which functions like a blueprint of the pages on your site and the links between them. If you're creating the site yourself, you go from the site map step to planning the directory (or folder) structure that sits on your web server; this forms the basic architecture of your site. If you are using a web shop, you can hand over the site map (along with basic descriptions, called *specs*, of the way you want the site to look), and the shop will have a clear picture of your project. And even if you create the site yourself, having a site map and specs will help you stay on track as you make the many decisions required to build a website. Let's get started.

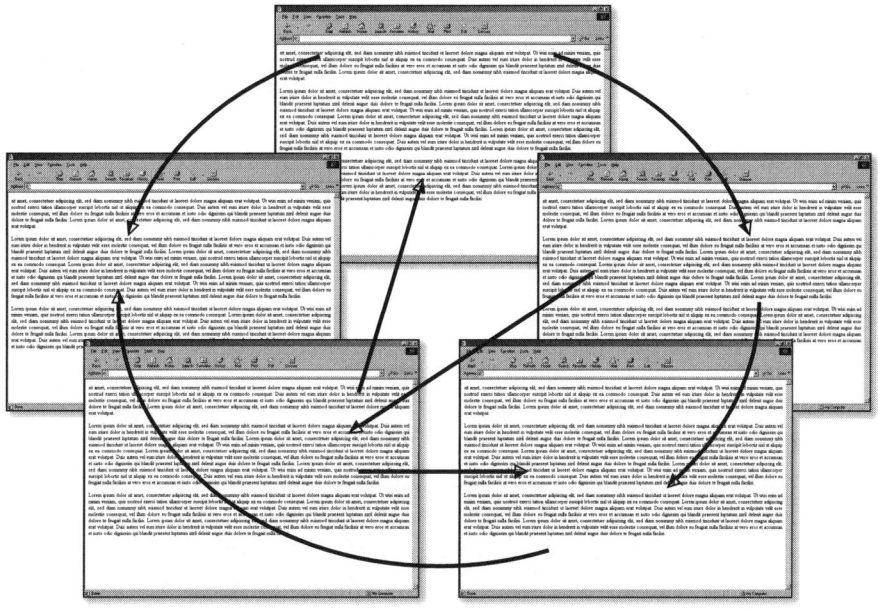

Figure 7.2
Website material is usually read nonlinearly.

Keep in Mind Your Goals and Expectations

Before you roll up your sleeves and begin the actual site plan, take a few moments to go back and review your website strategy. Refresh your memory. Take another look at the goals you set and the mission statement you wrote, at your budget, and at the decisions you made about branding and customer service. As you sort through your content, also consider any legal issues that might arise from the use of certain types of content.

> **Note**
>
> As you plan your site, always keep in mind the results you intend to produce and who your customers are. Those considerations drive everything.

If you build your website yourself, your desired results and your customers will obviously be in the forefront of your mind as you proceed. (You are, presumably, well informed about what you want to achieve.) If you hire a web shop, remember that although they might know more about building an e-commerce site than you do, you are more knowledgeable about your business and your e-commerce strategy. You also know more about where your e-commerce venture will be headed in the future. Communicating that knowledge will allow the web shop to fulfill your expectations; not communicating it will hinder them in giving you what you want.

Acquire Content

What content should you use for your website? The answer depends on what sort of site you are creating. For a sales site, the content might include a home page describing specials and innovative uses of a product, a product catalog, a customer or product support FAQ, and a few pages that describe the company and how to contact key people. The content for a more complex website such as an auction site, a distance learning site, or an information provider site would be quite different; exactly how it would differ depends, as always, on what the site is intended to accomplish.

Where the necessary content comes from is another question. Some of it will come from existing documents. For example, an "About the Company" section can often be pulled from documents that already describe the company; brochures, press releases, or flyers. Details about your company's products also probably already exist in printed or electronic form. A customer support FAQ might be adapted from existing customer support scripts. A "Jobs Available" section might include information about the company's benefits program and perhaps even information gleaned from community sources (such as the Chamber of Commerce) about the local culture and benefits of living and working in the area.

Some content will have to be created specifically for the site. New content might come from any of several sources—you can produce it yourself; you can hire a writer or some other professional to produce it; you can license it (see Chapter 3 for a discussion of the legal issues); your company marketing or public relations group can create it; or, if your budget allows, you can have an ad agency or web shop create it. It can be extremely helpful to make notes about each item of new content you think you need on separate pieces of paper, being as specific as you can. You can physically organize this content later; for now, all you need to do is identify it.

As you focus on content, also review the websites of your competitors. You have to improve upon their sites and ideas. What can you offer that would intrigue or serve your audience more than your competitors' offerings? What do your competitors do that seems off track? Do you have to keep up with them, even if what they're doing seems off track? If so, how can you refocus or repurpose their misguided efforts so you can better address your target market's needs or interests?

> **Note**
>
> As you plan your content, consider carefully whether each piece furthers your site's goals and adds value to your customer's experience. Also consider whether each piece will take extra effort and expense to implement or maintain. And finally, ask yourself whether the content you are planning to use works within the technical, navigational, and legal parameters of e-commerce. For insight into these issues, review the relevant chapters in this book.

Organize Content

After gathering together all the papers, documents, and notes that comprise your planned content, the next step is to organize that material. Sort it into related categories, and then organize the categories, setting aside or tossing out completely whatever doesn't make sense. Then look over your budding plan and move items around or even add or delete pieces. (Remember to consider the value of each item in the context of your e-commerce goals.)

Now, with your material roughed out, you can start planning the structure of your website.

Identify Pages by Type

Most of the pages that comprise your e-commerce website will probably fall into one of the following common types:

- The *home page* is also known as the *default page*, the *index page*, or sometimes the *front door*. The home page provides the first navigational entry into the site, establishing its purpose and personality (its branding message). Sometimes it displays links to the site's offerings, and in that sense it is like a cross between a book's cover and its table of contents. Some home pages offer actual content, but this content should clearly convey the site's branding. The most compelling and necessary items should be easily accessible from the home page; lesser priority pages can be linked from within the site. The home page's main purpose is to provide quick, easy entry into the site. Note that subsections of the site also often have index pages. For example, a software distribution site might include "index" pages that act as entries for the Products section of the site, for About the Company, and for Technical Support.

- *Content pages* often make up the bulk of a content-driven site (but might be a fraction of a whole sales site). Content *areas* are often entered through an index page that acts as that area's home page. Content should be well organized and the pages should have a similar look. (Content pages that look very different from one another can dilute branding and confuse the user.)

Tip
The simplest way to achieve a branded, consistent look is to repeat design elements and page layout from page to page. Having your color scheme, logo, and overall layout appear on every page reinforces your site's identity.

- *Navigational pages* help users navigate, or move around in, the site. Including some navigational pages can certainly boost your site's usefulness. These specialized pages should not attempt to carry content or product information, but should be clear and easy to use, uncluttered by other purposes than facilitating navigation.

- A *site map page* (different than the planning type of site map mentioned earlier in this chapter in that it is posted publicly on a website for users to see) is a navigational page that can act as a large table of contents that lists every significant page on the site and is much more comprehensive than the site's home page.

- A *search page* is a navigational page that enables users to efficiently search for items of interest, offering them a direct path to any item. Setting up a site search option involves creating a dedicated search page, but might also involve placing a search box directly on your home page or other pages. It also requires a page that shows the results of the search, and a page that helps customers to use the search pages correctly. You'll also need a page that lets a user know that a search has been unsuccessful (and perhaps why). Useful site-search tools include Microsoft Index Server, which provides search capabilities for web pages, Microsoft Office documents, and Microsoft SQL Server database content.

Tip

Most search engines available for use on individual websites (as opposed to Alta Vista, Yahoo!, and other search engines that search the Web rather than a single site) include sample query and result pages that you or your developer can customize. You'll want to do this so that another company's logo isn't littering your site, misidentifying your pages to your customers.

- *Help pages* (such as a FAQ list) empower users to help themselves in using your site, your product, or your services. Help pages are most useful for educating users about how to navigate your site and use your transaction system, your site search engine, and your products or services. It's wise to provide links to Help on your home page, as well as on every page a user might have questions, and to place a Help link on your navigation bar.

- *Company pages* are those that offer company background, provide location details, describe the company values or mission, list the top personnel, provide job descriptions and listings, and display other company information. Press releases and a list of awards can also fit in here, or they can go into a Press Room that is a category unto itself or a subsection of About the Company.

Tip

Unless you're building a corporate image site, avoid spreading company information all over. Place company information in one area where users with an interest in it can find it and where it is not tripping up those who have some other agenda—like making a purchase.

- *Transaction pages* are those that lead the user through a financial transaction. A financial transaction might include purchasing a single item or a whole shopping cart full, transferring cash from one account to another at a banking site, or buying an item from a third-party seller at an auction site. Navigation of transaction pages has to be a breeze; you do not want any speed bumps or barriers in the process. As you organize and oversee the design of these pages, job one is to make the flow simple and the process clear. Limit the number of pages it takes to get from selecting the product to completing the purchase, make sure everything that looks like a button acts like one, and make the necessary link or button that leads the user through a process the most obvious item on the page.

Refine Your Plan

Your next step is to group material into logical categories so that you can see the relationships between items and anticipate the paths users will follow to accomplish certain tasks on your site (like making a purchase). This is the time to decide what should appear on your site's navigation bar and finalize where links will lead.

Page Lengths and Linking

You can determine how long your pages should be by following this simple guideline: a single page should address one point or one issue and it should fit within one "screen" without requiring that the user scroll down. If you get stuck trying to organize lengthy pages, look for where material can be broken down. Shorter pages make for more interactivity, suit the dynamic nature of web content, and can easily be linked, leading the user along a suitable click path. But think about your overall linking strategy. In some cases, you might want to limit the number of links going into or coming out of certain pages on your site. You don't want to interrupt a transaction, for example, by placing on your transaction pages ads that link away from the sale (especially not to another site!). And in some types of pages, you'll want the user to follow a specific path through the material; this might be true in promotional sites or purchase-support sites, for example. Or you might want users to experience your content as a click path free-for-all. You can control user experience on your site, to a degree, by carefully planning page length, how links will work, and where and when to link.

Note

The navigation bar—that list of links that often appears along the left side or the top of web pages—is not a navigation page, though it is a navigational device.

Identify Material by Subject, Task, or Utility

Look over the documents and materials you've gathered to represent your content. To refine your vision, ask yourself which items are logically similar to others. You will probably soon see that your material naturally falls into groups based on its *subject* (what it's about), the *task* it allows a user of your site to accomplish (for example, making a purchase), or its *utility* (how you or site developers will use it).

For example, if your site sells gourmet foods, you might be able to group material into the big-picture subjects of products and cooking. Within that, you might subcategorize into appetizers, entrees, and desserts. Within the category of entrees you could even subcategorize entrees into meat, fish, and vegetarian.

In this case, grouping by task involves considering whether a user is looking for information about gourmet foods in general, looking for a specific product, looking for information about your company, or making a purchase.

Grouping by utility involves considering what you or developers will do with content. It's common practice to put the art or images that will appear on a site into one location so they can be stored and linked to efficiently. Following up on our gourmet foods example, you might place photos of various dishes (Ricotta Pancakes, Baked Alaska, Lemon Sorbet) together so you can later use those images in multiple areas of the site.

How you group your material depends a great deal on what it is, what your industry is, and what will best serve your needs (and, of course, those of your audience). As you refine the organization of your material, jot down as headings the various subjects, tasks, and utilities the material might fall into. Then go through the material and place it under the appropriate headings. You can do this by physically spreading the material out on a large surface and shuffling it, by drawing it on a whiteboard, by sketching it electronically using your drawing software, or even by creating an outline in Word.

Tip

You can also use Microsoft Excel to create a list of material that you can then sort and shuffle electronically. You can use the comment feature of Excel to take notes on your content, and other features in Excel (such as SUM, COUNT, and some statistics features) allow you to easily estimate and tally page counts.

If you find that some material doesn't fit in anywhere, you might have to rethink your headings. If you find yourself adding, changing, or deleting headings as you go, don't worry—refining is the goal of this exercise.

If the whole thing is working, in the end you will have categorized all of your material. Figure 7.3 shows material grouped into categories under headings appropriate to the topic of an example site.

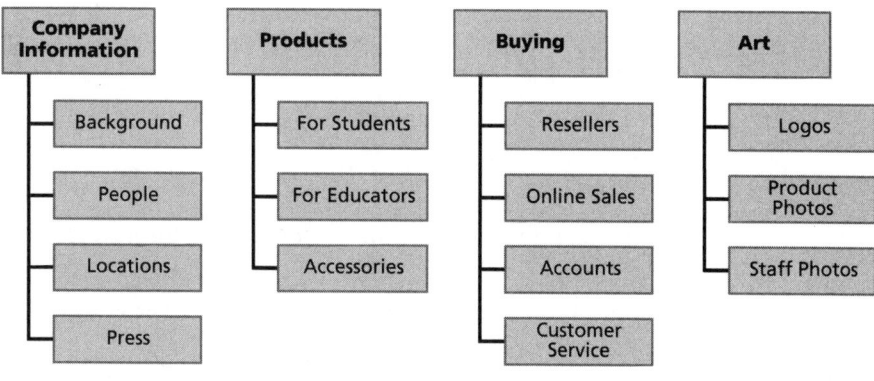

Figure 7.3

Material grouped into categories.

> **Tip**
>
> If you find that a given piece of material might fit nicely into two or more places, remember that you won't have to recreate the content; you can link to it. Make a note of the need for linking on the documents as you organize them.

Group Material into Hierarchies

Now you should establish hierarchies for the material you've categorized. Material in a hierarchy is in a system that goes from top, or more general, down to the more specific (see Figure 7.4 on the next page). Doing this with your website's material accomplishes several purposes. It creates a system that allows users and developers to find things more easily (just as placing your socks in a sock drawer helps you find your socks more easily), and it helps search engine indexing, site searches, and other automated processes work more smoothly and quickly. Establishing a hierarchy, then, is the beginning of creating URLs; the levels of the hierarchy will eventually translate into the segments of your web addresses.

Part 3: Build Your E-Commerce Website

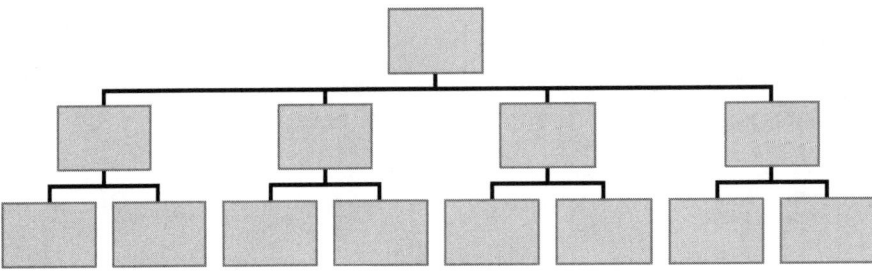

Figure 7.4
Material in a hierarchy goes from the top (general) down (to the specific).

The top of your hierarchy will be your home page. The second level down will be the large categories of material you have to work with. Within each of these might be third-level subcategories; in some cases, though, there might not be a third level. (In other cases, there might be a fourth level.) In general, don't make your site too wide (with many second-level categories and fewer third-level subcategories) or too deep (with few second-level categories and lots of third-level and fourth-level subcategories). But if you must err, go toward making your hierarchy deeper than it is wide. That will make organizing links onto your home page easier later.

Every piece of material you will use has to go someplace in the hierarchy. As you proceed, if something doesn't fit, place it into a "miscellaneous" category, but don't just leave it there. (This is similar to the process you went through for rethinking your categories, but here you are creating subcategories and making sure everything fits into them.) Later, look through the miscellaneous category for like items and group them together. In rare cases, a miscellaneous item might need its own stand-alone category.

> **Note**
>
> If a clear hierarchy for your material just doesn't gel, that might indicate that you need to revisit your general plan. Review the groupings you created, and think about whether the amount or type of content you project for the site is actually appropriate.

Define the Site's Architecture

Until now, you've been gathering information and materials. Now you are ready to create an actual blueprint for your website. You'll begin by converting the hierarchy you've created into a preliminary site map.

Chapter 7: Organizing Your Site's Framework

> ### *Understanding "Front End" and "Back End"*
>
> From a user's viewpoint, a website looks like images and text in a designed page, parts of which the user can, presumably, interact with by clicking items (buttons and links) on the page. That's the *front end*, also sometimes called the *interface*—it's the face of the site, with which the user interacts. The site also has a *back end*, which is the technical infrastructure, the behind-the-scenes computers, software, databases, and code that make up the site and insure its functionality. Think of a live theater production. A front end is like what the audience sees (a stage, action, lights, and smoothly working scenery), and the back end is like what the stagehands see (the scaffolding that holds up the scenery, the tables full of props lined up for actors to use, the switches the lighting technicians throw to change the lighting, and so on).
>
> Creating your site plan—also known as a site map—is a bit like planning what the audience will see so the stagehands can know what needs to be done.

Create a Site Map

The site map you chart now will provide you with an overview of your site. You (or the web shop or developers you hire) can work from this site map when it's time to create directories to hold the material that makes up your site. Much as in the construction of buildings, you have to start with a blueprint, making adjustments as you encounter variables you don't yet know about, so the directories you create might not match exactly the site map you chart now. Some considerations that you didn't see coming (technical, content, and so on) might come into play in creating directories as the site is actually built.

To create your site map, choose your drawing surface: a big piece of paper, a whiteboard, or software such as Microsoft PhotoDraw or Visio Professional 5.0. (Visio is optimized for drawings such as site maps, and integrates nicely with Office and other Microsoft products.) At the top and center of the page, draw a box and label it "home page." Then, under the home page box, draw more boxes along a horizontal line to represent the major groupings into which you placed your content and other material. Label each of those boxes with an appropriate name, and draw a connecting line from each of these second-level boxes to the home page box. Figure 7.5, on the next page, shows what the resulting drawing might look like. (Yours will look different because it will be based on your actual site plan.) Each of the lines between the home page and the other boxes on the map represent a link from your home page to a second-level page in the site. Now repeat the process, working further down, into the third (and, if necessary, fourth) levels. Not every page you plan for your site has to appear here, but if you can work up an estimated page count for each section you plan, you'll be in good shape.

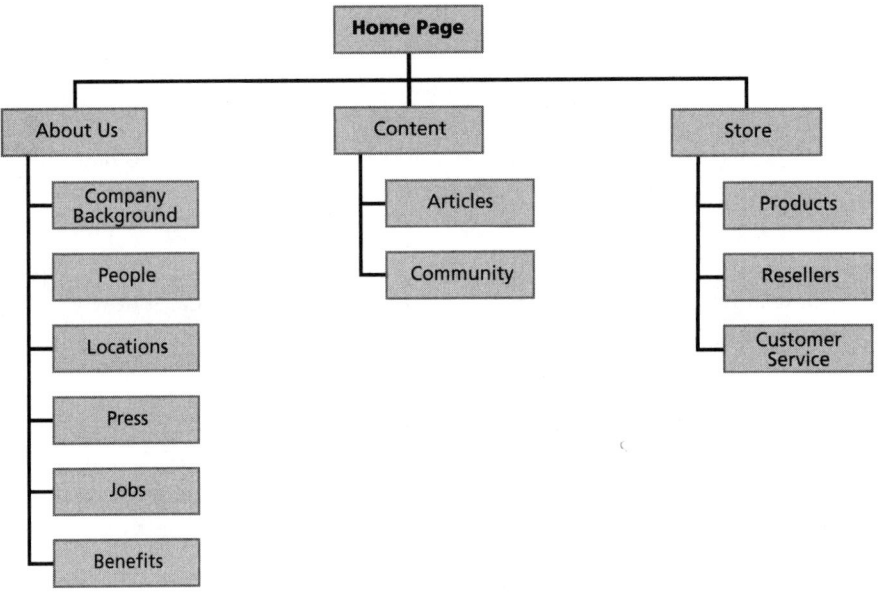

Figure 7.5
A site map beginning to form.

> **Note**
>
> If you use Microsoft FrontPage to create your site (see Chapter 8), you'll have the option to see a site map as you build. Keep in mind, though, that while FrontPage is a powerful, easy-to-use option for creating and managing a site yourself without knowing HTML, its capabilities are no substitute for solid pre-production planning.

Avoid Redundancy and Leverage Linking

Remember that you don't want to duplicate text. If you plan to talk about the company in an About the Company section, you don't have to repeat that text as supporting material in your product FAQ; you can simply link to it. Further, if an image or graphic (your logo, for example) is to appear in several places on the site, you can place the image in what is commonly called an *artbin*—a special place to store all the art. (Some people label this *images* instead of *artbin*.) You'll then be able to link to the image from various locations around the site.

Consider Navigation

After you've mapped out what you can, look for the paths users might take in browsing between the sections of the site or in completing tasks. To navigate from the home page to a page that allows the user to download a particular piece of software or a document, how would the user go? Draw dotted lines to show how the navigation through the most important tasks would occur. Figure 7.6 shows the example site map expanded to this stage.

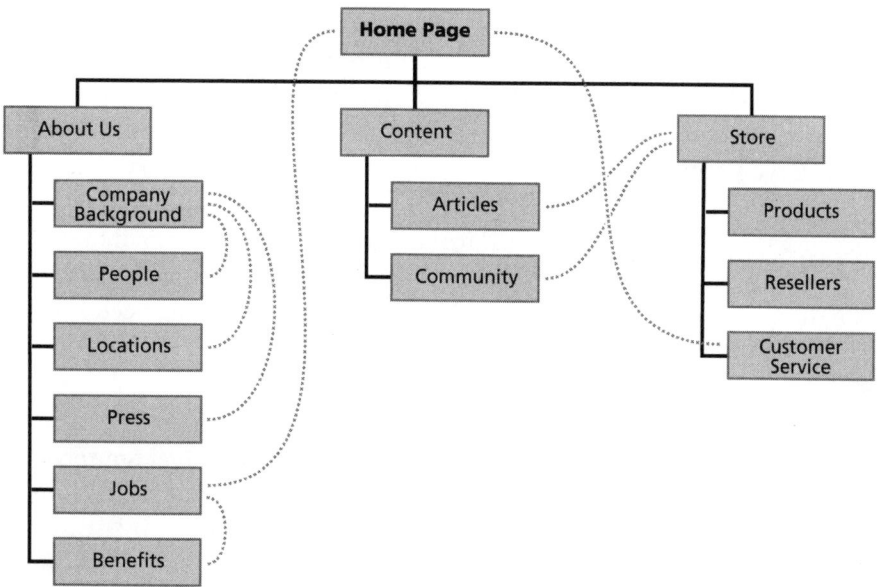

Figure 7.6
The site map with some linking paths shown.

As you chart potential paths, you might discover that the map isn't working quite as you'd imagined. That's fine—the point of all this planning is to iron out kinks now. Make adjustments as needed and move forward. And if the plan is just not working at all and you have to go back several steps to make a fix, remember that uncovering a major flaw in your plan now is better than encountering it just before the launch of your site, when you have too much invested to pause or reconsider. You are still in the pre-production planning phase. And the purpose of pre-production planning is to create a workable plan that will see you through implementation.

Build a Directory Structure

Having mapped your general site plan, now you can create a directory structure for the site. The directory structure is a plan for how the site will be stored on a server. It specifies in which directories on the server your site's items will exist. If you hire a web shop to create your site, you don't necessarily have to take this step. They will probably create a directory structure and pour the necessary files into it before they deliver your site to you. But it helps to understand enough about what the developers are doing to monitor whether they've done it properly. If you use FrontPage or Microsoft bCentral Site Manager to create your site, the software will create a directory structure for you. If you create your site yourself using HTML, you definitely need to know about creating a directory structure.

Why should you care about directory structures at all? Obviously because keeping things organized makes it easier to find and maintain your site files, but also because the directory structure on your server becomes the directory path that appears in the site's URLs. A user can access a web page by following a link or by typing in the page's URL.

Tip

An excellent directory structure includes directory names that are short, easy to remember, and descriptive. Building a good directory structure results in easier maintenance and easy-to-use URLs.

Chapter 7: Organizing Your Site's Framework

The "root" of your website site (the top of the hierarchy of directories and subdirectories) corresponds to a directory on your server called the *document root directory*. (It is not your home page, but it is a directory that contains your home page's file.) Where exactly that directory exists on a server depends on the server software that's running—for example, Microsoft Internet Information Server (IIS) handles things differently than Apache or other server software.

Understanding the Index File

When a user accesses a URL like *http://www.microsoft.com*, the server at that location serves an index file that exists in the server's document root directory. The index file (or default file) is served when no other document is specified in the URL. In other words, at *www.microsoft.com*, in the server's document root directory, there is actually a file named index.htm or default.html, which is in reality the site's home page file. When a user visits microsoft.com, the web browser at the user's end and the server at the other end "assume" the filename and don't require the user to type in a full URL such as *www.microsoft.com/default.htm*.

There are no clear-cut rules for creating a directory structure. For the most part, the structure to use is suggested by the flow of the site. However, some practices have become customary. Artbins, mentioned earlier in this chapter, for holding art, images, or graphics, are standard. Other special directories can hold *scripts* (pieces of programming code) or sound and video files. The simplest way to structure directories is to mirror the hierarchy you created earlier in this chapter. You can use the same logical groupings of files for your directory structure used to create your site map. Simply plot out a structure in which the files from the topmost page of the site (the home page) go in the server's document root directory, and then create directories under the document root directory for each major section of the site and subdirectories for the third level down. Ignore any lines in your site map that indicate linking; linking comes later. Figure 7.7, at the top of the next page, shows a directory structure for the site you saw mapped out earlier in this chapter.

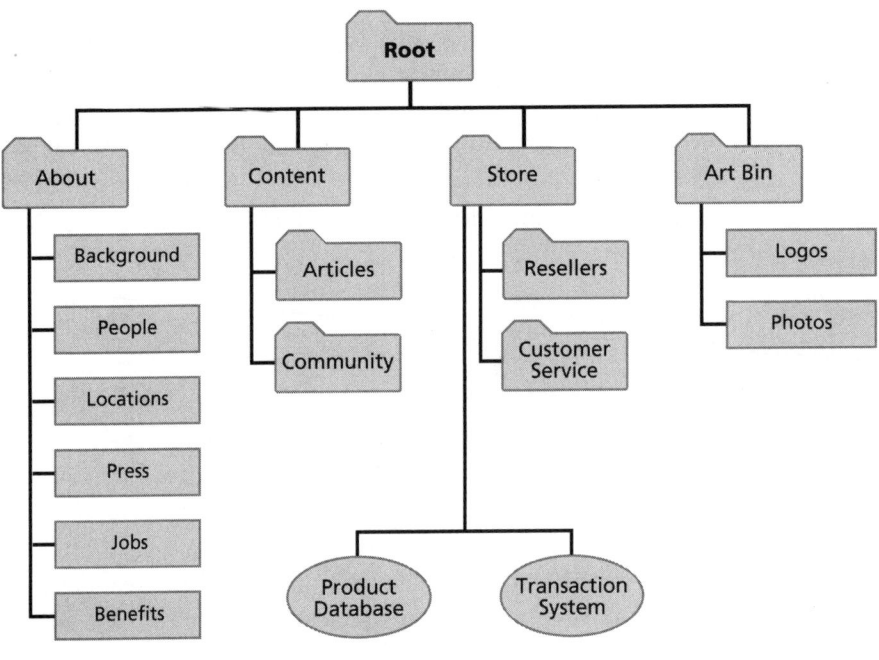

Figure 7.7
A directory structure emerges.

Think About the Back End

Many sites have as a big part of their back ends one or more databases. If you are creating a sales site with a catalog of products and a transaction system, your product catalog, for example, will be organized in a database, as will a list of resellers that is searchable by ZIP code. But certain other kinds of content can also be stored in a database. Chapter 10 discusses databases in more detail, but here, for a moment, let's consider the overall planning issue of whether your site is going to need a database. You will need a database if any of these circumstances exist:

- You plan to sell products through an online catalog. (You might need multiple databases, say, one including customer information and another that actually tracks the sales.)
- You plan to use the same content on multiple sites.
- You plan a site with pages that will change based on user input. For instance, on a page that lists search results, you might want to let users specify how many items will be displayed on the page.

Chapter 7: Organizing Your Site's Framework

You also might find a database handy if you plan a large site with many pages that will use common elements, such as repeated product specifications, a repeated lengthy copyright notice that must appear in its entirety on every page, logos, or other content. You don't actually need a database for this, but using one will make life a lot easier by making multiple changes a one-step process. As an example, if product specifications are kept in a database, you can simply link to the database in every instance where the specs are referenced. When something changes in the specs (for example, when an improvement is made to the product), you make the change in the database, all the pages that show the specs will then show the change. You won't have to go into each page manually and change the specs and then check each change for the typos that inevitably creep into such a matter.

Probably only small e-commerce sites that are not at all labor intensive can operate without databases. How deeply you need to dig into the building of a database is another question. If you use bCentral Site Manager as your solution for selling online, you pretty much don't have to attend to the database question; bCentral Site Manager is a turnkey product that does not require you to plan a database in order to create a catalog and a transaction system. Of course, if you need more functionality (bCentral Site Manager is a sales system and doesn't serve content or let users find resellers via zip code searches, for example), you need a more powerful database, such as a higher-end Microsoft SQL Server solution.

Chapter 10 goes into more detail about databases; if you need a database you'll have to plan its basic functionality. For now, review your site plan and directory structure, and think about whether you are including anything that suggests a need for a database. If so, pencil that into your plan.

Should You Build It Yourself?

Whether you should build the site yourself or "job it out" is an important consideration. The site plan you've developed will help you predict how big and complex (or small and manageable) the project of building your site will be. Now you can address what level of skill and expertise might be necessary to implement your plan. You can assess whether you're prepared to take on building the site yourself by answering a few quick questions:

- Do you have time? Can you take time away from your core business to create the pages? Can you afford the time it might take to learn HTML, for example, or software like Microsoft FrontPage, or any other technologies needed?
- How does your budget look? If you have a budget for development but can't take valuable time away from your core business, you might be better off hiring a web shop. If you have more time than money and your site isn't too ambitious, you might be in a position to build it yourself.
- How complex is the project? Is it a few basic HTML pages, dozens of pages, or hundreds of pages plus a catalog? Does it require a database and transaction system? Do they have to be custom-developed or are they pretty basic?
- Do you have the expertise? This is a question that really gets to the heart of things. Are you already proficient at HTML or with FrontPage? Is your site going to require database development, and if so, do you have those skills? Do you know what practices best lead to the building of successful transaction systems?

If you don't have the technical expertise and can't afford to take time off from your existing business to embark on a steep HTML and database development learning curve, you still have options. At the high end, you can hire a web shop (see Chapter 9), or at the low end, you can consider the option of creating your site with FrontPage. Easier still is letting bCentral Site Manager walk you through a series of wizards (dialog boxes that ask you simple questions about your preferences) that lead to the launching of an e-commerce site tailored to your industry and selections. If using bCentral Site Manager is your choice, you can move on to the building phase now. Your site plan will guide you. If you choose to build your own site or job it out to a web shop, to proceed, you will need to spec out the project.

Write Specs or a Design Document

If you are jobbing out the building of your site in whole or in part, if you are turning over parts of the project to your own staff, or if you are embarking on the adventure of creating the site yourself, you must now document the planning you've done in what's known as the *specs,* or design document. Doing so will provide anyone on the project with a plan they can know and follow. It will also help those who maintain the site after it is launched to stick with the design as they create, modify, and improve the site.

> **Note**
>
> Even if you have sole responsibility for your site, rest assured that a few weeks or months from now you will have forgotten some of what you've decided in the course of planning and building. Notes and documentation (starting with specs) will help you recall your decisions and how implementation occurred.

A typical spec sheet or design document includes:

- The site map you created
- The directory structure you created, along with notes associating pieces of the tree to pieces on the site map
- Descriptions of content and task pages as well as items in the utility category
- A listing of those navigation bar items that will appear on every page of your site

The design document should also include:

- The site's mission statement or goals
- The site's branding guidelines
- Sketches (a *storyboard*) showing your ideas for page look and layout
- Lists of the text elements your pages might use, including: titles and headings; lists (bulleted, numbered, simple, and multi-column); text that's set off as special notes; any special fonts or formatting of special text (bold, italic, or a font used for programming code on a software site); tabular information; "back to" links; linked headings; and so on

The design document can also include the following information, which is discussed in later chapters of this book:

- The server platform you are going to use
- The server software you plan to use
- Any database requirements, including as many specifics as possible
- Any information about the transaction system you would like to use, or what you would like a transaction system to do for you

Finally, the design document should describe any programming requirements you might know about, though they might be few at this early stage.

Note that your spec sheet or design document is no more etched in granite than any other aspect of your website. You can make changes to the specs; you just need to set them down now to get started. On the other hand, the more solid the plan the better; if you change everything, you will certainly slow the project and probably increase its expense, so do try to settle as much as possible in the specs.

Tip

If you are working with a team, place your spec sheet or design document online where everyone can use it as a reference. If you make changes to it, notify team members that they should look at the latest version.

Share your specs or design document with everyone who designs, implements, or posts content on your site. This will help them know how things should be and where new content should go. It will make the process of working with a team run more smoothly. It can also be the basis for a style guide (explained in detail in Chapter 11), which will make keeping your site fresh and maintaining its integrity and assuring its credibility a lot easier.

With your site plan and specs complete, you're ready to tackle design and implementation. For information about building the site yourself, turn to Chapter 8. For insight into hiring and working with a web shop or developers, turn to Chapter 9.

Chapter 8

Creating the Site Yourself

Each of the topics covered in this chapter could be a book unto itself. In fact, many hefty books have been written on every single subject covered here. This chapter offers you brief introductions and overviews that will help you make site-related business decisions. It will also help you understand some of the basics of what can and can't be done in website design so that you can deal effectively with designers and developers if you decide not to create the site yourself.

HTML 101

Basic HTML is easy—really. HTML, which you might recall stands for Hypertext Markup Language, is not programming, and it doesn't require a special college degree. HTML is simply a markup language, meaning that it is a codified method that allows certain elements (headings, body text, captions, and so on) to be interpreted by a computer in such a way that a web browser can display those elements according to a designated design. (Markup languages were first used long ago to tell typesetters how to place type so that it would look right.) HTML is based on another markup language, Standard Generalized Markup Language (SGML). SGML allows content to be marked up for display in any of a wide variety of media, while

HTML was originally created to allow scientists (for whom the World Wide Web was invented) to share information around the globe.

Many people think that nothing jazzy can be done using only basic HTML. It's true that to create the most sophisticated page layouts, complex coding and tricks of the trade are used, and to create interactivity that is more involved than simple linking, at least simple programming skills are required. Still, truly beautiful web pages can be created using basic HTML, and to understand how web pages work and what can and can't be done, you must start by understanding HTML.

> **Note**
>
> Most professional website designers and production people "hard code" in HTML rather than use WYSIWYG (what-you-see-is-what-you-get, pronounced *wizzywig*) tools that make creating web pages a snap. Hard coding offers much more control than do WYSIWYG tools.

How HTML Works

A web page is actually a text document. It contains instructions (code) that tell web browsers how to display the page so users can see it in formats that are conventional and easy to read. HTML uses *tags* (individual pieces of code) to code documents. Tags appear in *angle brackets* (< >), often in opening and closing pairs. For example, <HTML> is a code that signals the beginning of a web page and </HTML> (notice the addition of the slash) signals the end of the page. If tags are formatted correctly, they don't appear on the page. A very simple document with HTML coding looks like this:

```
<HTML>
<HEAD>
<TITLE>The Page's Title Goes Here</TITLE>
</HEAD>
<BODY>
The page's "body" text (its main text) goes here. It can be short or
long, but it must appear within tags that indicate that it is the body
text.
</BODY>
</HTML>
```

To a web browser, any piece of text that is surrounded by brackets is a tag. In our example, the title of the page (represented by the phrase "The Page's Title Goes Here") is surrounded by an opening tag (<TITLE>) that

Chapter 8: Creating the Site Yourself

indicates that it should be displayed as the page's title (in the browser window's title bar, as shown in Figure 8.1). Various other tags can indicate that an item is art, how that art should appear (at what relative size, for example), what page layout conventions are being used for that particular page, which phrases are linked, where the links "go," and so on. Because the tags themselves will not appear on the web page being presented, you can even include comments to yourself or others within special tags.

Tip

As you go along, document the decisions you make about how to use HTML. This will help you and others who work on your site create a consistent look. It will also save time in that you won't have to create a new solution every time you encounter a challenge. See Chapter 12 for tips about creating and using a style guide.

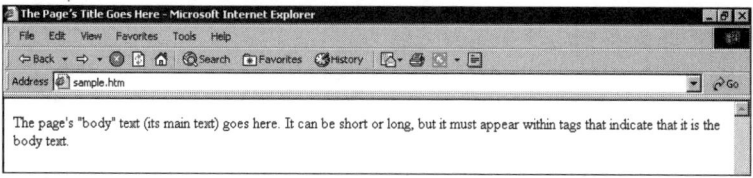

Figure 8.1
Very simple HTML appearing as a web page.

Note

In this book, tags appear in uppercase letters. HTML is not case sensitive; for your coding to work it does not have to be all in uppercase letters. However, many people use uppercase to make the tags more visible within the text that makes up a page.

To create a web page, you can write the content and the tags in simple-to-use software such as Notepad or in word-processing software such as Microsoft Word. You also have the option to bypass the basic HTML markup step altogether by creating documents in Microsoft Office applications, such as Word or Microsoft Excel, and then simply saving the file as an HTML file. Or, you can create entire sites or individual pages using Microsoft FrontPage. (More on the Office and FrontPage options will be presented later in this chapter; other special HTML authoring or editing software is also available. Simply search for "html editor" or "html tool" on any popular search engine to find a wide variety of options.) To do the markup (the HTML coding) yourself or to modify your site, you'll need to know a bit more about HTML and understand its possibilities and limitations.

Required Tags and Their Order

Certain tags simply must be in their place. The <HTML> tag indicates that the document in question is an HTML document, and it must always appear at the beginning of the document. Some HTML authoring tools automatically place it and other tags in their correct locations. If you create an HTML document using Notepad or using Word as a simple text editor (as opposed to creating a document in Word and saving it as HTML), you will have to place the <HTML> tag yourself.

The <HEAD> tag typically follows <HTML> to indicate to web browsers that some code invisible to the user—the page's title and related title information—are about to be specified.

Within the <HEAD> tag, you can also place two types of META tags. You can use the first to specify keywords that search engines can use when indexing your site. In the second, you can place a description that might be displayed on the search engine if your site is "found." (See Chapter 12 for specifics about using META tags.)

The <BODY> tag is also essential; it indicates, as mentioned earlier, the main text on the page. Open any web page using your web browser; on the View menu, click Source (your browser might use different names for this feature); and you can see the HTML coding that makes up the page. Look for these codes and, although other tags will usually appear as well, you'll see that the required tags are always there, always in the same order. If you scroll down, you'll see that a closing version of each of the essential tags also appears.

Opening and Closing Tags

Most tags come in pairs. An opening tag (<HTML>) indicates the beginning of the affected element, and a closing tag (a tag with a slash, as in </HTML>) indicates the end of the affected element.

Certain tags don't require closing tags. These include <P> (which indicates where a new paragraph should begin),
 (which indicates where a line break should occur), and <IMG> (which indicates an image).

Note

Tags are often nested between other tags. For example, among the essential tags described in the earlier example, <HTML> and </HTML> enclose the other tags. And to make the word "ponchos" both bold (<B>) and italic (<I>), the markup would be <B><I>ponchos</I></B>.

Tags That Do Special Jobs

Some tags, such as anchor tags, "mail to" tags, tags for fonts and colors, and comment tags, perform commonly used special tasks. The tag that indicates a link (confusingly enough) is the <A>, or anchor tag. To specify a link, you must add an *attribute* (special descriptive information) to the tag, which, in the case of an <A> tag, points to the destination of the link (the item to which the link leads). In the example

```
<A href="http://www.tauberkienan.com">Tauber Kienan Associates</A>
```

The opening anchor tag contains the attribute

```
href="http://www.tauberkienan.com"
```

specifying the destination of the link. The linked phrase "Tauber Kienan Associates" is enclosed by the entire opening anchor tag,

```
<A href="http://www.tauberkienan.com">
```

and the closing anchor tag,

```
</A>
```

"Mail to" links open the user's email software with a specified address prewritten in the To: line. They are like the <A> tags described, except that instead of the target being followed by a website URL, MAILTO: appears followed by an e-mail address. Here, the user is being encouraged to send me email:

```
Send comments to <A href=mailto:"ecommerce@tauberkienan.com">Brenda Kienan</A>
```

Fonts and colors are indicated by attributes within tags. Fonts have names such as Times New Roman and Helvetica; colors are indicated by numbers that can be found on many websites offering information about the web-safe palette (more on that in a moment). To indicate that a piece of text should be in the font Arial and in a certain shade of green (indicated by a number unique to that color), the coding would be

`<FONT FACE="Arial" COLOR="#336600">Tauber Kienan Associates</FONT>`

Note

The nesting of tags can get quite complex. To specify a certain font for the word "ponchos" as well as formatting it bold and italic, the markup would be `<FONT FACE="Arial"><B><I>ponchos</I></B></FONT>`. Note the "first-in, last-out" order of the tags; when the font is specified first, the bold tag second, and the italics tag third, all of those tags must be closed in the reverse order.

You can use comment tags to make notes within HTML. For example, you can include a tag like this `<!-- Updated 11/30/02 CET -->` to indicate that the page was updated on a certain date. (The initials CET indicate who made the update.) When a web browser encounters a tag that begins `<!--` and ends in `-->`, it will simply ignore what is within the tag.

Limitations of HTML (and a Few Workarounds)

Because HTML was originally created as a means for marking up text (research results) to be shared by scientists and not as a tool for sophisticated layout design, it was born with some basic limitations. In the early days, for example, only two fonts (Courier and Times, which is like Times New Roman) were available. As web browsers became popular, public interest in the Internet took off, capabilities of HTML expanded, and web designers came up with clever workarounds. The options have widened, but the limitations of HTML are still renowned.

- There is still a relatively narrow range of fonts available to HTML, and you can't know exactly which are installed on a user's computer. You can specify a font in your page design, but if it is not available to a certain user, his or her browser will substitute

Chapter 8: Creating the Site Yourself

another. (You can provide in your coding a list of fonts to be used as alternatives. This is done via <FONT FACE>.)

- You also can't specify the exact size of type, because different browsers interpret type sizes differently. You can choose among a range of sizes (1 is the smallest and 7 the largest). Any given user's browser will then translate the size you've chosen into a size it can display. As an example, you cannot specify "12 points" (a typical type size used by print designers) but you can specify "3" (a fairly standard size for web page text) or "2". (See Figure 8.2.) But exactly how large a size is when it appears in a user's browser window can vary.

- With headings, again, specifications cannot be exact. You can specify the levels of headings. (There are six possible levels, going from 1, the topmost level with the largest type, through 6, the lowest level, as shown in Figure 8.3 on the next page.) But doing so determines only whether the text in the heading will be smaller or larger relative to other headings. It doesn't specify an exact size.

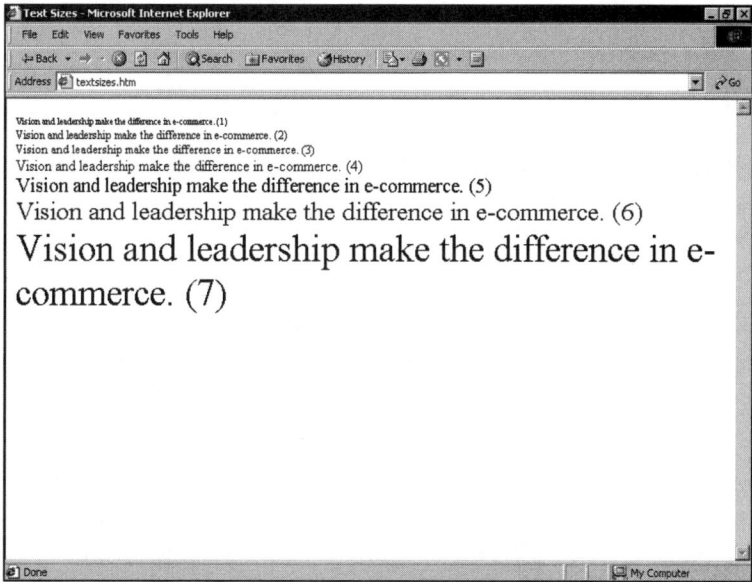

Figure 8.2
The relative sizes of text.

Part 3: Build Your E-Commerce Website

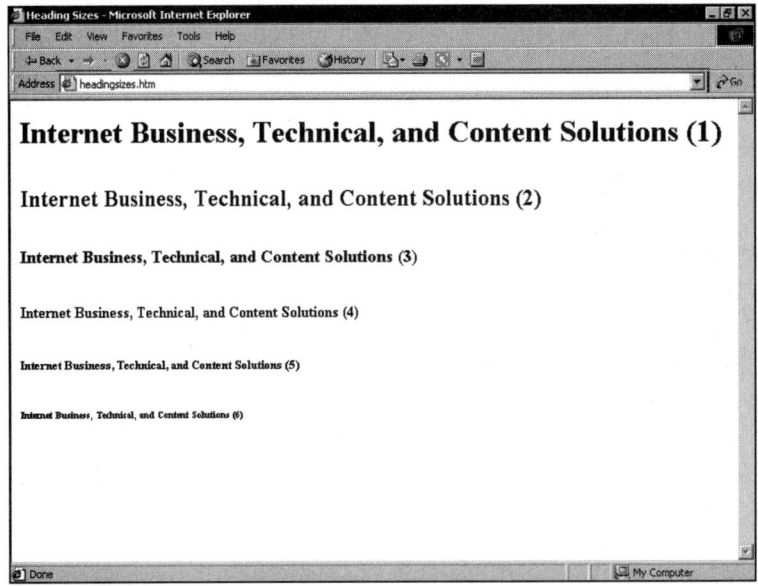

Figure 8.3
The relative sizes of headings.

> **Note**
>
> You can specify font and color for headings, but you can do so only within the same parameters as other type. The coding can then become cumbersome and the advantages of using headings can be lost. (Some crawlers or robots take headings into account as they index sites, and some automated document maintenance processes rely on the appearance of headings.)

- How to establish emphasis is a controversial topic. You can decide whether any text that you want to emphasize should be bold (`<B>`) or italicized (`<I>`), but many designers prefer to let the user's web browser determine how the emphasis will occur. The `<STRONG>` tag renders text in bold and `<EM>` renders text in italics.

- Some characters aren't readily available. You can use special characters such as ™, ©, and ®, but they require special coding made up of an ampersand (&) and an *alphanumeric code* (which consists of a blend of numbers, letters, and sometimes other

186

symbols) followed by a semicolon. (See *www.hotwired.lycos.com /webmonkey* to find out your options for handling special characters.) Other characters, such as *em dashes* (—) and *en dashes* (–), can be coded, but the code simply is not recognized by all browsers. As a workaround, you can use two hyphens to represent an em dash and one for an en dash.

- You cannot use every color known to humanity, and you might not be able to match your company's colors (brochures, business cards, and other items that you hope will fortify your brand). Only 216 colors are recognized by most web browsers. These are known collectively as the *browser-safe palette* (or the *web-safe palette*). Each color is assigned an identifying alphanumeric code. When you specify a background color or any other color, you'll provide the code. Lynda Weinman's website is a terrific resource for learning more about color and graphics (*www.lynda.com*).

Tip

Stick to the 216 color browser-safe palette when you design your site. If possible, choose the palette for your logo, letterhead, and print publications from the browser-safe palette; that will make translating your company look into a website much easier. Also, keep in mind that the browser-safe palette includes very few yellows. If yellow is among your preferred colors, be especially careful to choose one that's going to work for your website.

Page Layout Tricks

In the world of print, designers and typesetters have a great deal of control over page layout. But in HTML, there is no "absolute positioning." You can't specify that an element on the page should appear a specific distance from the left margin, for example. You also can't specify how much space will appear between one line of text and another. To get around these limitations, web designers use tables to lay out pages. These are not informational tables; instead, they invisibly stake out areas of the page (cells) within which text, images, and other elements can appear. (See Figure 8.4 on the next page.) Most websites today use tables as layout devices.

Part 3: Build Your E-Commerce Website

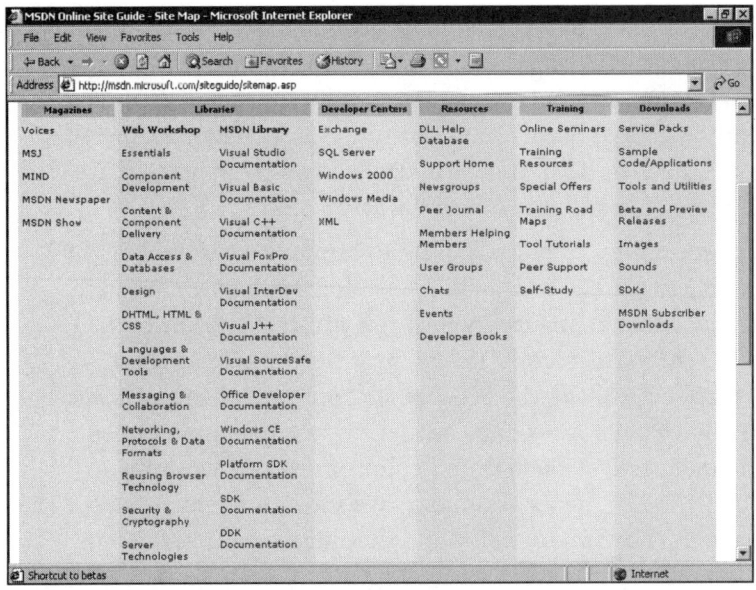

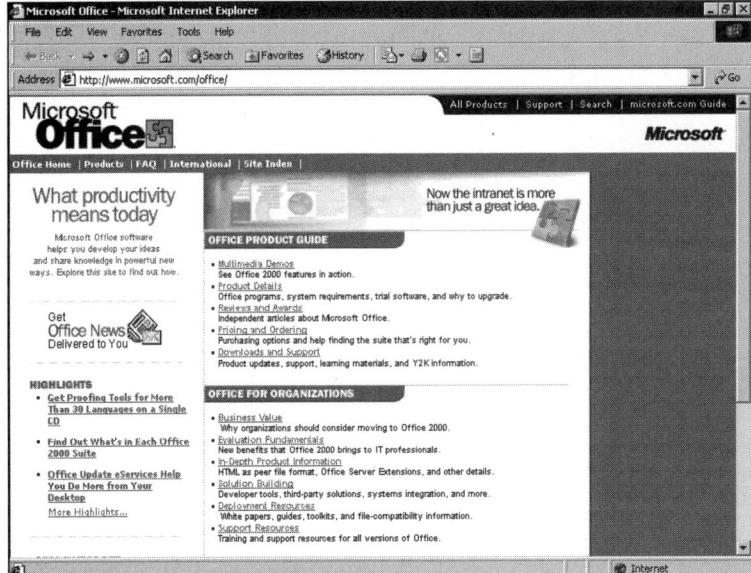

Figure 8.4
An informational table (top) and a web page created using a layout table (bottom).

To create some control over spacing, many designers use the *single pixel gif trick*. The designer creates a small GIF file (an image file) that is actually no image—it either matches the page's background color or is transparent—and places it where a bit of space is needed.

Chapter 8: Creating the Site Yourself

Tip

To minimize design time and maintenance overhead, create a *template* (a prototype). You can then drop your text and images into the template to create new pages instead of having to create them from scratch. Also, keep a copy of your template among your archived files so you'll always have a clean page to start with.

The use of *frames* ("panes" within the larger browser window, as shown in Figure 8.5) also offers some control over page layout. However, the use of frames on your site can prevent your pages from eligibility for indexing by search engines (see Chapter 12). This is because a page created using frames is actually the sum of several pages of HTML coding. Each frame is coded as a separate page; a *frame set* (yet another page of coding) holds instructions for how the frames should appear and function as a whole.

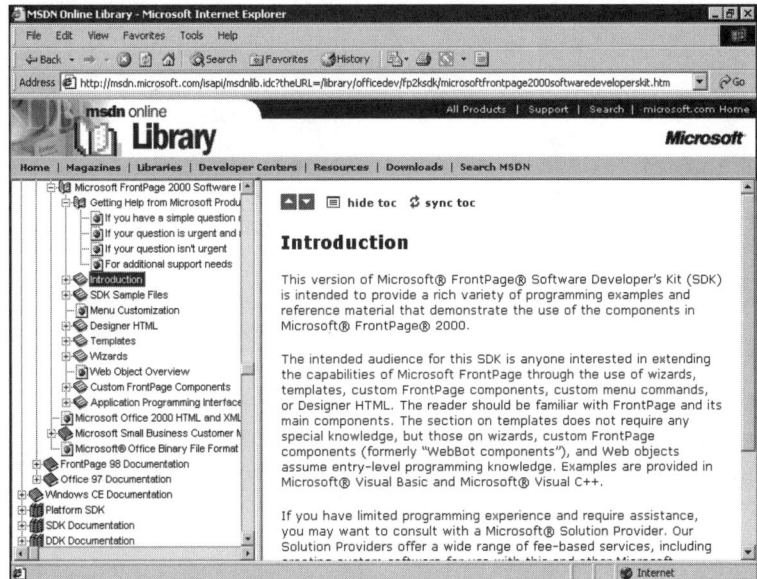

Figure 8.5
Frames offer layout control but carry important disadvantages.

Cascading style sheets are yet another option for controlling page layout. Use of cascading style sheets allows more specific formatting information (including layout, fonts, sizes, colors, and other attributes) to be stored in a file (the style sheet) separate from the actual HTML coding; the style defined in the style sheet is automatically applied to all the HTML pages involved. Unfortunately, cascading style sheets are recognized only by newer browsers (Microsoft Internet Explorer 3 or later and Netscape Navigator 4 or later), so if your audience is using older browsers, this option might not be yours to choose. Additionally, Internet Explorer and Netscape Navigator interpret style sheets differently (as do various versions of each), so style sheets don't actually offer as much control as one would hope.

Tip

Even veteran HTML coders sometimes have to look up a tag. For a complete online reference to HTML, including browser-specific extensions and information about cascading style sheets, see *www.htmlreference.com*.

Notes on Naming Files and Directories

As you save the files that make up your website, keep in mind a few tips that will make life easier. File names should be meaningful so they're both easy to remember in general and easy to identify when you're looking through a list of files. (As an example, classlist.html is better than cl.html or newpage7.html.) They should be short so you (and others) can type as little as possible. (The more brief name augclasslist.html is better than augustclasslist.html.) They should not include blank spaces, underscoring, other punctuation, or special characters like ampersands, exclamation marks, or vertical lines, because those symbols have special meanings to some operating systems. These tips also apply to naming directories (or folders). The discussion of directories in Chapter 7 includes additional information about organizing directories logically.

HTML files, by the way, always end in the extension .htm or .html. Make sure your web page files are saved with one of those extensions.

Posting Your Pages

If you're creating web pages using HTML, you'll probably use file transfer protocol (FTP) to transfer the files to the live server. You might create the files on your desktop computer and then assemble them on a staging server for testing, or, if the site is very small, you might do all the work on your computer and simply upload the files from there. Windows comes with a basic FTP program you can use; alternatively your ISP or IS department might have one it prefers you to use. A user name and password will be necessary when sending content via FTP. You can get these from your ISP or IS department, or from whomever is hosting the site (see Chapter 10 for more on hosting, servers, and ISPs).

Understanding Images

Placing art and images on a website is not difficult, but there are ins and outs. Properly prepared images can look stunning, while sloppily prepared images will slow the site down as well as look bad. Knowing the basics will get you started in handling images more adeptly.

The Basics of Image Files and Formats

Two types of images generally appear on websites. One is *true graphics* (images that are composed of pieces of relatively solid colors, for example, illustrations, clip art, text, and so on), and the other type is photographs (black-and-white or color). To appear in electronic media such as a website, any image has to be translated into digital form. This process transforms the image itself into little dots of color. (This is true even of black-and-white images.) More complex images—mainly those that have many colors or many gradations of colors or those that are more realistic looking—require more complexity in the dots. The more complex the dots, the bigger the size of the file, and therein lies the problem.

Because larger files take longer to download, and because you want your web pages to load in your users' browsers quickly, it's best to avoid large files. A web page generally should not be larger than 50K in size. That is, the sum size of all the files that make up the page should not exceed 50K. Yet a photographic image, for example, can easily be 12K or more, and the average banner ad is 10K.

Various file formats (methods for saving files) are used for various purposes; the two most commonly used for images on websites are GIF and JPEG. Both formats translate images into files by compressing them. GIF compresses some files more, making them smaller, and it is best used for true graphics. JPEG allows for much more complexity and is better used for photographs.

Is It Text or Is It Art?

Not every graphic on the Web looks like art. Some *text* is actually a graphic rather than straight HTML. For example, in Figure 8.6, the phrase "Web services to grow your business" is straight HTML; "Manage more efficiently" is actually a graphic. Because specifying fonts, sizes, colors, and placement is so difficult in HTML, sometimes it's best to create the text in a drawing program and place it on the page as a graphic to get exactly what you want.

Figure 8.6
Text as straight HTML and as a graphic on the bCentral site.

How can you tell which text is HTML and which is a graphic? Watch as a web page is loading, and you can see the graphics appearing first as lightly drawn boxes within which the images then appear. Any text that appears in this way is a graphic. You'll soon get a feel for this and know immediately when you look at text whether it's been created as straight HTML or as a graphic. Buttons, some headlines, and almost all ads (even if they contain only text) are graphics. Navigation bars are often built with buttons that are graphics.

Remember as you plan and create your site that HTML is much easier to alter than text that's a graphic. If, for example, you build your navigation bar with linked buttons rather than HTML links, you might have to get an artist to create the buttons the first time and then do them again any time you want to make a change. Microsoft PhotoDraw provides tools for creating buttons easily, so you can do it yourself, but it's still more time consuming than simply altering the HTML.

Page Size and Download Times

You've probably encountered web pages that took just about forever to arrive on your screen. This usually happens because the page was designed and implemented in such a way that the file sizes became bloated. The following table indicates in seconds how long pages of varying sizes will take to load with the types of connections indicated.

How Connection Speed Affects Download Time

Page Size	14.4K Modem	56K Modem	One ISDN B Channel	Two ISDN B Channels	DSL	Cable Modem
25K	13.89	3.57	3.13	1.56	0.52	0.03
50K	27.78	7.14	6.25	3.13	1.04	0.07
100K	55.56	14.29	12.50	6.25	2.08	0.13
200K	111.11	28.57	25.00	12.50	4.17	0.26

Each element on a page is an electronic file, as you'll recall, and the size of each file contributes to the overall size of the page. To a user with a 56K modem experiencing optimal conditions (no network delays, for example), a 50K page would appear in 7.14 seconds.

Preparing Images for the Web

Placing images on websites isn't a matter of simply slapping them into place. They must be properly prepared. Start by creating the image using drawing software or by translating it into digital format (by scanning it, for example). Save it in the appropriate file format (GIF or JPEG, essentially). Avoid *dithering* (dithering occurs when dots of color appear next to each other to produce a third color) by making sure GIF files use only the browser-safe palette—most current software can deal with this. Note that avoiding dithering is neither necessary nor advisable for JPEGs, however. JPEGs achieve the visual gradations required by photographs through their own processes. Sometimes dithering is part of those processes.

Other Image Types You Will Encounter

While true graphics formatted as simple GIFs and photographs formatted as basic JPEGs are very commonly used, website designers employ a number of variations, tricks, and conventions to achieve greater range in their work. You'll frequently run across:

- **Animated GIFs** Small animations that can be created by drawing a series of GIFs to appear, flipbook-style, in succession. Animated GIFs can be created using drawing software or a special utility.

- **Transparency** Graphics technique that allows a background color or image to shine through the area surrounding a logo or other image. When you save a file as a GIF, you will usually be offered the option to create a transparency.

- **Interlaced GIFs** GIF files that load in several passes. The first pass loads more quickly than a whole GIF would; this means that an image begins to appear on the user's screen more quickly. In subsequent passes, the image is clarified. Again, when you save a file as a GIF, the option to make the file interlaced will usually be offered to you.

- **Thumbnails** Small versions of larger images that are usually linked to the larger image on a separate page. Drawing software usually offers the option to shrink images into thumbnails.

- **Image maps** Large illustrations or other images, portions of which are clickable as links. A classic example is a geographic map (such as the state of Pennsylvania); users can click a spot on the map and jump to a page related to that region. Image maps are usually created via an HTML editor (such as FrontPage) or a special utility.

Tip

Use the <IMG> tag's ALT attribute to identify your images. The ALT attribute lets you specify a text description of an image that will appear before the image does, or when a user moves the mouse over the image. If a user has turned off graphics, the description will appear instead of the image.

Creating and Managing Your Site with Microsoft FrontPage

Using FrontPage, you can build and maintain a website with no knowledge of HTML. FrontPage includes a set of tools for creating and managing websites. The FrontPage interface is the same as the interface for other Office applications (such as Word or Excel), so if you're already an Office user, the learning curve for FrontPage is minimal. You can use FrontPage to build your site from the ground up, to create individual pages, or to edit HTML that's been written using, for example, Notepad or Word. A website created with FrontPage can have consistent look and feel across all its pages. Using FrontPage, you can monitor, manage, and update your site. You can work on the site individually, or, using FrontPage's management tools, you can work with a team.

A full discussion of using FrontPage is beyond the scope of the few pages that follow. For insight into using FrontPage, consult the bigger books. In this chapter, you will find an overview.

Conventions of Microsoft FrontPage

FrontPage uses some conventions and techniques that are unique, an understanding of which will help as you approach building your FrontPage website. First, note that you'll need web-server software installed on the computer you'll be using to create your website; FrontPage comes with what you need, so there's no need to worry. Just know that it has to be there and that it is distinct from the web-server software you'll need when your site goes live to the public. The web-server software that comes with FrontPage is only there to allow you to build a site and view it as you build.

Further, FrontPage uses the term Web to describe a website or an area of a website. A FrontPage Web is made up of web pages and is created in HTML (although FrontPage takes the HTML burden from your shoulders). In addition to HTML files, a FrontPage Web can contain image files, animations, Office files, audio and video, and whatever else generally makes up a website. You can import into FrontPage websites or areas of sites that have been created without FrontPage; if you do, FrontPage will call the imported material a Web as well.

Using FrontPage to Create a Site or a Page

To create a website in FrontPage, start the software, and then begin by using a wizard (which steps you through the process of simply adding content to a set of pages with prepackaged design), or a template (a page with a preformatted layout and design; you can create a whole site based on this template or use it for only one page).

You can then change the look if you like, by selecting any of a number of *themes*. Themes include such details as background and other colors; heading size and formatting; and the look of bulleted lists, links, and other elements. Alternatively, you can customize pages to give them a look that you prefer, even one that's been professionally designed.

As you work, the HTML coding will be done for you, behind the scenes. You will be able to see the pages you're working on in a WYSIWYG view that both looks like a web page and shows your changes as you make them, but that can be edited. You'll also have the option of seeing the HTML "source" (the code) as it develops or previewing the pages in Internet Explorer. You can add images, links, video, and audio, as well as alter the formatting of the pages.

Mapping the Site and Its Navigation

Using FrontPage's navigation tools and features, you can chart how your future users will make their way around your website. FrontPage will then generate navigation bars automatically based on what you've determined. (You can make choices about how the navigation will work and whether the navigation links will be buttons or text, among other options.) As you add new pages to your site, you can then add them to the navigation structure with ease.

A mapping feature is also provided to show you how the links on the site interconnect the site's pages. As you link to newly created pages, they will be added to this view of the site. This is a boon in that it helps you to identify content that should be linked but isn't. You can also see the potential clickpaths a user might have to travel to get from one area of the site to another. You can use what you learn to both modify the site and make decisions about the site's navigation.

Adding a Catalog, Transaction System, and Shopping Cart

You can easily use FrontPage to create product pages that describe your wares, or you can use FrontPage to design the look of your catalog pages and call forth the product information from a database back end (see Chapter 10). As of this writing, you cannot design a shopping cart or transaction system using FrontPage alone, but you can create your site and catalog using FrontPage. You can then create the shopping portion of your site using, for example, Microsoft bCentral Site Manager, linking it seamlessly from your FrontPage website.

Working with FrontPage and HTML

You can import pages that have been created via hard-coded HTML into your FrontPage Web. The HTML in those pages will not be altered. You can then edit the pages using FrontPage's WYSIWYG tools and its other features to integrate them smoothly into the site's overall look and navigation.

Caution

Not all HTML authoring and editing tools are compatible. Some versions of some tools add their own codes to the HTML code; these special codes are then unrecognizable to other tools. It's generally best, if you're working with a team or otherwise passing files around, to stick to one tool to avoid trouble.

You can also edit pages using HTML (as opposed to using FrontPage's WYSIWYG editor), which will give you finer control over the page layout and general look. For example, you can apply your company's colors to the background and text (within the limits of the browser-safe palette), and can even create a look that matches your print material's look and feel.

Managing Your FrontPage Website

FrontPage automatically generates a series of reports that outline and describe your website's status, making site management more efficient. You can easily find out about *orphan files* (those that are not linked in any path from the home page) as well as about files that load too slowly, files that are growing stale and need updating, files that have been recently modified, links that are no longer viable, and tasks that have yet to be completed. The Tasks feature in FrontPage allows you to note specific items to be done, mark them off as they are completed, and even assign them to various team members, who can then mark them "completed" for you to see. Use this task list feature to plot out for yourself or team members what needs to be done in as much detail as possible. Content management consultant Alicia Eckley advises that "people often look at big pictures and tend not to think about the details. The only way you can get everything done in the time you've usually got with a quality outcome is to think through, detail by detail, the elements of the site and the processes involved. Content has to be created, revised, coded, tested, and proofread. Scrambling at the end never gets the best result." (See Chapter 11 for further information about content management processes.)

Tip

You can put the directory structure you planned in Chapter 7 directly into action as you create your FrontPage Web, using a feature that allows you to view, create, and rearrange the folders that make up your Web.

Using FrontPage's mapping and navigation view features, you can generate a site map that can be printed. It can then be reviewed in meetings or included in printed documentation or reports. Other features automatically fix links when the files they lead to are renamed or moved, check spelling in the background as the site is created, and track revisions so that team members don't mix up versions of a single page as they make changes to it.

Making the Site Live

When your FrontPage Web is set to go, making it live is a simple operation. You'll have to move the site from the desktop computer on which it was created to the server that will host it (see Chapter 10 to find out about server options). You can do so via a series of dialog boxes that will step you through the procedure easily.

> **Note**
>
> For a FrontPage-created website to work as a live site, you'll have to verify that the server hosting it has *FrontPage Server Extensions* (a set of special scripts that enables FrontPage to work). Ask your ISP if the site is hosted there, or ask your tech people if the site is on a server at your location. A listing of ISPs that host FrontPage websites is at *www.microsoftwpp.com*.

Designing for Multiple Browsers

Regardless of how you're creating your site, in the design stage, always consider which browsers your audience is using. Various browsers recognize different tags. Even among the tags they all recognize, not everything will look the same on every computer. A simple example is that any given font appears two to three times larger on a PC than it does on a Macintosh. Further, different browsers support different technologies. Microsoft Internet Explorer, for example, supports Visual Basic Scripting Edition (VBScript), but not all browsers do.

Identify the browsers and operating systems you anticipate your audience will be using before you design your site. As you design, look at the pages you are creating in various browsers on various computers, matching as closely as possible the range you anticipate. (A chart in the E-Commerce Management Center at *www.tauberkienan.com* outlines which current browsers support what.) You needn't have every browser on every computer in your office; if you tested all of the most commonly used browsers and software versions as of this writing, you'd have to test at least 14! Instead ask associates and friends to view the pages from their computers and report what they see and what operating system and browser they are using. Then make adjustments and ask them to look again.

You can create multiple versions of your site (or individual pages within it) that are tailored to the operating systems and browsers you expect your audience to use. However, this option increases maintenance overhead quite a bit. Each change you make to any given web page will have to be replicated on all the versions of that page, and all the versions of the pages will have to be tested and maintained. Only the most mission-critical sites with the biggest budgets are likely to go this route.

General Design Rules

Following these general design rules will help you create an attractive and functional website.

- The colors you choose for backgrounds, links, and visited links should complement each other, not clash. Remember that dark text on a white or neutral color background is still the easiest to read.

- Place the most important items at the top of the page so users don't have to scroll to see them. Break pages longer than two screens into separate pages with a link leading to them.

- Everything that looks like a button must act like a button. Don't get tricky about this. If a user clicks something that looks like a button and it turns out not to be, the user will either be confused or think your site is broken. Either way, it's a bad impression.

- No two links placed near each other on the same page should go to the same destination—coming across duplicate links can startle and annoy a user. Also, two links with the same name (wherever they're located) should always have the same destination.

- For easier maintenance of items that have to be updated (including navigation bars), use HTML text rather than images.

- Avoid gratuitous animation, excessive art, blinking text, and anything that simply distracts the eye. Too many fonts on a single page will just look like a mishmash; too many colors can look like fruit salad. Balance large and small art and long and short blocks of text.

- Horizontal ruled lines are usually unnecessary. They act as a speed bump, tripping up the user's eye as it travels down the page. Paragraph breaks and other less obvious devices will do the job.

Chapter 8: Creating the Site Yourself

Tip

To get a clear picture of what does and doesn't work in website design, see Builder.com's tutorials and critiques of websites (*www.builder.com*) and Web Pages That Suck's reviews of lousy sites and counterproductive navigation (*www.webpagesthatsuck.com*).

Jazzing Things Up with Interactivity

Interactivity on websites takes many forms and can add plenty of pizzazz. Interactive elements can include:

- Navigational features such as mouseovers (see Figure 8.7) or clickable buttons that glow or change shape.

- Entertaining components such as puzzles, games, electronic postcards.

- Added-value or interactive tools such as calendars and mortgage calculators (see Figure 8.8 on the following page).

- Forms that gather data (online surveys) or allow users to self-assess (instant-response quizzes).

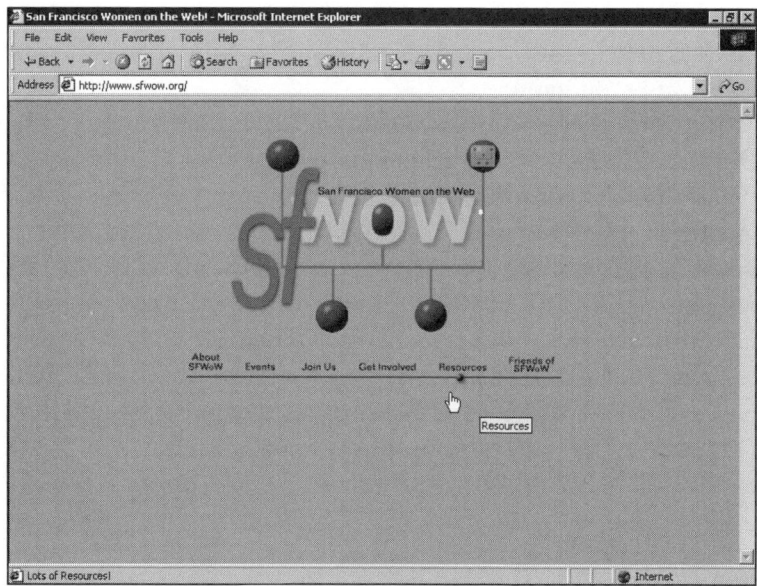

Figure 8.7

A mouseover on the SFWoW site is used as a navigational aid and visual punctuation.

Part 3: Build Your E-Commerce Website

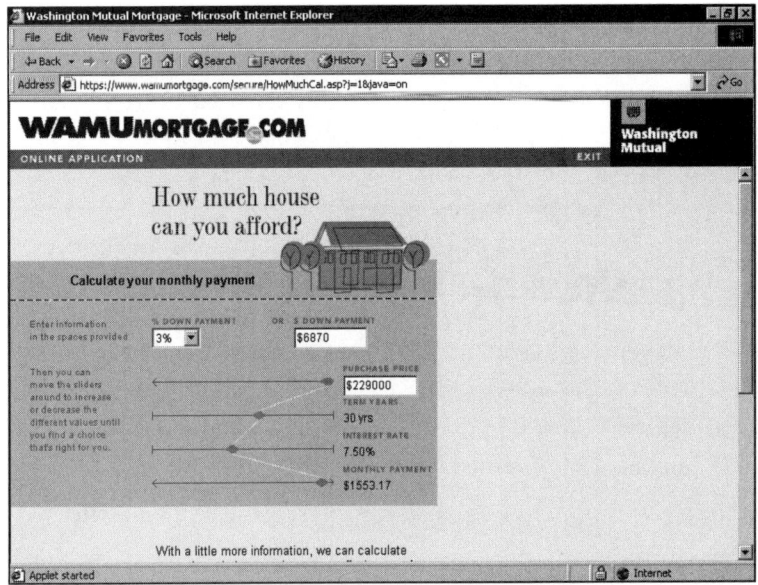

Figure 8.8

An interactive mortgage calculator on the Washington Mutual website.

On the other hand, if interactive elements are overused or done poorly, they can seem gratuitous or even silly. Use interactive elements only to further your cause. If a specific activity or gadget will enhance your audience's experience or support the goals and branding message of your site, fine. But be judicious.

Many of the nifty effects mentioned above require programming skills beyond the grasp of those without real experience. However, options do exist that are easy for the non-programmer to implement and that can add sufficient interactivity to your site. FrontPage offers several such options, such as components for mouseovers and discussion boards, and allows you to create interactive forms for surveys, quizzes, or other purposes.

You can also download some cool interactive components from websites such as *www.webmonkey.com* or *www.javascripts.com/scripts*. Download what you like—you'll have to pay any fees requested—and then incorporate it into your site. (Instructions are usually included with the download.)

Including Microsoft Office Documents

You can easily save documents created with Microsoft Office as HTML documents and upload them to your website, just as you would any other HTML document. You can edit these documents using NotePad, Word, or FrontPage (or other HTML editing tools). Web pages that were first created as Word documents, for example, can be tinkered with to add the same level of imagery and interactivity as any other web page.

Another option is to upload to your site the document file in its original format (.doc, .xls, or .ppt, for example). If you embed a link to the document in your HTML, users who have Office will then be able to access the file in its Word, Excel, or Microsoft PowerPoint format and use it. (This is how the spreadsheet mentioned in Chapter 2 was made available at the E-Commerce Management Center at *www.tauberkienan.com*.) The code from creating such a link is like the code for creating other links; it goes like this:

```
<A href="http://www.tauberkienan.com/ecommerce/
ecommercebudget.xls">Sample Budget</A>
```

FrontPage includes additional tools for publishing Microsoft Access databases online. Users can then query the database via a FrontPage-generated form; the results will appear as a new web page. Using this technique, you can create a product catalog, a customer support knowledge base, or a retail outlet locator.

Relying on Microsoft bCentral Site Manager

Microsoft bCentral Site Manager offers you the option of creating a website tailored to your industry. You can have a functional, attractive catalog, shopping cart, and transaction system up and running very quickly without any programming skills and without hiring developers. (You also won't have to install any special software on your computer.) You can include pages for customer support, for technical help, and for contacting your company in your bCentral Site Manager website.

To create a website using bCentral Site Manager, pull together and organize your content just as you would if you were hiring designers and developers. Then, with your content in hand, your next step is to sign up for the service; bCentral Site Manager is available through Microsoft bCentral, at *www.bcentral.com*.

Part 3: Build Your E-Commerce Website

At bCentral Site Manager you'll be stepped through the process of creating your site using wizards. Just answer the questions asked, choose the look you like, and as you set up the site you'll be able to preview the pages as they'll appear on the Internet.

Tip

You can customize your bCentral Site Manager website with FrontPage. A quick and easy tutorial is available at bCentral.

You can set up your own business rules and specify tax tables for your bCentral Site Manager website. You can also indicate the shipping methods you will provide and rate information. While you must make arrangements with your own bank to handle your merchant account (see Chapter 10), your bCentral Site Manager service can include credit card processing capabilities.

Site hosting, server maintenance, and order summarizing are included in the reasonable monthly fee charged for bCentral Site Manager's services. Tools for accounting and the tracking of fulfillment are also part of the package.

Small businesses and e-commerce managers who have almost no technical skills can launch and run a functional e-commerce website with a back end powered by Microsoft. The bCentral Site Manager solution is easy and economical.

Hiring a web shop, designer, or developer to build your website is a much higher-end solution and is the subject of the next chapter.

Chapter 9

Working with Web Shops, Developers, or Teams

If you're considering jobbing out the building and maintenance of your e-commerce website, you must decide whether to job out the whole project or just parts of it (and if so, which parts). You must also decide whether to use vendors or in-house resources.

Working with a vendor in the e-commerce industry has its ins and outs, and knowing how to find and work with good companies is essential. You need to know how to present your needs so you'll get good proposals from vendor candidates, how to assess their experience, and how to build good relationships so that the project goes smoothly. Maintaining vendor relations is also important in the event that you want your vendors to maintain your site or support you when you're ready to bring maintenance tasks in house.

> **Note**
>
> Even if you assign parts of the job to departments within your own company, knowing how to assess the experience of people in those departments is important. Read through this chapter to understand what skills and experience you might need in an in-house team.

Assess Your Needs

The type of shop you need (or whether you need one at all) depends on factors such as the scope of the project (whether it's the soup-to-nuts building of a full-blown site or just making some modifications, improving functionality, or creating fresh graphics). The size of your budget (and how it compares to the scope of your project) must be considered along with the level of expertise you or your team can bring to the project. Another factor is how much hand-holding you need throughout the project. If you don't have much experience at all and need a web shop to lead you through the process step by step, guiding you in making decisions, you can expect the shop to take that into account when they formulate their bid.

Consider Outsourcing and Insourcing

Keep in mind that in companies with multiple departments, in addition to the option of *outsourcing* (hiring a job out to another company) you have the option of *insourcing* (jobbing portions of the project to other departments within the company. You might, for example, have your in-house graphics department do the graphics and your tech department do the programming).

> **Note**
>
> Insourcing is often seen by companies as a logical strategy for avoiding the creation of say, two different art departments in the same company (one devoted to print and one to the web initiative).

Chapter 9: Working with Web Shops, Developers, or Teams

Tips for Effective Insourcing

When a team is pulled together from different departments to work on the e-commerce initiative, the politics can be difficult to navigate. These pointers can help smooth the way.

- **Evangelize.** Send out email now and then to let the company know what the web team has been up to and what results were achieved. This will help ensure that future web projects are taken seriously. When it's necessary to borrow employees to participate in a web project, that project won't seem expendable if the overall e-commerce initiative is seen as successful.

- **Don't poach.** Talk to the managers of any employees you want to borrow before you talk to the employees.

- **Look in unlikely places for insourcing candidates.** Is there an administrative assistant or programmer who is a writer in disguise? A page layout person in corporate communications who is eager to learn HTML? Look past job titles, and "hire" for potential.

- **Ask HR which departments are ramping down.** If you can absorb one department's downsizing casualties onto your roster, you might be recruiting grateful employees who will attack their new assignments with enthusiasm.

- **Cross-train by empowering other departments to post on the company intranet.** Orient staff in various departments in HTML and web processes, and you'll have a pool of trained insourcing candidates to draw from.

- **Give generous credit where it's due.** Remember to thank employees *and their managers* at every milestone and as publicly as possible. Send an email message up and down the ranks mentioning that without the support of those talented people and the generous managers (name them) who lent them, the work might never have gotten done.

- **Buy pizza.** Or take the gang out to lunch, the beach, or laser tag. Do something social that gives them time to gel as a team, and as the project progresses and important milestones are achieved, reward their extra efforts.

However, insourcing can have some disadvantages for the main web team. People from other departments assigned to the web initiative sometimes consider that assignment a lower priority than their usual work that supports the company's core business. That can leave the insourced tasks at the bottom of the "borrowed" employee's priority list and leaves the web team leader—who is responsible for producing results—with neither the authority nor the adequate resources to get the job done. Further, it is often the case that the "borrowed" staff is not web-savvy and has to be trained to work within the parameters of what can (and should) be done on the Web. This can be time consuming for all involved. Nonetheless, in some cases, especially when the need is short-term and limited in scope, or when the borrowed staff is actually web-savvy, insourcing might be a solution for avoiding redundancy in the company.

Tip

Microsoft Project can be a valuable tool for keeping team members informed and on track. Project lets team members access and share information, software, schedules, and documents across a network. It also includes project management features so you can organize and manage tasks and projects efficiently.

Consider Outtasking

Outtasking (jobbing out a specific task within the larger scope of the project) is yet another option. This is simply a matter of hiring freelancers or contract workers to complete a specific, definable, deliverable portion of the overall job. You can outtask the creation of some programming, some writing, some design, or some other portion of the project. The difference between outsourcing and outtasking is the size of what's being jobbed out; jobbing out the whole of database development, look-and-feel design, or even human resources functions would be considered outsourcing, while jobbing out a portion of one of those jobs would be considered outtasking.

Use Microsoft Products to Facilitate Collaboration

Microsoft products offer a number of solutions for keeping workgroups on track and in communication. Microsoft Exchange Server provides a platform for business communications and offers inexpensive administration while enabling collaborative features. Microsoft Office and its components, Microsoft Outlook, Project, and Microsoft NetMeeting, offer online access to shared calendars, contact lists, and project responsibilities. Project itself can be a valuable management tool; its project management features will help you track tasks and projects effectively. Team members or officemates working in a Project environment can easily share calendars, software, information, and documents. Outlook's everyday scheduling features can also be saved for viewing via your intranet. (See the Appendix to find out more about intranets.)

At the higher end, Microsoft Visual SourceSafe provides collaboration tools for team members to use during development. Using Visual SourceSafe, team members can develop web content, code, and supporting files in the same environment, and then deploy the files directly to the website. Version control is a key issue in team collaboration; team members working on the same document or file need to know they aren't mixing up the changes they're making as they go along. Visual SourceSafe provides easy-to-use version control capabilities, and it also generates site maps and tests links automatically.

Who's Who Among Shops and Developers

Whether you are choosing building contractors to remodel your home or web contractors to build your website, you will find that companies range in size from large to small. They all offer varying degrees of service, skills, and experience. Each approaches the building process from its own unique angle and will have its own recommendations about what you ought to do with your site. Let's take a quick look at the general categories of web shops and contractors.

What Are ISPs and IPPs?

You probably already have an Internet service provider (ISP). Your ISP is the company that provides you access to the Internet. It also offers you software you can use for email or web browsing and perhaps other services. You might recognize the names of larger ISPs, such as EarthLink, MindSpring, and America Online; smaller regional ISPs also exist in many areas. Most ISPs offer their customers the option to create a "free" website that is hosted on the ISP's server. Many people create personal websites using these services; however, creating a fully-featured, viable storefront for a mid-sized to large-sized e-commerce venture is not an option. The server space an ISP offers is simply not enough to hold a large site, and usually the ISP does not allow a customer to include the kind of programming and front-end features needed for selling and other types of e-commerce.

> **Note**
>
> Typically, the account you have with an ISP for your e-commerce site will be a different account with different features and options than the account you use for your personal Internet service. For more on choosing an ISP to host your e-commerce site, see Chapter 10.

Internet Presence Providers (IPPs) offer their clients a wider range of services than ISPs. They usually offer more robust options for hosting, often along with design, implementation, and even consulting services. An IPP then, provides a *presence* on the Internet as opposed to service for getting on the Internet. Sometimes a company calling itself an IPP provides only the more robust hosting options but no development, design, or implementation; if so, you can contract other companies for those services or your own staff can do it.

If you are considering a full service IPP to do development, design, and implementation, ask the company whether it has on hand a design team (and perhaps a content team) that works independently of the technical implementation and hosting team. A techie is not a designer, and asking a programmer who "does design" to lay out your website is unlikely to result in a professional image. Some key questions to ask an IPP under consideration include:

- What services does the IPP offer? What percentage of the time spent on a given project is devoted to which services?
- How many staff members are devoted to creative services like content or design? Who are they, and what is the scope of their responsibility in a project? What skills and experience do they bring to the table?
- To get the benefit of creative services, is it necessary to contract for hosting services? Are there any package deals available for both or for each?

What Ad and Marketing Agencies Do

Advertising and marketing agencies often have "creative" departments that forge words and pictures into full-blown campaigns to sell anything ranging from diapers to political candidates. (Sometimes they subcontract the actual work to design agencies and simply provide the strategy.)

Because they see the Web as yet another medium (augmenting TV, print, or radio) with a large audience available to be marketed to, most large ad agencies now have departments or subcontractors that specialize in creating Internet presences. Hiring ad or marketing agencies to create the e-commerce branding message holds some advantage for companies that have the budget for it. If it's an agency you've worked with before and it has creative, talented people on hand, it probably knows your message and style. But if you plan for them to actually implement the site, ask yourself and the agency what their background in e-commerce is. There is a big difference between creating ads or brochures and producing a compelling website that functions smoothly. Many designers who have been designing for print for years look at websites and think "I can do that," but the Web is a whole different animal with specific limitations and challenges. Question any agencies and designers you are considering closely; later in this chapter you'll learn more about the questions you should ask in assessing anyone's suitability for your endeavor.

> **Tip**
>
> One option for working with an ad or marketing agency is to retain them as your branding or creative consultant, but assign the actual implementation to a company that has the experience you need. This strategy adds to your management overhead, but it does net you the sum of two companies' best experience. Just remember to decide who is top dog.

If the ad agency you already work with is genuinely web-savvy, you might find hiring them to create your site is a successful path to putting forth an overall branding presence with just the right message delivered in all media.

What Specialized Web Shops Do

Some companies specialize in creating or building websites (without offering hosting or providing overall advertising or marketing campaigns). These companies come in various configurations and range in size, from large, renowned web shops that work for large clients to smaller outfits and even independent operators. Some smaller companies and independent operators are backed up by "virtual" organizations in the sense that they pull together freelancers or other small companies according to the needs of a given project. Choosing among the options here requires looking at your budget, at how much time you have for managing outsourced services, and, as always, at what you've determined to be your site's goals.

Innovative, exclusive design firms (Organic Online, Razorfish, and others) include talented, skilled staff that know cutting edge design tricks. They also are in high demand, are expensive, and can afford to turn away work that they don't feel will enhance their portfolios of clients. Large firms (whether renowned or not) often include on their staffs account managers, marketing and creative personnel, programmers, database developers, video and sound producers, artists, typographers, and other designers, and generally, a crew of HTML coders. While corporations with big budgets might consider these firms, small-sized companies (or those without big budgets) generally ought to look for more accessible options.

Smaller web shops, with perhaps five to twenty in-house employees, sometimes focus on a specific design style or a certain type of client. They might approach a given job only with their in-house staff of design and implementation people, or they might subcontract certain jobs such as the conversion of video and sound files to the appropriate web formats, the implementation of programming and database development, or HTML coding. When you make a contract with a shop like this, it might form a small team assigned to produce your site. This team might include any of a number of specialists necessary to get the job done:

- A producer or project manager to manage the design and production process
- A designer or creative director to create the site's look and feel
- Artists to create or edit graphics for the site (with direction from the designer)
- Programmers to code the scripts needed to make forms, applets, message boards, chat areas, and other specialized applications run on the site
- Production staff, or HTML coders, to convert into HTML the work of the designer, artists, and your copy writers

Note

The title a web team member uses differs from one company to another. "Webmaster" is generally considered too vague or broad these days; more specific terms are now common. Remember, from one company to the next you might be assigned a configuration of people with very different titles. Minimally, there ought to be a producer or project manager assigned who will be your primary contact throughout the project.

Most e-commerce initiatives will work with small, medium, or large web shops rather than large ad agencies. To sort through how to approach, get bids from, select, and work with web shops of any size or type, read on.

About Independent Contractors

Very small, independent operators in the web shop business sometimes consist of only the owner, a one-person-band who does…well, everything. That person might sometimes dip into the same pool of freelancers the mid-sized web shops do. If you consider working with an independent contractor, keep in mind that the skills and abilities of the contractor will define the boundaries of what you can do with your site. If your project requires a database, find someone who has those skills or has access to a proven subcontractor with those skills. If you need a designer but not much programming, hire someone with design skills, but make sure they're web design skills and that you've communicated about how production will take place. Who, exactly, is going to do the HTML work? Investigate the relationship between the independent contractor and any freelancers, and make sure everyone involved knows who is doing what and that they are qualified and can work as a team.

> **Note**
>
> One advantage of using smaller shops is that they often take on only one big project at a time. You can get the full attention of a project manager from beginning to end. But a disadvantage is that an independent operator who is in the middle of another project when you accept his or her bid might have to finish up that project before starting on yours.

Using Multiple Vendors

Mixing and matching vendors has the advantage of netting you the expertise of specialists; however, it can add to your managerial overhead. If two or more vendors haven't worked together before or don't have complementary work methods, ironing out project details, communications paths, and potential problems can drive costs (and your blood pressure) right through the roof.

Nonetheless, sometimes the most practical route is to outsource technical implementation of at least some portion of your site to a programming shop, and give design to someone else. In some cases, an otherwise highly-qualified shop is lacking one key player, compelling you to hire another shop to work alongside the first.

If you must work with multiple vendors, see to it that top-down understanding of roles and responsibilities is in place. Have high-level people representing each vendor attend the early meetings, and make sure they understand the project's scope as well as who's who and how they'll work together. Someone has to be top dog. Someone has to act as "general contractor." Decide up front who that will be and make sure everyone knows.

Chapter 9: Working with Web Shops, Developers, or Teams

Find the Right Vendor

Word-of-mouth referral is often the best method when it comes to finding a contractor or vendor. If you can (sometimes competitive rivalries rule this out), contact the managers of e-commerce sites you admire and ask who created their site. Alternatively, you can look online for potential contractors or vendors. Yahoo! provides listings of designers and other web shops, as does Microsoft bCentral. You can also find referrals through professional organizations such as the Association of Internet Professionals, Webgrrls, or SFWoW. Or you can ask around for local listings; in the San Francisco area, for example, people seeking web shops or contractors are often referred to Craig's List (*www.craigslist.org*), a well-known website.

When you get the names of various vendors, take a look at their sites and the sites they list as those of their clients. Later in this chapter, you'll learn in more detail what you should look for in assessing candidates; at this juncture, just get a sense of who's who and try to narrow the field to the vendors that are of real interest. To begin, let's focus on what the project is and how to communicate that to potential vendors.

Define the Project

The one single factor that leads to the bloating of a budget and failure to meet timelines is the lack of clearly-defined expectations. It's plain and simple—poorly defined or undefined expectations lead to poorly executed websites. Freelance project manager Gloria Keene says "I was asked to step in to complete a project when its manager left unexpectedly. A vendor had been hired to create the design and another to develop the back end. The outgoing project manager had little experience and she started everyone out with specs that were vague and incomplete. We soon found ourselves in a meeting where the goal was to finalize details and get started with the actual production. At one point one vendor turned to the other and said something about 'when you start coding,' and the other vendor said 'no, you're doing the coding.' It turned out none of the players had included doing the actual [HTML] coding in their bids."

To get the results you want in your website, whether you are jobbing it out to a shop, insourcing it, or outtasking parts of it, your first task (once you have developed your strategy) is to put in writing what you want. The more information you provide, and the clearer it is, the more likely you are to get the result you want. A written request for a bid is known as a *request for proposal* (RFP). Providing potential vendors with RFPs assures you that when the bids come in they'll be similar enough in scope to allow you to make an apples-to-apples comparison.

As you discuss (in writing) your project with those who might execute your plan, be prepared to cover these points:

- The deliverable product, described as clearly as possible. Use the specs or design document you wrote based on the discussion in Chapter 7 as the basis of a summary. You'll recall that you wrote that document to communicate to those working on the site how it would look and function; give vendor candidates an abridged version and follow up with a designated contact person by giving them the full details before work begins.

- Any approval points or benchmarks required on your end. (Examples include marketing approval, a legal review, signoffs from executives or others.)

- The timeline you anticipate. You'll set the deadline for launch; the vendor will describe its production process and tell you whether your dates can be met. An outline of the production process can translate into an overview of the project's schedule; both sides should understand whether these dates are simply goals or real deadlines. You might want to establish consequences for missed deadlines for both sides; the consequence of a missed deadline on the part of the client might be simply a delay, while the consequence of a missed deadline on the vendor's side might be a reduction in payment (a penalty). Alternatively and more positively, you can offer bonuses for meeting deadlines rather than penalties for missing them.

- Whether the vendor's services should include announcing and promoting the site (if it's a full-service vendor you're dealing with). Will you expect them to submit your site's URL to search engines, indexes, and portals? Are there any specialty portals you want included? Will your public relations people make announcements to the media and appropriate discussion groups, or will the vendor? (See Chapter 12 for more on promoting a site.)

- What maintenance services you expect to be included, if any. Will you want the vendor to stay with the project after launch to provide bug fixes or other improvements based on user feedback? (You'll have to discuss with potential vendors whether that will involve a separate contract or be included, as it might be in a full-service contract.)

Now refer again to the mission statement you created after reading Chapter 1. Keep those goals in mind as you review the style, experience, skills, and references of various candidates.

Look at Style

Although some design shops (and vendors of other sorts) can provide a wide range of looks, most work in a certain style or put a certain spin on what they do. You need to make sure the style of any designer you select fits the project at hand. If your mission is to provide customer support for your health care products marketed to seniors, for example, a shop that specializes in artsy, postmodern design and hip, leading-edge copy is just not going to be appropriate.

Similarly, programmers and developers put their own spin on what they do. Some might specialize in building custom transaction systems from the ground up (like a fully-tailored suit that will fit you and only you perfectly) while others customize existing products to provide a transaction system (more like an off-the-rack suit with the cuffs and sleeves altered as needed).

The best way to assess the style of various shops is to look not at their sites but at their clients' sites. Try to find out exactly what role the shop had in each case, consider how closely it matches what you need, and look to see how well the shop succeeded in those cases that most closely match yours.

Evaluate Skill and Experience

Experience counts in all matters, but in the e-commerce world just exactly what counts as experience and how much experience it is possible to have are big questions. To appropriately assess experience, research the backgrounds of the individuals who make up the shop's team. E-commerce is still in its infancy, so most people working in the field are either new to it or bring to it background from some other field. Some have rich experience gleaned from industries such as publishing, print design, marketing, and programming; others are fresh out of spanking-new certificate programs. Those who bring experience with them need to have a fresh take based on the differences between their former industries and e-commerce; those fresh out of school might not have the related experience you need. Consider carefully how much experience you need and of what sort.

Almost no one was working in web design, development, or business before 1995. Anyone who tells you in 2001, for example, that he or she has ten years of experience in e-commerce must have a unique perspective on what that means. Question exactly what that person claims to have been doing. Do they mean they had email in 1994? That's no credential for e-commerce or web design. Were they publishing content on gopher (a forerunner of the Web)? Were they designing electronic graphics first for computer game developers, then for multimedia companies? That's more relevant. "Years of experience" can mean relevant, related experience, but anyone who claims to have been directly involved in e-commerce or web design or development before 1995 is probably not understanding your question.

Also, while designers and artists in print and advertising media are required to have skill with color, layout, and visual balance, designers who work on websites also have to know how to convert graphics that include deeply saturated color into electronic files that are small enough to be transferred across the Internet quickly. Not just any designer can do web design: unfortunately, many fine designers don't know that the skills they've honed for designing for print don't prepare them for designing for the Web. It's unwise to hire a designer with no web experience to design your site, even if he or she is otherwise qualified in the field, and even if the site is to be implemented by someone else. A designer who has no web experience simply does not know the constraints and requirements of designing for the Web.

On the technical side, you might think that programming experience is programming experience, but it's not. Programming for the Web takes a variety of forms and some specific skills. Someone with experience developing spreadsheet applications or video games might not have the programming skills or mix of experience necessary for e-commerce programming. New technologies for e-commerce appear at lightning speed; talent, diligence, and even passion are required to keep up and to distinguish hype from practical utility.

Chapter 9: Working with Web Shops, Developers, or Teams

Any web shop can tell you quickly about the backgrounds and skills of its team members. How many jobs a shop or an individual has handled is less revealing than what the shop or individual did on those projects and how those contributions led to the client site's success. Relevant experience is what counts.

When a vendor offers examples of its experience, ask how success was defined in those projects. Also ask whether and when those success benchmarks were reached. If yours will be a sales site and the vendor is describing a successful endeavor that's similar, ask if the shop followed up after launch to find out whether success had been achieved? If so, do they know what impact their input had? Did sales increase as much as or more than predicted? Did the customer base grow into previously untapped markets? Was the client satisfied with the process of delivering and handling those sales?

Note
You can interview candidates after you get bids, or interview them briefly as part of a screening process before you get bids, and then follow up with a more detailed interview later.

Judge Quality of Interaction

How well vendors hear you as you communicate your plans, and how they respond to feedback, changes, and guidance has a big impact on the success of your endeavor and on your stress level. As you interview vendor candidates, do you sense that you will get what you need and have a good experience working with these people? How can you tell? Consider not just how often a vendor communicates and how quick their response to your communication is, but also in what style the candidate communicates. Do they understand you when you speak and respond appropriately to what you say or request? Do they use jargon without regard for your understanding? Do they ask questions to clarify what they need to know? How willing they are to maintain communications? What office hours do they keep, and how available are they (if necessary) during off hours?

Ask specific questions. How many clients do they expect team members to maintain? (Is your project going be put on hold for some other deadline?) Will the vendor work directly with your ISP or in-house IS group to coordinate installation and future updates of your new website? Does the vendor expect you to manage communications between them and your ISP? (If they do, you just need to know this up front and the vendor will have to provide you with the necessary information.) As you discuss details, note whether the vendor's people respond completely or with half comments or vague allusions. Ask how proactive the vendor will be in coordinating with your marketing or content development people, and whether the vendor expects complete, final copy to be delivered to them. Will they be able to accept last-minute changes? Listen to the content of the answers, but also to tone and nuances of vocabulary. Avoid vendors whose communications reveal the possibility of arrogance, griping, or blaming; it's generally a lot more pleasant to work with people who are respectful, positive, and responsible.

> ### *Tip*
>
> If you are going to be working with multiple vendors, try to get your final candidates together for a meeting before you sign everyone up. Note how they interact with each other as well as with you or your team. If, for example, one company is more responsive and communicative while the other is balking or suspicious of its new colleagues, the two are not going to work well together. It's better to know that and address it now than to find out during the project.

Watch Out for Red Flags

As you interview vendors, watch out for indicators of trouble. If you are trying to job out original site design, and a designer presents you only with a menu of predefined templates, you are not being heard. If you have described two or three goals your site should accomplish and the vendor comes back with a plan for addressing just one, you are not being heard. If you provide a potential vendor with a list of your competitors' sites and the vendor comes back with a plan mimicking one or more of them rather than presenting an original approach, you are not talking to a creative vendor. And if the vendor quotes a price or presents a proposal without first hearing in detail what you have in mind, you are probably dealing with an amateur. If red flags arise as you interview potential vendors, pause to investigate whatever makes you uncomfortable. Ask more questions. Clarify your intentions. And if you find that a certain shop has all the qualities you need but seems to communicate poorly, be especially diligent in getting details in writing.

Chapter 9: Working with Web Shops, Developers, or Teams

Evaluate Quotes

In a best-case scenario, you'll get quotes from perhaps three potential vendors and the quotes will cover points similar enough to allow you to compare these quotes directly. Your best tool for getting such quotes is the specs list detailed in the RFP (mentioned earlier). Of course, you will look at the bids to see which is lowest (an easy task if the quotes are based on similar specs); you'll probably also take into account the experience you've had in getting the quotes. The lowest bid is not always the best bid; sometimes the lowest bid is lowest because a lesser degree of service or commitment is involved. If the lowest quote is from a potential vendor who has been slow to get the quote to you, for example, you might consider that tardiness an indicator of the quality of service you'll get, which could counteract any potential savings indicated by the low quote.

Let's look briefly at what drives rates in website design and development. The scope of a project, how many staff-hours it will take to complete, and the expenses it might involve are clear determining factors. A web shop's prices can also be affected by the shop's experience, level of service, and reputation. Some shops are so well known they can afford to both charge more and select which clients they'll work with (based on their interest in a project or on the prestige a project might add to the shop's portfolio). That's certainly understandable. But keep in mind that geographic location is also a factor. Web shops and developers in New York City or San Francisco charge more than those in Buffalo or Sacramento. Do higher rates indicate more talent or ability? Maybe. It can be argued that the bigger city's talent pool is larger and that some cities (like New York and San Francisco) have a high concentration of talented people teaching each other new tricks daily, but question whether your site is in need of such cutting-edge skill.

If you have provided an RFP to your potential vendors and one comes back with a bid that is wildly different from the others, consider that a red flag. Look to see whether some piece of the project was dropped out of the bid, whether some cost-cutting shortcut was inserted, whether the shop might be charging more because it is in a different locale or simply because it can. An exceptionally high price might indicate an inflated opinion of worth or it might indicate better service. An exceptionally low price might indicate naïveté, or suggest that the shop is in financial trouble and hungry for business. Look for a shop whose fees are in an acceptable range, and consider that your best bet.

Negotiate Fees

Just about everything in life is negotiable. You can sometimes find room in an estimate to get a justifiable discount. If you decide to negotiate, a counteroffer of perhaps 10 to 30 percent less than the shop's bid might be reasonable, along with a rationale for the lower fee. Offering less, however, is often a good way to start things off on the wrong foot. To make negotiation easier, you can ask that estimates for your project be submitted in some modular form (so many dollars for this part, so many for that part, and so on) so you can scale back your plans if necessary. Also, if you get a bid that's beyond your budget but you want to work with that vendor for other reasons, you can ask for the vendor's assistance in reviewing the bid and determining where you can scale back to fit into your budget. You might be able to scan your own art, for example, or rely on a two-step approval process instead of endless rounds of review by heads of four departments.

Get References that Count

Ask prospective vendors to supply you with three or more references that include current or recent clients whose projects were similar to yours in scope and purpose. You can do this either before you get bids or you can wait until you've narrowed the field to one or two top candidates and get references only for them. When you request references, ask for the name of a decision-making person who worked with the candidate, their address and phone number, and a URL for the project involved. Start by looking at the websites. Then contact the reference and interview him or her, asking questions such as these:

- Who managed your project at the vendor's end? What was that person's name and title? How was his or her professionalism demonstrated? How did he or she handle challenges or problems? Did you deal directly with anyone else? Who, and how did that go?
- Did *deliverables* (certain items that have set due dates) arrive on time and in the form you expected? How did the vendor manage the schedule? If the schedule slipped, why, and how was that addressed?

Chapter 9: Working with Web Shops, Developers, or Teams

- Was the project completed within budget? What came up to affect the budget? Was feature creep a factor? Did the shop seem more concerned with staying within budget or with pushing extra features and enhancements?
- In general, did the vendor perform as expected? Was the quality of work up to the level of the vendor's stated expertise?
- Would you hire this vendor for another project? Why or why not? How would you work differently with this vendor in the future?

Ask specific questions, take notes, and thank anyone you speak to for their time.

Beware of Feature Creep

If you've ever remodeled your kitchen, you've probably experienced "feature creep": in the course of the project, you change your mind (or give in to persuasion) and get the higher quality sink fixtures, then go with granite countertops instead of faux granite, and maybe get the fridge with the automatic ice maker instead of a simpler model. This gradual adding-on of features or additions as you go along will drive up the cost of a project in no time.

To avoid feature creep, set a budget (see Chapter 2) and stick to it. Ask at every juncture and suggestion what the financial implications of your decisions or ideas might be. Don't be pressured into features that aren't in the best interests of the site. Get individual estimates for additional features, and consider those estimates in the context of whether that bell or whistle is going to contribute to your site's real success. Look for less costly alternatives. Above all, remember that the price you got at the outset of your project was based on the specs you provided. Most shops anticipate and account for a few minor changes in their estimates—small adjustments are inevitable in the course of a project. Major changes and feature enhancements, however, quickly bloat budgets. You can't expect your vendors to monitor how changes will affect your budget. It's your job to keep your costs in line.

Deliver Specs and Firm Up Details

Once you've sorted out the bids, talked to references, and finally selected a vendor, it's time to hand over detailed specs. You also need to settle a few more details. Clarify with the vendor these issues:

- The process for the project. Every company has its own way of working and you'll need to make sure you understand how this vendor does things. You might also need to ask for some adjustments in the procedures to accommodate how you do things. As an example, if you are having a full-service shop create your site, you'll need to know how the site will be placed on your server. Can the shop do this for you? Or will your files be delivered on a zip disk or some other portable storage medium? (See Chapter 10 for more on server and hosting options.)

- How contingencies will be covered. Things change, and things go wrong. That's just life. Of course the more prepared you are, the less likely it is that things will go wrong. Part of preparation is anticipating how you will cope when things do go wrong. Establish some guidelines for who will do what if and when the unexpected occurs.

- On what basis payment will occur. Payment is often tied closely to benchmarks such as the delivery of certain items (deliverables). But negotiating for *payment based on acceptance* of deliverables provides you with more certainty that you'll be paying for what you want rather than something that's just in the ballpark. It also provides you with the leverage you might need to get what you want. The agreement, then, is that when you get what you specified, you'll pay. Just remember that when payment is based on acceptance, you also need to specify to the vendor in advance whose approval is needed.

- How payment will occur. Most companies assume payment will be within thirty days of invoicing. But if, for example, your company issues checks only once a month or every two weeks and that means payment might sometimes take forty-five days, tell the vendor up front. This will keep everyone's expectations in line with reality.

> ### A Note on Nondisclosure Agreements
>
> A *nondisclosure agreement* (NDA) is a document that protects confidentiality. It specifies an agreement between the signing parties that confidential information disclosed in the course of doing business will not be revealed to others. NDAs are standard in many modern contracts, but you might not find one in the contract of specific vendors. NDAs can also exist as stand-alone documents that are signed before a project is described or when the project's contract is signed. If your website will include features, products, or services you do not want leaked to others before launch, you can ask that NDAs be signed. An attorney can draw up an NDA for you to use.

Understand the Contract

As the saying goes, a verbal contract isn't worth the paper it's printed on; before the project begins, you need one that's signed by both parties. A contract outlines what you expect from the vendor and what the vendor expects from you. It also spells out how and when payment will occur and what will happen if expectations aren't met. In a good contract, all the important questions one might ask about the business arrangement should be answered in writing. Remember that it's wise to have your attorney review contracts before you sign them, and it's unwise to try to write a contract yourself. Attorneys see things in contracts the rest of us don't see. As part of their jobs, they erase ambiguities and clarify language to avoid misunderstanding.

> **Note**
>
> Who owns what when a website is created is a deep and complex question. A single web page can contain many elements (writing, images composed of other images, code, and scripts) that might be licensed from others. For an introduction into the issues involved, review Chapter 3.

A contract is a document of mutual agreement. Until it's signed, its terms might be negotiable, but once it is signed it's binding. Before negotiations begin, have in mind which terms you feel might be negotiable and which could be deal breakers. (The vendor will have done the same.) You or your vendor might have a standard contract you can use as a starting point. Yours will have been written to your benefit, as theirs will have been written to their own. Theirs might be a better standard contract than yours for the type of work they do (and reading it might provide you with insight into their business practices). Yours will probably be written with your interests at its core but might not address their business or processes. If and when you get into any contract negotiations, consult your attorney.

Remember Maintenance After Launch

Your site is not going to take care of itself after launch. Like any business, it will need maintenance. You must clean up bad links, maintain and improve service, post new product offers, remove old products and pages, and change the site to adapt to an evolving market. You must also promote your e-commerce site to attract traffic and boost business. Who will do all this, and how?

It's easy to focus on launching the site and forget about what's going to happen the next day and thereafter. This is a common pitfall. It's urgent to consider who will do routine and special maintenance after launch—you, or the vendor? The web shop you hire might be interested only in producing your site, planning to hand all concerns thereafter back to you. If you and your staff have the skills for dealing with this, that's fine. But require a warranty or time period during which the shop is required to fix any problems that occur. You can also request basic training for your staff; the web shop might agree, for example, to deliver the site and then train someone at your end to make changes and handle maintenance tasks. The shop might provide templates, written instructions, or even on-site, hands-on training. This can be a great solution, but if you go with it, also agree on how your requests for assistance will be handled after basic training.

In a more full-service scenario, the web shop delivers and installs the site, announces it and perhaps submits its URL to search engines, and even performs day-to-day maintenance after launch. The shop might also implement daily updates to the content, upgrade the functionality, provide detailed performance analyses, and more. An ongoing relationship such as this requires a clear maintenance contract or retainer agreement.

Chapter 9: Working with Web Shops, Developers, or Teams

Manage the Project

Overarching management is one thing that should not be outsourced. Someone in-house—either you or another team leader—needs to be the one who manages your project. Good project management is crucial; it can lead directly to satisfaction at your end and to building the type of positive relations with vendors that result in the success of your project.

Ending a project on an upbeat note seals the business relationship and puts both parties in a position to extend or resume the relationship when other projects present themselves. A shop that has done its best work for you (and that now knows your site in detail) can be a time saver in the future. Such a vendor will be able to pick up future projects and run with them with little preparation and less supervision. You know you can trust them, and they know you are a good client.

A positive relationship results when both the vendor and the client define responsibilities, keep promises, manage expectations, and keep communications clear. It's up to the vendor to deliver what has been promised, but it's up to the client to specify the scope of the project, monitor delivery, and tend the budget. It's also a client's responsibility to pay on time. Thirty days means thirty days, not forty-five or sixty. To maintain good vendor relations, keep your part of the bargain. If you do this and work with solid companies, you could find yourself with more than just a vendor. You might find that you actually have a valued partner.

Chapter 10

Understanding the Back End and Hosting

You don't have to be a general contractor to own a house, and you don't have to be an automotive engineer to own and operate a car. Likewise, you don't have to be a programmer or a database developer for your company to have an e-commerce website. Even so, you should know enough about the back end of a website so that you can discuss the maintenance of your website intelligently and make smart business decisions. Just as being knowledgeable about construction enables you to buy a house with a sound structure and knowing the basics of mechanics enables you to see that your car is running smoothly, being at least conversant in back end technologies helps you to assure that your e-commerce website remains in good working condition. You'll be far better enabled to make solid business choices about your site and troubleshoot some issues yourself if you understand the general technological underpinnings.

Part 3: Build Your E-Commerce Website

> **Note**
>
> This chapter is meant to help you make effective management decisions about the behind-the-scenes technology that drives your e-commerce website. It will make you more conversant, but it is not meant to make you into a developer.

The components that make up the back end of a website were defined and described in Chapter 1. To refresh your memory, the backstage, technical stuff that makes your e-commerce website work includes the following components:

- The web server that delivers the web pages
- The database server that stores and delivers product information
- The mail server that sends out newsletters
- The transaction systems—*scripts* (special software programs), encryption systems, shopping cart software, and more—that enable your site to accept credit card payments

Let's start our exploration of the back end by looking at what a server is.

> **Note**
>
> If you create and run your e-commerce site using a packaged solution such as Microsoft bCentral Site Manager, you don't have to deal with the issues of choosing and maintaining the platform, servers, and transaction systems at all. The packaged solution will have made those choices for you and maintenance will be part of the package deal. However, if you are deciding whether to host the site yourself, host it elsewhere, or go with a more sophisticated packaged solution, you'll want to know what the issues are. Read on.

What Is a Server?

A server is essentially a computer that "serves" (by providing files or data in response to requests from client computers); the tricky part, though, is that several "servers" can exist on one computer, because what makes the

Chapter 10: Understanding the Back End and Hosting

computer a server is the *server software* that runs on it. On a single computer, you can have a web server serving your web pages; a database server enabling any databases (product information, content, a dealer or outlet locator); and a mail server handling your email newsletters or discussion group. Alternatively, you can have just one type of server on one computer and another on another computer. For the purposes of this chapter, when "server" is mentioned, it will mean a computer that has server software running on it. When server software is discussed, it will be referred to as a specific type of server software.

> **Note**
>
> Whether to run a database server and a web server on the same computer is a decision that's often based on performance. Requiring a server to do double duty can make it run more slowly, such that a user accessing the site might experience a slower response from the site.

Your server (or servers, if you need more than one) can be *hosted* (housed) *onsite* (within your premises) or *offsite* (at an ISP that accepts responsibility for maintaining your server on the ISP's premises). Alternatively, your server software can be run on a computer owned by the ISP, at the ISP's location. In that case, the server might be shared by many of the ISP's other customers.

> **Note**
>
> The difference between a website and a server is that a website runs on a *server*, which is a computer with *server software* running on it; the *website* is the sum of the content and back end systems running on the server.

To some degree, the questions you address in deciding what server, *platform* (operating system), and hosting options to go with are chicken-or-egg questions. For example, whether you host your server onsite or offsite can have bearing on which server solution you choose, and that influences which platform you use. If you have already determined the platform, your choices in server software will be narrowed. Let's take a look at platforms.

Part 3: Build Your E-Commerce Website

Selecting a Platform

The platform your website runs on is, simply speaking, the operating system used on the computer that serves your website. You cannot use a desktop operating system (such as Microsoft Windows 98) as the platform for your web server. While desktop operating systems are fine for your desktop computer or your laptop, they simply are not designed for serving a website 24/7 (24 hours a day, seven days a week). A web server must be very robust to perform the varied tasks required for serving a website (or a website's database, mail server, or transaction system). It also has to have especially powerful security features. So among Microsoft products, your best bet is an operating system such as those versions of Microsoft Windows 2000 created for hosting servers, or Microsoft Windows NT.

When choosing among all possible platforms for your website, take into account these issues:

- Any expertise you, your technical staff, your developer, or your web shop might already have; tapping existing knowledge can save the time, trouble, and expense of retraining people on a new operating system.
- The platform your preferred tools (such as HTML editors and scripting tools) work with, the servers they support, and the platform those servers run on. The tools you use might also come down to the expertise your team already has. As an example, Microsoft FrontPage creates websites that work best when hosted on Windows 2000 or Windows NT servers, because FrontPage takes advantage of certain features offered by those platforms.
- Your budget, obviously enough; some operating systems cost more than others. Don't forget to take into account, however, the expense of training people and the expense of hardware.

Note

You definitely don't want to pay for your developer's or web shop's time as they tackle the learning curve associated with new software. If your preferred developer or shop is proficient in a certain platform, go with that. If your preferred platform is unfamiliar to a developer or shop and you feel strongly about your preferred platform, interview other candidates.

Chapter 10: Understanding the Back End and Hosting

Choosing a Server

A server can be acquired through an outright purchase, a lease from the manufacturer, or a rental from your ISP. If you host your site on your ISP's server, you don't have to acquire a physical server at all; you will share the ISP's server with other organizations and individuals. The advantage to this is that you don't have to invest in your own server, while the disadvantage (as developers will tell you) is that you might encounter limitations in your platform and server options as well as with what you can do on the server. As you compare server options, pay special attention to performance, reliability, and support; these issues are described in the next few sections.

Issues of Performance

The level of performance a server offers is basically defined by the number of users the server can handle. A more robust web server with web server software on it can support more website users at any given time than a less capable server can. Performance is affected by many factors; the most important among these are the type of processor the server has, how much memory the computer has, and what type of hard disk it uses.

How Processors Affect Performance

Your desktop computer has a single processor, called the central processing unit (CPU). Unlike desktop computers, servers can have several processors. (This is part of what makes your desktop computer an inappropriate choice as a server.) It's actually quite common for a server running web server software, for example, to have two or even four processors. (You never have three or five processors; you can only have one of them or an even number of them.) While describing what level of performance a server offers is not as simple as saying "a computer with two processors is twice as powerful as one with a single processor," it is true that the more processors a computer has, the more powerful it is.

The speed of the processors is also a factor in performance. Speed is usually measured in megahertz (MHz), and the higher the number, the faster the processor (for example a 400MHz processor is faster than a 200MHz processor). And finally, the type of processor impacts the speed. More recent models are generally introduced to provide greater speed and better overall performance. Pentium II processors are faster than Pentium processors, for example.

How Memory Affects Performance

A server has to be capable of managing many tasks at once These tasks can include responding to requests for web pages, querying a database for information, or running the transaction software required to process credit card transactions. Each task the server performs requires memory (random access memory, or RAM), and the more memory your server has, the more tasks it can perform simultaneously. It is common for servers to have at least 128 megabytes (MB) of RAM, but more RAM is preferable. As of this writing, 512MB or even 1024MB of RAM is common in robust servers.

How the Hard Disk Affects Performance

The server's hard disk defines its potential in a number of ways. The size of the hard disk indicates how much can be stored on it, and given that a website is made up of software, code, art, other graphics files, and scripts—all of which need storage space—the size of the hard disk dictates how large and complex the site can be. These days, the smallest hard disks are between four and eight gigabytes (GB). To determine how much hard disk storage you'll need for your website, add up these components:

- Space required by the operating system (100MB to a few GBs or more depending on platform you select)
- Space needed for your website files (pages, images, video, sound files, and so on)
- Space for files required by the operating system, such as log files (at least 10 percent of the total disk space)
- A "cushion" of extra space that the operating system can use for its own purposes (another 10 percent of the total disk space)

Tip

You can't estimate the 10 percent you need for the log files and the 10 percent you need for a cushion until you add up how much you need, and that 20 percent is going to be part of what you need. What to do? Simply assume you need 10–30 times the amount of hard disk space the operating system needs and then work up or down from there. For example, if the operating system needs 1GB, assume you need 30GB plus 20 percent.

In addition to size, the type of hard disk your server has will also directly affect performance. Many desktop computers use Integrated Device Electronics (IDE) hard disks, which are optimized for access to a single file at a time. On your server, a small computer systems interface (SCSI) hard disk will be more up to the task at hand. SCSI (pronounced "scuzzy") hard disks are very fast and are optimized for accessing many files at once. This is crucial for multiprocessing and will make or break your website when it gets the traffic you hope it will have.

Note

Another aspect of server performance is based on the type of content your website delivers. Serving static HTML pages puts very little demand on a web server. But if your site serves dynamically, meaning pages are generated from a database, and uses some form of middleware (see the section on middleware later in this chapter), much more server power is required, even to serve the same number of pages. Your developer can help you determine what additional requirements there will be based on your middleware package and any dynamically-served content you plan to include.

Issues of Reliability

The importance of reliability boils down to this: if your server crashes, users cannot access your website. A crash can result in lost revenue, lost credibility and loyalty, and the lost time it takes to troubleshoot the problem and correct it. This downtime is expensive and should definitely be avoided. To ensure reliability, buy, lease, rent, or use a computer specifically built to act as a server. You can also beef up the hard disk by specifying a *redundant array of independent disks* (commonly known as a RAID disk) instead of the plain SCSI disk mentioned earlier. RAID uses multiple SCSI hard disks and stores files on them in such a way that if one of the disks fails, the system will continue to function.

To assure even greater reliability, ask your developer to build redundancy into your systems. *Redundancy* is simply a matter of using one or more additional components as backup systems so that if one component fails, another takes over automatically. An entire server can be added as a backup, ensuring that if the main server fails, the redundant server takes over some or all operations. Redundancy is also often provided for *power supplies* (components in all computers that convert the electricity provided by the power company into the type the computer actually needs) and *network connections* (components that plug computers into local networks or an ISP's network). When a redundant power supply is added to a server, the server can continue running even if its primary power supply fails. An acronym you might run across in discussions of redundancy and power supplies is *UPS*—it means uninterruptible power supply. A UPS provides a backup to the electricity supplied by the power company.

> **Note**
>
> Providing for redundancy does require more hardware and software, so it can bump up the cost of your back end pretty quickly. Whether this is an advisable investment depends on whether your e-commerce website can stand any downtime.

Issues of Support

Most of the time, your server will hum along just fine, but even well-maintained servers have been known to crash, and you must be prepared for that. A server might crash because it is overloaded, because its hard disk gave out, or because a power surge fried its power supply.

You (or your developer or your tech staff) can prevent some crashes by monitoring your system. This can be accomplished because servers track themselves and generate *log files* (regular listings of all the activities the server has performed in a given time period) to allow for such monitoring. Tech people also often monitor the system by using utilities that provide reports on usage. Some of these utilities convert the log files into reports, making them easier to read. Others monitor the server and present animated graphical charts showing current usage. If you or your tech people see that your server is running at 75 percent of its capacity, you are pushing its limits. Just as you don't want to run your car at its highest speed at all times (because that creates greater wear and tear and prevents you from having any capacity to accelerate when you need to), you don't want to max out your server. You need a cushion for when you get spikes in website traffic, for example.

Chapter 10: Understanding the Back End and Hosting

Support for a server includes monitoring it, troubleshooting any problems that arise, and solving the problems you find. Support can be provided by the hardware manufacturer, the server software developer, your ISP, or your tech staff; who is responsible for what depends on what the agreements with these entities are and on the nature of the problem. Your first line of defense is your tech staff or your ISP's tech staff if you have a server support agreement with your ISP.

Support contracts are sometimes sold separately from the server itself, so keep in mind that when you purchase, lease, or rent a server, the deal won't necessarily include support. Similarly, when you rent space on a server from an ISP, the deal might or might not include support. But getting a support contract is a very good idea; this is not the time to skimp. You might need support only rarely, but when you need it, you *really* need it. Without a contract for ongoing support, you'll find yourself scouting around for someone or some place to do the job. With poor support, it may take as long as a week to fix a problem. That's a lot of downtime for even the least mission-critical websites.

> **Note**
>
> If your company has an information services (IS) or information technology (IT) department, a vendor, in-house technicians, or an outside consultant might already be in place to provide support for your server. If your website is hosted at your ISP, support might be provided for in the contract with the ISP. You must have a support plan in place, but you don't necessarily have to purchase a support contract from your servers' manufacturer.

Some server vendors will sell you two-hour or three-hour support contracts. That means they'll guarantee a technician at your site within two or three hours of a reported problem, regardless of the day or time you call. Other contracts guarantee same-day or next-day response and repair. When you select among service contract options, remember that downtime can cost you dearly, and compare the cost of the service contract to the cost of lost revenue and credibility.

> ### A Word on Technical Support
>
> Technical support for your e-commerce endeavor should encompass three general areas: the hardware; the software, including the web server software and the database; and the website itself, including the content, the transaction system, and so on. It's unusual to get support for all of these areas from the same person or team. Even if you have a technical staff, they'll sometimes need assistance from others who have even more expertise with the specific hardware, software, or coding in question. When you purchase or lease a server, or when you rent space on one, clarify what the support agreements are for both the hardware and the software. Likewise, when you have a developer create a site, database, or transaction system for you, clarify what the support agreement is. Not all support is created equally. Prices and levels of service vary widely, and it's important to know what you're paying for as well as how diligently promises and guarantees are kept. Check references just as you would when hiring a web shop (see Chapter 9 for more detail).

All About Hosting

When people speak of hosting, they are referring to where a server is located. It can be at your location or at an ISP; it is also possible to rent space on your ISP's server (at the ISP's location) and host your site in that rented space. Each option has its special pros and cons.

Hosting Your Server at Your Location

Until recently, only mid-sized to large companies could consider hosting their own servers. This was because hosting a server required a dedicated connection to the Internet, which was prohibitively expensive or simply unavailable to smaller operations. (Small technology companies found this cost effective, but small non-technology businesses found it too expensive.) However, with the availability of high-bandwidth connections such as digital subscriber lines (DSL) and cable modems, hosting your own server is now a more viable option. It's possible, but is it a wise move?

Chapter 10: Understanding the Back End and Hosting

> **Note**
>
> Some companies that provide DSL or cable modem access do not allow web servers to be run on the lines they provide. They offer service only for personal use (such as web browsing). If you are considering DSL or cable modem service, review the provider's contract carefully.

If you host your own server, you will have full control over it. You can use the software you prefer (within limitations of the hardware) without having to consider what your ISP prefers or can support. On the other hand, you (or your staff) will be responsible for keeping the server running around the clock. When something goes wrong at 4:00 in the morning, you will have to fix it. Depending on what the problem is, this might mean getting the phone company or cable company out to address a connectivity issue, or it might mean someone (you or your staff) addressing a server crash. If you have full-time, expert technical staff hosting your site at your location on your server, the latter solution might be an option, but for most companies, it isn't advisable.

If you do host your own site, you'll want to install a firewall to protect your web server and the other computers on your local network from trespassers. A *firewall*, shown in Figure 10.1, is a system that simply puts up a selective roadblock. It allows outsiders to access your web server but prevents them from accessing any of your other computers.

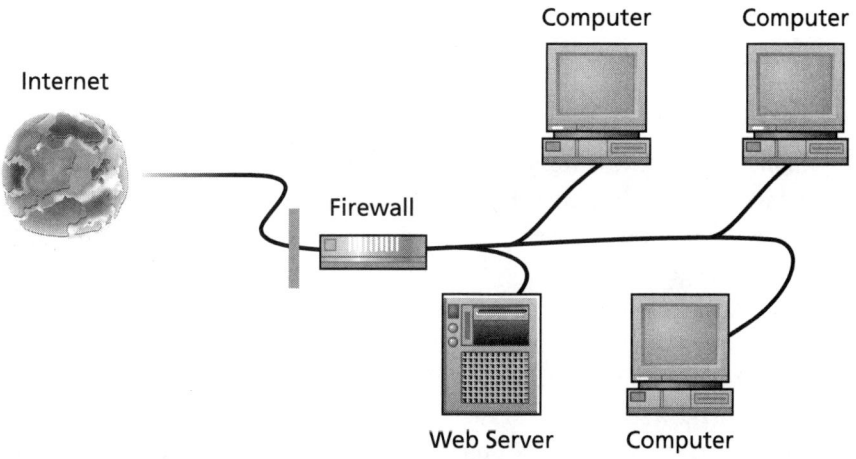

Figure 10.1
A firewall protects your internal systems from the outside world.

Hosting Your Server at an ISP

If you host your server at an ISP, you will gain access to their generally high-speed Internet connectivity (most ISPs have multiple T1s or even higher-speed lines). You might also gain access to their staff, which will be available up to full time to monitor and respond to problems. You might have to purchase a separate contract for full support, but at a minimum the ISP's staff will see to it that the connection between your server and the Internet is functioning. (Whether your server is functioning is a separate issue. See "Issues of Support" earlier in this chapter.)

Your ISP might specify some limitations on what platform, server software, and other technologies you can use. If so, this is not an arbitrary set of rules. The ISP is responsible for providing stable, secure, fast connectivity to its clients; to do this, it can't allow anything to disrupt any aspect of its systems. Within limitations imposed by the ISP, if you host your server at the ISP, you can install and use your own software on the server.

> **Note**
>
> The cost of hosting your server at an ISP can range from a few hundred dollars a month to thousands. The pricier options provide more service and usually guarantee that you'll experience less downtime. They generally accomplish this through reliable connections to the Internet and through hiring experienced staff to be on site around the clock. However, it is always wise to look into any guarantees carefully to be sure of both what is being promised and how the promise will be fulfilled.

Hosting Your Site on an ISP's Server

If yours is a smaller business and you want more sophistication than a site created with wizards (such as bCentral Site Manager) offers, you might find hosting your site on an ISP's server the most economical and attractive option. You'll get space on a robust server without incurring the cost of buying, leasing, or renting a whole server. You'll also get the advantage of a professional staff that monitors and maintains the server all the time. (These people will not, however, monitor and maintain your website, unless you make a separate contract for that.) You—and everyone else who's using space on the server—can have your own domain name. You can run your own database transaction system (within whatever limitations the ISP states), but the server software will be determined, provided, and maintained by the ISP. The next section describes issues you'll want to address in choosing and dealing with an ISP.

Choosing and Working with an ISP

You don't have to limit your search for an ISP to your immediate geographic region. Scout around for a good deal. (Both MSN and Microsoft bCentral provide information about specific ISPs you can consider.) Research whether the ISPs you're considering provide and are proficient in the platform and server options you prefer. Also consider the issues of redundancy and support described earlier in this chapter.

> ### ISPs, Connectivity, and Bandwidth
>
> Different ISPs offer varying levels of connectivity, and in a professional setting, that's of as much interest as redundancy and support. The issues you need to consider have to do with how the ISP is connected to the Internet. The Internet has several *backbones* (main arteries), which are interconnected. Some ISPs are connected to the backbones; some are simply connected to other, larger ISPs that are then connected to the backbone. The closer an ISP's connection to the backbone, the better the connection is. Also, ISPs that have multiple redundant connections are better able to provide continuous service.
>
> Additionally, ISPs have differing levels of bandwidth to offer. An ISP's *bandwidth* (how much data can be transmitted through the available lines) is affected by the type of lines used and their capacity. T3 lines are faster than T1 lines, for example, because they have more bandwidth. (The DSL or ISDN lines you might have in your office or home are not as fast as T3s and T1s because they have less bandwidth.) ISPs have differing numbers of, say T3s or T1s; this affects how much overall bandwidth they have. When you set up an account with an ISP, you'll be allotted a certain amount of bandwidth. If you need more later, the ISP might charge additional fees for the extra service.

> **Tip**
>
> You do want to choose an ISP within the country you'll be doing business in, because Internet connectivity between countries is unreliable. You also want technicians to be available to answer your questions during your business hours. If your ISP's business hours begin and end three hours earlier or later than yours, ask yourself whether that will that meet your needs.

Your ongoing relationship with your ISP will be well served by clarifying roles and responsibilities. Here are some issues you and your ISP should come to grips with:

- Who will talk to whom when problems arise? Designate a single contact person within your company, and keep in mind that your ISP will probably have several people at their end working various shifts.

- What types of changes on your site are they authorized to make, and what types do you expect them to make? You'll want them to address problems with the server immediately, but remember that it is your website, and you want control of changes to its content and functionality.

- Will they automatically notify you when they find a problem with your website? You certainly don't want to discover the site's down at the moment you try to show it off to associates or potential partners.

- How reliable is their service? What level of uptime do they guarantee? Various ISPs offer differing levels of connectivity, which affects how much uptime they can guarantee.

- How will they handle increases in site traffic? This is an issue regardless of how you've chosen to host your website. If you're hosting your site yourself, you'll need a plan for increasing the speed of your connection to handle any increase in traffic. If your server is located at your ISP or your site is on your ISP's server, you'll need to know what they'll charge for additional bandwidth.

- If you are renting space on your ISP's server, how much hard disk space will they allot to you and what will they charge for additional hard disk space? Usually they'll start by assigning you 20MB to 50MB of hard disk space; if you need more, you'll have to pay for it. Find out both what you'll pay and the procedure for getting more space.

Chapter 10: Understanding the Back End and Hosting

- Do they support the server technologies required to run your site (for example, Microsoft Active Server Pages (ASP) pages or Microsoft SQL Server database access)? Again, this is an issue only if you are hosting your site on your ISP's server. They will probably be willing to support only some technologies and won't want to install new technologies just because you want them.

How all of these issues are handled will vary among ISPs. As mentioned earlier, ISPs often support only the actual Internet connection. They probably won't support the server unless the server in question is theirs and you are renting space on it. If the server is yours and something goes wrong with it, you'll have to address the problem yourself or call someone (not the ISP) to troubleshoot. Some other ISPs provide basic support and will even back up your content on a regular basis. Others provide a higher level of support and will even go so far as to guarantee a certain level of uptime. Of course, one generally pays more for higher levels of support; which level of support is appropriate for you depends upon how crucial it is that your site remain up and running at all times.

Consider a Database

A database is a system that makes organizing, storing, and accessing data easier. It is made up of *records*; each record contains a number of pieces of data. For example, if we use a phone book as a sort of metaphor for a database, we can say that in the phone book, a single record exists for each person listed. Within a database's record are *fields*, which are empty cells into which data is placed. A typical record for a product catalog database would have separate fields for the product name, price, and other distinct pieces of data related to the product.

A collection of records in a database is known as a *table*. A database can be made up of a single table or many tables. There are two basic types of databases:

- Flat file databases include a single table, and all the data is stored in that one table.
- Relational databases allow for the creation of multiple tables. Fields within the tables can then be shared, so that data does not have to be repeated, and complex relationships can exist among the various tables.

A good database is the bedrock of many an e-commerce website. Product catalogs, customer information, and inventory tracking are typically all stored in databases. When a database is created for a website's back end, scripts are written to call forth the data in the database, apply HTML to it, and present it in the form of a web page to users of the website. When a user searches a website's database, he or she enters data into a web page form to submit a *query*, which is simply a question asked of the database.

That's the simple version of website databases. What you can do with a database-backed website is actually much more exciting than that.

The Power of a Database-Backed Website

Simply storing product data in a database allows you to update the information easily, but the real power in a catalog database comes from this one-two combination: users can search the catalog, and the catalog can be coordinated with inventory, ordering, and tracking systems to automate purchase and fulfillment processes. Customers can search on any of the attributes of your products (size, color, price, weight, power, and so on), but they can also make a purchase in just a few steps (or even in one step, if their credit card data has been stored in a customer record in the database). This is possible via database-generated catalog pages linked to the transaction system. Website users can virtually customize a product before purchase (selecting, for example, the color by viewing an image of the product and clicking a "color chooser" to change the product's color). They can find a local dealer or retailer by searching based on city, ZIP code, or the specific products the dealer or retailer carries. When the catalog database is tied into inventory management systems, the customer can be notified immediately as to whether an item is out of stock or on back order. Notification can occur in the form of a message appearing automatically on the order form web page or in the form of an email message generated and sent out automatically.

Databases can be applied to websites in other ways. For example, all of the data supplied by users or customers who register on your site, sign up for your mailing list, participate in your online survey, or complete an online transaction, can be stored in a database. That data can then be sorted, indexed, or categorized to provide you with reports detailing who is visiting your site or buying from your catalog.

A perhaps more surprising opportunity exists in that you can store text, images, and other media in fields in a database and then write scripts to call forth that material and place it into web pages. This is known as creating content dynamically.

> **Note**
>
> When you view websites, you can tell when web pages are being generated dynamically simply by looking at the URL. If the URL doesn't end in a filename with the .html or .htm extension, but instead looks like a line of programming code, a script (represented by the code you see) is likely to be pulling data from a database to create the page.

Storing content in a database and creating pages dynamically makes maintenance of large and complex websites a lot easier. Making changes to the navigation bar, for example, is less complicated if you can do it once in the database and then have the change appear on all pages on the site. That definitely beats making the change, say, 500 times! Also, it is quite possible for content producers who don't know HTML to enter content into a form that automatically drops the content into the database. They can simply type the text into a field, click a button on the form, and the new content will become part of the web page without the necessity of marking it up in HTML.

> **Note**
>
> It's quite common to include in an HTML document a *database call* (a query to the database) that dynamically pulls some content in from the database. This can be quite handy. It allows you to store content that's repeated often on the site in the database. You can then make any change to that content (for example, raising the price of a product) one time in the database, and the change will be automatically replicated wherever that content appears.

Relational Databases vs. Flat File Databases

Relational databases soar where flat file databases fall. A relational database allows you to store a lot of data in multiple tables. Fields can then be shared among the tables. The classic example is a database that contains one table for customers and another for orders. Each customer has a record in the customers table, and each order has a record in the orders table. Each order placed by a certain customer does not have to contain all the information regarding that customer; instead, a link from the order to the customer record (in the customers table) calls forth the customer information.

In a flat file database, only one table exists. Every order would have to include all of the customer information. That means that when Sally places an order on Tuesday and then again on Thursday, both orders have to include all of Sally's identifying data, including her address, credit card information, and so on. This gets really repetitive. What's more, having to manage all those big, bloated records put a severe load on a database server.

Even a relatively small flat file database can have negative impact on server performance; a fairly large and complex relational database places a far lighter load on the server. The downside of using a relational database can be expense. It can cost thousands of dollars just to license the software. Depending on the complexity of the database, you might also need a database server on which to run the database software. Then you generally have to bring in a developer to build the database. A flat file database has to be built by a developer, but it is built from the ground up using no licensed database products, and it requires no special server.

Note

Many small businesses find Microsoft Access a good solution for harnessing the power of relational databases. Access is a relational database designed primarily for desktop computers. It allows multiple tables of information, and lets you create relationships among these tables just as you would using other, more powerful database software. While Access databases cannot support hundreds of users accessing millions of records (like SQL Server can), it can support a few users accessing thousands of records and it performs far better than a flat file database would. And if your web business soars, it is relatively easy to migrate from Access to SQL Server.

Introducing Middleware

Operating between the database and the web server, special software known as *middleware* does the job of transporting data. Various types of middleware exist, each taking a radically different approach to the task it performs. Some allow you to simply add special code (much like HMTL code) into the HTML that defines your web pages to call forth data from the database. Others require you to insert special scripts into the HTML that defines the web pages. Still others require that you use specific authoring tools to create the entire website (rather than creating it with HTML); you then always have to work within the environment of the authoring tool.

When you are selecting middleware, look at compatibility with your database software. Consider, too, whether those who will be using the middleware have the necessary programming expertise. Some middleware requires programming experience, while other middleware requires none. One approach to middleware is Microsoft Active Server Pages, which allow you to insert scripts.

Note

Middleware is not the only option for transferring data from the database to the web server. Traditional programming languages (such as C++ or Visual J++) can be used to create programs that run on the server and manipulate your database. While this requires more expertise than using middleware, the result can be especially efficient and reliable. However, for most purposes, middleware is fine.

Maintaining a Database

Like nearly everything else on a website, the database must be maintained. Maintenance of the database content can be performed by even the most non-technically adept users via easy-to-use forms and other utilities. Some common maintenance tasks that fall into this category include:

- Adding and removing records as your data changes. For example, in the case of a product catalog database, you'll need to add new records as you add new merchandise and remove records as you stop selling items.

- Making changes to the data stored in the database. You might want to change the description of a product or some of the other information you keep in the database. (This is useful if, say, you begin to carry a product in a new color.)

The developer who creates your database system should provide you with simple, password-protected forms that will make adding and changing data easier. These forms might look like nothing more than HTML pages;

you can use your web browser to work with them. While you cannot do backups via a web browser, your developer should identify the procedure for making backups and give you complete, easy-to-follow instructions.

Other maintenance tasks include reviewing log files, monitoring server performance, and verifying that the hard disk is not overloaded. These tasks (similar to those necessary for maintaining a web server) are typically the domain of those more technically adept than the average manager. Do not wait until you have problems to find someone to handle such matters. Establish a maintenance agreement with your database developer when your system is first built. Regular maintenance will save you from unexpected downtime and poor performance.

Make sure someone creates a backup copy of your database regularly (as well as making a backup copy of the rest of your site). Backing up your database is not necessarily included in the regular backup of your site that you, your developer, or your ISP does. Because of the way some databases work, special tools might be needed. Verify with your developer that those tools are in place and backups are occurring.

Also, don't wait until your database crashes to find out whether the backups are good. Have your developer test your backups occasionally by randomly selecting a file or a table from your database and restoring it from the backup.

Caution

When restoring a file to test your backup system, don't overwrite the live database. If it turns out the backup data is bad, you will have caused the very situation you were trying to avoid. Instead, restore the data to your staging server, and test it there. Seeing something restored from the backup is the only way you know for sure that your data is being protected.

The Basics of Transaction Systems

A transaction system is the behind-the-scenes combination of programming, databases, payment paths, and business rules that enables you to sell goods and accept revenue from your customers. The elements that make up most e-commerce transaction systems include the following:

Chapter 10: Understanding the Back End and Hosting

- A catalog (in the form of a database) that lists products available for sale along with data, such as the price, descriptive information, and perhaps a photo, describing those products.

- A database that stores customer information (at least temporarily) as well as the customer's choices about shipping and payment methods, and tracks purchases during the transaction process.

- A shopping cart (a set of scripts or programming) that tracks what customers select for purchase while the customers continue to browse the website. When a customer clicks a Buy button, the scripts that make up the shopping cart system add the item of interest to a record in the database that deals with purchases.

- A purchase system (more scripts and programming) that pulls together the selections the customer made from the catalog (information from the shopping cart) and the payment and shipping information (from the customer database).

- A credit transaction processing system (usually consisting of licensed software) provided by a company, such as CyberCash (*www.cybercash.com*) or CyberSource (*www.cybercash.com*), that facilitates online credit transactions.

- A connection or interface triggering a fulfillment system that sends the order to a warehouse or otherwise sees to it that the ordered items will be shipped.

All of these elements work behind the scenes in tandem when a user makes a purchase. In the best possible scenario, the user will be aware only of a few steps in the sales and transaction process: select the item or items of interest, view the order, enter credit card information, select a shipping method, and submit the order. A confirmation web page or email will signal that the order was successfully entered.

But behind the scenes, a complex system of programming, security-enforcing encryption, databases, credit and financial information transmission, and order fulfillment is going on. From a business perspective, it is most important to understand the necessity of a high level of security and the nature of the relationships with the various financial institutions involved.

Security in E-Commerce Transaction Systems

Protecting the security of credit card data as it is stored and transmitted is crucial to the success of an e-commerce transaction system. Without assurance that their credit card data is safe, customers simply won't buy. And security breaches undermine the credibility of both the site experiencing them and the e-commerce industry as a whole.

When security is working well, it is such a behind-the-scenes process that it goes unnoticed. Security in e-commerce is accomplished through a combination of using *encryption* (scrambling data so that even if it is read by trespassers it will be unusable); placing barriers such as firewalls in the way of intruders; and creating policies regarding who has what sort of access to the confidential data. When you set up an e-commerce transaction system, a certain amount of the system will be within your area of responsibility. For example, it will be up to you or your staff or developer to make secure your servers and any forms into which users will enter confidential data. (Your developer will know how to do this, but it is your job to provide a reminder.)

Any purchase system that accepts payment from a customer and authorizes a charge to the customer's credit card should use the industry standard, Secure Sockets Layer (SSL) security. SSL accomplishes security by encrypting data. When you view a web page, you can tell that this type of security is in place because the page's URL starts with *https:* instead of the more common *http:*. A special icon (in Microsoft Internet Explorer 5 it is a lock) might also appear in the browser window.

For SSL to work, a *certificate* (a digital document that proves your identity) must be issued to you by a *certifying authority* (an organization that is entrusted with vouching for others in this way). Again, your developer will take care of this. Note, however, that you will have to provide documentation to the developer to send to the certifying authority. This might include bank references, a notarized statement or application, and other supporting documentation. Obviously, given that your developer is privy to your secure systems and confidential data, it's imperative that you select a knowledgeable, reputable developer and maintain a good working relationship with him or her; see Chapter 9 for pointers.

> **Note**
>
> A database of people's credit card numbers is a tempting target to unscrupulous, hacking thieves. Because of this, transaction systems normally store credit card numbers only temporarily. They are immediately passed to a third-party credit processing company, which sends back a transaction authorization number. It is that number that is actually stored in your database. Those numbers aren't useful at all to thieves. They pertain only to one transaction and don't provide an electronic path the thief can follow to the credit card number itself.

Occasional security audits will turn up any holes in your systems. A security audit might take the form of a review of the code and systems, or it might include the additional tactic of approaching the site as a user and attempting to retrieve information a user shouldn't be able to access. An example of the latter is that when a user enters data into the system in a manner the scripts are not set up to accept, that can (in an unsecure system) trigger access to confidential data. In other words, a perfectly innocent user could make a real mess of things in an improperly secured system.

Either you can hire a company that specializes in security audits to investigate your site, or you can ask a developer to do it. Hiring a specialized company is the more expensive option but the company will probably provide a certain level of expertise in such audits. If you go the developer route, keep in mind that the developer who created the site might not be the most objective judge of the site's security system. On the other hand, a different developer who is on equal footing with yours might audit the site with an eye toward wrangling away the job of beefing up your security and maintaining the site from your existing developer. Get references and scrutinize the experience and motivations of any developer you hire for an audit just as you would if you were hiring a developer to create your systems.

How Credit Card Transactions Work

From your customer's point of view, a credit card is a convenient means to making purchases and paying later. Credit cards can be viewed from several other vantage points. From the viewpoint of a business accepting payment, a credit card is both a convenient method for receiving payment and an assurance that the credit card user has enough credit worthiness for you to assume payment will actually occur. From your bank's point of view, a credit card is a short-term loan to your business. This is because your bank (the "acquiring" bank) makes payment to your merchant account days before it receives payment from the customer's bank. (The customer's bank—the "issuing" bank—actually makes payment to your bank before receiving payment from the customer!)

From the viewpoint of the banks involved, despite the general security of the credit card system, some risk is involved. A customer might decline the charge or (of more concern to the customer's bank) default on payment. In an e-commerce setting, from the viewpoint of the banks involved, there is additional risk. To understand why this is so, consider the steps involved accepting a credit card in the physical world:

1. The customer presents the credit card to the merchant. The card is "swiped" through a reader or imprinted on hard copy. The card numbers are recorded directly from the card held in the customer's hand.
2. The merchant gets an authorization number for the purchase amount from the customer's bank over a terminal or a phone line.
3. The merchant gets the customer's signature on a credit slip, which creates a legally binding contract.
4. The merchant provides merchandise in exchange for the signed credit slip.

At the end of this process, payment is authorized and transferred. Everyone is fairly well assured that payment will occur neatly according to longstanding systems. However, in an online setting, because the customer does not present the card in person, the signature cannot be affixed to a credit slip. The signature therefore cannot be visually verified, and the banks will not have in hand the assurance of a signed "contract" when it authorizes payment for an electronic sale. This makes banks nervous. It inspires them to want more assurance from e-commerce merchants that their systems are secure. It also inspires them to charge online merchants higher fees.

As of this writing, new technologies are being developed to address these issues. In the meantime, banks find the size of the e-commerce market and the level of security that is generally afforded by online systems persuasive arguments for accepting credit card transactions over the Internet.

> **Note**
>
> In a traditional credit card transaction in the physical world, you (the merchant) get an authorization number from the issuing bank and at that moment, the customer signs and receives the product. In an e-commerce transaction, it's best to follow a few simple rules when building the system. Verify that your developer includes getting the authorization number and verifying the billing address against bank records before the credit card is formally "accepted." Also confirm with the developer that the payment process will occur very quickly, while the product is being shipped.

Credit Card Setup, Step-by-Step

Because e-commerce transactions are riskier for banks than face-to-face credit card transactions, and because online payment systems have to be secure, the process for signing up to be an online merchant accepting credit cards is different than signing up to be a brick-and-mortar merchant accepting credit cards. First of all, the banks are a bit choosier. Also, the process involves different steps and some additional players. Not only do you have to deal with your bank and the credit card companies, you also have to deal with credit card–processing software companies. Let's look at the process step-by-step.

Open a Merchant Account

The first step is to go to a bank and tell them you want to accept credit card payment over the Internet. You can start with the bank that handles your existing business accounts. However, they might not offer e-commerce accounts. If not, they might refer you to a bank that does or you can also try to get references from other business people. Once you have a bank to work with, they will step you through applying for the account you need.

Note that this will most likely be a separate account from the one you might already have for your business. The bank will also provide you with an application and contract for the credit card companies you'll be dealing with; this is a matter distinct from the bank contract.

> **Note**
>
> The rules for taxing Internet sales are basically the same as the rules for taxing mail order sales. For most small to mid-sized businesses, that means you should collect and pay sales tax according to your regional laws.

Select Credit Card–Processing Software

In a brick-and-mortar store, customers swipe their cards through a device that transmits information about the sale to the banks and credit card companies in an instant. In e-commerce, that role is played by credit card–processing software companies. CyberCash and CyberSource are two such companies. They provide software that resides on your server and does the job of transmitting transaction data securely.

As you select a credit card–processing software company, take into account which companies your developer has worked with before. As always, you don't want to pay for the learning curve and you do want to tap your developer's expertise. Consider, too, which company's software your ISP already has installed (your ISP might not want to install new, unfamiliar software). You'll also want to take into account costs. Each of the credit card–processing software companies charges some combination of a setup fee and a per-transaction fee. Some also charge a monthly minimum fee when a merchant has not generated enough transactions to be a profitable client.

Integrate the Credit Card–Processing Software with Your Transaction System

Your developer will pull the account software and credit card–processing software together with your databases and the scripts that make everything work. To assure smooth integration, keep your developer in the loop, especially as you choose credit card–processing software. Your developer should be able to advise you on the fine points of your options as they compare to other choices you've made in your specific system.

Chapter 10: Understanding the Back End and Hosting

> **Note**
>
> As you are organizing your transaction system, remember to deal with *fulfillment* (the process of shipping the product to the customer). A small e-commerce endeavor's fulfillment system might consist simply of generating an email message that triggers shipment. In a more sophisticated system, scripts run automatically when an order is placed. The order then appears along with other orders in the warehouse or shipping location's existing fulfillment system.

About Fees and Charges

Banks charge your customers monthly fees and interest on any outstanding balances. They also charge you, the merchant, for every credit card transaction that occurs at your place of business. The specific mix of fees charged and their amounts varies from bank to bank. The following categories generally apply:

- Setup fees are processing fees charged for the work involved in opening an account.

- The discount rate is a percentage of each transaction; the bank keeps this percentage as part of its compensation. Discount rates vary drastically from bank to bank. They also vary based on the type of business you do. Generally, e-commerce companies pay a higher rate (that is, get a lower discount) than brick-and-mortar businesses.

- Special charges are often added for credits to the customer (which occur when a transaction is canceled or a product is returned). They might also be added for special services such as providing printed statements rather than electronic statements or transferring funds between accounts.

> **Tip**
>
> Make sure that any credits to customers for products that are returned or for canceled orders are processed quickly at your end. If you credit the purchase back to the customer, the fee you will pay might be fifteen cents. If the customer complains to the issuing bank and the charge is reversed, the fee you will pay can be $20 or even as much as $50 depending on the bank's policy.

Other Forms of Payment

Because credit cards offer such familiarity, ease of use, and the advantage of existing payment systems (which make the transactions between customers, merchants, and banks smooth), they are the dominant method of payment in e-commerce. However, other methods of payment do exist:

- In a direct debit system, the customer enters his or her bank account number along with some identifying information, and money is directly transferred from that customer's bank account to a merchant account when a sale occurs. This method is not commonly used in e-commerce because it doesn't provide the level of secure protection required in an online setting.

- A wallet system allows the customer to transfer funds from a bank account or credit card to an electronic "wallet." Once the funds are in the customer's wallet, he or she can use that amount to make purchases. This option requires the customer to have a special account with the wallet company. (Microsoft Passport is available at *www.passport.com*. Special instructions there for merchants will tell you how to set this up.) This technology is an alternative for companies selling products priced so low they don't warrant the expense (to the merchant) of credit card fees.

- Yet another system, offered by companies such as eCharge (*www.echarge.com*), allows the customer's telephone service account to be billed for e-commerce transactions. Essentially, the customer purchases a product or service through a website, and the charge then appears on the customer's phone bill.

Armed with some understanding of transaction systems, payment methods, and other backend issues, you are now in a position to consider just how your systems will be built.

Will You Build or Buy Your Transaction System?

In Internet years gone by, the only option for creating a transaction system was to build it from scratch. That is still an option, but these days you also have the choices of customizing a transaction system built on top of purchased components or of buying a complete, prepackaged transaction system (which you might be able to customize only slightly). Each of these options has advantages and disadvantages:

- Building from scratch involves hiring a developer (or team), specifying what you want the system to do, and paying for its development. The advantage is that your custom-built system will do virtually anything you want. The disadvantage is that this is an expensive and time-consuming way to go. Further, the end result (at least in its first iteration) is as likely to be as bug-ridden as the first version of any software. And finally, the system will not be familiar to those who must work on it after your developer does. For most companies (even large ones), building from scratch is not recommended.

- Customizing based on purchased components involves licensing a product such as Microsoft Site Server Commerce Edition and having a developer create custom programming to make it fit your needs. This method can net you almost the same level of customization you'd get if you built from scratch, but the economics are far better.

- Buying a fully functioning transaction system involves purchasing a complete system, which you can then customize minimally. Purchased transaction systems generally include all the components of a transaction system (catalog, databases, scripts, and so on). They can sometimes be customized to the extent that you can create your own look and feel for the transaction and catalog pages. They might, however, offer only limited functionality. For example, you might not be able to show two related products on a single web page, as you would be able to do with a more powerful solution.

Of course whether you build or buy a transaction system, one of the key issues you must address is support, which has been discussed earlier in this chapter, and which, along with factors discussed in the next section, affects keeping your site humming around the clock.

Keeping Your Site Running Night and Day

In the brick-and-mortar world, storefronts have posted hours. They open and close at specified times. But websites are expected to be up and running around the clock. A great advantage to doing business on the Web is that your products and services are available to your customers when *they* want them, regardless of whether they are viewing your site from their desks at lunchtime in California, from home in the afternoon in France, or in the middle of the night in New York. When you commit to doing business on the Internet, you commit to having your site up and running at all times. Unfortunately, servers sometimes crash, and because they are running day and night, they can crash at 3:00 in the morning, dinnertime, or other inconvenient hours. Regardless of who is hosting your site, you'll have to take this into account. You must specify who is going to handle server emergencies.

How seriously you have to take late-night server failures depends on how critical the constant operation of your site is to your business. How late-night server failures will be handled depends on your hosting arrangement and support agreements. If you are hosting your site yourself, you (or someone you designate) will have to handle late-night problems. If your site is hosted at an ISP, the ISP might provide 24-hour monitoring and (depending on your support agreement) might do basic emergency maintenance. In these cases, you might be in the enviable position of never knowing anything went wrong until an error report arrives via email the next day.

Note

Microsoft back-end and transaction products come with tools for maintenance and monitoring usage. Additionally, third-party tools and reporting agencies can monitor uptime and report site crashes via either email or pager (for a fee). One such system is Red Alert (*www.redalert.com*).

As is true in so much of life, preventing emergencies is far better than reacting to them. To prevent server emergencies—and website downtime—your best bet is to engage in a proactive program of server maintenance. Many managers don't fully comprehend the necessity of monitoring server logs, keeping an eye on usage, and preventing server overload by building redundancy into systems as needed. When your server is running smoothly, server maintenance might seem expendable. However, trust your developer and technical staff when they say it is necessary. Downtime leads to lost sales, which no manager or business owner likes to see. A very small investment in regular server maintenance can save you from experiencing inconvenient server emergencies and expensive downtime.

Part 4

Maintain, Promote, and Succeed

11 Maintaining Fresh, Compelling Content
12 Promoting to Your Target Market
13 Assessing Your E-Commerce Success

Chapter 11

Maintaining Fresh, Compelling Content

Every e-commerce website in existence has content. *Content* includes a site's offerings, the text and images that describe those offerings, and the features that make the site usable. Sites, such as CNN.com, Salon.com, and BabyCenter.com, whose main product is the content itself are called *content driven*. Yet even a site that is not content driven has content. Many sites provide data (product specs, stock quotes, or weather information, for example) or listings (such as a portal's list of links or an entertainment site's list of music, theater, and film events). Data and listings are content. Content is also the text and images on a site that describe any downloadable files. It can even be said that the downloadable files themselves are content, in that they are among the site's offerings. Whatever, the content, how well a site delivers it (the text, images, and offerings) can make or break a user's experience of the site.

Part 4: Maintain, Promote, and Succeed

Take a look at Figure 11.1, which shows the factors that drive repeat visitors to websites (according to a 1999 Forrester survey of 8,600 web-enabled households). Notice that 75 percent of the respondents in this survey said that high quality content was the factor that brought them back.

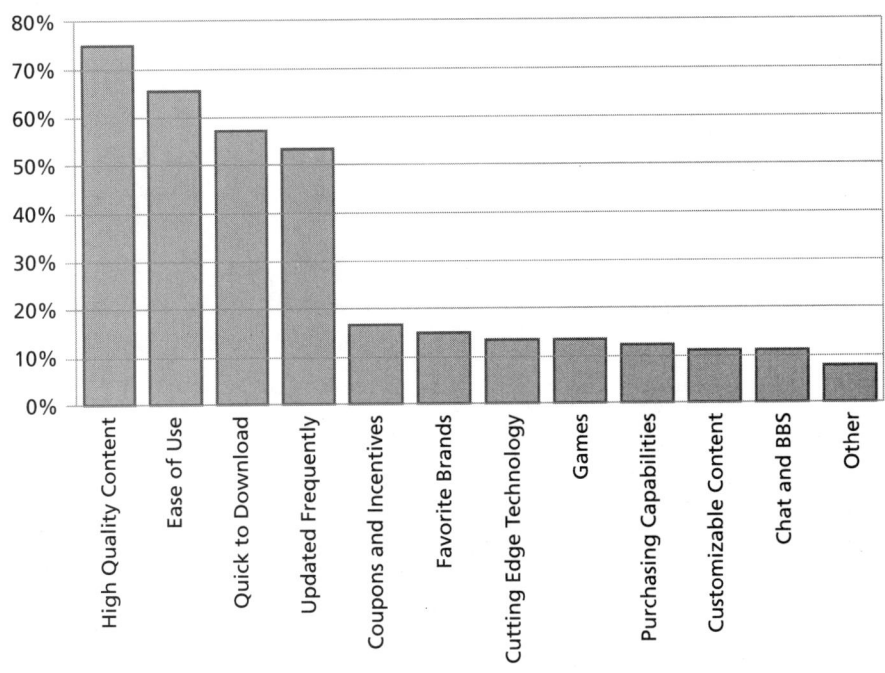

Figure 11.1
Factors that compel users to revisit websites, according to a Forrester survey.

The secret to maintaining accurate, fresh, compelling content is to start with a clear understanding of your branding, then organize your content before production, and finally, apply consistent quality assurance processes and strong content development to your site throughout its lifetime.

> **Note**
>
> Technology is not the driving force that compels users to keep clicking. Multiple technologies can be used to support and provide a back end for user experience, but they are not the ultimate answer. Just as a camera does not make fine photos, Internet technology does not make fine online content—people do.

Chapter 11: Maintaining Fresh, Compelling Content

Create Effective E-Commerce Content

Content can and should carry forth your branding. This is important in marketing sites or sites that promote or distribute a product or service. But all sites—even content driven sites—have branding; publishers and editors work hard to create a recognizable identity for their published works. You'll recall from Chapter 4 that branding is creating just such a recognizable identity.

Branding takes creative, aggressive putting forth of the brand message. Branding must be relentless at every level and in every iteration of the message; this extends to the content. To brand your content means to differentiate it from your competitors and from any preconceived ideas your audience might have. It means to establish a clear, recognizable, consistent identity.

Strong content development achieves a number of goals that are important in e-commerce. Done well, it can:

- Create a clear message
- Reach a specified audience
- Assure readability, usability, and quality of customer experience
- Expedite service and customer care
- Streamline processes
- Establish, maintain, and promote branding

Note

Relentless branding leads to *mind share* (meaning that your product, service, site, or company's brand will be the dominant one in the minds of your audience). Mind share, in turn, leads to market share. Thoughtful, consistent content development is paramount to delivering a clear message about your company, product, or service.

Content development includes consideration of the "four Cs" of the Internet: *content*, *community*, *commerce*, and *context*. We've discussed the first three Cs in other chapters; let's look at the fourth.

Context is the atmosphere or environment in which you understand or experience something. It's a total picture that is influenced by and informs each piece of the picture. Effective content development creates context, and the context you create when you design and build a website affects the message you deliver. In any e-commerce venture, the context is the sum total of the user's experience, and the context should support and further the branding message you have defined.

> **Note**
>
> Let's consider a fifth C to add to the lexicon: *consequence*. For many Internet users today, the novelty has worn off. Just surfing is no longer compelling; browsing has become purposeful. Users want to find what they seek immediately, and they want what they find to be both useful and easy to use. As you develop content, ask yourself what your site offers that is of consequence to its audience.

Just delivering information isn't enough. If it were, raw data could be provided to users without any thought about how the data appears on the web page, or how it might be interpreted. Creating the right identity for a website and creating the context in which the site's content can be effectively delivered is paramount; to do it well requires consideration of experiential and visual elements such as:

- Writing, word choice, tone, and other language devices
- Presentation of information in tables and charts
- Handling of graphics, illustrations, and photos
- Use of animation, video, and sound

Listings and data (such as entertainment schedules, stock quotes, product data, and catalog listings) are, in other words, just raw data until voice and style are applied to them. Content development provides context, and whoever addresses content development when your site is created should consider—in addition to issues of navigation, accessibility, comprehensiveness, and personalization—visual style and how language is used.

> **Note**
>
> Remember: First impressions are lasting. When a user comes to your site, he or she has an immediate impression of its readability, ease of use, and overall identity. Establishing that impression the first time is far easier than re-establishing the correct impression after you've allowed a less than favorable one to take hold.

Writing for E-Commerce

All good writing starts with compelling *leads*. Leads are the sentences that open the main text. Your first sentence has to grab the user's attention. Good leads are often short, assertive, and sometimes even provocative. Beyond that first sentence, focus on the goals you intend to achieve and make sure the points that are addressed in the text are furthering those goals. Point out the benefits of what you offer, and (as discussed in earlier chapters) add value wherever possible. Always speak the customer's language. Keep your promises. And to maintain the integrity of your information, double-check all the facts you cite.

What Is Stickiness?

Stickiness is a buzzword often heard at e-commerce conferences and seen in print. Everyone wants stickiness in his or her website, but what is it? Simply put, *stickiness* is what keeps users sticking around a website. It's also what keeps them coming back. What makes a site sticky is its relevance and appeal to the audience. It all goes back to who your audience is and what your site offers them that they want and need. Not every site should inspire users to stay and browse; a sales site, for example, ought to offer users what they need to quickly and conveniently make a purchase. But a sales site can be sticky, in the sense that it can be so terrific it inspires users to come back to it again and again. That, as much as browsability, is stickiness.

Make Blocks of Text More Readable

Lengthy text in any medium is tough to read. You can provide graphic relief by adding art to your text (as described in the next section), but in an online setting where the size of the paper doesn't limit the length of the text, it's also best simply to keep the pages short. Users aren't fond of scrolling. One or two screens of text is about the limit.

Some e-commerce sites include small or large blocks of text, for example, news stories, company information, or descriptions of services, by necessity. Look through this book and imagine what it would be like without the headings, lists, new paragraphs, and occasional art used to break up the text and organize the information to make it more readable. When longer blocks of text are necessary on your website, you can use distinct headings for sections of the material. Spread long articles (over 1,000 words, for example) across several separate pages and provide a short, linked table of contents at the top of each page. At the bottom of each page, a link leading to the subsequent page will pull readers along, especially if the link specifically describes what's of interest on the next page.

Spice Up Text with Art, Charts, Tables, and Lists

Art placed judiciously to illustrate a point or provide a helpful view of a product is well used. In some cases (as when text is dense), a piece of art can also help the eye continue reading. But gratuitous art is just that. Make sure any art you use serves the needs of your customers. *Infographics* (art that pulls together a lot of information and makes it easily understandable to readers) are often used in magazines. You can present product comparisons or instructions with infographics. Similarly, you can organize complex information into charts.

Lists are easier and quicker to read than longer text, which is good for explanations but not for scanning information quickly. Use bulleted lists in cases where the listed items do not need to be consecutively ordered:

- Apples
- Oranges
- Grapes

Use numbered lists in cases where the listed items are events that must occur in a consecutive order:

1. Lather.
2. Rinse.
3. Repeat.

When information is more complex than use of a bulleted or numbered list would suggest, you can use a table to present it in an organized, more visually friendly way:

Property	Bedrooms/Baths	Features	Cost per Week
California condo	Two/one	Near sunset beaches	$1,000
Kona Coast house	Three/one and a half	Oceanfront lanai	$1,400
Maine cottage	One/one	Wood burning stove	$800

Use Language That's Consistent with Branding

Content achieves a recognizable identity partly through the language used to convey information. Think about the sections of your Sunday newspaper. In the food and travel sections, the language is full of adjectives that evoke the senses. The goal is to help you, the reader, experience pleasure at the thought of the eating or travel experience being described. Turn to the business section, and you'll find no lush descriptions; instead, the language will be more to the point, more clipped, and full of business jargon. Open a typical computer how-to book, and you'll find that the language includes a lot of verbs; "How-to" is about doing. In short, the *editorial voice*—the tone and language used to reach your intended audience—should match the look and feel of your site. When you considered the branding of your site, you considered what message you wanted delivered. The language used in conveying your message is as important as the visual style of your site.

Tip

Word-processing software such as Microsoft Word offers many features that will help you edit and polish your text. You can check spelling and use the electronic thesaurus to add variety to your phrasing. You can also use other features in Word to track changes and record edits made while the text is being massaged, keep a running check on possible page length, and so on. Microsoft FrontPage also offers a spelling checker and thesaurus, but a word processor is specially designed to facilitate editing text in ways that HTML editors can't match, so it's best to revise your material using word-processing features before you convert the text to HTML.

Leverage Linking to Highlight What's Compelling

Links, or *hyperlinks*, are highlighted text that, when clicked, bring the user to a new area or calls forth a new web page. Links appear on web pages in a different color than the rest of the text and they are underlined to give the effect of highlighting or emphasizing the linked text. Use hyperlinks to your advantage. Make sure your phrasing conveys what a user will get if he or she follows the link. Rewrite or edit your text as needed to make the highlighted (linked) phrases—those that appear most loudly when a user accesses a page—fulfill your branding message and telegraph what the website offers.

Part 4: Maintain, Promote, and Succeed

The non-descriptive phrases "Back to" or "Go to" are not compelling, whereas "Back to <u>Recipe Search</u>" tells the user what to expect and why he or she might want to bother. Take a look at these lines of customer service text:

<u>How can I order</u> this product?
<u>Is it safe</u> to purchase online?
What <u>credit cards</u> can I use?
How can I <u>change my order</u>?
Can I <u>send this product as a gift</u>?

Notice that the questions are short and that in each case the linked phrases highlight the most relevant part of the question. Users can scan the text quickly and find the answer they seek in a snap. In some cases, including an adjective in the link makes a more specific or stronger point than would simply linking on a noun. For example, in describing your company's credentials and experience, which would you want to link on, <u>background</u> or <u>rich background</u>? Which makes the stronger highlighted phrase?

Tip

Avoid hackneyed phrasing. On your website, ban the use of phrases such as "check out" (as in "check out our products"), which is vastly overused on the Web and can be replaced with "see," "explore," "take a look at," or dozens of other phrases. I also discourage "click here" (again, overused and not benefit-oriented) and links to special "what's new" pages. (Why isn't what's new obviously presented on the home page or in some other prominent location?) Seek wording that differentiates your site from the millions of others that use those tired old terms.

Provide Complete Information

When you're writing catalog copy or other information about your products or services, place all the information a customer might need right there, in one place. It's extraordinary how many realtors who list vacation homes for rent on websites don't provide the rental price, the number of bedrooms and bathrooms, or some other information a potential renter might need. To close a sale, you must give customers all the information they need, including the product data, the benefit of buying, and a *call to action* (text that in essence urges them to take the next step). A classic call to action is "get yours today." Another is "subscribe now." Others include "step into

Chapter 11: Maintaining Fresh, Compelling Content

luxury," "get free email" and "win big." (Of course, you'll use phrasing that's specific to your industry in your calls to action!)

There are seeming exceptions to the general rule about offering all information up front. In cases where the product is very expensive (as in capital equipment), customers typically want to speak to a rep before making the purchase. In other cases (multimillion dollar real estate or industry-specific business reports), the company doing the offering might want to make sure the customers are qualified to make the purchase before revealing key information such as the price. But even in those cases, the information the customer needs (how to contact the seller's rep) and a call to action ("call for details") are advisable.

Keep It Fresh

In television and other broadcast media, the term "evergreen" is used to describe material that retains its fresh appearance over the course of time. To achieve an evergreen quality, a TV show avoids visual and verbal signs of a specific time period. For example, instead of dressing the stars in the day's fashions, the costumers stick to simple, classic looks. The script uses little slang and few hip terms or phrases. The show could then appear in many countries and over the course of years without looking too dated to be acceptable.

Borrowing from the television world, we can think of website content as *evergreen* (long lasting and thus requiring little maintenance) or *deciduous* (more "seasonal" and requiring more maintenance). While in the cases of news sites and online magazines, freshness and constantly changing content are paramount, in the cases of many e-commerce sites, relieving the staff of maintenance tasks is key to keeping the cost of labor down.

To keep your website content evergreen and lessen your maintenance load, follow these guidelines:

- Avoid using phrases that specify or imply dates ("now," "soon," "current catalog," "next version," "this summer"). And don't promise content that's "coming soon" or "under construction."
- Name only specific staff members you absolutely must name. People get promotions, change jobs, and sometimes leave the company. Except for people such as press contacts (as described in Chapter 12), and executives (who leave the company less

- frequently than other employees), avoid naming specific people on your website.
- Publish content that is reference-oriented rather than providing users with news.

In general, the more specific, timely, and oriented to the here and now your content is, the more upkeep it will require. That's not to say that specifics are to be avoided; obviously, you should provide all the specifics about your products and services necessary to enable customers to make decisions.

To facilitate keeping content fresh in a site that has among its goals delivering timely, more deciduous information, be prepared to spend staff time managing update cycles (setting the timing for updates, assigning tasks, managing a content calendar, and so on). Keep the content especially well organized, set up good quality assurance processes, and use technology tools to support your efforts.

Keep It Organized

Part of why you create a directory structure, as discussed in Chapter 7, is to make maintenance easier. Just as keeping your kitchen pantry organized makes cooking easier (knowing where the tomatoes are will save hunting for them when you're making cioppino), keeping your website organized makes content development and maintenance easier. Knowing where a specific piece of art is will save you time when you need to use that art or replace it with a fresher version. Consider the example of a site that a court ordered to remove certain content. The content had been placed in pieces throughout the site because it was believed that users would enjoy it that way. Because that content was spread all over the site and because it was stored in various directories using filenames that were not associated with each other, hunting that content down and destroying it was a very time-consuming task.

Tip

Use your directory structure and name files so they can be easily identified. If you break a brochure into several web pages, for example, either put all of those pages in one directory, give them all file names that indicate that they're associated, or both. See Chapter 8 for tips on naming files.

Chapter 11: Maintaining Fresh, Compelling Content

As your site develops, don't add areas willy-nilly. It might be tempting to simply tack on a new area when you believe a new type of content would serve your site's users, but try to tuck that new material into your existing structure instead. Imagine what would happen in your home if you simply added rooms without an overall plan. Showing little regard for architectural logic and navigation leads to dead-end paths, purposeless areas, and poor allocation of resources.

> ### Where to Get Content
>
> There are all kinds of ways to get content. You can create content (or hire freelance or staff content creators such as researchers, compilers, writers, or editors to create it.) You can repurpose existing material. You can buy or license existing material. For example, information wholesalers sell raw content for a licensing fee, and they often want a share of any ad revenue. (They don't usually create the front end or the branding. That will be up to you.) Or you can license content from sources such as iSyndicate (*www.isyndicate.com*).
>
> Other options include forming a strategic partnership with a content provider, in which case you can co-brand and even co-develop the content; working together in this way can extend both brands. Often ad revenue sharing will be part of the arrangement, perhaps with some additional fees included. You can also act as an aggregator or portal by indexing other people's content. And finally, you can simply link to content, but in that case, you'll have to add some value to your listings of linked content if you want it to be attractive to users. You should also consider the business and legal wisdom of the links you plan. See Chapter 3 for a discussion of who owns what, including content, on your website, as well as linking and the law.

Assure a Smooth Reader Experience

We've probably all had the experience of reading a book we were enjoying, falling into a reverie, and—oops!—stumbling across a little typo. In that brief moment, our experience was interrupted and for at least a split second, we thought, "How did that get in here?"

Because you don't want your customers distracted from the business at hand—perusing your e-commerce website—you want to banish typos and other distracting errors from your text. Details count: spelling and punctuation are to a user's experience of online content as the condition of the coffee pot on an airplane is to a traveler's impression of the airline's safety equipment.

Whatever your site's business goals, you want users to experience the site as you intended it. A stray typo, a broken link, a glitch in navigation, or inconsistencies in usage of language, fonts, or layout can, at best, distract visitors from your product or service, and at worst, damage your credibility. That's why it's important to have in place methods for guiding the changes that will inevitably occur to your website.

Tip

Validating links is a vital step in checking the quality of your site and the integrity of its content. You must check links regularly to make sure they're still live and working. If you're running your site on Microsoft Internet Information Server (IIS), you can get and use Microsoft Site Server Express, a tool that offers site analysis including the option to quickly and conveniently check links on your live site. Site Server Express also generates reports that will help you analyze traffic and determine which areas of your site are most visited. You can then decide how much effort to put into beefing up less popular areas and maintaining fresh material in more popular areas.

Monitor Quality and Assure Credibility

Monitoring the quality of your website content and assuring yourself that credibility standards are met is a two part process. Part one is creating a style guide that describes your policies and procedures; part two is establishing a workable quality assurance (QA) process. Some typically mentioned excuses for not having a style guide and QA process include:

- We just have to get the site launched; we don't have time to write a style guide.
- We only have one staff member available to review the pages; he knows our policies.
- We aren't writers; we can't write a style guide.
- We don't have a style guide, so we can't do QA.

Note, however, that:

- Hours spent on creating a style guide will shave days off your QA cycle.
- Passing information as verbal lore leaves you in a vulnerable position if and when the holder of the lore becomes unavailable.
- Creating a style guide is a simple matter of keeping lists; no fancy writing skills are necessary.
- Conducting QA without a style guide is a lot tougher and more time consuming; that's why creating a style guide is important.

A style guide documents the decisions that have been made about how the site's identity will be carried through. It defines the look and feel of the site, its language and tone, and all of the conventions that establish the site's personality to users and customers.

What Does an Editor Do?

An editor's basic job is to step in for the reader (or, on a website, the user). The editor smooths the text, but also considers issues of readability as affected by page layout, or use of art, charts, tables, and lists. If the editor encounters anything that will act as a barrier to understanding as the reader (or user) experiences the content, the editor will fix that problem or ask that the appropriate party fix it. In an online setting, an editor can (in addition to editing text and art) proofread, check links, and advise you on how the user will perceive many navigational issues. For a terrific explanation of the roles editors fulfill, see the Bay Area Editors' Forum at *www.editorsforum.org*.

Create and Use a Style Guide

You can create your style guide simply by keeping lists of the important decisions you made as you built the site. Word documents stored in a folder are easy to manage. As the project progresses, you can convert the Word documents into HTML, then link among various topics in the sections of the newly created HTML style guide, and make the style guide a living document your whole team can use. This checklist will get you going; you can modify it to suit your site:

- Format and Structure
    - A clear diagram of the directory structure, showing what types of files will be stored where.
    - A site map or index showing major areas of the site and major navigational paths.
    - Notes about the site structure's overall logic.
    - Guidelines describing what is stored in databases (your database software might include a feature for mapping and documenting the database).
    - A flowchart showing how transaction systems are organized.
    - Notes about how to place content into the site's structure.

Tip

Using Visio, a sophisticated diagramming program, you can draw directory structure plans and site maps. What's more, with Visio you can use a wizard to automatically draw an accurate, complete map of your existing website. Flowcharts are also easy to create with Visio. You can diagram almost any aspect of your site with this versatile tool.

- Visual Style
    - Notes about how style choices were made and by whom.
    - Records of which artist or designer created specific elements of the site (so you can go back to that person for more work on that style when needed).
    - Where and how to place page banners, navigational bars, buttons, company logos, advertising, or graphics.
    - Which colors to use (and which colors to avoid) for pages, backgrounds, logos, navigational bars, special elements, and so on.
    - Which fonts or font families to use for page banners, navigational bars, body text, informational tables, forms, and so on; where those fonts are located and in what size they can be used.

Chapter 11: Maintaining Fresh, Compelling Content

- Where art is located.
- How basic page layouts and special effects are accomplished.

Tip

Document information about who designed what (and how to contact those people) in a Word table or Microsoft Excel spreadsheet during the process of creating your site. When you are ready to convert your documentation to HTML, you can do so easily using Word or Excel.

- HTML and Page Layout
    - Fonts to be used (and alternate fonts, if you are using <FONT FACE>).
    - Colors (including their codes) for backgrounds and special elements.
    - Headings—the font, color, size, weight, and so on for headings of various levels.
    - Whether to use <B> and <I> or <STRONG> and <EM>.
    - How to code special characters such as ™, ©, and ®.
    - META tags to be used to optimize standing in search engines.
    - In page layout tables, the preferred table and cell widths, as well as cell padding, cell spacing, and information about where exceptions are allowable.
    - In frames, naming conventions, targeting and default targets, and directory structure for frame sets.
    - Any disallowed characters, such as em and en dashes, which are not part of the standard HTML character set.
- Graphics and Multimedia
    - The maximum size in bytes for a page.
    - What file types are allowable in what circumstances (in general, it's best to stick to Graphic Interchange Format (GIFs) for simple graphics and Joint Photographic Experts Group (JPEGs) for photographic images) and what is the maximum suggested size.

Part 4: Maintain, Promote, and Succeed

- How and when to indicate the size of downloadable multimedia and graphics files (this is a convenience for users, who can then decide whether or not their systems can manage the files).

- How and when to use ALT tags to describe images (for the benefit of users who've turned off graphics).

- Suggestions for how to avoid dithering, which reduces image quality, and how to use interlaced files that load in several passes.

- Limitations on use of logos, company colors, and other company-identifying elements (for this, you might want to link to the visual style, editorial style, and legalese sections of your style guide).

- Information on placement of banner ads.

- Notes regarding who designed and who approved various graphic elements, so that in the future you can contact those involved to make adjustments or have additional material created or approved.

- Editorial Style and Usage
    - Which reference guides your site uses as a basis for editorial style—*Chicago Manual of Style* or *Associated Press Stylebook and Libel Manual*? Which dictionary? Which edition of each?

    - The mission or philosophy of the site—the goal that making it public is meant to achieve.

    - How to handle punctuation—for headings, will you use *heading style* (with the first letter of all important words uppercased), or *sentence style* (with only the first letter of the first word capitalized)? How will you handle *all-cap* names like CNET? What about names that include punctuation, like Yahoo!? And what about terms like Web site? Will it be that or website?

    - Are there acronyms that can stand unspecified, such as AMA (for the American Medical Association, which is familiar enough to users of a medical site) or HTML? These can appear in an alphabetical list with those less well

Chapter 11: Maintaining Fresh, Compelling Content

   known acronyms that need to be spelled out, such as CSS for cascading style sheets.
- What to do with various compound words, for example, whether you will go with e-mail or email.
- How to handle such special elements as captions (how will they be formatted, and how long can they be?); the use of color or black and white in images; the format of informational tables and the headings and text within them; the length and tone of headings; and so on.
- Policies regarding the use of logos, linking, and legalese on your site.
- Online references that will be of use, for example The Slot (*www.theslot.com*), which provides insight into making editorial choices.

- Linking and Cross-Linking
    - How many links should appear in a paragraph or story.
    - Your policy on what sorts of words to link on. Again, avoid the generic "click here" and link on the most pertinent phrase instead; for example, the destination of the link (which is more enticing to users).
    - How to phrase links to downloadable files, graphics, and media.
    - When to use buttons for links rather than text and vice versa.
    - How to handle *jump links* (those that link to text within the same page).
    - Whether and in what circumstances it is acceptable to link outside of the site.

- Legal Matters
    - How copyright notices should be worded and where they should be placed on your pages.
    - How trademarks should be indicated.
    - Policies regarding gaining permission for use of copyrighted material from elsewhere.

- Policies regarding use of your own material; for example, when it is permissible and what procedures must be followed by others to gain permission to use your material.
- Notes regarding who among your staff is authorized to grant permission to use your material.
- Any forms or permissions agreements necessary for others to fill out in order to use your material.

- Review and Approval Procedures
  - Who's who on the review team as well as what they are authorized to review.
  - How the review and approval process occurs.
  - How approvals are recorded.
  - Who signals that the material has been fully approved and can be posted.

Establish an Effective Approval Process

Ask your developer to provide you with a staging server on which you can place pages before they go live. This will allow you to test for navigability and usability without posting your unfinished site in public. As part of your testing process, you might want to set up a standard review team that includes representatives from your company's marketing, legal, public relations, sales, editorial, production, and other departments. It's best to also have the site tested by some of your actual customers, but you'll probably want to do that only after the site has been found to be in pretty good shape. Start with an in-house review team and then bring in your customers.

Tip

Make sure each member of your review team knows which areas he or she is supposed to review. You might want the legal representative to focus on legal issues, for example, and not on the choice of colors. Similarly, you might want the marketing people to turn their attention away from the wording of the legalese. Let everyone know what the scope of their responsibility is. Let them know, too, what the deadlines are. (And set those deadlines a few days before your own "drop-deadlines" to give yourself a little room to maneuver.) You can use an Excel spreadsheet to track who has submitted their feedback, who has yet to do so, and where the files are in the production process.

Chapter 11: Maintaining Fresh, Compelling Content

Reviewing and getting approval for each page on your site might seem like a headache now, but it will certainly relieve the migraines that can be induced if you have to fix every page repeatedly after the site goes live. It might also save you from some embarrassing problems. Keep in mind the examples of one site on which the company had misspelled its own name three times in three different ways, and another site that had accidentally posted a public announcement of a merger that hadn't been finalized and in fact never occurred. Avoiding such blunders, along with maintaining the integrity of the site and upholding the credibility of the company, product, or service it represents, is the real value in creating and adhering to a good style guide. A style guide is among your best tools for building and maintaining a quality website that fulfills its intended purpose.

Tools for Managing Site Maintenance

Ongoing site maintenance is a project like any other, with deadlines, priorities, and often with team members working on various aspects of the project. Good project management is paramount. Say you want to add some features and functionality to your site or to freshen up an entire area of your existing site. You'll want to see how pursuing this project will impact others. You'll want to know whether the project can be completed on time with the resources available. Using Microsoft Project, you can predict how a project will play itself out and you can manage resources and people throughout the course of your projects.

Microsoft Project allows you to juggle what-if scenarios and put together complex project plans, and provides tools for following through by tracking who has done what and on what timeline. How missed deadlines will impact the overall schedule will be immediately obvious with Project's assistance. Project also works smoothly with Microsoft Outlook; if you assign tasks using Project, the assignee will see the tasks appear on his or her "To Do" list. Additionally, Project can show you how resources are being used; for example, if your project plan is unbalanced or a delay is going to occur, you'll see that some people on your team will have to work 60 hours a week to make up for others.

Similarly, FrontPage provides task management features that allow you to assign and watch the progress of various aspects of site creation and maintenance. Using these features, you can assign responsibility for various areas of your site to assorted team members, for example. You (or they) can then list the tasks they must accomplish and the assignee can update the task list as progress occurs. Updating, archiving, purging, and creating content can be listed as general tasks ("Refresh product list") with priorities and deadline dates noted. More specific tasks ("Write home page headlines") can be also be designated.

Another Microsoft product, Visual SourceSafe (VSS), is version-control software that allows multiple users to work on only the most recent version of a given file. VSS prevents people from making changes to separate copies of an individual file concurrently (which creates version control problems when no one is sure which version of the file or document is the correct one). VSS logs changes to files as they're being worked on and tracks the time and author of the changes. It stores a version of every set of changes to a file, so that if you later wish to restore a version, you can. VSS integrates into the menu structures of Word, FrontPage, and other development software.

Archive and Purge Content

Old web pages don't die, they languish—in public. When you remove a link from your website, that action does not remove the linked page. Old content will still appear in search engines and user searches of your site if you don't purge the page by placing old, outdated pages that you want to keep in a separate directory, far from the live site. Make yourself an archive that is yours and only yours, unavailable to the public and any search engines that come trolling around. Keep your website as tidy as you wish the closets in your home were, because users will accidentally stumble into unkempt corners of your website and those corners do not represent your e-commerce endeavor as you'd like them to see it.

Chapter 12

Promoting to Your Target Market

The bottom line in building traffic is marketing, marketing, marketing. Advertising and promoting your e-commerce site, both online and off, is crucial to success. Your content should soar, your design and technology should support your offerings, and your products must be backed up by service. Even with all that, if no one knows your site is terrific, no one will visit it. Which marketing, advertising, and promotion techniques you choose and how you mix and match them will depend on your budget (which has bearing on your strategy), and while it's true that a bigger budget can buy more exposure, using your budget wisely is just as important. Even on a smaller budget, you can implement numerous techniques for promoting your site and boosting traffic. What works for you is what matters.

Tip

The techniques for building website traffic can also work for building newsletter or discussion group traffic. Newsletters and discussion groups can be powerful tools for bringing traffic to your site. An investment in applying promotional techniques to newsletter and discussion group initiatives can pay back in an even greater boost in traffic.

Part 4:   Maintain, Promote, and Succeed

Attract Traffic with Your Site and Your Message

In traditional promotion, the modus operandi is interruption. Ads interrupt television, radio, print, and (in the form of billboards, taxi ads, and bus signs) the highways and byways we travel daily. On public television and radio, where commercial messages don't interrupt during the programming, sponsor messages still intrude between shows. Public relations efforts have as a goal placing a message in print or broadcast media. Again, this is an insertion of persuasive information into our experience.

But in Internet promotion, interruption is not the most effective technique. Users despise unsolicited commercial email, they resent intrusions into discussion groups, and they are jaded with advertising. To get your message across in most Internet venues, a combination of *attraction* and *permission* works far more effectively than interruption.

The foundation of your marketing plan should be a site that fulfills its promise, provides something of value to the customer, and establishes identity and credibility. (These were the subjects of earlier chapters.) Marketing is not just about selling; it's also about creating a need. It's about making people want something, and making them want it as badly as possible. Marketing is part product, part packaging, part pricing, and part *positioning* (establishing the product in the perception of customers and in comparison to competitive products). The first goal of your marketing plan must be not only to create a site that compels customers to visit again, but also to tell their friends what a terrific experience they had at your site and what value they received. Simply put, there is no better way to engineer word-of-mouth advertising than by offering a quality product. Your website should be this quality product. Your site can be a destination, a reference, a point of distribution, or a diversion. But it must first *attract* its customer base and then reward those whose visits are a result of your promotional efforts.

As you focus your site's marketing strategy, build on what you know about your site's goals and target market (the audience you defined in Chapter 4). Your marketing strategy and the promotion plan it includes will target the same audience and be aimed at furthering the same goals.

Chapter 12: Promoting to Your Target Market

Tip

Why reinvent the wheel? To find out what's working for others (and what isn't), join a discussion of marketing and promotion techniques. The discussions of a particularly focused group devoted to the exchange of online advertising, promotion tips, and other information are archived and searchable at *www.le-digest.com*. Search Alta Vista, Yahoo!, and other venues for trade associations and discussion groups related to your industry.

Take a look at Figure 12.1. This graph shows the results of a survey by Forrester Research, Inc. of 8,600 web-enabled households, indicating how people typically find web pages. Note that the most common avenues cited are search engines, email, other websites, and word-of-mouth. Note also that the numbers shown don't add up to 100 percent. That's because one person finds web pages using a variety of methods. And *that*, my friends, means that, whenever possible, a variety of avenues should be used when promoting a website. Let's take a look at the possibilities.

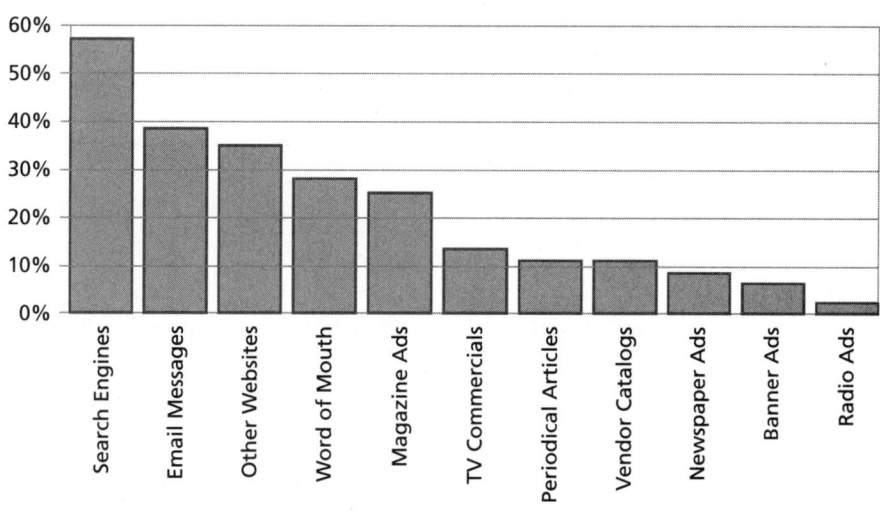

Figure 12.1

How users find websites, from a Forrester Research survey.

List Your Site

How will people find you? Get listed in search engines, directories, and portals. Sounds simple, but it's not necessarily that easy. Not all sites are listed, and more importantly, not all sites get high ranking. Let's examine what it means to get listed, and then explore a few methods that will help you do that *and* get the highest ranking possible.

What Are Search Engines, Directories, and Portals?

Search engines, more or less automatically, create the listings they contain. They are software-driven: the software crawls the Web and compiles a database that is searchable. You can submit your site to a search engine but the search engine also finds sites on its own.

Directories differ from search engines in that they are created by human beings. You submit your site to a directory and then people, not software, select those they consider appropriate to list. They manage the indexing of the list, too, by creating categories and subcategories. Alta Vista is an example of a classic search engine, while Yahoo! is a directory. Hybrids of search engines and directories also exist; for example, HotBot includes both a search engine and a directory.

A portal is a site that provides entry to other sites, a jumping-off place. Portals often provide feature content and special services (such as discussion groups or free email) in addition to listings or reviews of sites. MSN (*www.msn.com*) is a portal; it includes value-added content and services as well as MSN Search. FindLaw is also a portal, though it addresses only the topic of legal resources and not a broad range of topics in the style of MSN.

Tip

To get the latest scoop on search engines, directories, and portals, see Microsoft bCentral's SubmitIt! Search Engine Tips (*www.bcentral.com*) or check into Search Engine Watch at *www.searchenginewatch.com*. Search Engine Watch also offers a newsletter that will keep you up to date on search engine happenings.

How Search Engines Work

The typical search engine, if you look behind the scenes, consists of three parts:

- A software program (called a *crawler*, *spider*, or *robot*) that "crawls" the Web, visits sites, reads them, and follows their links. (This is one of the reasons you crafted the directory structure so carefully back in Chapter 7—to make it easier to follow the links.) Crawlers crawl to and around a site because its URL was submitted to the search engine or simply because the crawler encountered the site on the Web. Once it has identified a site, the crawler returns periodically to look for changes, but how often that occurs varies from search engine to search engine.

- A database (sometimes also called an *index*) into which the crawler dumps what it finds (URLs and data related to the web pages that were crawled).

- The actual *search engine software* that allows users to search the database.

When you use a search engine, the search engine software performs its function by sifting through the data in the database. It then provides you with a list of web pages that it has ranked according to its interpretation of the pages' relevancy to the terms you typed when you initiated the search.

Get to the Top of the List

Your goal is for your site to appear among the first 30 sites listed when a user searches for sites like yours. In other words, if your site sells western-style saddlery, you want a user searching for "saddle" to see your site as highly ranked as possible, preferably as the first site pertaining to the term "saddle," but certainly among the first 30. The following discussion can help you optimize your web pages to achieve better ranking. It's important, however, to remember that things change. Search engines, like other businesses, constantly improve their systems, and what achieves better ranking for you today might not work as well a few months from now. Nonetheless, following a few simple guidelines can boost your chances of a high ranking in most search engines.

First, keep in mind that, in the case of directories, a good site is more likely to be reviewed than a lousy one. Directories are created with human intervention, so the selection process can be subjective. Luck is also a factor, but building a site that's compelling and easy to navigate will attract attention and might make the difference between being indexed in a directory and not being indexed.

Second, in general, do not design your web pages using *frames* ("panes" within the larger window of the web page) or *image maps* (large graphics that contain within them the links that lead to interior pages of the site). Because of the technical structure of the HTML involved in creating framed pages or pages with image maps, search engines cannot index those pages and will simply skip over them during the crawling process. Similarly, search engines have a hard time with pages created *dynamically* (that is, using content and images stored in databases). Workarounds for these issues do exist, and you can find out about those workarounds at Search Engine Watch (*www.searchenginewatch.com*), but if you don't want to invest in implementing the workarounds, just avoid using frames, image maps, or database-driven content.

Third, optimize your site's design, layout, writing, and HTML development to maximize your chances for a boost in ranking. A lot has been made of the use of META tags for this purpose; META tags are special HTML coding that let you include, for example, a defined list of keywords and a description that many search engines use in their ranking processes. However, META tags are not the whole story.

Note

A few specialized HTML tags provide the opportunity to "tag" your site with specified words and phrases that will help the site to be categorized and indexed correctly. These tags include the TITLE tag, which defines the page's title (as it appears in the browser's title bar rather than on the page itself), and two META tags (one for a set of keywords and one for a description).

Crawlers, as mentioned, follow links. But different search engines work differently. They generally use some sort of mathematical formulae (based on algorithms) to determine ranking; the algorithms used at each search engine are closely guarded secrets. For the most part, search engines take into account how often certain words appear on (in some combination) the web page's URL, its title (as it appears in the title bar at the top of your web browser window), its text (including the title that appears on the page itself), and the keyword and description META tags.

As a very simplistic example (it's actually much more complex than this), among a group of websites devoted to 1966 Mustangs, the site that has the words "1966 Mustang" appearing most often in its URL, title, text, and META tags should theoretically come to the top of the list in a search for 1966 Mustang. However, rankings are actually generally based on the frequency and location of keywords in comparison to other words on the page. Search engines usually check for repeated words (assumed to be keywords) that appear near the top of the page, in the headline, and in the first few paragraphs. They also check how often those words appear compared to other words. But search engines aren't so bright; they take things quite literally. A search engine won't know, for example, that car, auto, automobile, vehicle, and Mustang all refer to essentially the same thing.

Knowing all this, you can build into your web pages a good foundation for maximizing your ranking in search engines. Here is a simple procedure for modifying a web page's HTML, taking into account how the major search engines work.

To start, jot down between one and four words that precisely match your topic and can appear in the page's title along with a broader list of perhaps a dozen keywords that closely relate to the topic. (If you need another approach, try crossing out all the irrelevant words on your page until you are left with just a few words; these are the most important ones.) While you're at it, write a very short sentence that describes your page clearly and simply, including in that sentence a few of the most relevant keywords you identified. With those items in your possession, follow these steps:

1. Open the page using an HTML editor.

2. Incorporate a few of the most relevant words you identified into the "title" portion of the HTML code. (They don't have to be the only words in the title section, but they must appear there.) Here is an example for a site that sells adventure camping equipment:

   ```
   <TITLE>Adventure Camping Outfitters: Equipment for camping,
   backpacking, climbing, hiking, canoeing, kayaking;
   everything for camping and adventure camps</TITLE>
   ```

3. Repeat the most important words (adventure, camping, camp, and camper, in the example) in the page's text, near the top of the page, and scatter them throughout the writing that comprises the page.

Part 4: Maintain, Promote, and Succeed

> **Tip**
>
> If your site design uses tables as a formatting technique, the table layout can sometimes push the text that appears at the top of the page down in the HTML file. See Search Engine Watch for tips that will help you deal with this and other dilemmas.

4. In the "head" portion of your code, enter a META tag for the keywords you identified. For example, this META tag could be used for the adventure camping site:

   ```
   <META NAME="keywords" VALUE="camping, adventure, camp,
   backpack, camper, hike, climb, kayak, canoe, adventure
   camping, backpacking, adventure camp, hiking, equipment
   for camping, climbing, sport camping, kayaking, canoeing,
   camping equipment, adventure sport">
   ```

> **Tip**
>
> Use lowercase letters in the keywords META tag, even for titles and proper nouns, and make everything singular (*sport*, not *sports*). Use synonyms liberally and make sure you include occasional synonyms in the page's text. However, do not simply repeat words (camp, camp, camp) because the search engines are onto that trick and might penalize for it by lowering your ranking or by even kicking your site out altogether.

5. Enter a "description" META tag, using the descriptive sentence you wrote. (Note again that the sentence must include some of your keywords.) Here is an example:

   ```
   <META NAME="description" VALUE="Equipment for adventure
   camping, backpacking, climbing, hiking, canoeing, kayaking;
   get everything you need for camping and adventure camps.">
   ```

> **Tip**
>
> In the description, don't use first-person references ("I"). Use third person references instead, because they are more descriptive and let you fit in another keyword. (As in "camping equipment for adventure campers.") Also, forget saying, "Welcome to...." The goal here is to use keywords, and "welcome" is not the descriptive, specific type of keyword that will get your site indexed properly.

Chapter 12: Promoting to Your Target Market

Some search engines also take into account the popularity of the web page; in other words, among groups of sites about 1966 Mustangs or about adventure camping, those with the largest number of *backlinks* (links leading to it from other sites) or with listings in other search engines or directories will get an extra edge in the rankings.

Caution

Don't think you can place your competitors' names and their product names into your META tags to lure potential customers your way. Not only is that unethical, but it might be grounds for a lawsuit.

One two-pronged strategy for leveraging the importance of popularity in search engine rankings is to develop a lot of backlinks *and* get your site listed in some specialized directories (travel, health, personal finance, or whatever is appropriate to your topic and audience). That will have the dual effect of driving traffic and boosting your rankings.

Note

Search engine ranking is not permanent. The search engines change their algorithms all the time, and more and more sites are indexed every day. Even if you achieve a good ranking, it pays to monitor your ranking and refine your techniques. SubmitIt! provides convenient features for testing and monitoring your ranking as well as for submitting your site to multiple search engines and directories quickly and easily.

There is another route for boosting your ranking; as of this writing, at least one search engine accepts payment for higher ranking. It remains to be seen whether others will follow the lead. However, it also seems unlikely that payment for ranking will become common; to many people, paid listings seem to lose their credibility, and after all, the search engine and directory industry runs essentially as a service to people.

Tip

To find out what works for others, view the source. Do a search on a term that closely matches your own site, go to the sites that show up at the top of the search results list, and use your web browser's view source feature to see what META tags and other tricks that site used to get where it is.

Protect Some Pages from Searchability

You might not want certain sections of your site indexed by search engines. Some pages require users to enter them through other pages in order for their content to make sense, and you might not want that sort of page indexed; you probably wouldn't want your transaction system pages to be indexed, either. A trick for preventing most search engines from trolling around where they aren't wanted is to include a specially formatted file called *robots.txt* in the root directory of the website's files. A list in robots.txt indicates which pages on a site are designated to be off limits to search engines. To find out more about robots.txt files and how to implement them, ask your developer, check with the major search engines, or look into Search Engine Watch.

Another method for preventing the indexing of specific pages is a bit easier. You can simply embed this line among the page's META tags:

```
<META NAME="ROBOTS" CONTENT="NOINDEX">
```

Note, however, that fewer search engines recognize and respect this method than the robots.txt method, so using the robots.txt file is preferreed.

Submit Your Site

You have two basic options for submitting your site to search engines and directories: You can go to each one and use its submissions page; generally the page provides a form to fill out and a Submit button to send the form in. Or you can use an automated service that lets you fill out just one form (which often includes a checklist so you can select the search services you want to target) and send your submission to many search engines and directories at once.

> **Tip**
>
> One strategy that has worked well for some is to start by submitting the most important pages of the site (perhaps two or three of them) to second-tier and third-tier search services and to appropriate niche search engines and directories. This can establish the site's "popularity" and make it more appealing to the more major search engines and directories. Once your site has been listed in the smaller venues, you can then go for the big leagues with more oomph in your submission.

While submission services that let you fill out a form and submit your site to dozens or hundreds of search engines and directories at once are a tremendous time saver, the pros generally think it best to submit to the major search engines manually, one at a time. This allows you to tailor your submission precisely. There are only a few major search engines and directories, so the time investment is in fact pretty minimal. If you're going to use an automated submission service, use it for the second-tier and third-tier search services.

Remember that it can take as long as a month for your submission to be processed. Don't spam the search engines; that only clogs the pipeline for everyone and is likely to hurt your chances. Do keep in mind that establishing and improving your search engine ranking is a project that might take months. It is, however, a worthwhile endeavor in that your traffic will improve dramatically with a top-30 ranking in the major search engines.

Before you submit your site to search engines, optimize it for ranking. It's always best to get the correct information in place first. While many of the search engines' crawlers do come around to check for changes, the Web is large and complex and they don't come by terribly often.

Get Others to Link to You

You want your site to have many entry points, offer content and service that inspires customers to stick around, and then provide as few exits as possible. Let's focus now on *entry points,* or ways in to your site. How is it possible to develop a lot of entry points? To create them, you must persuade as many other sites as possible to link to yours. Getting these backlinks is the direct result of providing something of value to others, but it also involves persuasion, negotiating, and sometimes trading.

Get Backlinks and Trade Links

Getting backlinks is easiest for sites that offer strong content or a unique service. Obviously, other sites will be more inclined to link to yours if your site's offerings deepen, add interest to, or complement theirs. To launch a backlink campaign, first identify sites that seem likely candidates. You might do well to get links (either reciprocal or nonreciprocal links) with vendors, suppliers, sister companies, trade associations, professional groups, or your college alumni association. If you link to others (say in a directory of related resources), let them know and ask them to link to you. Take a look at ReciprocalLink (*www.reciprocallink.com*), a site that lets you announce your intent to exchange links and matches sites with other sites by category.

> **Tip**
>
> Trade at the rate of real value. If, for example, your site gets five times the traffic of the site you're swapping with, you should get five times as much exposure on that site in exchange for what you're providing to them. That might mean better placement for you (on the home page rather than a little-trafficked interior page) or it might mean more placements or placement for a longer period of time.

If you offer something for free on your site—a screensaver, software demos, postcards, or a nice interactive tool—directories that index sites offering free stuff, such as *www.thefreesite.com*, can list your site.

If you have a logo you can provide to others as a linkable button, it will stand out on their pages more than a simple link. However, if you ask someone to use your logo as a link without giving them a compelling reason to use it, they might rightfully be reluctant because your logo will merely interrupt or dilute the branding on their site. If, however, you provide an incentive for using your logo—perhaps useful or entertaining software to download from your site—you can make a logo for that software available as a button that links directly to the download page.

Form Partnerships and Join Alliances

Partnerships and alliances can take many forms, ranging from simple agreements to trade links or ads to *affiliate programs* and *sponsorships* (both discussed in an upcoming section) to *co-branding relationships* (where two companies together release a product branded with both their identities). Because search engines often consider a site's popularity in the rankings and because publicity and prestige seem to beget more publicity and prestige, making your site prominent by joining forces with others is vital to your promotional campaign.

Develop relationships with any sites that complement or are related to yours (but not with competitors, obviously). As you visit other sites that cater to the same market, contact their managers and request a link or offer to trade a link. If you join a professional or trade association, have them list your website address and other contact information. Don't overlook *web rings*, which are loose agreements among a group of related sites to link to each other in a sort of "circular" path. While web rings can include some amateur sites and you might not know exactly where the path leads, a high-quality web ring can be an alternative, especially for smaller sites.

Offer or Achieve Awards

Consider entering your site into award competitions. These include design awards, content and presentation awards, "Best of the Web" awards, and general awards for notable sites. Examples range from the Webbys (*www.webbies.com*), to Cool Site of the Day (*www.cool.infi.net*), to an individual site's "best financial resources" awards. As always, don't just spam the awards sites. Make sure your site is actually qualified for the award and polish it up before you enter. Enter only those competitions you are ready for and have a shot at; otherwise you'll get the wrong sort of reputation.

Similarly, if you are in a position to legitimately offer an award, you can provide an attractive award button that links back to your site. For example, if your organization is a nonprofit association of professional editors, you might offer an award each month to a website that is particularly well edited; or if your company sells pet supplies you might offer an award to especially clever personal websites featuring pets. Awards appear legitimate and prestigious if they are offered by organizations or companies that have real standing. They can also start to look like cheap shots if they are handled poorly, so if you offer awards, be sure that you've set things up fairly and that you're recognizing real value in making the award.

Check Your Backlinks

Checking to see how many backlinks you enjoy (and who has provided them) is quick and easy. You can use online search engines such as AltaVista and HotBot to do it. (Others also provide this service, but as of this writing, Alta Vista and HotBot are the easiest to use.) To use AltaVista to check your backlinks, follow these steps:

1. Open your web browser, and navigate to Alta Vista (*http://www.altavista.com*).

2. In the search box (where you'd normally enter a word or phrase to start a search of websites), type the following (all lowercase):

   link:http://www.yourdomainname.com/ -host: yourdomainname.com

   Note that the - is a minus sign, and be sure that you replace "yourdomainname" with—what else—your own domain name (it appears twice).

3. Click the Search button. A list will appear showing the URLs of all the web pages indexed by Alta Vista that link to your site.

Part 4: Maintain, Promote, and Succeed

> **Tip**
>
> The list shows only backlinks to the page whose URL you gave; to find out about links to interior pages you'll have to run a separate search. To do so, simply include the page's entire URL in the search rather than just "yourdomainname.com."

You can check your backlinks using HotBot by following these steps:

1. With your web browser, open HotBot (*www.hotbot.com*).
2. In the search box (where you'd normally enter a word or phrase to start a search of websites), type your URL.
3. In the menu box labeled Look For, select Links To This URL.
4. Click the Search button. A list will appear showing the URLs of all the web pages indexed by HotBot that link to your site.

> **Tip**
>
> Again, this list shows only backlinks to the page you specified. To find out about links to other pages, perform another search specifying their URLs in the search box.

Create Affiliates

In setting up an affiliate program, you provide other sites with an incentive to send users, leads, or sales your way. Your affiliates will place links prominently on their sites leading back to you; you will offer them a reward or commission for results. Affiliates are also known as *associates* or, less commonly, as *resellers*. The types of rewards or commissions involved can include outright payment, finder's fees, bounties, or even barters such as ad placement or products in exchange for click-throughs (explained later) or sales.

When you organize your affiliate program, think of your affiliates as a kind of commissioned sales force. Plan a compensation package that provides a good base and lets them earn big bonuses. Some e-commerce sites report that their affiliates earn three percent or more (as much as 30

Chapter 12: Promoting to Your Target Market

percent!) of the revenue that comes from each sale generated. These figures vary according to the cost of the product involved and the level of competition among marketers that compete for affiliates in that target market. Because an affiliate program has almost no up-front cost (you have only to design a little logo and announce your program), your affiliate program can be infinitely scalable. You can have hundreds or thousands of affiliates if your product and program are attractive. Participation in this kind of affiliate program packs the triple advantage of getting you backlinks, extending your branding, and selling your product or site.

Tip

It is time consuming to manage and optimize affiliate programs; you have to do a certain amount of tracking and accounting. Joining an affiliate service such as that provided by Microsoft ClickTrade, (available through bCentral) can take the burden of finding potential affiliates from your shoulders, as well as make tracking and accounting for commissions easier, allowing you to concentrate on other important endeavors.

Setting compensation rates for your affiliate program is tricky. You have to decide how much a customer or sale will be worth and how much you can afford to pay. First remember to figure in processing fees and other customer acquisition costs. Then set the commission or payout as high as you can; that will get the quick attention of those who might opt in to your affiliate program. Also keep in mind that credibility is an issue. As always, having a good name or attaching yourself to one will persuade potential affiliates that you'll actually make payment and do it on time.

Tip

Encourage your affiliates to add value. If your site sells fresh lobster, your affiliates, like you, can add recipes and information to their sites to support the lobster program. Also, placing affiliate buttons throughout an affiliate's site rather than in one spot three levels down will help generate more visibility and more return for both the affiliate and you. Provide tips to your potential affiliates along with links to other sites that have successfully implemented your affiliate program.

Part 4: Maintain, Promote, and Succeed

Use Banner Ads

Advertising is typically an expensive venture. For premium, national ad space on respected, highly trafficked websites, and the creation of ads to go in the space, a minimum budget of $40,000 per month is quite typical. However, there are ways to advertise no matter what your budget. You can advertise through banner ads on targeted niche sites, and even on high profile sites like Yahoo!, Excite, and Microsoft.com. Before we get into how to use them, let's take a look at what a banner ad is.

The Basics of Banner Ads

A banner ad is simply a message delivered in the form of a piece of art, usually a GIF image, that appears on a website and is linked to another website. The typical banner ad measures 468 pixels wide by 60 pixels high and appears at the top of a web page. Smaller ads (often known as postage stamp or thumbnail ads) are usually placed elsewhere on a page.

Ad rates are set by the sellers of the ad space and are based on how much traffic the site gets and how targeted the market is. (A *broad* market, meaning one that includes a broad range of people, is reached by Yahoo!; a *targeted* market or *vertical* market, meaning a market that is narrowly focused, is reached by Golf.com, for example.) For the purposes of selling ad space, traffic is discussed not in *hits* (the number of files downloaded when a user accesses a page) but in *impressions* or *page views*. (Both terms refer to the same thing; an impression or page view occurs when a pair of eyes falls on the page.) The price of ad space is described in *cost per thousand* (CPM), meaning what the ad space costs per thousand impressions or page views. CPMs vary widely; as mentioned, more highly trafficked sites get higher CPMs, but smaller sites with highly targeted and much-sought-after markets can, too.

Do They Work?

There's an old saying in advertising that half your advertising works but you never know which half. This, of course, refers to traditional media, where the size of the audience an ad space seller claims to be reaching can be measured according to agreed upon standards and even verified via a trusted third-party auditing company (Nielsen for TV, Arbitron for radio, and MediaMark research (MRI) for print.) But no one knows exactly how many of those reached by a specific ad appearing in a specific venue at a specific time actually bought the product as a result of that appearance of the ad.

Online media turned that whole business on its ear. For a long time, there was no third-party auditing system to verify claims of high traffic; even today, while there are companies engaged in verifying traffic numbers (ACNielsen, I/PRO, and Media Metrix, for example), standards that compare to the systems of measurement used in traditional media aren't fully set. (See Chapter 13 for more information about this.) In that context, and because it was easy to count how many users clicked on an ad to visit the site it led to, measuring *click-throughs* or the *click rate* came into vogue.

These days, banner ad rates tend to be based on CPM and advertising success tends to be measured in click-throughs. (Some companies even try to compare the click rate to conversion-to-sales.) Unfortunately for advertisers, users seem to be suffering from banner-ad overkill; they no longer see banner ads because the ads are so ubiquitous. As a result, overall click-through rates have dropped from an average of 2 percent in 1997 to less than 1 percent in 1999. Furthermore, measurement of the click rate does not take into account the level of brand awareness that was achieved or supported via the banner ads, and so, in a sense, we are back at square one: probably half your advertising works but you don't know which half.

Get Real Results

As we go forward, marketers are putting more emphasis on affiliate programs and email campaigns, but banner advertising remains an avenue for supporting brand awareness, and as such is in the mix of most big e-commerce promotion campaigns. To make the most of a banner ad campaign, first set realistic expectations. A banner ad campaign probably isn't going to drive traffic through the roof, and it isn't a direct response medium. But it can be effective in furthering brand awareness, and if you plan your campaign well you can achieve a reasonable level of cost-effective click-throughs.

Create Targeted Ads with a Call to Action

Your first step in building an effective banner ad campaign is to create effective ads. Hire a professional designer or use a good service. (bCentral offers design services through a partnership with a professional design firm that charges a very reasonable rate.) Whatever designer you use, if he or she is savvy to banner ad design, you'll be asked whether the ad is meant to drive click-throughs or further brand awareness, so be prepared to describe your goals.

The text in your ad must include a call to action. "Click here" is a call to action; but luring the user to click by clearly communicating the benefit of doing so would be a better call to action. A time-limited offer can work, but be sure that when the user arrives at your site by clicking the ad that the benefit offered is actually there. Scour the Web looking at banner ads, note those that intrigue you, and look at their messages. Generally you'll want to shape ads to appeal to different demographics on different sites; you'll also do well to rotate ads. People get tired of an ad after seeing it even a few times, and they tune it out. Brand names in banner ads might draw in the loyal customer and the curious clicker, but the brand name should be secondary to the branding message (see Chapter 4).

The typical ad's on-screen size is 468 x 60 pixels. The file size (including all panels and animations and everything) should be less than 10K. That's because you want it to load very, very quickly. You want it to pop into view before the user clicks away. To keep the file size under 10K, your designer will make the ad visually simple and will, as usual, use web-safe colors. Animation is a must these days, but as always, use it judiciously. Using two or three panels with some simple animation is fine; you don't want your ad to look like a circus—unless you are a circus.

Buy the Right Ad Space

Websites tend to sell ad space in three forms. The first, *run of the site,* means the ad might appear anywhere on the site; it will be "in the rotation," meaning that it will be rotated among the other ads that have been sold on a run-of-the-site basis.

A second alternative is to buy placement on a designated page. This allows you to target a page with a topic that would intrigue your target audience. For example, you might place an ad for gourmet dog treats on a page devoted to dog health on a site that deals more generally with pets.

> **Tip**
>
> It can be more effective to place your ad on a page *leading* to the page that's more closely aligned with your target audience. Why? Because you might then capture the target audience, luring them away with your own offerings, as they seek what interests them.

Chapter 12: Promoting to Your Target Market

The third form of ad space you might buy is based on a keyword search. In this case, you'd "buy a word," meaning that you'd purchase the privilege of popping your ad in front of anyone who searches on the target keyword. If the word you select is *anniversary*, for example, every time a user searches that site for anniversary, your ad for fresh flowers will appear.

To reach new customers, when you buy ad space, go broad. Broad in this sense might mean run-of-the-site on a general interest site, a search engine, or on a site devoted to a topic that is generally of interest to your target market. (Notice that in the print world, cars are advertised in magazines as varied as People, Esquire, and Time.) To reach highly targeted audiences, buy keywords on a big site or run-of-the-site ads on niche or vertical market sites.

Remember that in the ad space market, rates are set with the expectation of being negotiated down. You can offer less than the going rate; as much as 30 percent less as a starting point is not unreasonable.

> **Note**
>
> There are slow times in the industry when special bargains can be had. Midwinter is such a time; ad sales are slow for the weeks following the winter holidays, and you can get some nice deals for January.

You can also find good bargains through bCentral's AdStore, where you can purchase ad space with big sites (even the major search engines and directories) as well as targeted sites in a variety of industries. Using AdStore, you can purchase ad space for as little as $50 or as much as $2,000. You can also tailor your campaign by viewing demographics and other data, and you can log in to see the results of your campaign or to modify your ad.

Trade Ads

Trading ads can be as simple as trading ad space on one site for space on another. It can also be wonderfully creative. One e-commerce manager reports that he is bartering ad space on his site for discount hotel club memberships, which he then offers as prizes to his email newsletter subscribers and as incentives to affiliates. Another company describes approaching trade show producers within the target market and trading banners ads on the company's site for print ads in the trade show directory.

You can trade ads with many of the same types of sites you trade links with: sister companies, vendors, clients, and sites that offer complementary services or products. Yet another good option for trading banner ads is to get involved with Banner Network, a service offered by Microsoft via bCentral. Banner Network offers its members the opportunity to trade banner ads, target the sites on which the ads will appear, and track and measure results.

Sponsor Another Website

Sponsorship is not just a revenue source (as described in Chapter 2): if you turn it around so that you are the sponsor rather than the one being sponsored, it is also an alternative for promoting your site. In a sponsorship scenario, you pay to "sponsor" someone else's site; in return for this you get prominent placement on the site, usually with links back to your site. The relationship here is a deeper partnership than occurs when you buy banner ad space. A sponsorship deal can include the sponsor having a say in the content, for example. It can also include a combination of banners and buttons to indicate the sponsorship, and it can include distribution of co-branded content or interactive tools (such as financial planning tools). In a sponsorship arrangement, you can leverage content and a target audience without having to create the content or build the audience.

As you consider a specific sponsorship arrangement, ask yourself whether the site you'll be sponsoring is an appropriate venue for you. Appropriate questions to ask yourself are:

- Does the site's content, design, and functionality reflect well on your brand?
- Does the site reach the target audience you seek?
- Does the site attract a large enough audience to achieve your goals?
- Is the site's content updated frequently?

In a best-case scenario, you'd do well to survey the site's users to find out how effective they feel the site is. At the very least, ask the site's producers for some indications of that; perhaps the site's producers have surveyed users themselves and have results available for you to see.

As mentioned, one of the differences between buying ad space and entering a sponsorship arrangement is that as a sponsor, you can have some input into the site's content. You can, for example, object to content that might offend or undermine your appeal to your target audience. If such an objection is not addressed to your satisfaction, you can withdraw your sponsorship. But beware of actually controlling the content. To maintain audience loyalty and the site's credibility, the integrity of editorial content should remain free of interference. After all, you chose a site to sponsor presumably because the content was popular and well done. A good content provider should be just that, and your job is really to pay for—not to develop—content.

Establishing a sponsorship can provide you with the advantages of riding the crest of a wave of popularity without having to generate the attraction. The downside is that the up-front deal making can be time consuming. But be honest with yourself as you evaluate this option. Do you really have the resources and time to create such compelling content yourself? Above all, will sponsorship achieve your promotional objectives as well as or better than another method of promoting your site?

Leverage Newsletters and Discussion Groups

Email newsletters and discussion groups are some of the most effective methods available for boosting traffic. For example, one e-commerce venture reports that it has achieved a 25 percent click-through rate from its newsletter and a six to seven percent conversion-to-sales rate. This is such an important topic that Chapter 6 discusses in detail the ins and outs of launching and optimizing newsletters and discussion groups to drive traffic.

Briefly, email is a good way to drive traffic because it is effective and it's inexpensive to implement, but you must respect the universal resentment of getting junk email. Content has to be of value and interest, and to avoid the stigma of spam, it's best to allow people to opt in to your newsletters and email announcement lists. As you develop your email program, apply traditional direct marketing techniques by testing to find out what combination of content, offer, copy, and recipient list really works for you.

Make Your URL Prominent Everywhere

It probably goes without saying these days that you should make your URL obvious on every piece of print and every email message that goes out of your office. Add it to your stationery, business cards, brochures, sales sheets, and product packaging. Include it in a signature file that appears automatically at the end of every email message. (A signature file of half a dozen lines of text is just about right; longer ones start to look tacky.) Have all your employees do the same.

Also include it in your phone book yellow pages ads, and in any advertising you do on taxicabs, billboards, TV, radio, and matchbook covers. Paint it on your trucks. If you don't have trucks, you can rent them. Some "dot com" companies pay for the privilege of splashing their branding across other companies' trucks, cars, or even across city buses. It's believed in some quarters that moving ads like these attract extra attention. But it's also possible that seeing a "dot com" company's branding on something as tangible as a truck inspires a perception of brick-and-mortar solidity (and the attending credibility) in consumers.

> **Tip**
>
> Follow these quick tips in forming an offline campaign's message: Focus on value to the consumer, include a call to action, and include a human being to give consumers someone to identify with easily. These are the same guidelines you'd adhere to in any branding message. See Chapter 4.

Whenever possible, go beyond just showing your URL in promotional pieces. Showing the URL during an entire TV ad as well as working it into the ad's script increased results 25 percent for one company. Even in print, on billboards, and elsewhere, a branding message that tells customers what your site offers can improve results. A quick tagline that identifies your site, telegraphs its benefit or value proposition, and attracts attention is going to get more notice than a generic URL. Tauber Kienan Associates along with the URL *www.tauberkienan.com* doesn't say much about the company's promise; the tagline "Internet business, technical, and content solutions" says more.

Get Coverage in Magazines and Newspapers

Get your name out there, favorably and inexpensively and as often as possible, using traditional public relations (PR) techniques in non-traditional ways. PR does not require the capital an ad campaign does; instead, it takes time and energy. Remember that public relations is *relations*. It involves a relationship with the press: building a relationship, nurturing it, and leveraging it. Successful PR professionals hone their interpersonal and organizational skills to a fine edge. They know who's who, what their media contacts care about, and how to approach them. They also know how to set priorities, plan and manage time, and control torrents of paper and endless rounds of telephone calls and emails. They know when to trumpet successes and how to put the right spin on trouble to perform damage control. You can learn and use professional PR techniques to inexpensively promote your e-commerce venture.

Your goal is positive exposure in business journals, trade magazines, newspapers, other local and regional publications, and on the Web. Getting your website's address into print or broadcast has the extra value (in addition to simple exposure) of being like a third-party endorsement. You can do a lot with no budget and just an investment of your time; with a small budget you're even better off. While a $20,000 budget for promoting a website over the course of a year buys nothing but stale peanuts in the advertising world, in the public relations world it can land coverage in major news media, garnering both exposure and credibility. For far less than that, you can launch a very successful local or regional campaign. Let's take a look at how you can launch a PR campaign.

Gather Materials

Your first order of business is to pull together tools. You need to identify a few phrases that describe your company, product, and site. Like the words and phrases you developed earlier in this chapter (to use in creating your site's title and META tags), these should be precise and descriptive. Use them to work up brief descriptions. Create a very short description (just a few words), a mid-sized description (perhaps 15 words), and a longer description (perhaps 25 words) of your company, product, and site.

> **Tip**
>
> Esther Schindler, along with members of the Internet Press Guild, has written a wonderful piece on establishing and maintaining press relations, which can be found at *www.netpress.org/careandfeeding.html*. Kirk Hallahan, at Colorado State University, provides a great Publicity Primer (*http://lamar.colostate.edu/~hallahan/hpubty.htm*) that includes checklists of materials. And the Voyager Group at *www.voyagergroup.net/press.htm* offers a comprehensive list of PR links along with PR advice.

You should also pull together the following resources:

- A professional photograph (slide, 8x10 glossy, or TIFF or JPEG) of your store, website, product, or your own face, whichever seems most appropriate to your campaign
- A list of key information (specs, data, dates, timelines, graphs, charts, awards)
- A few testimonials, endorsements, or quotes you can use (with permissions)

Write a Press Release

Armed with these materials, when you have news to publicize, you can write a press release. To get noticed, your press release must be, above all, newsworthy. What makes news? That's a big question, and the answer depends on the size and focus of the publication, on how your story compares to others received on the same day, and, frankly, on which way the wind is blowing. Here are a few possibilities:

- New products, services, locations, distributors, or personnel
- Sponsored events, rallies, awards, or seminars
- Receipt of awards, grants, honors, or designations
- Offerings of awards, grants, honors, or designations
- Formation of strategic partnerships, alliances, or co-branding ventures

As you write your press release, follow the standard format. Many books and websites describe this in detail; here is a primer to get you started.

- At the top, provide the date as well as complete information about who can be contacted for further information.
- Provide a concise headline that telegraphs your message.
- Place your most important message in the first paragraph.
- As you write the follow-up text, focus on the topic you are presenting, making clear what makes it unique and worth covering. Keep the press release short and to the point; it should never be more than one page long.
- In the text, use the active voice; avoid verbs that end in *ing*, for example. Eliminate unnecessary words or phrases, and avoid corporate-speak or industry jargon. "Leveraging our core competency, Fabrikam Incorporated's value proposition is a unique offering to our e-commerce partners" says just about nothing and takes a long time to do it. "Fabrikam Incorporated offers business support services to e-commerce companies" is more immediate and clear.
- In the final paragraph, provide company information and a brief paragraph of background. Include URLs that go directly to a page on your site that provides more information.

Launch Your Press Campaign

Send your press release to every appropriate person, avoiding those who are not appropriate. You can find out who's who via services or publications that list editors and honchos at major media outlets (MediaMap at *www.mediamap.com* lists technology and computer editors) or by checking the *mastheads* (listings of personnel and information) in print publications you've targeted. When you send out your press release, address it to individuals, not "the news desk." And please, spell people's names correctly. You want to show these people respect and demonstrate your competence.

> **Tip**
>
> To reach new customers, focus your press efforts on consumer and news media. For the deepest penetration into an existing market, reach into narrowly focused media; for example, if you sell pet supplies and are trying to reach deeply into a market of dog owners, go for highly targeted dog magazines.

When writing and sending press releases via email, make the header informative; don't let it look like spam. Avoid the phrases "press release," "demo," or "e-commerce solution" in your header; instead, use one of the headers you came up with for this occasion. Place your full contact information (name, phone number, address, email address, and URL) in your signature file. And while you will probably send the press release out to a number of contacts, don't include your entire press contact list in the To: line. Instead, send out individually if you must, or put the list in the Bcc (blind courtesy copy) line available with most email applications. Keep your electronic press release short, and follow standard pointers for writing press releases such as those described earlier in this section.

Post to Your Online Press Room

Of course you should post your press release in an online press room on your site. When you do, follow these guidelines:

- Make the contact information obvious. Ideally, your online press room should include a list of each PR person you have on staff (as well as any PR agency staff assigned to your account) along with their email addresses, surface mail addresses, and phone numbers. If your company offers more than one product or service and various people act as PR reps for those products or services, list each person's area of responsibility.
- Link to a page listing your company's executives with photos, titles, and correctly spelled names.
- Also provide a link to a product page with information and perhaps another link to actual product specs.
- Use minimal graphics in your press room area—time is of the essence to the press. A downloadable product photo is fine, but only if download is quick. Gratuitous graphics, heavy visual branding, animations, and trendy adornments are only barriers to meeting deadlines and will drive the press away.

Under no circumstances should you make press people register for access to your press room. These are deadline-driven people who work at a high clip; they are disinclined to be inconvenienced. And your goal is *relations*, remember? You want to make things as easy for these folks as possible, so you can set up a long-term, productive relationship with them.

After you've sent out a press release, don't follow up by calling and saying "Did you get my press release?" It's extraordinary how many editors just despise being intruded upon, especially with that hackneyed line. In addition, don't attach digital demos or photos to your email. Don't assume editors will automatically look at any demos you include; again, they are busy people and will ask for a demo if they want to follow up with you.

PR can be a very effective and inexpensive (though labor-intensive) technique for promoting your site. The downside, of course, is that it takes a while to build press relations and that you must constantly be generating buzz. But especially for sites with strong content or newsworthiness, the results of a PR campaign will build over time and can certainly pay off.

Become a Presence in Discussion Groups

If you create a discussion group, you or someone on your staff will probably be involved in moderating or hosting it. Obviously, in such a setting, you can subtly or not so subtly evangelize your site, product, or service. Alternatively, you can participate in other online or email discussion groups, offering advice, counsel, tips, and, incidentally, pointers to your website.

You do not, however, want to do this willy-nilly. Because you don't want to waste your own time and because you don't want the effort to backfire, you must target appropriate venues and behave appropriately within them. To find discussion groups that fit your target, start with bCentral's ListBot groups and the directory called Liszt (*www.liszt.com*) as well as chat hosts and calendars.

Before you start actively evangelizing in an electronic discussion, be sure to find out about the group's ground rules. Some allow outright advertising and promotion while others do not. You can still be an authoritative presence on those that do not, and the combination of your signature file (showing your URL) and the wisdom of your commentary will, presumably, do the job just as well as or better than a more blatant ad or announcement.

Part 4: Maintain, Promote, and Succeed

Mix Online and Offline Promotion

While some methods of promoting your e-commerce venture will suit your needs better than others, it should be clear by now that an integrated campaign is the way to go. Traditional (offline) advertising focuses on awareness, repeating a branding message with frequency to a mass audience. A maximized online campaign with mixed, interlocked media can leverage messages tailored to targeted groups of customers. Ironically, offline media seems to reach a broader audience; its use also builds credibility and drives significant traffic. But online media (links, search engine listings, email) reaches a more targeted audience.

> **Note**
>
> Employing a number of techniques, including both offline and online efforts, certainly nets you more than the sum of their parts. A diligent backlink campaign creates popularity, boosting your search engine ranking, which in turn makes the site both more popular and attractive to the media. This makes it more interesting to prestigious sites that might backlink, and further boosts search engine ranking. The overall result is a dynamic interweaving of promotional wizardry.

But how do you know exactly what's working? There is simply no great method at this juncture for tracking overall response to specific promotional activities, especially in the short term. It's always been difficult to know and measure the results of advertising; often, you'll see a spike in traffic but not know exactly what caused it. You can match traffic data as closely as possible to advertising schedules or watch for jumps after a PR success. You can compare the zip codes of those who buy to the locations of your current regional ads or PR campaigns. You can also try giving customers a discount that's tied to use of a unique code, or you can push them to a unique URL to see whether they're taking the bait.

To best measure the progress of individual aspects of your promotional efforts, you will have to change one thing at a time and watch closely to isolate what works. As you get a feel for what's working for you, it's best to cut back on efforts that show marginal returns and focus on what's apparently successful. Don't limit your thoughts to what drives traffic, but instead focus on what drives sales and what is cost-effective. If you get most of your customers from full-color advertising in a niche magazine but the advertising costs a pretty penny, and you also have to mail out brochures to provide more information and close the sale, that represents both expense and legwork. If you get fewer sales from your website but the costs are comparatively minimal, your dollar might be better spent on website promotion.

Keep in mind that Internet publicity is still in a "try everything" phase. As a group, 47 marketing managers surveyed by Forrester Research reported that they had been allocating 44% of their budgets to offline efforts and the rest to online efforts, but they did not report conclusive results from their efforts. Your best bet, then, is to promote your site using as wide a variety of techniques as you can envision. As you market, track what works and focus your efforts there.

Chapter 13

Assessing Your E-Commerce Success

To many business people, the key measurement of success is dollars earned. Profitability drives most business. But profit and revenue are not the only benchmarks of success. The goals you've set for your website will define the terms of its success, and the terms might not be based on profit. For a site that promotes a product or service, for example, the amount of media presence generated might be a better measure than profitability. Other sites might use the level of community involvement that's created, or a reduction in customer service calls to define success. In the case of a research site, for example, the quality of the data acquired in the site's surveys and the level of credibility the site's reports are achieving are likely to be the best measure of success.

Most e-commerce endeavors can be considered start-up ventures; it usually takes a while to ramp up to profitability. As you build toward profitability, you will need benchmarks that measure your venture's progress. How much revenue a venture produces (as opposed to how much profit it creates) is one measure of business viability. The number of customers served can be another useful benchmark. In print publications, circulation is often cited to measure a company's success both before and after the company achieves profitability. To satisfy potential advertisers, investors, any media that takes an interest in your venture, and your own basic business interests, you must have methods for quantifying your success.

Measuring traffic is such a method. In addition to quantifying your success, measuring traffic can help you focus your business development and marketing plans, buy and sell advertising, and allocate resources effectively. Additional statistics about the who, what, why, and when of your website's audience will help you refine your strategies, develop better tactical solutions, and point your resources in the right direction.

> **Note**
>
> Measuring traffic is equally important to sites that have non-profit, profit, cost savings, media presence, purchase support, or other goals. Measuring traffic and getting a complete picture of who uses your site and how they use it will help you direct your e-commerce endeavor regardless of its goals.

What Does Success Mean to You?

The measurements you put your trust in as you assess your success must match the goals you set when you planned your site. For a retail sales site, some obvious measures of success are traffic, how many users are making purchases, how few returns occur, how few customer service events are experienced, how much revenue is produced, and ultimately, how much profit is created. In business-to-business settings, the best measurements might be those that account for getting and keeping customers. In a case where the product is capital equipment (for example, expensive biotechnical devices), the number of calls received and the number of sales generated by website leads and closed later by sales reps can be the milestones.

Depending on your site's mission, its overall success might be measured in a variety of ways. Here are some examples:

- If your goal is to promote (a company, product, service, person, or viewpoint), you can measure your success by:
    - Media presence (print, broadcast, online)
    - Number of registrants at the site or for your newsletters
    - Rising traffic

Chapter 13: Assessing Your E-Commerce Success

- If your goal is to inform, you can measure your success by:
  - Growth in subscriber base or traffic levels
  - Increased credibility with audience and other media (as shown by how the product or service is described or referenced by others, for example)
  - More ad sales at higher rates
- If your goal is to educate, you can measure your success by:
  - Number of registrations
  - Number of graduates from courses or programs
  - Number of repeat students
  - Raised scores on tests or evaluations
  - Increased recognition as a learning center
- If your goal is to distribute, you can measure your success by:
  - Number of visitors who download the product or files
  - Decreased number of support events
- If your goal is to sell, you can measure your success by:
  - Number of customers and repeat customers
  - Number of sales
  - Revenue generated
  - Profit produced
- If your goal is to research, you can measure your success by:
  - Quality of data gathered
  - Credibility with the target audience
  - Media presence
  - Number of participants in online surveys and quality of their participation
- If your goal is to provide customer service or technical support, you can measure your success by:
  - Decreased costs
  - Quicker resolution of problems
  - Fewer events requiring staff response

> **Note**
>
> Standards and methods differ depending on what you're measuring. Successfully analyzing an online community or an intranet, for example, requires an approach different than that described in this chapter. For more information about other approaches to analyzing information, see Chapter 5 (conducting surveys), Chapter 6 (measuring community success), and the Appendix (measuring intranet and extranet success).

The Benefits of Measurement

The benefits of setting the right standards and measuring success are many. With good measurement of traffic, you can:

- Maximize ad revenue by quantifying and verifying traffic to advertisers; make informed decisions about buying and selling ad space; and set your ad rates accurately
- Time your promotions to leverage what you know about traffic and your audience's habits
- Increase the response rate for promotions, surveys, registrations, and other ventures
- Demonstrate return on investment (ROI) to yourself, your company's executives, and your investors
- Monitor and forecast trends so that you can provide the best possible service when it's actually needed
- Tune your site's performance and make better technology decisions
- Structure and enhance your site's content, navigation, and usability based on real user feedback and observations about how the site is actually used
- Allocate resources wisely to further improve efficiency and optimize content and design when needed
- Know your customers better, meet their needs, expand what you offer them, and extend your brand and your business reach to meet the right target audience

Consider the case of one research and information site that launched with strong expectations of achieving its intended goals. Within a few months, monitoring of the site's traffic and usage patterns along with analyzing a survey of site users revealed that unexpected areas of the site were getting attention, while one area that had been planned as a real traffic-getter was languishing with low numbers. The company quickly decided to spend time and attention on the more popular areas and jettison the loser. In another example, the management of a casino found through monitoring its website that Wednesday night was the most active night for booking weekend reservations and was able to plan its promotions and staffing accordingly. At an education site, managers discovered many site users taking an interest in a web page that described a certain course, but few people were registering for it. What was the problem? A little tinkering with the wording of the course description resulted in a sudden spike in registrations.

Getting to Know Your Audience

Long before you launch your site, you will have defined your intended audience. As an entrepreneur or manager, that's part of the basic planning you must do to assure yourself (and potential investors) that your endeavor is a viable business venture. Defining your audience allows you to focus strategy for your offerings, branding, and your overall marketing plan. It also allows you to assess your expected return on investment (ROI).

As time goes on, your initial speculation might need some adjusting, and as you monitor your site, the information you gather can be transformed into more accurate knowledge of the audience you are actually reaching. One great promise of e-commerce is that you can stay close to your customers. You have a more direct connection with them than is possible in many business environments. Email, online surveys, and other direct feedback loops give your customers the opportunity to communicate more directly. Those avenues, along with other methods of tracking customer activities and responses, provide you with knowledge of your audience that can help you tailor your offerings and services to their interests and needs. The more you know about what your audience is doing at your site and when and how they are visiting, the more closely you can align your business with their needs. And that, most assuredly, spells success.

Part 4: Maintain, Promote, and Succeed

> **Note**
>
> Your online audience might differ dramatically from that of your brick-and-mortar store. For example, your online audience might be more concerned with convenient, quick delivery than with product merchandising. Or they might be more technically savvy—it's true that online book buyers buy more Internet books per capita than book buyers at brick-and-mortar stores do. Don't assume that you know your e-commerce customers based on your knowledge of your "3-D" customers. Get to know your market as it exists rather than as you believe it exists.

What Can You Know?

Just a few years ago, Internet professionals had to rely on their judgment and overall intuition for a sense of what worked. Of course, user feedback could be immediately received via email or online surveys, but objective data was scarce, and what there was of it came from detailed *log files* (long lists of electronic events as recorded by the server). These log files (shown in Figure 13.1) were hard to read and harder to interpret into trends. (Log files are further explained later in this chapter.)

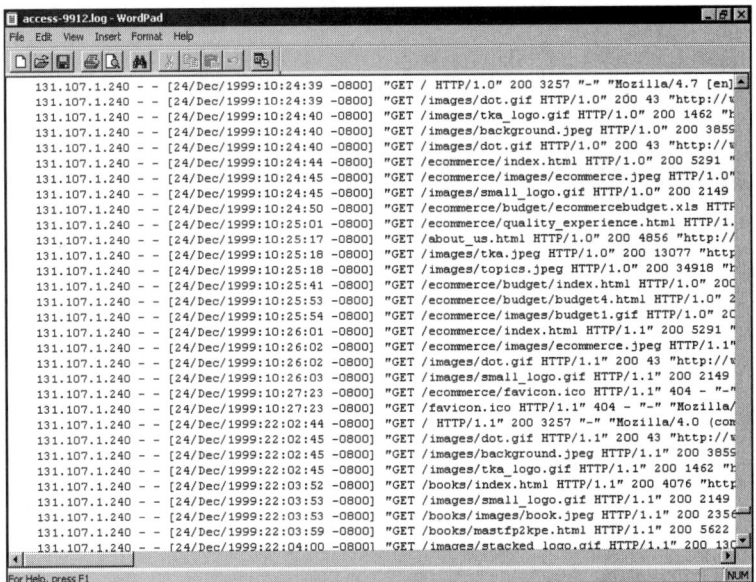

Figure 13.1

Log files aren't especially user-friendly.

Chapter 13: Assessing Your E-Commerce Success

Log files serve a fine purpose for server administrators and other tech types, but executives and managers want reports. They want readable facts about their site's visitors. As of this writing, detailed, accurate accounting for website statistics is still in its infancy. The whole question of what should be counted and how it will be counted is more complex than it might seem at first glance.

Consider, for example, these variables:

- One server can host multiple websites (see Chapter 10)
- One website can be served by multiple servers (either because it is mirrored on another server or because pieces of a single site are served by several servers)
- Any URL can be redirected to another URL

Further, the very question of how to identify and count *unique users* is a problem—which computers are accessing the site (and how many of them) can be counted, but several people can use the same accessing computer. There is simply no way to know how many *users* are truly using the site as compared to how many *computers*. (Unless you force them to register and log in each time they use the site, in which case they can still register under different names and skew the numbers. In addition, registering and logging in can be a barrier that many people will find daunting or annoying enough to keep them away.)

Another problem is that it's difficult to take accurate measurements and compare them to each other in an industry where standards of measurement have yet to be defined. While many tools exist for measuring impressions and other information, no two tools base their measurements on the exact same set of criteria. Different tools make different assumptions about, for instance, how (from a technical perspective) an impression or page view is defined. So you can use two tools to measure one site's traffic for a specific time period and come up with different numbers. You can know what is going on with your website's traffic and audience with, at best, a high degree of probability. But at this juncture, you cannot know exactly—at least not enough for business statisticians to be happy. If it's any comfort, however, your competitors are in the same boat, and many smart people are working feverishly to solve this problem.

In the meantime, unfortunately, no one data source can provide everything you need to know to run your site effectively, and no single tool or technology exists to bring data together into meaningful information you can use. The most complete, accurate information is obtained through analysis and cross analysis of:

- Server, network, and operating system log files
- User registration databases
- Transaction system databases
- Reports from third-party services that compile and verify data

But even without sophisticated feedback systems, high-powered technology, or pointed surveys, you can know or infer quite a bit about your site's users. You can know such basic information about your audience as:

- How many users or customers are visiting the site or a specific area of it
- How many users return as compared to how many are new visitors
- What customers do at your site, including what areas or pages they visit, how long they stick around, whether they make a purchase, or how they otherwise partake of your site's offerings
- What users want or need and what you can do better or differently to address those needs

This information allows you to focus your strategy and efforts to:

- Create one-to-one, custom communications
- Build strong and lasting business relationships
- Further your existing goals and further develop new goals

If you know you are getting a lot of traffic from a specific geographical region, for example—a simple matter that can be deduced from log files—you can target that region as a new market or one worth expanding. If you run a radio ad and provide both a phone number and URL in the ad, you can track the number of calls and spike in traffic you receive immediately after the ad is aired. If calls go up 10 percent and traffic 23 percent, you can demonstrate that the target audience has an interest in the website. You can also open the door to immediate user feedback. If you survey users about your products, you can incorporate their suggestions as you develop new products or improve existing offerings.

Chapter 13: Assessing Your E-Commerce Success

While user profiling and measurement of website statistics is still in its infancy, you must learn what you can in order to focus your efforts. Even using the most basic data sources and tools, you can be aware of:

- **What is accessed** The most requested pages (top 5–10 on a weekly basis); the most frequently used entry and exit pages; and the files most often downloaded.

- **Activity levels** The amount of activity measured by the day of the week and by the hour of the day.

- **Demographics** The number of new users and the number of authenticated users most often visiting. (Authenticated users are those whose identities can be verified, usually via a username and password.) Also from which countries or states most users are coming. The information on states, however, can be skewed; if many visitors are using the same ISP, their access might be routed through the ISP's state. (This is the case with America Online, for example. Its millions of users all appear to be in Virginia but might be in any state.) Remember, too, that traffic reports identify *computers* as users rather than people.

- **Technical statistics** Which pages are not found when requested by users, which pages load most slowly, and what other server errors are occurring. (A website that's working well experiences no technical errors.)

- **Browsers and platforms** Which are most often used (by both name and version number).

- **Referrals** Which sites, URLs, and search engines are sending traffic your way, as well as which phrases and keywords users are using to find you. (You can also identify visits by crawlers or spiders.)

You can also glean information from surveys that encourage users to "tell us about yourself," from site registration systems, and from how many views and clicks your online ads receive. (If you store such information in a database, you can then use Microsoft Access or Microsoft Excel to analyze the data.) Coding print ads or coupons or providing in them a special URL for accessing your site can also help you track information; again you can use Access or Excel to compile or index the results.

> **Note**
>
> You can also infer some information. If people are accessing your site or a specific page between 8 AM and 5 PM, for example, you can assume they are using a fast business connection. If they are primarily visiting in the evening or on weekends, they are probably at home, with a 56K modem, at best.

By using a few tricks of the trade, conducting some clever online surveying (discussed later in this chapter), and understanding how traffic measurements and user profiling work, you can go much deeper in your analysis of what's working for you.

Understanding Measurements of Traffic

Let's start with that old standby, hits. Every time a user accesses a web page using a browser, the user's computer is actually requesting the electronic files that make up the page from a server. Each request is a hit on the server. (A *hit* occurs every time a user's computer requests a file from a server.) But remember that a single web page can be made up of many files. Also, two pages that look very similar can be created using different methods, which means that (at least hypothetically) two web pages that look identical can generate a wide range in numbers of hits. One might generate four hits, for example, while the other might generate twenty or thirty. This makes counting hits a poor measurement of traffic. Comparing the number of hits one site or web page gets to the number another gets is a crude system and an inaccurate comparison.

A better method of comparison is to count impressions. An impression occurs every time a user's eyes fall on a page. Actually, from a technical perspective, it's the number of times a page is requested from the server. And as mentioned earlier in this chapter, while impressions represent a more accurate method for counting traffic, what really constitutes an impression (what combination of electronic data gleaned from the log files) has not been established within the industry. Nonetheless, traffic is often measured in impressions.

Chapter 13: Assessing Your E-Commerce Success

> **Note**
>
> When an advertising space sales rep talks about *guaranteed impressions*, he or she is describing the number of impressions the buyer is promised; that number of impressions (sets of eyes falling on the ad) will be delivered despite potential dips in traffic during the specified time period.

How many unique users a site or page gets is also of great interest. While most executives and managers asking about unique users would like to know how many individual people are using the site, the reality is that only unique computers can be counted. If half a dozen people are using the same computer, that computer will still register as only one unique user.

Clicks are very measurable. The click-through rate, also known as the response rate, increases whenever a link, button, or banner ad is clicked.

How "Cookies" Work

Cookies are a feature of some web browsers that allow the storage of a kind of a "note" to the browser among the browser's files on the user's computer. A cookie is placed among those files when the browser requests a web page from a server that uses cookies. Cookies get a bad rap among some users; those who don't like the use of cookies worry about someone else placing a file on their computers. They are also concerned about what cookies can be used to accomplish and whether cookies will be misused.

Most cookies are used for harmless and even useful tasks like identifying users and storing their passwords. Cookies can also be handy in user profiling: because a cookie actually can identify an individual user, the use of cookies provides a technique for measuring unique users. Cookies provide developers with options for tying surveys to transaction histories and accomplishing other sophisticated feats of correlation. For marketers and developers, the use of cookies opens up opportunities for serving the needs of customers by tracking their activities and preferences more closely.

Those users who worry about cookies sometimes think they open doors to increasingly intrusive marketing and perhaps even manipulation by commercial ventures. As you develop your website and its systems, keep in mind that how you use cookies is of as much concern to users as are other privacy issues.

> **Note**
>
> Many people consider viewing to be a passive response; in e-commerce, you want a more active response from users. You generally want them to click through, buy, or otherwise act on what you've presented. The rate at which passive viewing becomes active response is known as the *conversion rate*.

Analyzing Hits, Impressions, and Page Views

Now that we know what these terms mean and what the limitations and capabilities of website measurement are, how can we know what sort of traffic we're actually getting? Most of the data used to analyze traffic comes from log files. Even many third-party auditors base their reports on your log files. (Auditors verify traffic for the purpose of assuring advertisers that you are experiencing the boom you say you are.) Other data can be obtained from surveys, registrations, and the reports offered by banner exchanges and other programs. But because log files are so prevalent as a basis for reports, let's start there.

Looking into Log Files

If your site is hosted at an ISP on their server, the ISP will usually provide weekly or monthly log files for you to download and review. Note that in most cases, you must get the log files right away; they won't be available forever. If your site is on your own server (either at your location or elsewhere), retrieving and reviewing log files is your job (or your technical staff's job). To begin with, server log files record:

- The date and time of the hit
- The name of the host from which the request that resulted in the hit came
- The visitor's login name (if the user is authenticated)
- The referrer
- The visitor's IP address and host
- The number of bytes that were transferred

Chapter 13: Assessing Your E-Commerce Success

- The path (name and location) of the file that was served (which file it was, in other words, and exactly where it was located on your server)
- A listing of messages that indicates whether the file was actually served or an error occurred; if an error occurred, an error code will be provided

From this data, other data can be deduced; for example, log file analysis software will generate lists of the log file data. In those lists, the top-most item in the "path of the file that was served" list is the most popular page, while the bottom-most item in that list is the least popular page. An impression occurs (very roughly speaking) when a request is made to the server for an HTML file (as opposed to an image file or some other sort). A unique user is counted based on a combination of data, including the date and time, the name of the host, and the IP address.

Selecting Tools

Once you have the log files, you will have to use some type of analysis software tools to be able to measure traffic and understand your audience using the files. Select the tools you use to analyze traffic and create reports based on your real needs. Consider, for example:

- **Price** It can range from free or cheap, for basic software, to over $300,000 for custom solutions.
- **Capacity compared to your volume of traffic** Some software is better at crunching big numbers and large files than other software.
- **Customization** Some software offers only a predefined set of reports while other software enables you to write your own queries and specify what will be included in your reports.
- **Platform** You will probably run the software on your desktop computer rather than on the server; choose software that runs on the operating system used by the computer you'll use.
- **Service** Everything said about service in Chapter 10 applies here.
- **Company's stability and growth potential** If you rely heavily on your website and need reliable reporting, choose software from a known, reputable source that is likely to continue to service the software for the length of time you plan to use it.

Part 4: Maintain, Promote, and Succeed

Microsoft Site Server Express is website traffic analysis software that translates log files into useful information about requests to the server as well as to the users and organizations that interact with a website. It provides reports in an HTML format or in formats that can be used in Microsoft Office applications such as Word or Excel. Find out more about Site Server express at *www.microsoft.com*.

Tip

You can barter for traffic analysis reports by running a company's ad, for example, and by getting their premium reports package. Another option is to sign up with beta programs to minimize the cost of using pre-release software that offers more complete statistics and tracking reports.

Auditing Your Data

If you plan to sell ad space, you will quickly find that potential buyers want independent confirmation of your website's reported traffic. (This was discussed in Chapter 12.) They also like to know key information about the audience your site reaches. As of this writing, industry standards for exactly what to measure and how to measure it are still needed. For example, different software and different companies use different technical definitions of impressions. As a result, they use differing data to count impressions for any given website, and this leaves the entire system of counting impressions deeply flawed. (Although it is not as wildly inaccurate a basis for comparison as counting hits.) Despite all of these issues, media buyers want third-party confirmation and it must be provided. Various companies are in the game; they each do the job their own way.

Media Metrix (*www.mediametrix.com*) estimates site popularity based on consumer sampling. Consumer sampling generally works by providing groups of users with software to install on their computers. As the users go about their online routines, the software tracks what they do (what they click on, how long they stay, and so on). The sampling company retrieves this information from the group of users and compiles it into reports.

Both I/PRO Index (*www.ipro.com*) and Nielsen Media Research (*www.acnielsen.com*) provide software you can run on your server to glean the types of reports that media buyers appreciate: those that offer information about the most frequently accessed fields and directories, geographic distribution of the site's audience, which organizations are visiting the site, and so on.

ABC Interactive (*www.abcinteractiveaudits.com*) audits traffic based on your log files and the verified monitoring of a selected group of users. Their reports are based on this data and are in a format that's familiar to media buyers.

Note

Developments in third-party auditing are emerging quickly. Check the websites of the companies mentioned to find out what's new in the world of site traffic verification and audience profiling.

Soliciting and Analyzing User Input

Part of the beauty of doing business on the Web is that you can get input directly from the user or customer with fairly minimal effort. Offering an online survey and using automated tools to store, retrieve, report on, and analyze the data is a dream compared to sending out printed surveys, getting people to return them, and then compiling the data to make usable reports. (Chapter 5, in its discussion of staying close to the customer and providing top-notch customer care, discusses techniques and tools in detail, including how to leverage email for better communication with customers.) As you organize and write your surveys, follow these guidelines:

- Use interception or incentives to encourage participation. Either you can intercept every tenth or twentieth visitor with a request to fill out a quick survey (this will also facilitate a more random sampling), or you can offer those who participate an incentive such as a chance to enter a drawing for a free prize. (Keep in mind, however, that this will encourage participation by people who want the prize and will not represent the most random group possible.)

- Make the survey and the questions themselves short. Generally, specific questions with a few multiple choice responses get the best results. Keep the questions brief and offer between two and five possible responses. (A site geared toward education might ask users to identify themselves via a question such as "I am a: student/alumnus/potential student/parent of a student.") Include one or more open-ended questions as needed, but remember that few people enjoyed essay questions in high school and your users might find a survey full of open-ended questions off-putting, too.

- Ask the most personal questions last. Structure the order of questions so the less personal ones build to the more personal ones. If you must ask about income level, for example, place that toward the end of the survey, so that participants will have warmed up to responding and be more likely to answer. Place questions about your product or services earlier in the line up.

Note

Keep in mind that the Internet is a public place. If you ask for highly personal data, protect the privacy of survey respondents by using a secure server. And as you create your survey, don't ask questions that will reveal your confidential strategies to your competitors.

In your analysis, separate first-time users' responses from those of return visitors—they'll have differing viewpoints. (You can include a question in the survey to ask whether the respondent is new to your site.)

What to Do with All That Information

All too often, companies solicit customer feedback, look briefly at any statistics and reports they have, and then stack that valuable data in a closet to gather dust. Someday, they tell themselves, they will take all that information into account when they rebuild the website. Often, they simply aren't sure what the information suggests about what they ought to do. Remembering your site's goals and the methods of measuring traffic discussed throughout this chapter, consider Table 13.1. It will help you determine what data to analyze most closely and which areas of site development might need attention.

Table 13.1 Base Improvements on Appropriate Data

When Your Goal Is	Analyze This	And Improve This
To promote (a company, product, service, person, viewpoint)	Media presence, registrants, impressions	Branding message, price, promotion, how site's offerings, content, and design fulfill the branding
To inform	Number of subscribers, impressions, media presence, ad sales	Content, navigation, usability
To educate	Number of registrations, graduates, repeat students; scores on tests or evaluations; recognition	Course content, pricing, promotion, and branding; site content, navigation, usability
To distribute	Number of visitors and downloads, number of support events	Placement and descriptions of product, navigation, speed of download, customer service FAQ
To sell	Number of customers and repeat customers, number of leads and sales, revenue generated, profit produced	Call to action, value proposition, promotion, ease of use, navigation of transaction system
To conduct research	Quality of data, credibility, media presence, number of participants in surveys and quality of participation	Call to action, method of generating random or targeted sampling, ease of participation
To provide customer service or technical support	Cost per event, time to resolution, number of events requiring staff response	Customer self-service tools (FAQ and other methods), writing for the target audience, ease of use
To foster community	Number of participants, quality and frequency of participation, loyalty to the group or sponsor	On-topic interaction, quality of moderating, recognition of leaders, spin-off topics

Is the Customer Always Right?

Your job, as an e-commerce entrepreneur or manager, is to assess trends and make changes to your site, your products, and your services as needed. Few businesses that don't adapt to changing markets stay in business. Whatever your business, you have to take user feedback into account and give the customer what he or she wants and needs. The customer is not just always right; the customer is your reason for being.

You must always reply to user input and make changes based on trends, but it's important to recall that you don't have to do what every individual user demands. You cannot be all things to all people, and to try to do so leaves your company, site, product, or service undifferentiated in the eyes of the public. How can you know when to implement a user's suggestion and when not to? The answer will be different for each business, but it is usually based on clear understanding of your target market and how your product or service meets the market's needs.

E-commerce management is all a loop: know what your audience needs, build a site, launch and promote it; build up business and garner customer support and feedback; modify your product, service, and site based on your new understanding of your audience and their needs; and then rebuild, relaunch, and so on.

Buzzwords come and go, and trends swell and recede. You can ride the crest or fall behind. The real promise in e-commerce is that those who stay close to their customers can compete and succeed. To win, you must be flexible in the face of change, able to identify opportunity, and first to market. You must also be the best at what you do. You must harness the technology you need to support *smart* business solutions. And you must create a website that's of consequence to those who use it.

Appendix

Amending Your Site with an Intranet or Extranet

If you have an existing website, you can use technologies that are already in place to create an *intranet* (an exclusively internal website for communication and collaboration among employees) or an *extranet* (a secure external website for communicating with vendors, buyers, or partners). A Forrester Research survey has shown that 96 percent of the Fortune 1000 companies polled had intranets in place already or were building them. Secure intranets are widely reported to be a quick-growing segment of the Internet; they are much less expensive to build than private networks and can streamline processes, procedures, and the dissemination of information. CMPnet (*www.cmpnet.com*) has reported that leveraging existing web development infrastructure (to create an intranet or extranet, for example) can result in a return on investment of 1,000 percent or more! And according to a Computer Economics (*www.computereconomics.com*) study, 78 percent of the surveyed companies that had launched extranets had experienced returns equal to or in excess of their investments.

Appendix

There is simply no doubt that use of an intranet or extranet can be profitable both financially and in terms of increased efficiency. The benefits of implementing an intranet or extranet might include the following:

- Improved communication between users and the individuals and organizations they regularly interact with
- Decreased paperwork
- Streamlined processes and procedures
- Better use of human resources (HR) personnel through employee self-service
- Increased loyalty from customers and business associates

The key advantage of using web technologies in this way is that you can establish a *knowledge base* (a collection of experience and information about processes and initiatives of significance to a company). An intranet empowers employees in much the same way that a FAQ empowers customers: it provides a tool for keeping employees informed and assists them in quickly locating information without having to call on others. If an employee can quickly find answers, inquiries to other employees are reduced. Many human resources "events" are routine inquiries that eat up valuable HR staff time; each HR event costs a company roughly the same as a customer service event. As a comparison, an interaction that costs one dollar face-to-face might cost 10 cents by phone and less than three cents if it occurs via website-based or intranet-based employee self-service. Further, an intranet allows information such as the employee handbook to be updated quickly and easily without reprinting and redistributing it to all employees.

Note

If your organization is small and the employees are all based in the same place, you probably don't need an intranet. A simple network will allow you to share resources, and you'll probably communicate effectively via email and face-to-face conversation. However, if you work with virtual teams, have a decentralized organization, or if your company has expanded beyond 50 employees, you could find an intranet invaluable. Similarly, an extranet will be of more value to larger companies with a broad base of associates requiring frequent interaction.

What Are Intranets and Extranets?

An intranet is simply a website created for the internal use of an organization. It uses the same general technologies as a public website but is accessible only to employees or authorized agents of the organization. The language used on the intranet might differ from the language used to communicate to the public, and sometimes the visual branding apparent on the company's public website isn't carried through on the intranet site. Users access the site with a web browser just as they would a public website. An intranet is "protected" from the outside world by a firewall. (For more information about firewalls, see Chapter 10.)

An extranet, unlike an intranet, is accessible to authorized *off-site* users; these include people and organizations with whom the company does business. Only those users who have been provided with a valid username and password can use the extranet. Even then, some users might have their access limited to specific sections of the extranet. For example, a buyer to whom your reps sell might have access only to their own company's account information, a sales rep working in the field might have access to all of his or her accounts, and a receptionist logging in from home to check email probably would not have access to any financial information.

Typical Uses of Intranets and Extranets

The basic goal of all intranets and extranets is to facilitate communication. In a typical scenario, human resources information is placed on an intranet so that employees can look up information in a snap. For example, an employee who wants information about benefits can access it without going to an HR professional and can access it 24 hours a day. Reports, white papers, software manuals, and website style guides can all be placed online as well. All employees can then benefit from this legacy of wisdom and focus time and energy on the productive aspects of their jobs. Other examples of shareable information include training schedules, newsletters, vendor information, and internal job postings. Consider the following examples of material that can be placed on intranets by various departments.

- **Human resources** Procedures and policies related to hiring and firing; orientation and training; benefits (medical and dental plans, vacation, pension, 401K, and stock options); grievances; drug and alcohol policies; employee records (you can make these available only to a select group or allow employees to update their own records, for example, when a change of address occurs); and downloadable forms to be used for insurance enrollment, vacation requests, and changes to tax status or pension plans.

- **Sales and marketing** Product information (prices, specs, and manufacturing or delivery schedules); information on new marketing initiatives; advertising schedules; press releases; "best practices" advice on sales techniques; and customer leads. You can also link customers to internal systems.

- **Product development** Documents and charts regarding research, planning, and project status; schedules and timelines maintained via group and individual calendars; contact information for team members working on a project; and discussion groups or message boards for direct communication. An electronic whiteboard and other collaborative software can allow a group to work together despite geographic distance; this software can be available for download via the intranet.

- **Customer service** Reports of issues, problems, or customer service events; problem-tracking information; price and product information; policies about returns and exchanges or service agreements; scripts and training materials for customer service reps; and links to a knowledge base.

- **Management** "Managers' Tool Kit" applications that provide access to a system for processing new employees, conducting reviews, giving raises and promotions, and processing terminations; and employee pay stubs (some high tech companies, where it is assumed that every employee is on the intranet, have dispensed with paper pay stubs entirely).

- **Information Services (IS, also known as *Information Technology* [IT])** Internal technical support via online documentation, FAQs, and email; lists of company-approved software that employees can download from the intranet; and computer-based training (CBT) systems that allow for self-paced study of new software.

- **General** Job postings and procedures for applying for in-company transfers; employee directories (with a search engine that makes finding staff and their contact information easy); organizational charts for the company or department; and company or departmental newsletters.

The use of an intranet facilitates the effective exchange of information and sharing of resources between departments. Employees, team members, or business associates can be encouraged to post their Microsoft Word documents, Microsoft Excel spreadsheets, Visio drawings (such as organization charts), Microsoft PowerPoint presentations, or Microsoft Project timelines to the intranet. In a more innovative example, a product group might post a dozen different packaging proposals to the intranet so that the employees can vote for their favorite.

Former intranet site manager Maureen Nelson reports that where she worked, webmasters responsible for a wide range of sites met weekly to discuss issues and offer each other strategies. Because the group was geographically scattered, the meetings were conducted by conference call, and any material presented at the meeting was later posted to the intranet for those who missed the meeting. Maureen says, "All attendees were required to 'sign in' over the intranet, so meeting leaders could tell who had attended. As people signed in, their email addresses were made available so everyone could contact each other after the meeting to discuss things further."

The examples are endless. As your company grows, you can place a company "library" on the intranet where designated employees can conduct research or download PDF files or electronic books that the company has licensed for its use. A company store can offer employees special discounts; a company travel center can facilitate travel planning for executives, sales reps, or other frequent travelers; a company directory can offer maps and directions to various locations or campuses; an online registration system can offer employees the opportunity to sign up for training sessions that are then conducted either online or offline.

As with intranets, the uses and applications of an extranet can range from A to Z and back again. For example, a temporary employment agency that uses a paper-based payroll system could have a problem if its growth exceeds the capacity of that system. To manage the growth of a widely dispersed "staff" of on-site temporary employees, the employment agency could build an extranet using Microsoft systems and technologies including Microsoft Internet Information Server (IIS), Microsoft SQL Server, and Microsoft Internet Explorer. Employees and client companies could then use these technologies to log in time sheets and other information, enabling the employment agency to cut its costs and its payroll processing time dramatically, despite its growth.

Appendix

Assess Cost and Return

The cost of creating an intranet or extranet can vary widely depending upon the breadth of the site's purpose, the technologies used, and whether you have to build it from the ground up. If you can piggyback on existing systems built for your public website, and if the intranet or extranet is simple, costs can be negligible. The process could be as simple as converting some company documents to HTML and posting them on a password-protected portion of your web server. Using the design templates created for your public website will also keep costs to a minimum.

If your intranet or extranet endeavor is more complex, or if you have to build it from the ground up (meaning that a back end and a design have to be generated), the development and implementation costs will be comparable to those of a public website of the same size and complexity. To find out more about the range of possibilities, refer to the discussion in Chapter 2 of the expenses involved in building a website.

As you consider return on investment, ask yourself how the intranet or extranet will genuinely help your business. It should provide you with some combination of the following benefits:

- Improved competitive edge, perhaps through shared knowledge
- Increased sales as a result of faster access to the information required to support and close a sale
- Reduction in labor, production, or distribution costs resulting from the automation of everyday functions
- Better productivity through access to information, resources, or tools, or through online access to traditionally available data
- Faster time to market
- The capacity to share more information with vendors or partners
- More effective customer support
- New and more practical support for collaboration among virtual or decentralized teams

All of these are potential returns on your investment. Quantifying these returns might be challenging before you launch your intranet or extranet, but given what many companies report, evidence of return can quickly be apparent. Still, keep in mind that an intranet or extranet, once launched, is likely to require as much care and upkeep as a public website.

Address Management and Technology Issues

As in the building and management of a public website, pre-production planning of the intranet or extranet is vital to the initiative's success. A great deal of the planning in this case, however, concerns issues of internal management. To begin with, you'll have to determine in whose portfolio of responsibility the day-to-day management of the site (or sites) will reside. (In other words, who will "own" it?) How will it grow? And of all the groups that might be served, which must be served first? You simply cannot serve all groups at once; it's best to choose one or two to participate in a pilot program as you develop your plan and then expand your efforts later. Human resources and perhaps product development are generally good candidates for a fledgling intranet. Once these efforts are in place and the kinks are ironed out, you can expand to include other groups.

> **Note**
>
> Like other company efforts, the intranet or extranet will be the focus of departments' or individuals' varying agendas. Upper management must specify a vision and purpose for the endeavor. What are its highest priorities? You cannot do everything for or be all to all groups; in most cases effort must be focused on doing the most good for as many beneficiaries of the site as possible.

Information on an intranet can be organized by department, by professional interest, by function, or by extracurricular interest. All the HR information can go in an "HR" area or site; an internal publication of interest to all the IS people can be posted in an "IS" area; a newsletter for managers only can be placed in a cross-departmental "Management" area; and information about the softball team, the safety group, the diversity group, or the company branch of Toastmasters can go in an "Extracurricular" area. On an extranet, information can similarly be divided according to the needs of the business associates the extranet serves.

You will have to determine who the content providers will be. Will the group that launches the site also be the group that maintains it? Once these decisions have been made, you'll also have to specify standards for publishing or posting to the site (see Chapter 11). Is a standard look and feel or editorial tone required? In the case of multiple-site intranets or extranets, is each site allowed its own look? Will all users have the same browser (freeing you from the multitude of design decisions you have to make to serve an audience that has several versions of a variety of browsers)?

Tip

In an organization that offers more than one intranet site serving the needs of various internal groups, you'll want to establish one portal or home page that will serve as an entry point to the other sites. Providing a portal makes it easier for staff to navigate a group of sites and provides room for the overall intranet effort to expand through the addition of more groups' sites.

Creating Consistent, Clear Policies

Rules may be made to be broken, but they also provide people with a set of parameters they can work within. In that sense, rules help keep the peace. Providing your staff with written policies addressing key aspects of your intranet or extranet plan will keep everyone on track. It will also help to avert challenges from individuals and groups within the company who have special agendas. At times, you might want to grant privileges or bend the rules for special circumstances, but in general, good policies are just that, and applying them consistently will help everyone avoid unpleasant surprises.

- An **access policy** should state who (among the employees or business associates served by the intranet or extranet) gets access to which information or areas of information. A certain amount of training and orientation might be needed to ensure that those who have access know how to use the applications.

- A **publishing policy** should define the strategic vision for the intranet. Without a publishing policy, your intranet could become a chaotic jumble of information that slows rather than facilitates communication; navigation will be awkward, and the whole effect will be an impression of weak credibility. The publishing policy should also address who can publish and what can be published. (Not everything that *can* be published should be—you might not want your quarterly profit and loss statements posted for all employees to see). Appoint an "editor-in chief" or intranet manager to watch over the publishing policy and make sure it is followed.

(continued)

> **Note**
>
> Remember that content posted to an extranet is subject to quality assurance (QA) and approval, just as content posted to the public website would be. See Chapter 11 for more on QA cycles.

> ***Creating Consistent, Clear Policies*** (continued)
>
> - **Content policies** prevent intranet content from quickly becoming redundant, conflicting, and outdated. You can empower departments within your company to publish their own information on the intranet or extranet. Indeed, they can each have their own sites as needed and as is advisable. Remember, however, that you must provide parameters. Must they use the standard look-and-feel or editorial guidelines? Are only certain technologies to be used? Can only certain types of content be posted? What review and approval process will you require? Ultimately, someone will have to watch over the efforts of the various departments or offer technical support. At the very least, communication is required to ensure that the same information is not posted and updated by different teams, and at different times. A single portal to common information and to the various departmental sites, along with clear publishing policies, is often a good solution to this problem.
>
> - A good **security policy** will put employees, business associates, and your network administrator at ease. Some employees might be concerned, for example, that an intranet that asks them to post their social security numbers in an online application form is not adequately secure; someone must maintain security and notify the employees that it exists. On an extranet, you want to make sure that those accessing password-protected areas are reaching only the servers they're authorized to reach.
>
> As with all guidelines, policies about access, publishing, content, and security will evolve with time, but thinking them through at the outset will keep you from scrambling to address problems (and force compliance) later.

Appendix

Following along in the publishing and posting track, you'll have to decide who can actually publish to the intranet or extranet. Who will be in charge of the accuracy and reliability of the information? How fresh will the content be? Who will set, enforce, and monitor publishing policies for the site? Policies will have to address access, publishing, content, and security. Who will be in charge of creating them and making sure they are followed? This might be the charge of one person or of a cross-functional or cross-departmental team. If you go with an individual, he or she might be accountable, but if you go with a team, all its members might feel they have a stake in the site and develop an appreciation of its potential.

Caution

As always, it's important to manage expectations. Do this both up and down the ladder. It's quite typical for people new to the power of online media to first dismiss its potential and then, when they see what's possible, to expect the world. At first, HR might see only the possibility of posting job openings, but when they get a whiff of what others are doing, they might request a pie-in-the-sky list ranging from online job application processing to video interviewing over the intranet! In such a case, a little communication is necessary; the limitations of available technologies, the company's overall agenda, and the current priorities have to be explained clearly to the now enthusiastic supporter of the intranet or extranet.

Providing for Security

Security is of enormous concern in a website whose content is private employee material or confidential company information. As the executive or manager who oversees management of this sort of site, you'll want to be assured that appropriate security policies and systems are in place. Someone will have to specify, for example, who has access to what information on the site. Will there be different levels of security for various types of information? In the case of one company, it was determined that three levels of access were necessary just for the HR intranet. The broadest access was for employees (who accessed the same policies and procedures found in the employee handbook); medium-restriction access was provided to HR specialists (who accessed information on how to handle employee issues such as hiring and termination as well as how to communicate about a recent merger); and the most restricted access was for staffing specialists (who accessed information about which departments were cutting back on staff and which were recruiting). Security policies must be documented, communicated, and enforced for the intranet or extranet to succeed.

> ### Tip
> If you are using IIS as your web server software and people on the intranet are using Internet Explorer as their web browsers, security can be both simplified and made more powerful. Users can log in to the intranet and the network in one step, and the security established for your network will carry over to your intranet without much additional effort.

Which technologies will be used and what equipment is needed are issues integral both to security and to the overall effort. Standard questions in this area include: Who will make regular backups of the site and its information? How will new users be provided with access and browser software? How will scalability (the ability of the site to grow as needed) be assured? Someone must monitor usage and the server's load capacity. Who will that be? And who will decide when it's time to upgrade or add servers? You or your technology staff will have to determine what software and hardware to use, as well as what staff will be needed. Will you train existing technology staff or hire new people? If you train existing staff, remember not to spread them too thin. Unless your company is very small, your main IT person can't also be your intranet or extranet webmaster. Each of those jobs can easily be a full-time responsibility.

> ### Note
> Whether you hire new people or use employees you already have, remember that they'll have to be trained and retrained as tools and technologies evolve. Sending them to a class or a conference allows them to buff up their skills and network with their peers, from whom they can pick up time-saving tips. Buying them software or art CDs lets them work faster with better tools and produce a more professional looking site. The Web changes very fast, so be prepared to invest in this group continuously.

You'll have to address basic infrastructure issues such as how people will access the intranet or extranet. Keep in mind that not everyone might have Internet access. You also need to know if your business associates—not to mention your staff—have computers and browsers. If not, how will those without computers be served? (You might provide one or more general-use computers staff members can use on their lunch hour or

Appendix

during key times of the year, such as open enrollment periods for insurance.) One manufacturing company was so convinced of the long-term cost savings of an intranet that they bought PCs for every employee. Even factory workers could access the intranet from home—all they needed was a password. Another manufacturing company placed a single computer in a kiosk on its plant floor for the workers to use.

> **Tip**
>
> Tie everything into the business. If, for example, an intranet doesn't support the people who support the business, it will be seen as a cost center (otherwise known as an unprofitable drain on revenue). Have high-level executives on the planning committee to make sure the issue of the intranet's business relevancy is raised and answered. This will avoid the uncomfortable necessity of "making up" a business justification later. And make sure the company management is leading the intranet or extranet movement, not following it. An "underground" movement might be viewed with suspicion or seen as a hobby by the company owners or executives.

Remember to consider how the intranet or extranet will be connected to *legacy systems*, including existing databases and order-fulfillment systems. (A legacy system is one that has been carried over from the past.) On the HR intranet, will employees be able to access their own records? Can they just look at them, or can they update them and see their changes reflected in the records in the legacy system? Think about integration of the extranet with the customer service call center, if there is one. Some companies require their business associates to use the company extranet in order to conduct business. For example, a printing company might require its clients to upload print-ready files to the printing company's extranet, or a car parts dealer providing parts to smaller auto supply retailers might require that orders be placed via the extranet. In either case, the status of the project or order could also be tracked via the extranet.

> **Note**
>
> Using technology such as Microsoft Active Server Pages, it is possible for developers to create web page front ends on some legacy systems. Whether your legacy system can be converted in this way will depend on its age, what type of database it uses, and other factors. Ask a qualified developer for advice.

Getting the Support of Management

For funding to be adequate, support of upper management is needed. Upper management's first concern is rightfully what the return on investment will be, and return on investment for an intranet or extranet might be difficult to measure. A savings in the cost of distributing information printed on paper might be evident, but the savings in employee time is less immediately quantifiable. Good indicators of whether or not an intranet is being used can be the site's traffic and the volume of email the site receives. For more information, see "Measure Intranet or Extranet Success" later in this chapter as well as the discussion in Chapter 13 about assessing the success of a public website.

> **Note**
>
> Evangelizing must be constant. Let employees know the intranet or extranet is there. Add its URL to print and email documents wherever appropriate, and if employees calling within the company hear a different message than customers while they're on hold, add it to that message. Send out a monthly email newsletter telling employees what's new on their intranet or describing to business associates (who have opted in to the newsletter) what's new on the extranet. Include links to new or featured pages. Evangelizing the intranet or extranet will remind others to use it and will keep the company as a whole informed about what the endeavor is accomplishing.

Be Conversant: What You Must Know

Just as the budget for building an intranet or extranet from the ground up parallels the budget for building a public website from scratch, the issues you need to understand are roughly parallel. The technical concepts involved are similar; it is mainly the level of security and the method of restricting access that varies. An intranet or extranet is comprised of a back end and perhaps middleware (see Chapter 10). It has a front end that looks like a public website and is accessed via a browser. The design of its pages is bound by the same general limitations of HTML and graphics as a public website. (It is possible to require employees to use one version of one web browser on all their computers. Although you might not then have to design for multiple browsers and versions of browsers when you design

Appendix

your intranet pages, you still have to cope with the basic limits of what can be done using the available technology.)

To work effectively with intranet or extranet developers, you'll need a basic understanding of servers, databases, ISPs, and security. Your developer will talk about intranet-specific and extranet-specific concepts such as authorization, authentication, encryption, and firewalls. These concepts are generally described in Chapter 10. Remember: as a manager, you don't need a developer's level of knowledge, but you do need to address some basic strategic questions, which are, again, similar to those you were introduced to in Chapter 1. For example, you'll want to define the goals of your intranet or extranet initiative. To focus your strategy, consider the following:

- What you want the site to do—for the employees it serves if it's an intranet, or the business associates it serves if it's an extranet
- How you'll measure success; in other words, how will you know when the intranet or extranet has succeeded? What will have been accomplished for your company?
- Who will be responsible for (or "own") the intranet or extranet? In a small company, the intranet, extranet, and public websites will probably all be managed by the same individual or group. In a mid-sized company, a specific team might be responsible for the intranet or extranet, perhaps within the department that's most directly associated with the site's goals or purpose. A larger company might have multiple departmental intranets or extranets, with each department managing its own site. In that case, overall strategy would be set at the corporate level, with a task group or committee consisting of representatives from the various departments assigned to develop overarching policies for the sites.

Note

Extranets are usually owned by the person or department that interacts the most with the business associates who use the extranet. For example, an extranet devoted to supporting sales would be managed by the sales department, while an extranet supporting product development might be managed by the research and development team.

Measure Intranet or Extranet Success

Like any other online venture—and indeed any business venture at all—the intranet or extranet will be expected to meet goals. These goals are likely to be set in a business or project plan; they might be "soft" goals (such as improved internal communications) or "hard goals" (such as revenue produced from new customers).

Assessing success based on soft goals is not the easiest task. A measurement of the amount of use an intranet or extranet site gets suggests its usefulness (see Chapter 13). You can also survey employees or business associates to find out more about whether the site meets their needs. Ask them whether they have access to the intranet or extranet; whether they use it and how often; what other sites they visit most in the course of their work; and what kind of information or applications they would like to see on the intranet or extranet. One large company reports that it originally had a "company store" in the form of a print catalog, but when employees said that they'd prefer to buy over the intranet, the company added an e-commerce component to the internal site.

Soft benefits, such as (in the case of an extranet) wider reach, improved processes, quicker time-to-market, and a boost in customer loyalty, also won't win the day when budget time rolls around. A measurement of reduced costs in the areas the intranet or extranet addresses is a more apparent success. Specifying hard goals, such as (again in the case of an extranet) increasing revenue or the size of the customer base, makes the measurement of success much more tangible. In the end, to be seen as a business asset rather than as a cost center, an intranet or extranet must support a business plan with specified, attainable goals.

Glossary

acquiring bank A bank that handles merchant accounts, allowing companies to receive payments (from customers) made via credit cards. *See also* issuing bank.

affiliate program A system in which other website owners display your ad, link, logo, or template to direct traffic or sales your way; compensation can be fee-based, commission-based (pay per click-through or per order), barter-based, or some combination.

American Standard Code for Information Interchange (ASCII) Simple text that includes no formatting; ASCII text looks essentially the same on most computers.

anchor A text or image link from an HTML coder's point of view. Also known as HREF because the <A> (anchor tag) demands an HREF (hypertext reference) attribute.

anonymous FTP A feature of File Transfer Protocol that allows users to transfer files between a server and a local computer without a unique user name and password.

applet A "small" application (or program) created to exist and work within a web page or another program. Applets can add extra functionality to web pages; for example, an interactive calendar or puzzle might be created as an applet.

ASCII *See* American Standard Code for Information Interchange.

audience penetration The percentage of a potential audience that a site, service, or product has reached.

authentication The process of identifying a user to a secure system, usually by requiring the user to provide a valid, known user name and password.

backbone Any of the several high-speed networks that are the main arteries of the Internet.

back end For a website, the database, transaction system, and the server-side scripts that interact.

Glossary

bandwidth (a) The capacity of a communications channel such as a network or a modem as measured by the amount of data that can be sent through. (b) (slang) The capacity of a person or company to get something done based on available resources.

bitmap An image file in which the image is made up of dots.

branding The creation of an immediately recognizable identity for your company, product, service, or website.

brick-and-mortar (slang) Describes a "real-world" business with a physical location as opposed to an online (or digital) business. An e-commerce site might have a brick-and-mortar component, however, as Barnes & Noble does. *See also* dot com.

broad market A general target audience for a site, product, or service. *See also* vertical market.

business-to-business Describes a business whose clients or customers are other businesses rather than consumers.

cable modem A device that uses television cable (the same cable that carries cable TV service to millions of homes and businesses) to connect to the Internet. The use of television cable allows for more bandwidth than is possible with the ordinary telephone lines a dial-up modem uses. *See also* bandwidth.

cache (a) To temporarily store data such as image files or web pages. (b) A place (a portion of a computer's memory, for example) where such storage occurs.

certificate Data that cannot be forged and that uniquely identifies a user to a server or vice versa. Certificates are provided by certifying authorities. *See also* certifying authority; secure transaction.

certifying authority An organization that issues certificates and assures their authenticity. *See also* certificate.

channel Thematically related content (travel, news, finance, and so forth) presented on a website or sometimes via push technology. *See also* push technology.

chat To communicate via typed messages that are received and can be responded to in real time (meaning almost immediately).

click rate (Also called click-through rate.) A measurement of how often users click on a given link.

click-through The act of clicking a link in a website. Occurs when a user clicks a link or a banner ad, for example, and is transported to the site it represents. *See also* click rate.

client A computer that receives, via its connection to a server. *See also* server.

Glossary

community (a) A feeling of identification and bonding with a group based on shared affinities and a common purpose. (b) A group of people who gather to exchange ideas and information on shared interests frequently enough to identify and feel a bond with the group.

compressed (a) Describes data that has been condensed, packed, or "zipped." WinZip and other utilities allow users to compress files to conserve storage space and enable faster transfer of the files. In addition, compressing is often part of the process of preparing audio and video files for use on the Web.

configure (a) To set up programs, applications, or computer systems. (b) To make programs, applications, or computer systems work together.

conversion-to-sales rate Describes the number of actual purchases that result from contacts (electronic or otherwise) with customers.

copyright The right of ownership to a Work (such as a document, art, or music) and the right to make copies and profit from the Work. *See also* public domain.

cost per thousand (CPM) A pricing method applied to advertising space on a website. For example, if a website is selling ad space at a cost per thousand of $8, this means that for $8 the ad space buyer is being promised 1,000 impressions. *See also* impression.

CPM *See* cost per thousand.

crawler A software program that travels the Internet, following links and gathering data about websites to be compiled into a database that will form the basis of a search engine. (Also known as a spider, wanderer, or robot.)

cross-platform Describes a computer program that works on more than one operating system.

data Distinct facts or pieces of numerical or textual particulars that when combined in a meaningful way become information. For example, a first name and a last name are both data. When they are combined and applied to an actual person, they become information that identifies the person.

database An organized, searchable set of records. In terms of e-commerce, a database could contain records of all your customers, their contact information, and their latest purchases. *See also* flat-file database; relational database.

dedicated Describes a line, server, or other piece of computer-associated equipment that has only one purpose. A dedicated line, for example, might be a phone line that leads only to your PC (or modem).

development server *See* staging server.

dial-up The type of connection that occurs when a modem dials a phone number to access the Internet.

Glossary

Digital Subscriber Line (DSL)   A technology that provides fast online access via existing telephone lines. DSL is faster than ISDN (which also runs on existing telephone lines) but not as fast as T1 access, which requires special cabling.

directory   (a) A portion of an organizational system roughly similar to the folders within a filing cabinet. (Sometimes known as a folder.) (b) An organized index or listing of websites or other resources that is always browsable and sometimes searchable, meaning that a search feature is provided, enabling you to find what you seek with more immediacy. *See also* index.

discount rate   The percentage of each credit card transaction that's kept by the bank as a service fee.

discussion group   A forum for interaction among multiple users via email. Discussion groups can be centered around a single theme or group of topics. They might be small (half a dozen participants) or large (hundreds or thousands of participants).

dithering   A technique used to create the illusion of shades of color by varying a pattern of dots that make up the color. Dithered images look blurrier and load more slowly than non-dithered images. *See also* Joint Photographic Experts Group; graphics interchange format.

DNS   *See* Domain Name System.

domain   A unique name that identifies a computer or a set of computers on the Internet. Examples of domain names include *microsoft.com* and *tauberkienan.com*. *See also* Domain Name System.

Domain Name System (DNS)   The system through which domain names are assigned.

dot com   (slang) Describes a business that is online but that has no traditional or brick-and-mortar counterpart. Amazon.com is an example. *See also* brick-and-mortar.

download   To transfer files from another computer to your computer.

down time   An interval during which a computer, network, database, or other system is not functioning. *See also* lag time.

DSL   *See* Digital Subscriber Line.

encryption   A method of disguising or protecting a message or any other data (for example, credit card numbers or the specifics of a transaction) to prevent the unauthorized reading or use of it.

extended partnership   A sales model in which businesses form strategic partnerships to leverage their assets and add value and functionality for customers.

Extensible Markup Language (XML)   A technology that lets developers create their own markup tags, so they are not limited to the tags available in HTML and to the functionality HTML allows. XML, for example, allows links that go to multiple locations (including other pages or specific text on pages); HTML allows for links that lead to only one destination each.

extranet   A secured website (or a portion of a website) that is available to people outside the firewall. Extranets can be used by a company's business partners or salespeople on the road who need to access confidential information. *See also* firewall.

fair use   The privilege (not the right) to use a small portion of a copyrighted Work for the purpose of reviewing that Work, teaching, reporting events, or creating a parody.

FAQ   *See* frequently asked questions.

field   In a database or on a form, the space provided for entering data.

file transfer   The movement of a file from one computer to another over a network or via a modem.

File Transfer Protocol (FTP)   A standard, agreed-upon way for files to be transferred from one computer to another over the Internet. *See also* anonymous FTP.

firewall   A security system that creates an electronic barrier protecting part or all of an organization's network and its computers from access by outsiders.

flame   An unfriendly written attack against someone in an electronic discussion group. (A *flame war* occurs when both parties engage in and continue such an exchange, perhaps even inspiring others in the newsgroup or message area to take sides.)

flat file database   A simple database with one table; usually that will be a plain text file. *See also* relational database.

frames   "Panes" within the larger window of a web page. Each frame is actually a distinct web page and can have its own scroll bar and other navigational features; each can also contain text, images, and other media as well as links.

freeware   Programs that are distributed free of charge by those who developed them. *See also* shareware.

frequently asked questions (FAQ)   A list of questions and their answers intended to help people help themselves. A well-constructed and easily accessible FAQ can be a powerful customer service tool.

front end   (a) The interface of a web page or program; the part you see. (b) the software that provides an interface to a back end. For example, a web browser acts as the front end to a website or a transaction system.

Glossary

FTP *See* File Transfer Protocol.

fulfillment The last part of processing an online order, including the logistics of distribution, warehousing, and shipping.

GIF *See* graphics interchange format.

GIF89 (also known as GIF89a). A method of saving a GIF to allow a transparent background in the image. The advantage in using a transparent background in the image is that the background does not have to match the background of the web page on which it's being placed. GIF 89s can be stacked to create animations. *See also* graphics interchange format.

graphics interchange format (GIF) A file format used for web graphics. GIFs (pronounced *jifs*), like JPEGs, can be saved at a variety of qualities; however, the higher the quality (the more colors they include), the slower they will appear on a web page. GIFs can also be animated. Inside an animated GIF, several images are stacked in what amounts to a flipbook so they appear to be one animation. If you look at animated GIFs with a plain graphics viewer, the animation is not apparent. *See also* GIF89; Joint Photographic Experts Group.

hack To manipulate a program or system "behind the scenes," presumably to make improvements or to find out how it works. Hacking is not necessarily malicious, although malicious hacking is of great concern and should be prevented.

hard-deliverable A product that must be shipped, such as food or a computer, as opposed to a product that can be downloaded, such as music or software.

hit A request to a web server for data, a file, or an object. Because each web page might be comprised of dozens of files (text, graphics, animations, and so on), and what looks like a single piece of art might be comprised of several image files, counting hits does not indicate the number of visitors to a website. *See also* impression.

home page The front page or main page of a website, also known as a default page or index page. Note that a visit to a website doesn't have to start at the home page but can actually start anywhere in any site.

host To house a server. *See also* server.

HTML *See* Hypertext Markup Language.

HTTP *See* Hypertext Transfer Protocol.

HTTPS *See* Secure HTTP.

Hypertext Markup Language (HTML) The coding used to create web pages.

Hypertext Transfer Protocol (HTTP) The agreed upon, standard way for web documents to be transferred across the Internet.

ICE *See* Information & Content Exchange.

IIS *See* Internet Information Server.

image map A complex image, sometimes large enough to fill one whole screen of a web page, that includes several areas of clickable links. The first image maps actually were maps; they offered links to information about the places on the map.

impression One look at a web page or banner ad by a user. Counting impressions indicates how many pairs of eyes fell on the page, ad, or website being assessed. Also referred to as page view. *See also* hit; unique user.

index (a) A data file that lists the information to be found in a specific directory. (b) To organize data according to specified criteria. (c) A website (also known as a directory) that lists in categories other websites and perhaps other Internet resources. Indexes are usually searchable as well as browsable. *See also* directory.

Information & Content Exchange (ICE) A protocol developed to enable the syndication of content. ICE is based on XML. *See also* Extensible Markup Language.

inline Describes an item that appears directly on a web page. Graphics (or video or animation) that must be downloaded manually are not inline. *See also* inline image.

inline image A graphic in a web page; a graphic that does not have to be downloaded manually to be viewed.

insourcing Jobbing out portions of a project to other departments within a company or borrowing employees from other departments.

Integrated Services Digital Network (ISDN) A type of communications access that allows transmission of voice, data (such as the code that makes up web pages), and video via the ordinary telephone cables (digital or otherwise) that already lead into homes and businesses. With ISDN, you can have a line for voice and one or two lines for data; this is because ISDN allows two lines to operate over a single cable. ISDN is faster than a standard dial-up connection but not as fast as DSL or a cable modem.

intellectual property A piece of work (code, art, a trademarked image, or product specs, for example) that is intangible until it is fixed or made tangible through printing or some other method of recording it. Intellectual property is owned by its creator unless ownership is transferred; it is also a business asset. *See also* copyright; trademark.

interface The "face" a piece of software or website shows you, with which you interact. *See also* front end.

Internet Information Server (IIS) Microsoft's web server software that runs on Windows NT.

Internet presence provider (IPP) A company that provides hosting as well as some combination of content and design. *See also* Internet service provider.

Glossary

Internet Protocol (IP)   An agreed upon set of standards that allows computers to exchange data over telecommunications lines. IP is somewhat like the postal system in that a direct connection between sender and recipient is not required. Instead, when a file is requested from a server by a web browser, for example, the file is dropped into the system for delivery to the addressee (the requesting web browser).

Internet service provider (ISP)   A company that provides access to the Internet but does not necessarily provide site design or content. *See also* Internet presence provider.

intranet   One or several connected websites contained wholly inside a company's firewall. Intranets can facilitate interdepartmental exchange and streamline human resources tasks by providing self-service for employees or team members. *See also* firewall.

IP   *See* Internet Protocol.

IP address   A unique number assigned to a single computer on the Internet as an address. No two computers can share the same IP address at the same time, but Internet servers can rotate the IP address assigned to a set of computers.

IPP   *See* Internet presence provider.

ISDN   *See* Integrated Services Digital Network.

ISP   *See* Internet service provider.

issuing bank   A bank that offers credit cards to consumers. *See also* acquiring bank.

Joint Photographic Experts Group (JPEG)   A type of file format used for graphics, JPEGs (pronounced *jay-pegs*) can be very high resolution, can use many different colors, and compress very well. JPEGs are the file format of choice for photographs online. *See also* graphics interchange format.

JPEG   *See* Joint Photographic Experts Group.

knowledge base   A collection of information or wisdom about a particular subject or technology.

lag time   The interval that occurs between the time data is requested and the time it arrives; for example, the time between when you click a link and when the page that it is linked to appears.

LAN   *See* local area network.

legacy system   A computer, network, database, or other system that already exists or that an administrator "inherits" from an outgoing administrator.

liability   Accountability to customers, co-owners, business affiliates, the government, and the public, for example; false advertising, for instance, incurs liability that might result in legal repercussions.

libel Negative or false information about someone or something; to be libelous, that information must be written or publicly broadcast. *See also* slander.

licensing The act of obtaining (usually for a fee) permission to use a Work, generally within specific guidelines such as length of time, types of use, and geographic location of the use.

local Describes something that is near you; the computer on your desk, for example, is local, as compared to a remote computer, such as a server, that is elsewhere. *See also* remote.

local area network (LAN) Several computers that are connected by cables so they can share resources such as printers and software.

log A data file on a server that lists events such as every instance of users accessing a web page.

look and feel The tone and style of a site determined by the colors, fonts, graphics, and language used in it.

lurker Someone who only observes the conversations in a discussion group without contributing. It can be seen as courteous to lurk before joining a discussion group; this allows you to learn the group culture and avoid transgressions.

mailing list A compilation of email addresses. An electronic discussion group that broadcasts email messages to all of its participants can also be called a mailing list.

mail server An Internet computer that sends and receives email for a group of users.

merchant account A business bank account that accepts credit card payments from consumers.

moderated discussion A discussion in which a specific person ensures that the conversation sticks to the stated topic, that administrative issues are handled, and even that disputes are resolved. In an unmoderated discussion, members regulate themselves. *See also* discussion group.

mouseover An effect that occurs on a web page when the curser controlled by the mouse rolls over an item and the item changes its appearance. Mouseovers, also called rollovers, often occur in navigation bars or pop-up boxes, often to indicate a link.

multimedia Describes the use of a variety of media (graphics, audio, video, and text) in combination within a document or a presentation.

NDA *See* nondisclosure agreement.

network A system in which a number of computers are cabled together to share software, printers, and other resources.

Glossary

network administrator Someone who organizes, maintains, troubleshoots, and manages a network.

newbie (slang) A user who is new to the Internet or to a specific part of the Internet. The word newbie by itself is not usually derogatory.

nondisclosure agreement (NDA) An agreement between the signing parties specifying that confidential information disclosed in the course of doing business will not be revealed to others.

opt in A method for gaining subscribers to a mailing list that allows potential subscribers to sign up. *See also* opt out.

opt out A presumptuous and unpopular method for gaining subscribers to a mailing list that automatically signs up everyone whose email address is known to the mailing list's owner or is provided in online interactions, for example, a transaction or a request for customer service. Those who are automatically subscribed must then take action to unsubscribe (or opt out) if they are not interested in participating. *See also* opt in.

outsourcing The act of hiring a job out to another company.

outtasking The act of hiring out a part of a job to another company.

packet A piece of data that carries a destination address with it as it is transmitted over a network such as the Internet. On its arrival at the destination, the packet is reassembled (according to instructions that it also carries with it) with other pieces to form a message or a web page.

page view *See* impression.

path The complete description of the location of a file on a specific computer.

ping (a) To contact a computer to find out if it's active. (b) (slang) To contact a person to check in about something.

port (a) To rewrite a program so it runs on another platform. (b) A number that identifies a particular Internet server. (c) One of a computer's input/output plugs.

portal A site that serves as a gateway to many other sites. A portal might be theme-based (such as FindLaw), general, or customizable (such as those offered by MSN and Excite).

post To make public by publishing, for example, as a message in a discussion group or as a web page. You post a message to the discussion group by sending e-mail; you post a web page to a web server by sending an HTML document.

posting ratio In an online community (such as an email discussion group), the number of times participants post compared to the number of impressions (or page views). *See also* impression.

Glossary

project plan A plan that describes what you want your website to accomplish and how you're going to get there.

public domain A Work that is available to the public at large without the necessity of getting permission to use it (or paying a licensing fee) is said to be in the public domain. *See also* copyright; intellectual property; Work.

push technology A method for sending (or "pushing") content to users. In a client/server scenario—for example, when a web page is viewed—the client (the web browser) requests that the web page be served. In push, the content is served (perhaps at regular intervals) without request. As an example, push is used to deliver updated news or stock quotes; a news site might push new headlines to people without requiring them to reload the news site's home page.

record In a database, a set of data that forms complete information. A record contains fields, which contain data; in a relational database, a record exists within a table of records.

redirect page A page that automatically loads another page; that is, it redirects traffic from the variations of a domain name to the main domain name. For instance, people who enter *www.hewlittpackard.com* are taken to the same page as those who enter *www.hp.com*.

relational database A database in which the data in several tables is linked through one or more fields that they have in common.

remote Describes an entity that exists elsewhere. (For example, a remote computer is not near you; it is somewhere else.) *See also* local.

request for proposal (RFP) A written request for a bid from any outside resources or vendors you're considering using.

return on investment (ROI) The proceeds or results garnered from the money paid for a project or venture. The ROI for websites is sometimes intangible (such as greater name recognition) or not easily tied to the website (such as increased purchases at the brick-and-mortar store), but it can also be measured in revenue.

revenue model The plan for generating income for a business. Examples of revenue models might include product sales, ad sales, sponsorship, paid placement, subscription, fee for services, licensing, affiliate programs, and cost savings.

RFP *See* request for proposal.

robot *See* crawler.

ROI *See* return on investment.

rollover *See* mouseover.

router A computer that transfers packets of data between networks.

scalability The ability of the site to grow as needed.

Glossary

script A simple computer program that adds functionality (to a website) that cannot be accomplished using HTML alone; for example, a script must be written in order to make a form on a web page function.

Secure HTTP (HTTPS) A form of HTTP that allows secure transactions to take place over the Internet.

Secure Sockets Layer (SSL) The protocol used for Secure HTTP. *See also* Secure HTTP.

secure transaction An interaction (that might or might not involve a monetary exchange) over the Internet that is always encrypted to protect against harm or loss. *See also* encryption; Secure HTTP.

server (a) A computer that provides files or data to clients who request it. (b) A computer that manages files and resources on a network such as a local area network. *See also* client; network.

service level agreement (SLA) An agreement between your company and another company detailing the maintenance or technical infrastructure they will provide for your website for a fee.

shareware Software that is offered to others for trial use by its developer; those who want to continue to use shareware are generally required to register it and pay a fee. *See also* freeware.

shopping cart Software that creates the interface between a company's website and its catalog database, allowing customers to choose products to buy; review the items on their order; add to or delete items from their order; and make their purchases.

signature file A file that you can create to be automatically added to the end of every email message you send. This file (sometimes called a sig file) can include your company's name, motto, and contact information.

SLA *See* service level agreement.

slander A spoken message that reflects on someone or something negatively or falsely. *See also* libel.

spider *See* crawler.

sponsorship A revenue model in which another company supports your company financially in exchange for a prominent mention on your website and perhaps other considerations.

SSL *See* Secure Sockets Layer.

staging server A computer that mirrors the contents of a live server, allowing the functionality of web pages to be tested before they go live. (Also called the development server.) *See also* server.

strategic partnership (Also called strategic alliance.) A formal relationship between two or more companies aligning their resources or assets. Can be used to provide greater service or a co-branded product, for example.

style guide A document establishing guidelines that ensure a consistent look, tone, and style on your website; an essential element of quality control. Style guides can discuss page specs, graphics, linking, review processes, and editorial and legal matters.

support (a) To provide for, as in providing information to a customer to support his or her choice of one product over another (purchase support) or as in providing support of a product or service after it has been acquired (product support or technical support). (b) To enable the use of, as when a web browser enables users to experience the functionality of forms (form support) or when a network supports multiple users of a single server.

system administrator (Also called sysadmin or sysop.) A person who organizes, maintains, troubleshoots, and generally manages a computer system such as a server or network. *See also* network administrator.

table (a) A compilation of organized data or information into columns and rows on a printed page. (b) A method in HTML for controlling page layout by creating a (usually invisible) grid on a web page into which text and graphics can be placed. (c) A set of records in a database. *See also* relational database.

tags HTML or XML code, which tells a web browser how to interpret a web page.

target market The audience you intend to reach regarding your site, product, or service.

template A prototypical page or document with no data or content in it. On a website, a template shows the layout of the page, into which content can be entered without the necessity of each page being newly designed. In spreadsheets and databases, a template shows the cells or fields and defines the data that can be placed there.

template-driven Describes a site that uses templates as the basis for laying out content rather than requiring each page to be freshly designed.

thread A chain of messages on a single topic, written by different people posting to one discussion group.

trademark A symbol, word, or name that identifies a business or product and is the intellectual property of a company, organization, or individual.

traffic-analysis software Software that reads a server's log files and massages the data into meaningful information, such as number of pages served or number of site visitors in a given time period. Some traffic-analysis software also provides insight into "clickpaths" or traffic patterns through a site.

Glossary

transaction system An automated system for taking orders, accepting payment, and triggering fulfillment of an order. It might be a secure server and a custom-built payment system or a complete payment system built by a third party.

unique user An individual user as identified to traffic-tracking software. It's difficult to track individual users accurately because only individual computers can be counted and several people might use the same computer.

Uniform Resource Locator (URL) An address or a location of a document on the World Wide Web. URL is pronounced "you-are-ell."

URL *See* Uniform Resource Locator.

vertical market A focused, narrow audience with a deep interest in a single topic or a very narrow range of closely related topics. *See also* broad market.

WAN *See* wide area network.

wanderer *See* crawler.

web crawler *See* crawler.

web-safe palette A palette of 216 colors that will appear in web browsers without dithering and without substantial distortion. *See also* dithering.

wide area network (WAN) Computers networked together over long distances (across a city or across the nation, for example). A general rule is that if data travels over cables you don't own (such as the phone company's) it's a WAN. *See also* local area network.

Work A creation that is intellectual property. Examples include art, writing, code, maps, music, and so on. A Work is owned by its creator unless the creator transfers or assigns ownership. *See also* copyright; trademark.

work for hire A legal term in copyright matters that refers to work prepared by an employee or contractor within the scope of his or her employment, or a work specially commissioned for use as a contribution to a larger work. For a Work to be considered work for hire, both parties must agree to that, in writing.

XML *See* Extensible Markup Language.

zipped *See* compressed.

Index

A

ABC Interactive, 325
access to intranets/extranets, 336, 338, 339
acquiring banks, 345
ad sales, 48, 49
ad space, 298–99
advertising, 12, 282
   measuring the results of, 308
   using attraction and permission, 282
   your URL, 302
affiliate and affinity programs, 50, 345
affiliates, creating, 294
affinity, 130–31
alliances, joining, 292
ALT attribute, 194
anchors, 345
anchor tags, 183
animated GIFs, 194
anonymous FTP, 345
applets, 345
applications for e-commerce, 4, 6
approval process, establishing, 278
archiving
   email, 152
   pages, 280
artbin, storing images in, 171
artists, print vs. web, 218
art, placing, 191
ASP. *See* Microsoft Active Server Pages
attributes, 183, 194
audience
   assessing, 312
   clarifying, 90
   communicating with, 315
   getting to know, 315
   online vs. brick-and-mortar, 316
   penetration, defined, 150
   targeting, 265
auditing, 49
audits, security, 251
authentication, 345

AutoReply, using in customer service, 116
awards, 293

B

backbones, Internet, 241, 345
back end, 10, 18, 58, 229, 345
   components, 230
   in websites, 169
background images, 194
backlinks, 71
   checking, 293
   importance of, 291
backups of databases, 248
backup systems, 235
bandwidth, 241, 346
   and connectivity, with ISPs, 241
bank fees, 255
banks, and credit card transactions, 252
banner ads, 296–97
bCentral. *See* Microsoft bCentral
bCentral Site Manager. *See* Microsoft bCentral Site Manager
Berne Copyright Convention, 62
bitmaps, 346
branding, 21, 77, 80, 262, 315, 346
   content, 263
   on intranets and extranets, 331, 335
   Martha Stewart, 79
   market share, 263
   message, 95
   mind share, 263
brick-and-mortar, 346
broad markets, 346
browsers
   intranet/extranet considerations, 335, 339
   multiple, designing websites for, 199
browser-safe colors, 90
browser-safe palette, 187, 193
budgeting for deployment, 46

Index

budgets, 43, 44
   considerations, 223
   maintenance, 47
   promotion, 47
   models for, 33
   sample, advantages of, 34
   spreadsheets, 42
business plan, importance of, 8
business-to-business, 20, 346
business viability, measuring, 311

C

cable modems, 238, 346
cache, 346
call to action, 268
cascading style sheets, 189
catalogs, and FrontPage, 197
central processing unit (CPU), 233
certificates, 250, 346
certifying authorities, 250, 346
changes, approval process, 278
channels, 346
chat, 346
   areas, 136
   sessions, marketing, 136
click rates, 346, 357
clicks, 321
click through, 346
clients, 346
clip art, 56
collaboration tools, 209
colors, browser-safe, 90, 187
.com, using in domain names, 87
comment tags, 184
communication
   with customers, 109, 315
   in email newsletters, 133
   internal, streamlining, 329
   with vendors, assessing quality, 219
community, 12, 347
   building, 130
   extending invitations to, 139
   goals, determining, 138
   measuring success, 154
   offering value, 141
   providing security, 141
company pages in your website, 164

competition, 23, 24
   identifying, 44
complaints of e-commerce customers, 105
components, 235
compressed, 347
confidentiality, 225
configure, 347
connectivity
   and bandwidth, with ISPs, 241
   international, 242
consequence, 264
consumer sampling, 324
content, 59, 60, 162, 261
   branding, 263
   creating dynamically, 245
   creation options, 271
   delivery, 261
   development, goals, 263
   on extranets, and QA, 337
   fresh, 261, 269
   of intranets/extranets, 335
   licensing, 12
   monitoring quality, 272
   old, removing, 280
   organizing, 40, 161
   simplicity, 41
   tracking down, 143
   updating, with databases, 245
   website, monitoring quality, 272
   website, and server performance, 235
content driven, 261
content pages on your website, 162
content policies for intranets/extranets, 336
context, 263
contingencies, covering, 224
contracts, 225
conversion rate, 322
conversion-to-sales rate, 347
cookies, 321
   and unique users, 321
   user concerns about, 321
   user profiling, 321
copyrights, 23, 60, 61, 347
   articles, 61
   fair use, 64
   infringement, 63
   laws, 55, 60, 61
   licensing, 59, 67
   notice, 62

Index

copyrights (continued)
  public domain, 65
  registering, 63
  symbol, 62
  terms 62
  transferability, 62
  transfers, 67
Copyright Website, 63
costs
  cutting, 12, 13
  of website design and development, 221
Cost per thousand (CPM), 347
Cost savings, 51
CPU. *See* central processing unit
crashes, preventing, 236
crawlers, 347
credit cards, 18
  and bank fees, 255
  numbers, protecting, 251
  processing software, 254
  refunds, processing, 255
  transactions, 251–53
credit transaction processing systems, 248
cross-platform, 347
"Cs," fifth, 264
"Cs," four, 263
customer relations, 13, 16
customer service, 16
  around-the-clock, 5, 6
  breaching security, 109
  effect on revenue, 13
  via email, 106
  employees, managing, 118
  goals of, 101
  handling complaints, 111
  importance of, 103
  and intranets, 331
  marketing, 102
  and Microsoft NetMeeting, 112
  personal interaction, 111
  positive communication, 109
  preventing problems, 122
  supported by FAQ pages, 119
  using AutoReply in, 116
  using email, 115
  using online surveys, 107
  using website, 102
customers
  building loyalty, 108

customers (continued)
  communicating with, 109, 315
  complaints about e-commerce, 105
  creating positive experience for, 96
  disgruntled, handling, 111
  establishing trust, 98
  first impression, 104
  offering choices, 106
  protecting privacy, 109
  retaining, 104
  staying close, 91, 107
  understanding, 21
CyberCash, 248, 254
CyberSource, 248, 254

D

data, 347
  auditing, 324
  defined, 52
  transferring, 247
  transporting, 246
database-backed websites, 244
database call, 245
databases, 243, 347
  backing up, 248
  backups, testing, 248
  flat file, 246
  function of, 10
  maintaining, 247
  manipulation, and programming languages, 247
  redundancy in, 34
  relational, 245
  server, 230
  types of, 243
  and websites, 174, 244, 245
  when required, 10
dated content, 269
deciduous, 269
dedicated, 347
deliverables, 222
demographics, 319
departments within companies, avoiding duplicate, 206
design document
  elements of, 177
  sharing, 178

Index

designers, print vs. web, 218
design of websites, rules for, 200
dial-up, 347
differentiation, 80
digital images, 191
digital subscriber lines (DSL), 238, 348
direct debit system, 256
directories, 284, 348
directory structures, 270, 274
   building in websites, 172
discount rates, 348
discussion groups, 348
   hosting, 135, 151
   email, 134
   moderating, 134, 149
   offering, 148
   outsourcing, 151
   participating effectively, 307
   using to boost traffic, 301
dithering, 193, 348
DNS. *See* Domain Name System
document root directory in websites, 173
domain names, 80, 82
   checking availability, 88
   investigating, 86
   numeric address in, 88
   registering, 89
   registering multiple, 86
   reserving vs. registering, 83
   understanding system, 87
   using .com in, 87
Domain Name System (DNS), 87, 348
domains, 348
dot com, 348
download, 348
   time, and size of web pages, 191
down time, 348
DSL. *See* digital subscriber lines
dynamic content creation, 245

E

eCharge, 256
e-commerce, 4, 8. *See also* specific topic entries
   assessing appropriateness of, 7
   common errors, 28

e-commerce (continued)
   goals, 8, 9, 21, 80
   lingo, 34
   myths, 5
   public perception of, 3, 6, 7
   types of, 14
   winning strategies, 5, 6, 7, 18
editors, roles and responsibilities, 273
education, and e-commerce, 4, 5
efficiency, increasing, with
      intranets/extranets, 329
email
   archiving, 152
   discussion groups, 134
   etiquette with customers, 115
   newsletters, 133, 142, 301
   tracking feedback, 125
   using in customer service, 106, 115
   using Microsoft bCentral, 118
   using Microsoft Exchange, 117
   using Microsoft Outlook, 117
employees
   communicating with, 329
   training, 339
encryption, 250, 348
evergreen, 269
expenses
   fixed, 42
   hourly, 43
   ongoing, 43
   sample spreadsheet, 42, 47
experience, of vendors, evaluating, 217
extended partnerships, 348
Extensible Markup Language (XML), 349
extranets, 349. *See also* intranets/extranets

F

fair use, 64, 69, 349
FAQ. *See* frequently asked questions
feature creep, 223
feedback
   assessing, 328
   tracking in email, 125
fee for services, 50
fees
   bank, 255
   negotiating, 222

Index

fields, 243, 349
files
  changes to, controlling, 280
  image, 191
  naming, 190, 270
  transfers, 349
File Transfer Protocol (FTP), 190, 349
firewalls, 239, 250, 331, 349
first impressions, 264
flames, 349
flat file databases, 243, 246, 349
fonts, 56
"four Cs", 263
frames, 189, 349
  in websites, disadvantages of, 286
freeware, 349
frequently asked questions (FAQ), 13, 19, 349
  pages, 119
front end, 10, 349
  in websites, 169
FrontPage Server Extensions, 199
FTP. *See* File Transfer Protocol
fulfillment, 255, 350
funding, seeking, 8

G

GIF. *See* Graphics Interchange Format
GIF89, 350
Giga Information Group, projected e-commerce sales, 3
goals
  hard, 343
  identifying, 44
  setting, for intranets and extranets, 342
  soft, 343
Graphics Interchange Format (GIF), 188, 274, 191, 193, 350
  animated/interlaced 194
guaranteed impressions, 321
guest books, 137

H

hack, 350
hard-deliverables, 350

hard disks
  server, 234
  size, determining minimum necessary, 234
  type, 235
hard goals, 343
help pages in your website, 163
hits, 350
  analyzing, 322
  as measurement of traffic, 320
home pages, 162, 350
  for intranets/extranets, 336
host, 350
hosting, 25, 229, 238
  discussion groups, 135, 151
  onsite vs. offsite, 231
  servers, 231–240
HTML. *See* Hypertext Markup Language
HTTP. *See* Hypertext Transfer Protocol
HTTPS. *See* Secure HTTP
human resources (HR), expediting events/tasks with intranets, 330
hyperlinks. *See* links
Hypertext Markup Language (HTML), 179, 350
  editing web pages, 197
  limitations, 184
  source code, 196
  tags, 180–84
  WYSIWYG, 180
Hypertext Transfer Protocol (HTTP), 350

I

ICE. *See* Information & Content Exchange
IDC. *See* International Data Corporation
identity, creating with branding, 263
IDE. *See* Integrated Device Electronics
IIS. *See* Microsoft Internet Information Server
image maps, 194, 351
  in websites, disadvantages of, 286
images, 191
  background, 194
  dithering, 193
  files and formats, 191
  preparing for the Web, 193

Index

images (continued)
  storing in artbin, 171
  types, 194
impressions, 351
  analyzing, 322
  counting, 317, 320, 324
  first, 264
  guaranteed, 321
independent contractors for website development, 213
indexes, 351
index file, 173
industrial property, 60
infographics, 266
Information & Content Exchange (ICE), 351
Information Services (IS), and intranets, 331
Information Technology (IT), and intranets, 331
infringement on trademarks, 85
inline images, 351
insourcing, 351
  effective, 207
  vs. outsourcing, 206
Integrated Device Electronics (IDE), 235
Integrated Services Digital Network (ISDN), 351
intellectual property, 54, 55, 351
  articles, 61
  five areas, 55
  types, 60
  violating rights, 57
interacting with vendors, assessing quality, 219
interactivity on websites, 201
interfaces, 351
  in websites, 169
interlaced GIFs, 194
internal communication, streamlining, 329
International Data Corporation (IDC), projected sales in e-commerce, 3
Internet
  connection lines, 241
  connectivity, international, 242
  distribution of art, 61
  "four Cs", 263
  researching demographics, 44
  sales tax, 254

Internet Information Server (IIS), 351
Internet presence provider (IPP), 210, 351
Internet Protocol (IP), 352
Internet service provider (ISP), 210, 352
  agreements with, 242
  choosing, 241
  connectivity and bandwidth, 241
  hosting servers, 240
  hosting your server, 231, 233
intranets/extranets, 331, 341, 352
  access policy, 336
  access to, 331, 338, 339
  assessing need for, 330
  benefits of, 329, 330, 334
  branding, 331, 335
  content decisions, 335
  content policies, 336
  cost and return, assessing, 334
  cost effectiveness of, 330
  creating, 329
  establishing a vision, 335
  goals, 342
  homepage, 336
  and legacy systems, 340
  maintaining, 334, 335
  management support, 341
  managing, 335
  measuring success, 343
  and meetings, 333
  portal, 336
  posting departmental information, 331
  posting to, 333, 335
  promoting, 341
  publishing policies, 336, 338
  return on investment, 334, 341
  security, 336, 338
  technology considerations, 335, 339
  tying into business, 340
IP addresses, 352
IPP. See Internet presence provider
I/PRO Index, 324
IS. See Information Services
ISDN. See Integrated Services Digital Network
ISP. See Internet service provider
issuing banks, 352

Index

J
jobbing out tasks, 205
Joint Photographic Experts Group (JPEG), 191, 193, 274, 352
JPEG. *See* Joint Photographic Experts Group 274

K
keywords, ranking websites by, 287
knowledge base, 330, 352

L
lag time, 352
language
  and branding, 267
  editing text, 267
  hackneyed phrasing, 268
  use on websites, 264, 265
LAN. *See* local area network
leads, 265
legacy systems, 352
  and intranets/extranets, 340
legal information, online source, 54
length of pages in websites, 165
liability, 72, 352
libel, 353
Library of Congress. *See* United States Library of Congress
license agreements, online, 68
licensing, 12, 50, 59, 353
  exclusive rights, 67
  issues, 225
  nonexclusive rights, 67
  to others, 12
  types, 67
linking, 71
links, 267
  and anchor tags, 183
  and the law, 71
  mapped, 196
  removing, 280
  validating, 272
ListBot, managing mailing lists with, 148
listing websites, 284
lists, using in websites, 266
local, 353
local area network (LAN), 353
log files, 236, 316, 322
  reviewing, 322
logos, choosing, 91
logs, 353
look and feel, 57, 80, 353. *See also* trade dress, determining
loyalty, building with customers, 108
lurkers, 353

M
mailing lists, 353
  creating, 147
  managing with ListBot, 148
  selling, 19
mail servers, 230, 353
maintenance
  lessening, 269
  of intranets/extranets, 334, 335
  website, 226
  website, and databases, 245
  website, tools for, 279
management, 6, 328
  of intranets/extranets, 331, 335, 342
  support for intranets/extranets, 341
Management Center, The, 84
maps
  of websites, 274
  site, 198
market, defining target, 5
market forecasts, 20
marketing, 281
  and cookies, 321
  with customer service, 102
  knowing your audience, 315
  materials, 46
  positioning, 282
  strategy, focusing, 282
  and website traffic, measuring, 314
market share, 263
markup language, 179
Martha Stewart, 79
Media Metrix, 324

Index

memory server, 234
merchant accounts, 253, 353
message boards, 135
META tags
   entering, 288
   optimizing websites with, 286
Microsoft Access, 246
Microsoft Active Server Pages (ASP), 242, 247, 340
Microsoft bCentral, 4, 39, 48
   ListBot, 118
Microsoft bCentral Site Manager, 197, 203, 230, 240
Microsoft Excel, 52, 333
Microsoft Exchange, using with email, 117
Microsoft Exchange Server, 209
Microsoft FrontPage, 232, 267, 279
   conventions, 195
   and HTML, 197
   link maps, 196
   navigation tools, 196
   Tasks feature, 198
   websites, building/managing 181, 195, 196, 197
   websites, live, 198
Microsoft Internet Explorer, 333
Microsoft Internet Information Server (IIS), 272, 333
   and intranets, 339
Microsoft NetMeeting, 209
   using in customer service, 112
Microsoft Office, 209
   documents, including on websites, 203
Microsoft Outlook, 209, 279
   using email with, 117
Microsoft PowerPoint, 333
Microsoft products, as project collaboration tools, 209
Microsoft Project, 208, 209, 279, 333
Microsoft Site Server Express, 272, 324
Microsoft Small Business Financial Manager, 52
Microsoft SQL Server, 242, 246, 333
Microsoft Visual SourceSafe (VSS), 209
Microsoft Windows 2000, 232
Microsoft Windows 98, 232
Microsoft Windows NT, 232
Microsoft Word, 267, 333

middleware, 235, 246
   and database software, compatibility, 247
mind share, 263
mission statement, writing, 26
moderated discussions, 353
moderating discussion groups, 134
moderators, etiquette of, 150
monitoring your system, 236
mouseovers, 353
multimedia, 353

N

names, using on websites, 269
navigation, 81
   tools, in FrontPage, 196
navigational pages on your website, 162
NDA. *See* nondisclosure agreements
network
   administrators, 354
   connections, 236
   domains, 82
networks, 353
newbies, 354
newsletters
   in email, sending, 142
   formatting, 144
   tools to use, 146
Nielsen Media, 324
Nielsen/NetRatings, 22
nondisclosure agreements (NDA), 235, 354
numeric address in domain names, 88

O

Office. *See* Microsoft Office
offsite hosting, 231
online
   payment options, 256
   surveys, guidelines for, 325
onsite hosting, 231
opportunity cost, 25
opt-in/opt-out, 145, 354
orphan files, 197
outsourcing, 354
   discussion groups, 151
   vs. insourcing, 206
outtasking, 208, 354

Index

P

packets, 354
pages. *See* web pages
page view. *See* impressions
paid placement, 49
partnerships, 16, 18
  forming, 292
Patent and Trademark Office, 70
patent law, 55, 59
paths, 354
payment
  based on acceptance, 224
  options, 256
  systems, online, 253
PBS. *See* Public Broadcasting Service
performance
  and hard disks, 234
  and memory, 234
  and processors, 233
  and website content, 235
  server, and database types, 233, 246
photographs as website images, 191
ping, 354
plagiarism, 63
planning pre-production, 157, 158
plans, refining, 164
platforms, 231
  selecting, 232
port, 354
portals, 284, 354
  for intranets/extranets, 336
positioning in marketing, 282
post, 354
posting
  to intranets/extranets, standards, 335
  ratio, 354
  to your online press room, 306
power supplies, 235
pre-production planning, 157, 158
presentation of information, 264
press campaign, launching, 305
price quotes, evaluating, 221
privacy
  concerns, addressing, 146
  protecting, 109
problems, preventing, in customer service, 122
processors, 233
product
  development, and intranets, 331
  sales, 48
programming
  languages, and database manipulation, 247
  for the Web, 218
  scripts, 45
projects
  adding features, 223
  confidentiality, 225
  deliverables, 222
  expectations, 215
  management, 44, 227
  plans, 216, 355
  process, 224
  staffing, from within company, 206
  staffing, outsourcing, 206
  team, organizing, 208
  timeline, 216
Project. *See* Microsoft Project
promoting websites, 283
promotion, mixing online and offline, 308
proprietary, 56
Public Broadcasting Service (PBS), paid sponsorship, 49
public domains, 355
  laws, international, 65
public relations, 303
publishing, 53
  on intranets/extranets, 336, 338
purchase systems, 248
push technology, 355

Q

QA. *See* quality assurance
quality assurance (QA)
  for extranets, 337
  process, benefits of, 273
  process, establishing, 272
quality of website content, monitoring, 272
queries, 244
quotes
  evaluating, 221

Index

R

RAID. *See* redundant array of independent disks
RAM. *See* random access memory
random access memory (RAM), 234
ranking on websites, 285
records, 243, 355
Red Alert, 258
redirect pages, 355
redundancy, 235, 241
 in database, 34
redundant array of independent disks (RAID), 235
references, 222
registering domain names, 89
relational databases, 243, 245, 355
reliability of servers, 235
remote, 355
repeat visitors, 262, 265
request for proposal (RFP), 216, 355
resources, managing, 279
restoring from backups, 248
retail, traditional vs. online, 15
return on investment (ROI), 329, 334, 341, 355
 assessing, 315
 demonstrating, 314
returns, handling, 105, 124
revenue models, 8, 355
RFP. *See* request for proposal
right
 of privacy/publicity, 66
rights. *See* copyright
ROI. *See* return on investment
routers, 355

S

sales
 and marketing, and intranets, 331
 models, traditional vs. e-commerce, 15
 projections, 3, 6
 tax, Internet, 254
scalability, 355
scripts, 58, 230, 356
 inserting in web pages, 247
SCSI. *See* Small Computer Systems Interface

searchability, protecting websites from, 290
search engines, 284
 "crawling" with, 285
 databases, 285
 popularity in rankings, 289
 ranking in, 287
 software, 285
search pages in your website, 163
secure
 server, 18
 transactions, 356
Secure HTTP (HTTPS), 356
Secure Sockets Layer (SSL), 250, 356
security
 audits, 251
 breaching, 109
 in e-commerce transaction systems, 250
 intranet/extranets, 338
 policy for intranets/extranets, 336
 secure server, 18
serial discussions on message boards, 135
servers, 230, 356
 backup systems, 235
 capacity, 236
 crashes, alerting mechanisms, 258
 crashes, preventing, 236
 database, 230
 and hard disk, 234
 hosting, 231–240
 location, 238
 log files, 236
 mail, 230
 and memory, 234
 multiple, on one computer, 231
 performance, 233
 performance, and database types, 246
 processors, multiple, 233
 reliability, 235
 selecting, 233
 support, 236, 237
 web, 230
 and website content, 235
server software, 231
service, 102
service level agreement (SLA), 356
servicemark, 69
shareware, 356
shopping carts, 248, 356
 and FrontPage, 197

368

Index

shopping online, 8
signature files, 356
Simulations Interactive Media, 80
site maps, 198
   building, 158
   creating, 169
   pages in your website, 163
size of web pages, and download time, 191
SLA. *See* service level agreement
slander, 72, 356
small businesses, 3
Small Business Financial Manager. *See* Microsoft Small Business Financial Manager
Small Computer Systems Interface (SCSI), 235
soft goals, 343
software traffic analysis, 323
sound and video, using with branding, 94
specs, 224
sponsorships, 49, 356
SSL. *See* Secure Sockets Layer
staging servers, 34, 356
standards for intranet/extranet posting, 335
stickiness, 265
storyboard, 45
strategic partnerships, 357
style guides, 272, 357
   creation checklist, 273
style, of vendors, 217
submitting websites, 290
subscription, 50
success
   assessing, 311, 312
   of intranets/extranets, measuring, 343
   measuring, 312, 314
support, 357
   contracts, 237
   hosting, 240
   for servers, 236, 237
   technical, 238
surveys, 78, 127, 149
   guidelines, 325
   online, using for customer service, 107
system
   administrators, 357
   monitoring, 236

T

tables, 243, 357
   using in websites, 266
tags, 184, 357. *See also* HTML
target markets, 357
Tasks feature in FrontPage, 198
Tauber Kienan Associates, 6
technical support, 238
   providing, 5
technology
   back end, 229
   choosing, 132
   intranet/extranet considerations, 339
telephone billing, 256
templates, 196, 357
testing database backups, 248
text
   vs. art, 192
   editing, 267
   on websites, breaking up, 265
   on websites, dressing up, 266
   on websites, making more readable, 265
themes, 196
threaded discussions on message boards, 135
threads, 357
thumbnails, 18, 194
tools
   using in newsletters, 146
   web page editing, 197
   website maintenance, 279
   website traffic measurement, 317, 323
tracking
   customer information, 13
   projects, 4, 6, 13
   user data, 319
trade dress, 58
   law, 55
trademarks, 68–70, 357
   domain names, 68
   infringement, 70, 85
   law, 55
   Patent and Trademark Office, 70
   registering, 70
   symbols, 70
trade secret law, 55
trading ads, 299
traffic-analysis software, 357

Index

traffic on websites, 312
   analysis software, 323
   analyzing, 272, 322
   auditing data, 324
   counting impressions, 320
   and hits, 320
   log files, 316, 322
   measuring, 314–17
transaction pages on your website, 164
transactions
   credit card, 251–53
   importance of keeping simple, 122
transaction systems, 10, 230, 248, 358
   building or buying, 256
   and credit card processing, 254
   elements of, 248
   and FrontPage, 197
   security, 11, 250
   when required, 10
transparencies, 194
true graphics, 191

U

uninterruptible power supply (UPS), 236
unique users, 317, 358
   and cookies, 321
Uniform Resource Locator (URL), 358
United States Copyright Office, 61
United States Library of Congress, 61, 63
unsubscribing options, providing, 146
update cycles, 270
UPS. *See* uninterruptible power supply
URL. *See* Uniform Resource Locator
users
   data, auditing, 324
   data, tracking, 319
   demographics, 319
   feedback, assessing, 328
   information about, 318
   information, log files, 316
   information, using, 326
   input, soliciting/analyzing, 325
   surveys, guidelines for, 325
   unique, 317, 321
   website impression, 261, 271
utilities for system monitoring, 236

V

vendors
   assessing type, 206
   communicating with, 329
   communication, assessing quality, 219
   contracts, 225
   evaluating, 219
   experience, 217
   fees, negotiating, 222
   multiple, 214, 220
   price quotes, evaluating, 221
   red flags, 220
   references, 222
   relationships, establishing 227
   selecting, 215, 224
   services, 216
   style, 217
   trouble indicators, 220
   website maintenance, 226
version-control software, 280
vertical markets, 358
Visio, 274, 333
visual elements, on websites, 264
Visual SourceSafe (VSS). *See* Microsoft Visual SourceSafe
VSS. *See* Microsoft Visual SourceSafe

W

wallet system, 256
WAN. *See* wide area network
Web, the, preparing images for, 193
web pages
   archiving, 280
   editing, 197
   inserting scripts, 247
   layout tricks, 187
   old, purging, 280
   posting, 190
   protecting from searchability, 290
   security, 250
   size, and download time, 191
web rings, 292
web-safe palette, 358
web server, 230
web shops, advantages/disadvantages, by type, 212

Index

websites, 312
  acquiring content for, 160, 161
  activity levels, 319
  appropriate content, 19
  architecture, 168
  around the clock operation, 257
  art and design, 218
  ascertaining ownership, 58
  audience, assessing, 312–15
  back end, 169, 229
  and bCentral Site Manager, 203
  building, 4, 43, 51, 157, 175
  changing, approval process, 278
  community-based, 153
  company pages in, 164
  consequence, 264
  content. *See* content
  context, 263
  copyright, 61
  cost efficiency, 40
  cost of building, 5, 37–39
  creating, 179
  database-backed, 244
  databases in, 174
  design rules, 200
  designing for multiple browsers, 199
  development, 205–13
  development fees, negotiating, 222
  directory structures, 172
  dynamic pages, 286
  editor, role and responsibilities, 273
  frames, disadvantages, 286
  front end, 169
  and FrontPage, 195–98
  goals, 159
  grouping material, 166
  help pages, 163
  hierarchies, 168
  home pages, 162
  hosting, 229
  identifying material for, 165
  image maps, 286
  images, 191
  including Office documents, 203
  interactivity, 201
  interfaces, 169
  investigating competitors, 161
  language, 267, 268

websites (continued)
  linking, 71
  links, 267
  links, removing, 280
  listing, 284
  maintenance, 35, 41, 226
  maintenance, and databases, 245
  maintenance, lessening, 269
  maintenance, tools for, 279
  management, 328
  META tags, 286
  naming. *See* domain names
  navigation, 196
  navigational pages in, 162
  organizing, 158, 270
  ownership, 56
  page length, 165
  privacy policy, 19
  programming, 218
  promoting, 283
  ranking, 285, 287
  referrals, 319
  repeat visitors, 262, 265
  reviewing, 278
  search pages, 163
  simplicity, 18, 81
  site map pages in, 163
  stickiness, 265
  submitting, 290
  success, assessing, 311, 312
  surveys, guidelines, 325
  technical statistics, 319
  text, making more readable, 265
  themes, 196
  traffic. *See* traffic on websites
  transaction pages, 164
  update cycles, 270
  users. *See* users
  using names on, 269
  vendors. *See* vendors
  viewing specifications, 57
wide area network (WAN), 358
wizards, 196
Work, 358
work, jobbing out, 205
work for hire, 68, 358
writing for e-commerce, 265
WYSIWYG, 196

The manuscript for this book was prepared and submitted to Microsoft Press in electronic form. Text files were prepared using Microsoft Word 97. Pages were composed by Online Training Solutions, Inc. (OTSI) using Adobe PageMaker 6.52 for Windows, with text in Berkeley and display type in Frutiger. Composed pages were delivered to the printer as electronic prepress files.

Cover Graphic Designer
Tom Draper Design

Interior Designer
James D. Kramer

OTSI Editorial Team
Joyce Cox
Leslie Eliel
Joan Lambert
Steve Lambert
Rachel Moorhead
Gabrielle Nonast

OTSI Production
R.J. Cadranell

Contact OTSI at:
- Email: joanl@otsiweb.com
- Website: *www.otsiweb.com*

Proof of Purchase

0-7356-0846-6

Do not send this card with your registration.
Use this card as proof of purchase if participating in a promotion or rebate offer on *Small Business Solutions for E-Commerce*. Card must be used in conjunction with other proof(s) of payment such as your dated sales receipt—see offer details.

Small Business Solutions for E-Commerce

WHERE DID YOU PURCHASE THIS PRODUCT?

CUSTOMER NAME

mspress.microsoft.com

Microsoft Press, PO Box 97017, Redmond, WA 98073-9830

OWNER REGISTRATION CARD

Register Today!

0-7356-0846-6

Return the bottom portion of this card to register today.

Small Business Solutions for E-Commerce

FIRST NAME   MIDDLE INITIAL   LAST NAME

INSTITUTION OR COMPANY NAME

ADDRESS

CITY   STATE   ZIP

( )

E-MAIL ADDRESS   PHONE NUMBER

U.S. and Canada addresses only. Fill in information above and mail postage-free.
Please mail only the bottom half of this page.

For information about Microsoft Press® products, visit our Web site at
mspress.microsoft.com

BUSINESS REPLY MAIL
FIRST-CLASS MAIL   PERMIT NO. 108   REDMOND WA

POSTAGE WILL BE PAID BY ADDRESSEE

MICROSOFT PRESS
PO BOX 97017
REDMOND, WA 98073-9830

NO POSTAGE
NECESSARY
IF MAILED
IN THE
UNITED STATES